Washington Environmental Law Handbook

FIFTH EDITION

Washington Environmental Law Handbook

FIFTH EDITION

Theda Braddock

STATE ENVIRONMENTAL LAW HANDBOOK SERIES

Lanham

Published by Bernan Press
A wholly owned subsidiary of The Rowman & Littlefield Publishing Group, Inc.
4501 Forbes Boulevard, Suite 200, Lanham, Maryland 20706
www.rowman.com
800-865-3457; info@bernan.com

Copyright © 2015 by Bernan Press

All rights reserved. No part of this book may be reproduced in any form or by any electronic or mechanical means, including information storage and retrieval systems, without written permission from the publisher, except by a reviewer who may quote passages in a review. Bernan Press does not claim copyright in U.S. government information.

The fourth edition of this book was previously cataloged by the Library of Congress as follows:

Washington environmental law handbook / Theda Braddock Fowler. —Fourth edition.
    p. cm. — (State environmental law handbook series)
  Rev. ed. of: Washington environmental law handbook / by the law firm of Preston Gates & Ellis LLP. 3rd. ed. 1997.
  Includes bibliographical references and index.
  1. Environmental law—Washington (State). Fowler, Theda Braddock.
  KFW354 .W37 2006
  344.79704'6   2005020681

ISBN 978-1-59888-750-1 (pbk. : alk. paper)—ISBN 978-1-59888-751-8 (electronic)

∞™ The paper used in this publication meets the minimum requirements of American National Standard for Information Sciences—Permanence of Paper for Printed Library Materials, ANSI/NISO Z39.48-1992.

Printed in the United States of America

Summary of Contents

INTRODUCTION	xxi
CHAPTER 1: THE STATE ENVIRONMENTAL POLICY ACT	1
CHAPTER 2: GROWTH MANAGEMENT	17
CHAPTER 3: SHORELINE AND COASTAL ZONE MANAGEMENT	31
CHAPTER 4: REGULATION OF DEVELOPMENT IN ENVIRONMENTALLY SENSITIVE AREAS	53
CHAPTER 5: AIR QUALITY	63
CHAPTER 6: WATER QUALITY	83
CHAPTER 7: WATER RESOURCES	101
CHAPTER 8: SOLID WASTE MANAGEMENT	117
CHAPTER 9: HAZARDOUS WASTE MANAGEMENT (RCRA)	127

Summary of Contents

CHAPTER 10: HAZARDOUS WASTE CLEANUP — 143

CHAPTER 11: OIL SPILL REGULATION AND NATURAL RESOURCE DAMAGES — 175

CHAPTER 12: REGULATION OF UNDERGROUND STORAGE TANKS — 195

CHAPTER 13: ENVIRONMENTAL CONSIDERATIONS IN BUSINESS TRANSACTIONS — 213

CHAPTER 14: ENVIRONMENTAL TORTS — 227

CHAPTER 15: ADMINISTRATIVE PROCEDURE AND JUDICIAL REVIEW — 237

ABOUT THE AUTHOR — 255

Contents

INTRODUCTION xxi
Overview of Environmental Programs xxi
Elements of the Environment xxi
Pollution Control: Key Laws xxii
Land and Natural Resources Management: Key Laws xxii
Environmental Management: Key Laws xxii
Overview of Washington Environmental Agencies xxiii
State Agencies xxiii
Department of Natural Resources (DNR) xxiv
Department of Fish and Wildlife xxiv
Department of Health xxiv
Other Key State Offices xxiv
State Regional Agencies xxv
General Purpose Local Government: Cities and Counties xxv
Special Purpose Regional or County-Wide Municipalities xxv
Special Districts xxvi
Indian Tribes xxvi
Abbreviations xxvi
Acknowledgements xxvi

THE STATE ENVIRONMENTAL POLICY ACT 1
Introduction 1
SEPA Overview 1
Avoiding Analysis under SEPA 2
Making the Threshold Determination 2
Lead Agency Determination 3
Definition of "Action" and Categorical Exemptions 3

    Environmental Checklist..4
    Threshold Determination...4
    Determination of Nonsignificance ("DNS")..5
    Mitigated DNS..5
    Determination of Significance ("DS") and Scoping..6
The Environmental Impact Statement ("EIS")..6
    Content and Format..6
    Social and Economic Impacts..7
    Draft EIS, Public Comment and Timing...7
    Legal Adequacy of the EIS..7
    Using Existing Environmental Documents...8
Substantive Authority and Mitigation...8
Appeals..9
    Appeal To Local Legislative Body..9
    Agency Administrative Appeals...10
    Judicial Appeals..10
    Notice of Action...11
    Attorneys' Fees..11
Notes...12

GROWTH MANAGEMENT 17
Introduction..17
Planning for Growth: An Overview of the Planning Requirements..18
    Local Level Planning...18
        Comprehensive Plans..18
    Regional Level Planning..19
        Countywide Planning Policies..19
        Regional Transportation Planning..19
    State Participation...19
        Technical and Financial Assistance...19
        Sanctions..20
Comprehensive Plans...20
    GMA Goals...20
    Plan Elements...21
    Urban Growth Areas..22
    Open Space Corridors...22
    Public Facilities and Difficult-to-Site Facilities..22
    Transmittal to State..23
Development Regulations..23
Public Participation...23
Appeals..23

 Administrative Appeals: Hearings Boards 23
  Matters Subject to Review 23
 Finding of Noncompliance or Invalidity 24
 Sanctions 24
 Judicial Appeal 24
Relationship to Other Laws 24
 State Environmental Policy Act ("SEPA") 24
 Shoreline Management Act (SMA) 24
  Vesting 25
Notes 26

Shoreline and Coastal Zone Management 31

Overview 31
Jurisdictional Reach of the SMA 32
 "Where": Geographical Reach of the SMA 32
  Shorelines and Shorelands 32
  Lands Outside Shorelands 32
 "What" Actions Subject to Regulation 33
Substantive Requirements: Policies and Programs 34
 State Shoreline Policies 34
  The Public Interest Test 34
  Use Preferences and Priorities 34
 Local Shoreline Master Programs 35
  Content of Shoreline Master Programs 35
  Approval and Amendment Process 35
  Appeals of SMPs or Amendments 37
Procedural Requirements: Shoreline Permit Process 37
 Shoreline Permits With Conditions 37
 Shoreline Conditional Use Permits 38
 Shoreline Variance Permits 38
 Permit Processing 38
  Application 39
  Notice 39
  Local Hearings and Decisions 39
  Ecology Review 39
  SHB Appeal 40
 Modification, Duration, and Extension of Permits 40
Appeals: Shorelines Hearings Board 40
 Jurisdiction and Authority 40
 Composition 41
 Procedures 41

Who May Practice Before the SHB 41
Filing a Petition For Review 42
Prehearing Procedures 42
Scheduling Hearings and Presenting Motions 42
Conduct of Hearings and Rules of Evidence 43
Disposition of Contested Cases: Reconsideration and Appeal to Superior Court 43
Enforcement 44
Permit Rescission 44
Suits for Damages or Equitable Remedies 44
Enforcement Orders and Penalties 44
Coastal Zone Management Program 45
Jurisdiction of the Coastal Zone Management Act 45
The Washington Coastal Zone Management Program 46
Consistency Determination Procedure 46
Notes 47

REGULATION OF DEVELOPMENT IN ENVIRONMENTALLY SENSITIVE AREAS 53
Management of Environmentally Sensitive Areas in Washington 53
Regulations to Control Development in Wetlands and Aquatic Environments 53
Federal Regulations 54
CWA Section 404 (Dredge and Fill) Permits 54
Exemptions 54
Mitigation and Mitigation Banking 54
State Water Quality Certification 55
Nationwide Permits 55
Coastal Zone Management Act (CZMA) Consistency Determination 55
Other Federal Regulations 55
State Regulations 56
Wetlands Regulation Under the Growth Management Act 56
Regulation of Wetlands and other Aquatic Areas in the Shoreline Zone: Shoreline Management Act (SMA) 56
Hydraulic Project Approvals (HPA) 57
Regulation Under The Forest Practices Act RCW §76.09 57
Regulations to Prevent Flood Damage 57
Federal Programs 57
State Programs 58
State Management of Floodplains 58
State Regulation in Addition to Local Controls 58
Local Programs 58
Regulations to Protect Other Sensitive Areas 58
Geologically Hazardous Areas 59

    Aquifer Recharge Zones and Fish and Wildlife Habitat Conservation Areas 59
    Notes 60

AIR QUALITY 63
    Introduction 63
    Sources of Law and Regulation 63
    Regulatory Framework 64
        State Implementation Plan (SIP) 64
        National Ambient Air Quality Standards (NAAQS) 64
        Attainment and Nonattainment Areas 64
    Regulatory Agencies 65
    Registration and Operating Permits 65
        Registration 65
        Operating Permits 66
    New and Modified Sources 66
        Minor Source NSR 67
        Major Source NSR 68
            Key Terms 68
            Prevention of Significant Deterioration ("PSD") 69
            Nonattainment Area NSR 70
    Toxic and Hazardous Air Pollutants 71
        Federal HAP Program 71
        Washington TAP Rules 72
    Emission Standards 73
        General Standards 73
        Standards With Specific Applicability 74
    Enforcement and Appeals 76
        State Enforcement 76
        Federal Enforcement 76
    Notes 78

WATER QUALITY 83
    History of State Water Pollution Control Programs and Relationship to Federal Program 83
    Agencies Responsible for Water Pollution Control 84
        The Washington Department of Ecology 84
        The Pollution Control Hearings Board (PCHB) 84
    Regulation Of Water Pollution 84
        Discharge Permits 84
        NPDES Permit Program 85
            Pollutant 85
            Addition 85

    Point Source 86
    Waters of the State (or Waters of the United States) 86
    Permit Application Process..86
 State Waste Discharge Permit Program 87
 General Permits..88
 Combined Permit...88
 Stormwater Permits 88
    Discharges Associated With Industrial Activity 89
    Discharges From Municipal Sewer Systems 90
 How Permit Effluent Limitations are Derived 90
    Technology-Based Effluent Limitations 91
    Water Quality-Based Effluent Limitations...91
    Total Maximum Daily Load (TMDL) 92
Sediment Management Standards..93
Ground Water Quality Standards...93
Permit Appeals 94
Enforcement 95
 Agency Enforcement..95
 Citizen Enforcement (Citizen Suit Actions) 97
Notes 98

WATER RESOURCES 101
Introduction 101
 Surface Water Allocation: In General 101
 Ground Water Allocation: In General...102
Allocation of Water: In Washington..102
 Riparian Rights..102
 Prior Appropriation Rights..103
 Statutory Laws of Water Appropriation 103
Current Water Allocation System..104
Water Right Appropriation Process...104
 Permitting System...104
 Nature of Appropriative Rights 106
 Water Right Registration System 106
Water Right Adjudication System..106
Transfer and Loss of Water Rights...107
 Water Right Transfers 107
 Loss of Water Rights...107
 Beneficial Use Requirement 108
Water Reuse 108
 The Reclaimed Water Act..109

Contents   xiii

    Water Rights in Reclaimed Water...109
  Federal and Indian Water Rights 109
    Indian Treaty Rights...109
    Reserved Rights 110
      Indian Reserved Water Rights..110
      Non-Indian Reserved Water Rights...111
      McCarran Amendment Adjudications..111
  Notes 112

SOLID WASTE MANAGEMENT 117
  Introduction..117
  Local Governments and Comprehensive Solid Waste Management Planning...........................117
    Solid Waste Management Plans (SWMPs) 117
    Planning Procedures..118
    Legal Effect of Solid Waste Management Plans 118
    Implementing Local Solid Waste Management Plans..119
    Financing Solid Waste Management and Disposal 119
  Regulation of Solid Waste Handling Facilities and Activities 120
    General MFS Requirements...120
    Permit Procedures 122
    Appeals and Enforcement 122
  Laws Affecting Solid Waste Generators: Homes, Offices and Businesses 122
  Notes 123

HAZARDOUS WASTE MANAGEMENT (RCRA) 127
  Introduction..127
  Dangerous Waste Identification 128
    Definition of Solid Waste..128
    Definition of Dangerous Waste..129
      Listed Wastes..129
      Characteristic Wastes 130
      Mixture and Derived-From Rules 131
      "Contained-In" Policy..131
      State-Only Dangerous Wastes 131
      Exclusions...132
      Special Wastes..133
  Generator Requirements...133
    Generator Management Responsibilities 133
  Transporter Requirements 134
  Requirements for Owners and Operators of Treatment, Storage and Disposal Facilities (TSDs) 134
    General Performance Standards..134

- Permit Application Process ... 135
  - Existing Facilities ... 135
  - New Facilities ... 135
- Siting Standards ... 135
  - Notice of Intent ... 135
  - Siting Restrictions ... 136
- Closure and Post-Closure ... 136
- Corrective Action ... 137
- Enforcement and Penalties ... 138
- Notes ... 139

Hazardous Waste Cleanup ... 143

- Introduction ... 143
- History of Washington Legislation and Regulations ... 143
- Overview of Statutory Structure ... 144
- Analysis of Statute ... 144
  - Policy Declarations ... 144
  - Definitions ... 144
  - Ecology's Powers and Duties ... 145
  - Liability Standards ... 146
  - Enforcement and Settlement Provisions ... 147
  - The Toxics Control Accounts ... 148
- Overview of MTCA Regulations ... 149
  - Site Reports and Cleanup Decisions ... 149
    - Site Discovery and Reporting ... 149
    - Initial Investigation ... 150
    - Site Hazard Assessment ... 150
    - Hazardous Sites List ... 151
    - Biennial Program Report ... 151
    - State Remedial Investigation/Feasibility Study (RI/FS) ... 151
    - Selection of Cleanup Actions ... 152
  - Site Cleanup and Monitoring ... 152
    - Cleanup Actions ... 152
    - Compliance Monitoring Requirements ... 153
    - Periodic Review ... 154
    - Interim Actions ... 154
  - Administrative Procedures For Remedial Actions ... 154
    - Determination of PLP Status ... 154
    - Administrative Options For Remedial Actions ... 155
    - Consent Decrees ... 155
    - Agreed Orders ... 156

    Enforcement Orders 157
    Payment of Remedial Action Costs 157
    Prospective Purchaser Agreements and Brownfields Redevelopment 157
  Public Involvement 158
    Public Notice and Participation 158
  Regional Citizens' Advisory Committees 159
  Cleanup Standards 159
    Overview 159
    Setting Cleanup Levels 159
    Cleanup Standard Methods 160
    Cleanup Standards For Ground Water, Surface Water, Soil, Air and Sediments 161
    Identifying "Points of Compliance" 161
    Waiver of Cleanup Standards 162
  Selecting a Cleanup Remedy 162
  Cleanup Cost Considerations 163
  General Provisions 163
    Property Access 163
    Worker Safety and Health 164
    Sampling and Analysis Plans 164
    Laboratory Analysis Procedures 164
    General Submittal Requirements 164
    Recordkeeping Requirements 164
    Endangerment 165
  Notes 166

OIL SPILL REGULATION AND NATURAL RESOURCE DAMAGES 175
  Introduction 175
  Oil Spill Regulation 176
    Financial Responsibility Requirements 176
    Penalties for Failure to Meet Financial Responsibility Requirements 177
    Contingency Planning Requirements 177
      Parties Subject to the Contingency Planning Requirements: Facilities and Covered Vessels 178
      Planning Deadlines 178
      Plan Requirements 178
      Agency Review and Plan Updates 179
      Spill Response 179
      Primary Response Contractor Standards 179
    Spill Prevention Plans 180
      Vessel Spill Prevention Plans 180
      Facility Spill Prevention Plans 180
    Penalties for Violating Planning Requirements 181

Facility Operation Standards...181
　　Oil Spill Liability...182
　　　State and Private Causes of Action 182
　　　State Oil Spill Response Account 183
　　　Civil Penalties 183
　Natural Resource Damages 183
　　State Water Pollution Control Act..184
　　　Natural Resource Damages Provision 184
　　　Natural Resources Defined..184
　　　Pre-assessment Screening and Damage Assessment Process................................185
　　　Natural Resource Damages Computation Without Compensation Schedule 186
　　　Natural Resource Damages Computation Using Compensation Schedule 186
　　　Limits on the Use of Funds Recovered 187
　　Model Toxics Control Act (State Superfund)...187
　Notes..189

REGULATION OF UNDERGROUND STORAGE TANKS 195
　Introduction 195
　　Federal UST Program 195
　　State UST Program 195
　　Leaking Tanks 196
　Scope of the UST Program...196
　　What Is an Underground Storage Tank?..196
　　Exempt and Deferred Tanks..196
　　To Whom Do the UST Regulations Apply? 196
　Permit Requirements..197
　　Obtaining and Renewing a Permit 197
　　Display of Permit 197
　　Revocation/Removal of Permit..197
　Program Administration 198
　　Investigation and Access 198
　　Enforcement..198
　Notification, Reporting and Recordkeeping..198
　　Notification Requirements 198
　　　New UST Systems..198
　　　Existing UST Systems..198
　　　Emergency Replacement 199
　　　Changes to UST System..199
　　　Seller Disclosure 199
　　Reporting Requirements 199
　　Recordkeeping Requirements 199

UST Design and Performance Standards 199
    Design Standards 200
        New UST Systems 200
        Upgrading Existing UST Systems 200
        Deferred UST Systems 200
    Operating Standards for All UST Systems 201
        Spill and Overfill Control 201
        Compatibility 201
        Corrosion Protection 201
        Repairs 201
        Release Detection 201
Releases and Spills 202
    What To Do If You Suspect a Release? 202
        Report the Release 202
        Investigate and Take Necessary Corrective Action 202
    What Do You Do If There Is A Spill? 202
        Contain and Cleanup 202
        Take Corrective Action 203
        Report the Spill 203
Closure Requirements 203
    Permanent Closure 203
    Temporary Closure 203
    Previous Closure 204
    Closure Records 204
Financial Responsibility Requirements for Petroleum USTs 204
    Who Is Required to Demonstrate Financial Responsibility? 204
    When? 204
    To Cover What? 204
    How Much? 205
    Methods of Financial Assurance 205
    Recordkeeping and Reporting Requirements 205
    Reinsurance 206
UST Service Providers and Supervisors 206
    UST Services Must be Performed by Certified UST Supervisors 206
    Responsibilities of Certified UST Supervisors 206
    Penalties 207
Notes 208

ENVIRONMENTAL CONSIDERATIONS IN BUSINESS TRANSACTIONS 213
Introduction 213
Types of Real Property Likely to Involve Environmental Problems 213

    Industrial Properties..................213
    Commercial Properties..................214
    Agricultural Land..................214
    Landfills..................214
    Environmentally Sensitive Areas..................214
  Liability Concerns..................214
    Federal and State Superfunds..................214
      Liabilities of Purchasers and Sellers..................215
      Liabilities of Lenders..................215
      Liabilities of Landlords and Tenants..................215
      Statutory Exemptions from Liability..................215
    Other Environmental Laws..................216
      Environmental Management Laws..................216
      Laws Governing Real Estate Development in Environmentally Sensitive Areas..................217
    Special State Laws Governing Real Estate Transfers..................217
    Common Law Liability..................217
  Strategies for Minimizing Liability..................217
    Protecting Purchasers from Liability..................218
      Environmental Investigation..................218
      Contract Mechanisms..................219
      Prospective Purchaser Agreements..................220
      No Further Action Letters..................221
      Corporate Structuring to Minimize Third-Party and Off-Site Liabilities..................222
  Notes..................223

ENVIRONMENTAL TORTS: COMMON LAW AND OTHER REMEDIES 227
  Introduction..................227
  Nuisance..................227
    Elements of Cause of Action..................227
    Public and Private Nuisance..................228
    Recoverable Damages..................228
    Examples of Environmental Nuisance Cases..................228
  Trespass..................229
    Elements of Cause of Action..................229
    Recoverable Damages..................229
    Examples of Environmental Trespass Cases..................229
  Negligence..................230
  Strict Liability..................230
    Elements of Cause of Action..................230
    Recoverable Damages..................230
  Inverse Condemnation..................231

    Elements of Cause of Action...231
    Nonregulatory Takings 231
    Regulatory Takings 231
    Recoverable Damages..232
  Notes 233

ADMINISTRATIVE PROCEDURE AND JUDICIAL REVIEW 237
  Introduction 237
  Administrative Procedure in Washington 237
    Washington's APA: Scope and Application 237
    Rulemaking Proceedings 238
      In General..238
      Significant Legislative Rules 239
      Emergency Rules and Amendments...240
      Joint Administrative Rules Review Committee...240
      Public Access to Agency Rules, Rules Coordinator..241
      Interpretive and Policy Statements...241
      Challenges to Rulemaking Under the APA 242
    Adjudicative Proceedings..242
      In General..242
      Procedures for Adjudicative Proceedings 243
      Brief and Emergency Adjudicative Proceedings 245
      Administrative Safeguards..245
  Judicial Review of Agency Action 246
    Judicial Review Under the APA 246
      In General..246
      Civil Enforcement of Agency Rules and Orders..247
    Judicial Review of Actions by Local Agencies 248
  Notes 249

ABOUT THE AUTHOR 255

Introduction

ENVIRONMENTAL LAW IN WASHINGTON

Washington's environmental laws are intricate, extensive, and complex. This updated and expanded text is intended to introduce the regulated community to the most frequently applied laws and regulations. It is intended as a general guide to what can become a confusing and sometimes contradictory process whenever development takes place. Frequently several statutes administered by several agencies will apply to require some level of permitting. Failure to obtain all of the relevant permits can have expensive and painful consequences. Since knowing the players is part of meeting this challenge, this chapter provides a snapshot of the roles of the key government agencies in the state.

OVERVIEW OF ENVIRONMENTAL PROGRAMS

This book describes the state's key environmental programs. It does not try to discuss in any detail how federal agencies operate within the state or to focus on conventional zoning and land use development, even though these areas are intertwined with environmental management and regulation.

Elements of the Environment

Before highlighting the key state laws and programs, a strong cautionary note and recommendation may be in order: the more readily one can keep in mind what is meant by the "environment," the easier it is to avoid regulatory pitfalls and to address inevitable cross-media issues and programs. Fortunately, there is a relatively simple way to accomplish this in Washington. The State Environmental Policy Act (SEPA)—the most pervasive state environmental law because it applies to all state and local actions and regulation of the private sector—contains a convenient list of the "elements of the environment."

The first five comprise the natural environment, based on the classic Greek elements of earth, air, fire (energy) and water. They are:

1. earth;
2. air;
3. water;
4. plants and animals; and
5. energy and natural resources.

The second four comprise the "as built" environment:

1. environmental health;
2. land and shoreline use;
3. transportation; and
4. public services and utilities.

This list is all the more important because, for all practical purposes, the environmental impact of nearly every substantial action regulated by one of the laws in this book will need to be considered. By anticipating this analysis, the approach and the design of particular proposals can avoid many environmental and regulatory problems.

Similarly, the field of environmental law typically views these environmental elements in three ways: laws relating to pollution control, including waste management; laws relating to the quality and use of land and natural resources; and laws relating to management systems to maintain or achieve environmental quality along with other societal goals.

Pollution Control: Key Laws

The four state laws that form the foundation of pollution control are the:

1. Clean Air Act, RCW §70.94;
2. Clean Water Act, RCW §90.48 RCW;
3. Solid Waste Management, RCW §70.95;
4. Hazardous Waste Management and Cleanup, which includes petroleum, RCW §70.105, especially the Model Toxics Control Act, RCW §70.105D.

Land and Natural Resources Management: Key Laws

The four state laws that contain substantive standards and most broadly govern land and natural resources management are the:

1. Growth Management Act, RCW §36.70A;
2. Shoreline Management Act, RCW §90.58;
3. Forest Practices Act, RCW §76.04; and
4. Critical and Sensitive Areas laws, which consist of a number of local ordinances to protect these resources.

Environmental Management: Key Laws

Other than state or local administrative procedure acts, which generally govern administrative action (but generally do not govern environmental permit or hazardous waste cleanup processes), there is one law that provides the basic environmental management framework for the state, the State Environmental Policy Act (SEPA), RCW §43.21C. SEPA bears a close resemblance to its federal cousin, NEPA (the National Environmental Policy Act of 1969).

OVERVIEW OF WASHINGTON ENVIRONMENTAL AGENCIES

State Agencies

Department of Ecology (Ecology)

Ecology is the state analog to the federal Environmental Protection Agency (EPA), with some additional natural resource responsibilities. Ecology is responsible for administering most of the state's pollution control laws, including the federal and state clean water acts, clean air acts, and solid and hazardous waste management and cleanup laws. Local authorities administer some air and solid waste permit programs, usually with Ecology oversight.

Ecology is also responsible for overseeing and issuing statewide rules for carrying out SEPA and the Shoreline Management Act (which includes the state's coastal zone management program). Ecology's responsibility for water resources and ground water, including water rights permits and instream flows, has played a central role in Eastern Washington agriculture as well as development of hydropower facilities, and has become increasingly critical to urban growth and to fish habitat throughout the state. Ecology currently has the lead role among state agencies on wetlands protection and has a role in implementing the state's new growth management and land use legislation. Ecology provides the official comments and position of the state to the federal government for coastal zone management consistency and water quality certifications on US Army Corps of Engineers dredge and fill permits.

Ecology also administers various grant programs, including mixed funding for hazardous waste cleanups, grants to localities for planning and for development of pollution control facilities and activities, and public participation programs. The Governor has designated Ecology as the lead natural resource trustee agency for the state.

Ecology was created in 1971. It has a single director, appointed by the Governor with Senate confirmation. The director has always been part of the Governor's cabinet. Ecology has been reorganized several time since its creation. The relatively constant aspect of the organization has been a central headquarters located in Olympia (actually in several buildings in Lacey, just north of Olympia) with four regional field offices: Northwest (in Bellevue), Southwest (in Olympia), Central (in Yakima), and Eastern (in Spokane). Ecology has maintained its "central programs" at headquarters, such as the SEPA, shorelines, industrial section (which regulates industries of statewide significance, such as pulp mills and aluminum plants), policy development, public affairs, budgetary, and legal staffs. EPA has a liaison officer at Ecology's headquarters.

The legal staff is actually part of the Attorney General's office, which handles the hiring and managing of the state's environmental attorneys. Ecology, like other state agencies, has a senior attorney general designated for the department. The senior attorney general often organizes the legal staff into groups that correspond with key program areas. The role of the attorneys is somewhat different than the federal system. The attorneys officially report to the state's Attorney General, who is not appointed by the Governor, but is publicly elected. Although they are located within Ecology, the attorneys therefore have a certain independence from the agency. This is important in understanding certain key laws and working relationships, especially under the hazardous waste cleanup law and the Shoreline Management Act.

Because of the central role Ecology plays in most of the laws and programs described in this Handbook, it is described throughout in considerably more detail than the other agencies. Like the federal government, however, the other agencies play crucial roles in the areas of their jurisdiction or expertise, which may sometimes overlap with Ecology's.

Department of Natural Resources (DNR)

DNR was established by RCW §43.30. DNR is the state's principal public lands agency, similar to many of the functions performed by the US Department of the Interior and US Forest Service. Traditionally, the three key areas of DNR's involvement have been forestry, mining, and aquatic lands (the state generally owns the beds of rivers and bodies of water, which DNR leases for shellfish or harbor development). Because of these responsibilities, DNR interacts with many other state and local agencies and Indian tribes on environmental issues. As urbanizing pressures increase, DNR is also faced with "transition lands" issues, such as retaining the natural resource land base for forestry and mining while possibly acquiring new public lands in urbanizing areas for open space and recreation.

It also administers a number of constitutional provisions relating to public lands, commerce, and navigation. DNR is headed by the Commissioner of Public Lands, who is a publicly-elected official, independent of the Governor. The Commissioner appoints a supervisor as a chief administrative officer for the department and about a dozen managers for each of DNR's main programs. Although policy making is focused at headquarters in Olympia, DNR has reorganized and decentralized its operations, sending many of its managers and staff to its field offices.

Department of Fish and Wildlife

The Department of Fish and Wildlife is responsible for the management of game and non-game fish and wildlife. The agency has a key environmental regulatory role through its hydraulic project approvals (HPAs), as these permits are required for most construction activities in coastal and inland waters and streams. The agency also administers state wildlife protection statutes and comment on federal permits through its consultative role under federal wildlife laws, such as the Endangered Species Act, Fish and Wildlife Coordination Act, and international conventions. The department is headed by a director appointed by the Fish and Wildlife Commission with Senate confirmation. The agency has a decentralized organization, with half a dozen regional offices, as well as policy and coordinating functions in its headquarters office in Olympia, shared with DNR.

Department of Health

Created in 1989, the Department of Health was formerly part of the largest state agency, the Department of Social and Health Services. The agency head, the Secretary of Health, is appointed by the Governor with Senate confirmation.

Although the bulk of the department's efforts relate to health care services, the department has environmental health responsibilities in a number of areas, including drinking water, on-site sewage (septic) systems, food and shellfish, radiation, and public health laboratories.

The departments of Health and Ecology coordinate in a number of areas because of similar regulatory issues. In addition, the local health districts, which administer most environmental health and solid waste permit programs in the state, work closely with both agencies.

Other Key State Offices

From an environmental standpoint, the Department Commerce is responsible for comprehensive planning under the Growth Management Act, including protection of critical areas, such as wetlands.

With the growing interest in long term preservation of agricultural lands and rural lifestyles and public concern over the use of pesticides, the Department of Agriculture has taken its place at the table with other state environmental and natural resource agencies. The department also has a major role in water quality and water resource issues because of the importance of water in agricultural and aquaculture activities.

The state Environmental and Land Use Hearings Office includes the Pollution Control Hearings Board (PCHB) and the Shorelines Hearings Board (SHB). Both are quasi-judicial administrative appeal tribunals, which issue opinions that have precedential value. The PCHB mainly hears appeals of Ecology's pollution control permit and compliance actions, while the SHB mainly hears appeals of local shoreline permits. Especially significant, both hear cases and make the record *de novo*, regardless of how extensive the record may be.

The Growth Management Hearings Board, created under the Growth Management Act hear administrative appeals on plan-level issues arising under the GMA, including appeals on Shoreline Management Master Programs and SEPA compliance.

State Regional Agencies

There are nine regional air pollution control authorities (APCAs) authorized under the state Clean Air Act to issue permits and enforce air pollution laws within the jurisdiction defined by the boundaries of counties that agree to establish the APCA. These include the Puget Sound Air Pollution Control Authority (PSAPCA), Northwest Air Pollution Authority (NWAPA), Olympia Air Pollution Control Authority (OAPCA) and the Southwest Air Pollution Control Authority (SWAPCA).

General Purpose Local Government: Cities and Counties

General purpose units of local government, including counties, cities and towns, are responsible, for example, for: environmental (SEPA) review of all nonexempt projects and nonproject (policy, plan, program) actions, shoreline management plans and permits; comprehensive planning, zoning and land use regulations; development controls on subdivisions and critical environmental areas, such as wetlands; and grading, building and construction permits. In addition, most general purpose local governments adopt functional comprehensive plans and administer the following programs and regulations: drainage and surface water plans and permits; area-wide or local wastewater treatment plans and systems; solid waste management and disposal plans; and permits.

The state constitution and planning enabling acts as well as other statutes classify general purpose local governments and enumerate their powers.

Special Purpose Regional or County-Wide Municipalities

Environmental management and regulation sometimes may be placed in county-wide or regional municipalities. For example, there are over sixty port districts in the state that are responsible for most harbor and airport development. The port districts may also have management agreements with DNR to manage the aquatic lands within their jurisdictions on behalf of the state.

Counties have the authority to create metropolitan municipalities that may have a variety of regional environmental responsibilities granted by public vote, such as water pollution abatement, water supply, solid waste management, land use, transportation, parks and open space.

Special Districts

State law provides for numerous special districts for specific public service needs, such as public utility districts (PUDs), sewer districts, water districts, fire protection districts and soil conservation districts. These districts usually have broad powers for limited functions. They review and comment on projects that affect their services, and their approval may be involved on a project.

Indian Tribes

Indian tribes play a pivotal role in environmental management in Washington State, especially where natural resources, water quality and fisheries are involved. Unlike the preceding agencies, the recognized tribes are officially sovereign nations that have entered into a treaty with the United States.

The relationship is not entirely independent in law or practice. The US Department of the Interior, through its Bureau of Indian Affairs, has a trust responsibility for actions affecting tribal resources.

The larger tribes have developed expert environmental technical staffs, particularly in the areas of fishery biology, water quality, and wildlife habitat. Their advice is often heavily relied upon by the environmental regulatory agencies. The professional staff of the tribes participate regularly in the state and local permit and SEPA processes, as well as the solid and hazardous waste management and cleanup area. In addition, the tribes have established some coordinating bodies, such as the Northwest Indian Fisheries Commission.

ABBREVIATIONS

Other than abbreviations or shortened names specifically defined in the text, the following abbreviations have the following meanings:

Washington State:
    Ecology = Department of Ecology
    RCW = Revised Code of Washington
    WAC = Washington Administrative Code
Federal:
    CFR = Code of Federal Regulations
    US = United States Code

ACKNOWLEDGEMENTS

The author is extremely grateful for the generous assistance provided by the following employees of the Washington State Department of Ecology in reviewing selected chapters: Tom Cusack (hazardous waste management), Lori Crews (oil spills), and Stuart Clark and Gary Palcisko (air quality). Nonetheless, any remaining errors or omissions are completely those of the author.

CHAPTER 1

The State Environmental Policy Act

INTRODUCTION

The Washington Legislature enacted the State Environmental Policy Act ("SEPA")[1] in 1971. SEPA Rules were adopted by Ecology in 1984.[2] In March 1995, new rules authorized cities and counties subject to the Growth Management Act ("GMA") to incorporate SEPA into planning and decision making under the GMA.[3] These localities are authorized to merge SEPA and GMA procedures and to issue documents satisfying both laws.[4] The revisions also incorporated the concept of "critical areas," a designation local governments are required to make under GMA,[5] into the SEPA provisions on categorical exemptions.[6] Another revision integrated SEPA with the procedural requirements for remedial action under the Model Toxics Control Act.[7]

Also in 1995, amendments to SEPA made clear that local governments should incorporate SEPA review into the procedures adopted for project permit review[8] and that SEPA should supplement, not displace, the inquiries and decisions required under GMA and other land use laws.[9]

SEPA OVERVIEW

The purpose and policy sections of SEPA are extremely broad,[10] including the recognition by the Legislature that "each person has a fundamental and inalienable right to a healthful environment . . . ."[11] SEPA contains a substantive mandate that "policies, regulations, and laws of the State of Washington shall be interpreted and administered in accordance with the policies set forth in [SEPA]."[12] It also contains the procedural mandate that all branches of state government take a variety of steps to develop and coordinate information.[13] The most important of these procedural mandates requires a responsible official to prepare a "detailed statement" on environmental impacts and reasonable alternatives, including mitigation measures, for every proposal, legislation, and "other major actions significantly affecting the environment."[14] As is the case under the National Environmental Policy Act (NEPA),[15] the "detailed statement" is referred to as an environmental impact statement, or "EIS." Even proposed actions which will improve the environment require an EIS.

SEPA applies to all branches of government within Washington, including state agencies, municipal and public corporations, and counties, but not to the Legislature or the judiciary.[16] Each agency to which SEPA applies is required to adopt its own SEPA procedures, which implement and supplement the requirements of SEPA and the SEPA Rules. Therefore, in addition to the statute and rules, the SEPA procedures of the pertinent agency should always be consulted.

SEPA authority is supplemental to any authority otherwise granted to an agency by the authorizing statute, regulation, charter, etc.[17] Any government action may be conditioned or denied based on environmental considerations, regardless of the agency's statutory mission.

SEPA applies only to government action. However, because "government action" is defined to include the issuance of licenses, permits, and approvals,[18] it impacts almost all private development that has the potential to affect the quality of the environment. Thus, as in NEPA, private proposals are evaluated and may be conditioned or denied through the permit process based on environmental considerations. SEPA does not create an independent permit requirement, but overlays all existing agency permit activities (as well as other government actions).

AVOIDING ANALYSIS UNDER SEPA

Local governments planning under the GMA have two ways in which to avoid SEPA analysis. First, GMA local governments may make an initial determination that analysis under SEPA is unnecessary. This determination can be made only if the local government discovers, in the course of reviewing a proposed action, that the "specific probable adverse environmental impacts" of the action are adequately addressed by the regulations or requirements of the comprehensive plan or other land use laws.[19] Having made such a determination, the GMA local government need not issue a formal SEPA threshold determination or EIS. Second, GMA local governments may designate certain types of projects as "planned action." This designation is limited to types of projects for which the significant impacts have been adequately addressed in an EIS prepared in conjunction with a comprehensive plan or a planned development.[20] Planned actions do not require a SEPA threshold determination or the preparation of an EIS—but are, according to the statute, subject to mitigation and other requirements under SEPA.[21]

MAKING THE THRESHOLD DETERMINATION

The initial determination of whether a government action, such as adoption of legislation or issuance of a permit for a private or public proposal, will have a significant effect on the quality of the environment and therefore require preparation of an EIS is known as the "threshold determination." A threshold determination is required for any proposal that meets the definition of action and is not categorically exempt.[22] The threshold determination is made by the "responsible official" of the "lead agency."[23]

The lead agency is required to prepare its threshold determination early in the planning process so that the proposal and its impacts can be identified.[24] The threshold determination and EIS, if required, must precede the first government action on a proposal.[25] Preliminary steps that are necessary before a proposal is sufficiently definite for environmental review are not precluded,[26] but decision making must not be allowed to proceed to such a point that consideration of environmental factors is foreclosed.[27] The SEPA Rules also allow "phased review," e.g., review of a non-project document followed later by site-specific analysis.[28]

Lead Agency Determination

To ensure coordination of SEPA's requirements, especially proposals involving more than one agency with jurisdiction, the SEPA Rules provide for the identification of a "lead agency" for every proposal requiring SEPA compliance.[29] These rules are complex and should be specifically consulted, but to summarize the most common situations:

1. the lead agency for a government proposal is the agency initiating the proposal;[30]
2. the lead agency for private projects with only one agency with jurisdiction (i.e., permitting authority) is the agency with jurisdiction;[31]
3. the lead agency for private projects requiring licenses from more than one agency is the county or city within whose jurisdiction the project is located;[32]
4. the lead agency for private projects requiring licenses from a local agency, not a county or city, and one or more state agencies, is the local agency;[33] and
5. the lead agency for private projects requiring licenses from a number of state agencies is determined by consulting a list of ordered priorities.[34]

There are also rules designating lead agencies for specific proposals,[35] for transfer of lead agency status to a state agency,[36] for agreements to assume or divide lead agency duties,[37] and for resolution of lead agency disputes by Ecology.[38] The lead agency designates its responsible official according to the method established by the agency's own SEPA procedures.[39]

The lead agency is required to make its threshold determination "as close as possible to the time an agency has developed or is presented with the proposal."[40] The time to complete a threshold determination is not to exceed fifteen days in the usual case.[41] The rules recognize, however, that under certain circumstances, such as where additional information is required or the proposal is unusually complex, the threshold determination may require more time. In these situations, the applicant may request that the responsible official select a date for making the threshold determination and notify the applicant of this date in writing.[42]

Definition of "Action" and Categorical Exemptions

Threshold determinations are required for all proposals that meet the definition of "action" unless they are categorically exempt.[43] Actions are defined to include any project or program "entirely or partly financed, assisted, conducted, regulated, licensed, or approved by agencies," "[n]ew or revised agency rules, regulations, plans, policies or procedures," and "[l]egislative proposals."[44] Actions include both project actions (i.e., decisions on a specific project) and non-project actions (i.e., decisions on policies, plans or programs)."[45]

The categorical exemptions are set forth in Part Nine of the SEPA Rules. The exemptions are intended to cover actions that do not normally cause environmental impacts and therefore require no threshold determination. A categorically exempt action may not be conditioned or denied under SEPA.[46] Even though an action is listed in Part Nine as categorically exempt, however, it may nonetheless require a threshold determination for one of several reasons. First, GMA local governments may select certain categorical exemptions that will not apply within areas designated as "critical areas" by the locality under GMA.[47] In addition, a proposal that would otherwise be categorically exempt is not exempt if it is part of a series of related actions some of which are not exempt[48] or if it is part of a series of related exempt actions that together may have a probable significant adverse environmental impact.[49] Finally, a categorically-exempt action is not exempt from the threshold determination requirement if it, in fact, does have a significant adverse environmental impact.[50]

Environmental Checklist

The threshold determination in most cases is based on an environmental checklist prepared by the applicant (in the case of private proposals) or by the agency (in the case of public proposals). The SEPA Rules contain an environmental checklist form.[51] The form is designed to be filled out by the applicant, to the best of his knowledge. For complex proposals, the form should be filled out by someone with technical expertise, such as an engineering or architectural consultant. The checklist may also be supplemented with more detailed or extensive information than called for by the questions, usually in the form of appendices.

The lead agency uses the checklist to make its threshold determination, unless the proposal is a public proposal and the lead agency has already decided to prepare its own EIS, or the lead agency and the applicant agree that an EIS will be prepared.[52] The items in the checklist are not weighted.[53] In other words, an EIS is not required simply because numerous adverse impacts are mentioned in the checklist. On the other hand, a single probable significant adverse impact may require preparation of an EIS.

Threshold Determination

The responsible official reviews the environmental checklist, the proposed action, and any additional information supplied pursuant to WAC 197-11-335 in determining whether the proposal significantly affects the quality of the environment and, therefore, requires an EIS (the "threshold determination"). WAC 197-11-335 allows the lead agency to require, develop, or collect additional information if there is insufficient information in the checklist to make its threshold determination. WAC 197-11-350 allows the applicant to propose mitigation measures that might result in a negative threshold determination.[54]

In addition to making the threshold decision, the responsible official determines whether the proposal, alternatives, or impacts have already been analyzed in another environmental document that can be adopted or incorporated by reference, as allowed by Part Six of the SEPA Rules, and whether environmental analysis would be more appropriately performed at a future date, pursuant to the "phased review" rules of WAC 197-11-055 through -070.[55]

The rules recognize that a proposal must be considered in the context of the environment by directing the responsible official to consider that a proposal that would have a significant adverse impact if it were to be located in one environment may not have the same impact in another environment.[56] The Rules also, however, direct the responsible official to consider the "absolute quantitative effects" of a proposal that "may result in a significant adverse impact regardless of the nature of the existing environment."[57] Finally, the Rules note that the cumulative effect of several non-significant impacts may result in a significant impact requiring an EIS.[58]

The Rules provide additional guidance on the threshold determination by stating that a proposal may have a significant adverse impact if it adversely affects environmentally sensitive or otherwise special areas,[59] or endangered or threatened species or their habitat,[60] conflicts with environmental protection laws or requirements,[61] or "establish(es) a precedent for future actions with significant effects, involves unique or unknown risks to the environment, or may affect public health or safety."[62] The Rules expressly prohibit balancing the environmentally beneficial aspects of a proposal against its adverse impacts and they provide the example of a sewage treatment plant or other pollution control.

If, after following the process and considering the factors outlined above, the lead agency "reasonably believes that a proposal may have a significant adverse impact, an EIS is required." A determination of significance ("DS") is then issued.[63]

Determination of Nonsignificance ("DNS")

If the lead agency determines that a proposal will not have a probable significant impact, it documents this decision in a determination of non-significance ("DNS").[64] The DNS is issued in combination with or attached to a notice of adoption if any other environmental document has been adopted in support of the DNS.[65]

For DNSs for certain proposals that are likely to be more complex, controversial or involve significant impacts, the timing, circulation, and comment procedures of WAC 197-11-340(2) apply. This section applies to DNSs for proposals that involve: (1) GMA actions, (2) multiple agencies with jurisdiction; (3) demolition of any structure or facility not categorically exempt; (4) issuance of a clearing or grading permit not categorically exempt; (5) a mitigated DNS; or (6) a DNS issued for a proposal for which a DS was issued and then withdrawn.[66] For these proposals, the DNS and environmental checklist are circulated to agencies with jurisdiction, Ecology, affected tribes, and any local or state agency whose public services would be affected by the proposal.

Proper public notice of issuance of the DNS is also required. Public notice can take any of the forms described in Part Five of the Rules, including publication, posting on the property, and mailing. An agency may not act upon the proposal for fifteen days following issuance of the DNS,[67] during which time public comment is received.[68] Also, during this fifteen-day period, any other agency with jurisdiction may assume lead agency status pursuant to the lead agency rules (WAC 197-11-948).[69] Based upon comments received during the comment period, the lead agency retains or modifies the DNS or withdraws the DNS and issues a DS.[70]

Mitigated DNS

SEPA also allows a procedure whereby proposals may be clarified or changed prior to the threshold determination to eliminate any significant adverse impacts.[71] In addition, an agency may always take into account mitigation measures that the agency or the applicant will implement.[72] The Rules specifically allow an applicant to ask the lead agency whether it is considering a DS, and if so, the applicant may change the proposal to mitigate impacts to below the threshold of significance. The environmental checklist must be revised by the applicant if necessary to reflect these changes. The agency then makes its determination based on the proposal as modified. If the agency determines that an EIS is not required, it issues a mitigated determination of non-significance (MDNS) outlining the mitigation measures that are part of the proposal and follows the timing, circulation, notice and comment provisions outlined above.

Determination of Significance ("DS") and Scoping

If the lead agency determines that a proposal will have a probable significant adverse impact on the environment, it issues a DS. For most proposals, it then begins the "scoping" process, the first phase of developing an EIS.[73] Scoping is simply the process of identifying the proposed actions, alternatives, and impacts that should be discussed in the EIS. The lead agency is required to narrow the scope of every EIS to the probable significant adverse environmental impacts and reasonable alternatives, including mitigation measures. Scoping provides a method for doing this by requiring an opportunity for other agencies, interested parties, and the public to identify the scope of the EIS.

The scoping process is initiated with issuance of the DS and scoping notice.[74] The notice sets forth the areas identified by the lead agency for discussion in the EIS and requests comments on the scope from the public. The process may result in alternatives or impacts being added or eliminated from the scope of the EIS.

The Rules encourage creative use of scoping and establish an optional expanded scoping process.[75] Expanded scoping may include questionnaires or information packets, meetings or workshops, consultation among agencies prior to the comment period for the draft EIS, or any other method the lead agency finds helpful. Scoping is intended to focus the environmental analysis on only the truly significant impacts and issues and to produce a genuinely useful document. In practice, a well-run scoping process may preclude future challenges to the adequacy of the EIS.

THE ENVIRONMENTAL IMPACT STATEMENT ("EIS")

Content and Format

Part Four of the SEPA Rules discusses the format and contents of the EIS and how these differ between an EIS for non-project and project proposals. Two features of the EIS format in Washington are worth noting: (1) there are strict page limits intended to produce shorter, more usable documents;[76] and (2) freedom to organize the text in the most logical way. The EIS is required to contain:

1. the environmental impact of the proposed action;
2. any adverse environmental effects which cannot be avoided by implementation of the proposed project;
3. alternatives to the proposed action;
4. the relationship between local short-term uses of the environment and maintenance and enhancement of long-term productivity; and
5. any irreversible and irretrievable commitments of resources involved in project implementation.[77]

The material can be organized in any logical way within these sections.

The analysis of alternatives is to include "reasonable" alternatives, including "no action."[78] The SEPA Rules explain that "reasonable" is intended to limit both the number and range of alternatives that must be discussed and the level of detail required in the analysis.[79] Reasonable alternatives are those courses of action that could achieve the objectives of the proposal at a lower environmental cost.[80] Reasonable alternatives include alternatives over which an agency has authority to control impacts, directly or by imposing mitigation measures.[81]

The elements of the environment that must be discussed in an EIS are enumerated in WAC 197-11-444, which divides the elements into the "natural" and the "built" environment. This section provides that analyses may be required only for these elements of the environment. The lead agency may discuss other elements, but an applicant may not be required to supply this information.

Social and Economic Impacts

Those areas of "urban concern" that must be discussed in an EIS are specified in the environmental checklist.[82] Examples of items that must be discussed include housing, aesthetics and historic and cultural preservation.[83] WAC 197-11-448(3) lists information not required to be discussed, including methods of financing, economic competition,[84] profits, personal income and wages and social policy analysis. These considerations and others may be included in the EIS, but, if the lead agency decides to include these optional items, it may not require the applicant to supply the information.[85]

Draft EIS, Public Comment and Timing

Following scoping, the lead agency or the applicant[86] begins preparing the draft EIS ("DEIS"). The DEIS is issued by the responsible official to Ecology, federal agencies with jurisdiction, other agencies with jurisdiction over the proposal or environmental expertise on the proposal, affected cities, counties, local agencies, affected tribes, and any other person requesting a copy.[87] Public comments are then received for thirty days.[88] The comment period may be extended by the lead agency by up to fifteen days.[89] Public hearings or meetings may be held but are not required.[90] It is important to note that lack of comment by an agency or the public is construed as lack of objection to the environmental analysis contained in the DEIS and that lack of comment by a consulted agency affirmatively bars that agency from alleging any defect in the lead agency's compliance with Part Four of the SEPA Rules.[91]

The lead agency must respond to all comments in the final EIS ("FEIS"). Response to comments can take any of several forms, including modifying the alternatives, developing new alternatives, supplementing the analysis, making factual corrections, or explaining why the comments do not require agency response.[92] The FEIS must be issued within sixty days of the end of the DEIS comment period under most circumstances.[93] Agencies are prohibited from acting on a proposal prior to seven days after issuance of the FEIS.[94]

Legal Adequacy of the EIS

The standard of legal adequacy of an EIS document is the "rule of reason."[95] This is the same standard developed in the federal courts for EISs produced under NEPA.[96] Courts will not "flyspeck" the EIS but instead will examine whether the proposal and a reasonable range of alternatives are sufficiently disclosed, discussed and substantiated by supportive opinion and data.[97] Less detailed analysis is required for a "nonproject" EIS than for a "project" EIS.[98] The issue of the range of alternatives that must be discussed for a proposal by a private applicant is discussed at WAC 197-11-440(5).[99]

Using Existing Environmental Documents

The SEPA Rules specify the conditions under which SEPA can be satisfied by the use of "existing" documents.[100] An agency may comply with SEPA by "adopting"[101] all or part of an existing environmental document. When preparing an original environmental document, an agency may "incorporate by reference" all or part of an existing document,[102] and/or the use of environmental analysis prepared under other laws (i.e., non-SEPA documents).[103] If an agency wishes to add analysis or information that does not substantially change the analysis of impacts and alternatives in an existing document it may prepare an "addendum"[104] to the existing document. An agency is to prepare a "supplemental EIS" (SEIS) if there are substantial changes to the proposal so that it is "likely to have significant adverse environmental impacts," or if there is "[n]ew information indicating a proposal's probable significant adverse environmental impacts."[105] The SEPA Rules expressly approve of combining one or more of the above methods.[106] For example, an agency may adopt an existing EIS and provide additional information in an addendum or SEIS.[107]

An agency also may adopt "any environmental analysis" prepared under NEPA. This is in contrast to NEPA, which does not allow federal agencies to adopt environmental documents prepared under local procedures; however, NEPA does allow the coordination of joint state/federal environmental documents. The SEPA Rules specify when and how a NEPA environmental document may be used to satisfy an agency's SEPA requirements.[108]

The SEPA Rules allow any SEPA environmental document to be combined with any other agency documents.[109] For example, an EIS could be combined with a solid waste management plan prepared under the State Solid Waste Management Act, as long as the combined document satisfies SEPA's requirements governing content, notice, commenting and the like. If the combined document contains a separate summary of environmental considerations at or near the beginning of the document, the page limits for EISs need not be met.[110]

SUBSTANTIVE AUTHORITY AND MITIGATION

SEPA provides supplemental authority to government agencies to condition or deny proposals based on adverse environmental impacts.[111] This authority is limited by regulation:

1. conditions or denials must be based on policies, plans, rules or regulations in effect when the DNS or DEIS is issued formally and designated by the agency as grounds for the exercise of SEPA authority;[112]
2. mitigation measures must be related to specific impacts identified in an environmental document on the proposal (e.g., DNS or EIS) and must be stated in writing by the decision maker;[113]
3. conditions must be "reasonable" and "capable of being accomplished;"[114] and
4. an applicant can be required to implement mitigation measures only to the extent attributable to the identified adverse impacts of its proposal.[115]

In addition, in order to deny a proposal under SEPA, an agency must find that the proposal would likely result in significant adverse environmental impacts identified in a final or supplemental EIS[116] and that reasonable mitigation measures are insufficient to mitigate the impact.[117]

The SEPA Rules define "mitigation" as:

1. avoiding the impact altogether by not taking a certain action or parts of an action;
2. minimizing impacts by limiting the degree or magnitude of the action in its implementation, by using appropriate technology, or by taking affirmative steps to avoid or reduce impacts;
3. rectifying the impact by repairing, rehabilitating, or restoring the affected environment;
4. reducing or eliminating the impact over time by preservation and maintenance operations during the life of the action;
5. compensating for the impact by replacing, enhancing, or providing substitute resources or environments; and/or
6. monitoring the impact and taking appropriate corrective measures.[118]

GMA local government mitigation authority is limited following a determination that its comprehensive plan or other laws adequately address the project's environmental impact. Having made this determination, the local government may not impose additional mitigation.[119]

In reviewing agency decisions conditioning or denying proposals on SEPA grounds, the courts have applied a "clearly erroneous" standard. A decision is "clearly erroneous" when after reviewing the decision of the administrative agency, the court is "left with the definite and firm conviction that a mistake has been committed."[120]

APPEALS

SEPA's appeals provisions are described at RCW §43.21C.075, and construed in the SEPA Rules at WAC 197-11-680. SEPA appeals may be to legislative, administrative or judicial bodies. Appeals provisions vary depending on the underlying action, the SEPA decision, and the agency involved. Therefore, the statute and rules should be read carefully in conjunction with the agency SEPA procedures for any given situation. Also, as discussed below, many SEPA appeals are now subject to the requirements of the Land Use Petition Act.[121]

SEPA appeals must be linked to a specific governmental action. The appeals provisions set forth two general rules. First, appeals are of the underlying governmental action together with its accompanying environmental determinations.[122] Second, the SEPA portion of the appeal, i.e., the appeal of the environmental determination, must be filed within the time required to challenge the underlying governmental action.[123] There are exceptions to these rules, as set forth below.

Appeal To Local Legislative Body

Any decision of a non-elected official to condition or deny a proposal under WAC 197-11-660 is appealable to the local legislative body. For example, the decision by a city planning department to condition a construction permit could be appealed to the city council. The SEPA Rules provide that agencies may establish procedures for this type of appeal or may eliminate such appeals altogether.[124]

Agency Administrative Appeals

Agencies are also authorized, but not required, to provide for an administrative appeal of SEPA determinations in the agency's SEPA procedures. If an agency does provide for administrative appeals, the agency appeals procedures must comply with the requirements of WAC 197-11-680(3)(a). The following decisions are subject to administrative appeal: threshold determinations, supplemental threshold determinations, EIS adequacy, substantive conditions, and denials. Ordinarily, an appeal must wait until an agency has reached a final decision on the underlying action[125] but threshold determinations may be appealed, within the agency, prior to and separate from the agency's final decision on the underlying action.[126] No more than one appeal can be raised within the same agency.[127] Also, there can be no more than one open record and one closed-record appeal for each permit application.[128]

If an agency has made a decision on the underlying governmental action, the SEPA appeal must consolidate all allowable agency appeals of procedural and substantive determinations.[129] For example, if an agency has prepared an EIS for a rezone decision, and there is an agency appeals process for the rezone decision, an appeal of the adequacy of the final EIS must be combined with the appeal of the rezone decision. Procedural determinations made by the responsible official are to be given substantial weight on appeal.[130]

If an agency does provide for an administrative appeal, that procedure must be used before any judicial review is permitted.[131] This requirement codifies the common law doctrine of exhaustion of administrative remedies. Therefore, if an administrative appeal procedure is provided, an administrative appeal must be timely filed or all review, both administrative and judicial, will be barred.[132] Administrative appeals of local government action and SEPA determinations must be filed within fourteen days[133] from the date notice of the decision is issued.

The Shorelines Hearings Board (SHB) has jurisdiction to hear any SEPA appeals, whether or not a shoreline issue is involved, upon consent of the parties to the action. The parties may transfer all or part of the appeal from any agency or superior court. Once the SHB has ruled, a party may appeal its decision, but such appeal may only be taken to an appellate court.[134]

Judicial Appeals

Since SEPA claims must be combined with an appeal of the underlying action,[135] the applicable appeal process and time limits depend on the underlying action. SEPA claims connected to permits and other "land use decisions"[136] under the Land Use Petition Act (LUPA) are subject to LUPA and are initiated by filing a land use petition in superior court within twenty-one days of issuance of the land use decision.[137]

SEPA claims connected to other decisions not covered by LUPA are appealed along with those decisions, typically by filing a statutory writ of review.[138] SEPA challenges must be brought within the time limit applicable to the underlying action (not within thirty days).[139] In the event that an action is not subject to the Land Use Petition Act, and there is no applicable time limit for appeal, , SEPA establishes no statute of limitations for judicial appeals.[140] However, common law principles such as laches, still apply.[141]

If there is a time limit applicable to the underlying action, official notice of the date and place for commencing an appeal is required.[142]

Notice of Action

SEPA also contains an optional "notice of action" procedure.[143] This procedure may be used by either the lead agency or the applicant. If notice of action, or notice of subsequent action, is provided, any challenge on the grounds of noncompliance with SEPA must be commenced within twenty-one days of the last newspaper publication. In addition, subsequent governmental actions on the proposal may not be challenged on the basis of noncompliance with RCW 43.21C.030(2)(a) through (h) (procedural compliance with SEPA) unless the proposal has undergone a substantial change that is likely to have adverse environmental impacts beyond the range of those previously analyzed, or the action was identified in an earlier governmental document as one that would require further governmental review.[144]

Attorneys' Fees

The SEPA Rules give a court the discretion to award reasonable attorneys' fees not to exceed $1,000 to the prevailing party, including a government agency, if the court finds that the legal position of the opposing party is frivolous and without reasonable basis.[145]

NOTES

1 RCW §43.21.

2 WAC 197-11. Frequently referred to as the "SEPA Rules" or the "Green Book." Ecology has also published a handbook to guide interpretation, available at http://www.ecy.wa.gov/programs/sea/sepa/handbk/hbintro.html. Local governments may also have their own interpretation found in local zoning ordinances.

3 WAC 197-11-210.

4 WAC 197-11-228.

5 WAC 197-11-908.

6 WAC 197-11-305.

7 WAC 197-11-250. *See also* RCW §43.21C.036.

8 RCW §43.21C.240.

9 RCW §36.70B.

10 RCW §§43.21C.010 and .020.

11 RCW §43.21C.020(3).

12 RCW §43.21C.030(l).

13 RCW §43.21C.030(2).

14 RCW §43.21C.030(c). *See also Anderson v. Pierce County*, 86 Wn. App. 290 (1997).

15 42 U.S.C. §§4321 *et seq.*

16 RCW §43.21C.030(2).

17 RCW §43.21C.060; WAC 197-11-660; *Polygon Corporation, Inc. v. Seattle*, 90 Wn. 2d 59 (1978); *Sisley v. San Juan County*, 89 Wn. 2d 78 (1977).

18 WAC 197-11-704.

19 RCW §43.21C.240.

20 RCW §43.21C.031.

21 RCW §43.21C.031(1).

22 WAC 197-11-310(1); 197-11-704.

23 WAC 197-11-310(2).

24 WAC 197-11-055.

25 *Juanita Bay Valley Community Association v. Kirkland*, 9 Wn. App. 59 (1973); *Lassila v. Wenatchee*, 89 Wn. 2d 804 (1978).

26 WAC 197-11-055(2)(a)(ii).

27 *Eastlake Community Council v. Roanoke Assoc., Inc.*, 82 Wn. 2d 475 (1973).

28 WAC 197-11-060(5). *See also Cathcart-Maltby-Clearview Community Council v. Snohomish County*, 96 Wn. 2d 201 (1981) (EIS for rezone held adequate even though it did not evaluate impacts of future development because it provided a meaningful framework for future environmental analysis).

29 The lead agency is determined by the rules set forth in WAC 197-11-922 through -948. *See also* WAC 197-11-253 (determining lead agency under the Model Toxics Control Act).

30 WAC 197-11-926. See *Trepanier v. Everett*, 64 Wn. App. 380 (1992) (without a showing of bias, city council acting as lead agency in reviewing its own proposed zoning code revision did not violate appearance of fairness doctrine).

[31] WAC 197-11-930.

[32] WAC 197-11-932.

[33] WAC 197-11-934.

[34] WAC 197-11-936.

[35] WAC 197-11-938.

[36] WAC 197-11-940.

[37] WAC 197-11 -942 and -944; see also WAC 197-11-985 (form for assumption of lead agency status).

[38] WAC 197-11-946.

[39] WAC 197-11-910.

[40] WAC 197-11-310(2).

[41] WAC 197-11-310(3)

[42] WAC 197-11-310(3); *Eastlake Community Council v. Roanoke Assoc., Inc.*, 82 Wn. 2d 475 (1973).

[43] RCW §43.21C.031(1); WAC 197-11-310.

[44] WAC 197-11-704(1). *See Pease Hill Community Group v. County of Spokane*, 62 Wn. App. 800 (1991) (agency approval of private project by granting of permits constitutes "action").

[45] WAC 197-11-704(2). *See Indian Trail Prop. Assn. v. Spokane*, 76 Wn. App. 430 (1994) (SEPA is triggered when request for zoning interpretation is coupled with application for building permit).

[46] RCW §43.21C.110(1)(a).

[47] WAC 197-11-305(a); WAC 197-11-908(1).

[48] WAC 197-11-305(1)(b)(i).

[49] WAC 197-11 -305(1)(b)(ii).

[50] *Downtown Traffic Planning Committee v. Royer*, 26 Wn. App. 156 (1980); RCW §43.21C.110(1).

[51] WAC 197-11-315; 197-11-960.

[52] WAC 197- 11-315(1)(a).

[53] WAC 197-11-315(3).

[54] WAC 197-11-330(1).

[55] WAC 197-11 330(2).

[56] WAC 197-11-330(3)(a).

[57] WAC 197-11-330(3)(b).

[58] WAC 197-11-330(3)(c).

[59] WAC 197-11 330(3)(e)(i).

[60] WAC 197 11-330(3)(e)(ii).

[61] WAC-197-11-330(3)(e)(iii).

[62] WAC-197-11-330(3)(e)(iv).

[63] WAC 197-11-360.

[64] WAC 197-11-340; 197-11-734; 197-11-970 (DNS form).

[65] WAC 197-11-340(1).

[66] WAC 197-11-340(3)(a)

[67] WAC 197-11-340(2)(a)

[68] WAC 197-11-340(2)(c).

[69] WAC 197-11-340(2)(e).

70 WAC 197-11-390(2); *City of Olympia v. Drebick*, 156 Wn. 2d 289 (2006), *cert. den.* 127 S.Ct. 436.

71 WAC 197-11-350; *Anderson v. Pierce County*, 86 Wn. App. 290 (1997); *Pease Hill Community Group v. Spokane County*, 62 Wn. App. 800 (1991).

72 The mitigation required by an agency is not unlimited. RCW §82.02.020; RCW 43.21C.065. *Dolan v. City of Tigard*, 512 US (1994); *Burton v. Clark County*, 91 Wn. App. 505 (1998).

73 WAC 197-11-360.

74 WAC 197-11-980.

75 WAC 197-11-410.

76 WAC 197-11-425 through 197-11-440.

77 RCW §43.21C.030(c).

78 WAC 197-11-440(5).

79 *Id.*

80 *Id.*

81 *Id.*

82 RCW §43.21C.110(1)(f) and WAC 197-11-440 and 197-11-444.

83 WAC 197-11-444. See *Klickitat County Citizens Against Imported Waste v. Klickitat County*, 122 Wn. 2d 619 (1993), opinion amended, 866 P.2d 1256 (1994); *See also Concerned Citizens of Hosp. Dist. No. 304 v. Public Hosp. Dist. No. 304*, 78 Wn. App. 333 (1995).

84 *See Indian Trail Prop. Assn. v. Spokane*, 76 Wn. App. 430 (1994).

85 WAC 197-11-440(8), -448, -450, -640 and -100(3).

86 Regardless of who prepares the EIS, the EIS is the responsibility of the lead agency. WAC 197-11-420.

87 WAC 197-11-455(1).

88 WAC 197-11-455(6).

89 WAC 197-11-455(7).

90 WAC 197-11-502(6).

91 WAC 197-11-545; *Kitsap County v. Dep't of Natural Resources*, 99 Wn. 2d 386 (1983), *appeal after remand*, 107 Wn. 2d 801 (1987).

92 WAC 197-11-560(1).

93 WAC 197-11-460(6).

94 WAC 197-11-460(5).

95 *See, e.g., King County v. Boundary Review Board*, 122 Wn. 2d 648 (1993); *Cheney v. Mountlake Terrace*, 87 Wn. 2d 338 (1976).

96 *See, e.g., Trout Unlimited v. Morton*, 509 F. 2d 1276 (9th Cir. 1974); *Natural Resources Defense Council, Inc. v. Morton*, 458 F. 2d 827 (DC Cir. 1972).

97 *Leschi Improvement Council v. State Highway Comm.*, 84 Wn. 2d 271 (1974).

98 WAC 197-11-442; *Ullock v. Bremerton*, 17 Wn. App. 573, *rev. den.* 89 Wn.2d 1101 (1977).

99 *See Organization to Protect Agricultural Lands v. Adams County*, 128 Wn. 2d 869 (1996); *Citizens Alliance to Protect Our Wetlands v. Auburn*, 126 Wn. 2d 356 (1995); *Weyerhaeuser v. Pierce County*, 124 Wn. 2d 26 (1994).

100 RCW §43.21C.034; WAC 197-11-600.

101 WAC 197-11-600(4)(a).

[102] WAC 197-11-600(4)(b); *see also Klickitat County Citizens Against Imported Waste v. Klickitat County*, 122 Wn. 2d 619 (1993).

[103] RCW §43.21C.240(6).

[104] WAC 197-11-600(4)(c); *See also Nisqually Delta Association v. DuPont*, 103 Wn. 2d 720 (1985).

[105] WAC 197-11-600(4)(d). *See Citizens for Clean Air v. Spokane*, 114 Wn. 2d 20 (1990.

[106] Specific procedures for preparing addenda and SEISs and for adoption and incorporation by reference are set forth at WAC 197-11-620, -625, -630 and -635, respectively. An "adoption notice" form is contained at WAC 197-11-965.

[107] WAC 197-11-600(4)(e).

[108] WAC 197-11-610.

[109] WAC 197-11-640. *See also* WAC 197-11-235 (SEPA documents may be integrated into documentation of GMA actions).

[110] WAC 197-11-640.

[111] The authority to condition or deny was made explicit in RCW §43.21C.060, enacted in 1977 and amended in 1983, and further clarified in the 1984 Rules at WAC 197-11-660. *See Polygon Corp. Inc. v. Seattle*, 90 Wn. 2d 59 (1978).

[112] WAC 197-11-660(1)(a).

[113] WAC 197-11-660(1)(b).

[114] WAC 197-11-660(1)(c).

[115] WAC 197-11-660(1)(d).

[116] WAC 197-11-660(1)(f).

[117] *Id.*

[118] WAC 197-11-768.

[119] RCW §43.21C.240(3).

[120] *Ancheta v. Daly*, 77 Wn. 2d 255 (1969).

[121] RCW §36.70C.

[122] RCW §§43.21C.075(1) and (2)(a); WAC 197-11-680(4)(a) and (b).

[123] RCW §43.21C.075(5)(a).

[124] WAC 197-11-680(2).

[125] WAC 197-11—680(3)(a)(ii).

[126] *Foster v. King County*, 83 Wn. App. 339 (1996); *Saldin Sec. v. Snohomish*, 80 Wn. App. 522 (1996), *rev. granted*, 129 Wn. 2d 1022 (1996).

[127] WAC 197-11-680(3)(a)(iv); *See West Main Assoc.*, 49 Wn. App. at 517-519. *See also* RCW §43.21C.075(3)(a).

[128] RCW §36.70B.060.

[129] WAC 197-11-680(3)(a)(v). *See* RCW §43.21C.075(3)(b).

[130] WAC 197-11-680(3)(a)(vi).

[131] RCW §43.21C.075(4); WAC 197-11-680(3)(c).

[132] *See State v. Grays Harbor County*, 122 Wn. 2d 244 (1993).

[133] If public comment is allowed on a DNS, the fourteen-day period is extended by an additional seven days. RCW §36.70C.110(9). See also WAC 197-11-340(2).

[134] RCW §43.21C.075(7).

[135] RCW §43.21C.075(1).

[136] RCW §36.70C.020.

[137] RCW §36.70C.040(3)-(4).

[138] *See* RCW §7.16.

[139] RCW §43.21C.075(5)(a).

[140] WAC 197-11-680(4)(g). *See Concerned Organized Women and People Opposed to Offensive Proposals, Inc. v. Arlington*, 69 Wn. App. 209 (1993).

[141] See *Marino Property Co. v. Port of Seattle*, 88 Wn. 2d 822 (1977.

[142] WAC 197-11-680(5); *See also Felida Neighborhood Assn. v. Clark County*, 81 Wn. App. 155 (1996).

[143] RCW §43.21C.080.

[144] RCW §43.21C.080(2)(b).

[145] RCW §43.21C.075(9). *See also* RCW §4.84.185. *Environmental Legacy Issues*

CHAPTER 2

Growth Management

INTRODUCTION

In 1990, the Washington legislature enacted the Growth Management Act ("GMA"), upon the Legislative finding that

> uncoordinated and unplanned growth, together with a lack of common goals expressing the public's interest in the conservation and the wise use of our lands, pose a threat to the environment, sustainable economic development, and the health, safety, and high quality of life enjoyed by residents of this state. It is in the public interest that citizens, communities, local governments, and the private sector cooperate and coordinate with one another in comprehensive land use planning. Further, the legislature finds that it is in the public interest that economic development programs be shared with communities experiencing insufficient economic growth.[1]

In 1991, the legislature added three regional Growth Management Hearings Boards, each consisting of three members ("GMHB") to resolve disputes over compliance with the GMA.[2] In 2010, the three GMHBs were consolidated into one statewide Board consisting of seven members. Hearings are still held on a regional basis (Eastern, Central Puget Sound, and Western Washington) by panels made up of two members who reside in the region in question, and one drawn from one of the other regions. Decisions of the GMHB are available online in digest forms as well as a searchable database at http://www.gmhb.wa.gov. Finally, in 2011, the GMHB was administratively consolidated with the Environmental Hearings Office to become the Environmental and Land Use Hearings Office.

In 2002, the Legislature added, without discussing environmental considerations at all, that rural areas could stress economic development by exhorting the counties to:

> [h]elp preserve rural-based economies and traditional rural lifestyles; encourage the economic prosperity of rural residents; foster opportunities for small-scale, rural-based employment and self-employment; permit the operation of rural-based agricultural, commercial, recreational, and tourist businesses that are consistent with exist-

ing and planned land use patterns; be compatible with the use of the land by wildlife and for fish and wildlife habitat; foster the private stewardship of the land and preservation of open space; and enhance the rural sense of community and quality of life.[3]

In 2003, the Legislature required counties to ... ensure that, taken collectively, adoption of and amendments to their comprehensive plans and/or development regulations provide sufficient capacity of land suitable for development within their jurisdictions to accommodate their allocated housing and employment growth, as adopted in the applicable countywide planning policies and consistent with the twenty-year population forecast from the office of financial management.[4]

PLANNING FOR GROWTH: AN OVERVIEW OF THE PLANNING REQUIREMENTS

The GMA established roles and responsibilities for planning at the local, regional and state level. Before passage of the GMA, local governments were responsible for land use planning, and the state played a limited role. The GMA changed this system by establishing a statewide planning framework and requiring many local governments to plan.

Local Level Planning

Comprehensive Plans

The principal mechanism for implementing the GMA's growth management goals[5] is planning at the local level by cities and counties. At the outset, the GMA required the state's largest and fastest growing counties (counties with more than fifty thousand people and a population increase of more than twenty percent in the past ten years) and the cities within those counties to develop new comprehensive plans by July 1, 1993, and implementing regulations by July 1, 1994.[6] Failure to adopt comprehensive plans on schedule disqualifies local governments from receiving loans or pledges to fund construction of public works and from receiving public funds to construct water pollution control facilities.[7]

Counties not required by the GMA to plan may elect to do so.[8] The requirements for preparing comprehensive plans, which are extensive, are discussed in detail below.

Natural Resource Lands and Critical Areas. All counties in the state must designate agriculture, forest, and mineral resource lands that have long-term commercial significance.[9] Counties planning under the GMA must adopt development regulations to assure that the use of lands adjacent to these resource lands does not interfere with their continued use for producing food, agricultural products, timber, or minerals. These interim regulations may not prohibit uses permitted before their adoption, and they remain in effect until final regulations implementing comprehensive plans are adopted.[10]

Similarly, all counties and cities must designate critical areas and adopt development regulations that preclude land uses or developments that are incompatible with such areas.[11] Critical areas are defined as wetlands, aquifer recharge zones, fish and wildlife habitat conservation areas, frequently flooded areas, and geologically hazardous areas.[12] Cities and counties are required to use "best available science" when developing policies and regulations to protect critical areas.[13]

Regional Level Planning

Countywide Planning Policies

The Act required counties, in cooperation with cities located within their boundaries, to adopt Countywide Planning Policies ("CPPs") by July 1, 1992.[14] These policies are to be used to guide the development of comprehensive plans.[15] Comprehensive plans must be consistent with the CPPs to ensure that the counties' and the cities' plans are consistent with each other as required by the Act.[16]

The CPPs must, at a minimum, address the following issues:

1. location of urban growth areas[17] and related services;
2. promotion of contiguous and orderly development;
3. siting of public capital and transportation facilities;
4. countywide economic development and employment;
5. affordable housing; and
6. joint planning within urban growth areas.[18]

Only the Governor and cities may appeal an adopted Countywide Policy Plan to the Growth Planning Hearings Board.[19] Such an appeal must be made within sixty days of the CPP's adoption.[20] The GMA requires counties with a population of 450,000 or more with contiguous urban areas to adopt "multi-county planning policies"[21] but does not specify the content of these policies or a deadline for their adoption. As an incentive to adopt countywide planning policies, the state may give preference when awarding grants to those counties, or the cities within those counties, that have prepared county-wide planning policies.[22]

Regional Transportation Planning

The Act establishes a coordinated planning program for regional transportation systems and facilities throughout the state.[23] The Act authorizes local governments to form regional transportation planning organizations[24] to develop regional transportation plans and to certify that local comprehensive plans are consistent with such plans and other requirements of the Act.[25] All transportation projects within the region that have an impact on regional facilities or services must be consistent with the regional transportation plan.[26]

State Participation

Under the GMA, the state provides technical and financial assistance, mediates disputes between counties and cities, establishes minimum standards to ensure consistency in regional transportation planning, and enforces the Act through sanctions and a process for identifying and managing natural resources of statewide significance. State agencies must comply with local comprehensive plans adopted under the GMA.[27]

Technical and Financial Assistance

The Department of Commerce ("DOC") is the state agency charged with implementing the GMA.[28] DOC provides financial and technical assistance and incentives to counties and cities to help them prepare comprehensive plans and development regulations.[29] DOC also coordinates the state agencies' review of comprehensive plans and development regulations.

The principal form of financial assistance provided by DOC has been direct grants to local governments for preparing interim measures, comprehensive plans, and development regulations. DOC technical assistance includes the development of guidelines to implement the Act. For example, DOC issued guidelines to help local governments classify critical areas as well as agriculture, forest, and mineral land.[30] DOC is also available to mediate disputes between counties and cities regarding regional issues and the designation of urban growth areas.[31]

To ensure state-wide consistency in regional transportation planning, the Act requires the Washington State Department of Transportation ("WSDOT") to provide minimum standards for the development of regional transportation plans.[32] WSDOT also distributes funds to regional planning organizations to develop these regional plans.[33]

Sanctions

The Governor may impose sanctions on state agencies, counties, or cities that fail to comply with the GMA.[34] These sanctions are discussed in greater detail in Section 3.7, which covers appeals and enforcement.

COMPREHENSIVE PLANS

The GMA establishes goals to guide the preparation of comprehensive plans; prescribes the elements that plans must include; and creates special mechanisms for preserving open space, concentrating growth in urban areas, and identifying and planning for public facilities, including those that are difficult to site. By July 1, 1994, local governments were required to implement comprehensive plans with consistent and supportive development regulations and capital budgets. In addition, comprehensive plans of counties and cities with common borders or related regional issues must be coordinated and consistent with each other.[35]

GMA Goals

The GMA establishes thirteen goals to guide cities and counties in developing comprehensive plans and development regulations:

1. Encourage development in urban areas.[36]
2. Reduce the conversion of undeveloped land into sprawling, low-density development.[37]
3. Encourage efficient multimodal transportation systems.[38]
4. Encourage the availability of affordable housing.[39]
5. Encourage economic development throughout the state.
6. Provide compensation for "takings" of private property.
7. Process applications for permits timely and fairly.
8. Maintain and enhance natural resource-based industries.[40]
9. Encourage the retention of open space and development of recreational opportunities.
10. Protect the environment and enhance the state's quality of life.
11. Encourage citizen involvement.[41]

12. Ensure the availability of public facilities and services necessary to support development.[42]
13. Encourage historic preservation.

These planning goals are not listed in order of priority.[43] Rather, local governments are to use the goals to develop plans and regulations that reflect their own sense of balance among the often competing objectives of growth management. Unlike the objectives of State Environmental Protection Act[44] and the Shoreline Management Act[45] that apply generally to governmental actions, the GMA's goals are to be used exclusively for the purpose of preparing plans and development regulations.

Plan Elements

The GMA requires comprehensive plans to include six sections or "elements."

1. *Land Use Element.* The plan must designate the general location and extent of uses for agriculture, timber, housing, commerce, industry, recreation, open space, public utilities, and public facilities. Issues such as density, future population growth, water quality, and drainage must be taken into account.[46] In addition, this element must protect the quality and quantity of ground water used for public water supplies.[47]
2. *Housing.* The plan must inventory existing and future housing requirements, plan for preserving and upgrading existing housing stocks, and provide for low income and affordable housing needs.[48]
3. *Capital Facilities.* The plan must inventory existing public facilities and their capacity, forecast future needs, identify proposed locations and capacities of new facilities and provide a financing plan for a minimum of six-years to meet requirements for new facilities.[49]
4. *Utilities.* The plan must inventory existing facilities and outline proposed new facilities requirements, including electric, telecommunications, and gas lines and other utility facilities as appropriate.[50]
5. *Rural Element (Counties Only).* The plan must identify lands that are rural in character either as not designated for urban growth or as natural resource lands. The plan must permit uses that are compatible with the rural character of such lands.[51]
6. *Transportation.* The plan must specify the land use assumptions used in estimating travel needs, project the facilities and services required to meet those needs, provide a financing plan for necessary facilities and services and assess the impacts of the transportation plan on adjacent jurisdictions.[52] The elements of the comprehensive plans must be consistent with each other and internally consistent.[53]

Comprehensive plans may also include optional elements addressing such issues as conservation, solar energy, and recreation[54] and may provide for innovative land use regulation techniques such as density bonuses, cluster housing, planned unit development and transfer of development rights.[55] Comprehensive plans may also include an economic development element, an environmental protection element, a natural resource lands element, and a design element.[56]

Urban Growth Areas

Counties that plan under the Act must designate "urban growth areas" ("UGAs"), within which urban growth is to take place and outside of which only non-urban growth can occur.[57] Urban growth is growth that uses land intensively for buildings, structures, and impermeable surfaces to such a degree that it precludes using the land to produce food, other agricultural products, fiber, or minerals.[58] This requirement focuses much of the new residential, commercial, and industrial development in urban areas.[59]

Counties designate UGAs in consultation with the cities within their boundaries. These areas must include all cities, and may include unincorporated areas that either are already characterized by urban development or are adjacent to areas characterized by urban development. The overall size of UGAs will be limited to lands needed to accommodate the population growth forecasted by the Office of Financial Management ("OFM") over the next succeeding twenty-year period.[60]

If the county and a city do not agree on the boundary, the county must justify its action in writing and DOC may mediate the dispute.[61] In addition, cities may appeal the urban boundary to the Growth Planning Hearings Boards, discussed below.

A county may approve new fully contained communities outside of the UGAs if the development provides infrastructure; implements transit-oriented site planning and traffic demand management programs; provides for uses that result in jobs, housing, and services for the new community; provides affordable housing; mitigates impacts on designated agricultural, forest, and mineral resource lands; and is consistent with critical areas regulations. The county must also reserve a portion of its twenty-year population projection for use by the new community and subtract this reserve from the population projection for planning the remaining UGAs within the county.[62]

Counties may also develop short-term visitor recreational facilities (master planned resorts) outside UGAs. The county may do so, however, only if the comprehensive plan specifically identifies policies to guide development and includes provisions that restrict new urban or suburban development and uses in the vicinity of the resort. The county must also find that the land is better suited for resort use than for commercial timber or agriculture and must ensure that the project mitigates on-site and off-site infrastructure impacts.[63]

Counties may also establish a process for siting major industrial developments in the rural areas, which include natural resource based industries or activities that require very large parcels of land.[64]

Open Space Corridors

Planning counties and cities must identify open space corridors within and between urban growth areas. "Open space" includes lands useful for recreation, habitat, and trails; and must be coordinated with designated critical lands. Counties and cities may seek to acquire a fee simple or lesser interests in these corridors.[65]

Public Facilities and Difficult-to-Site Facilities

Planning counties and cities must identify lands for public facilities (i.e., public rights-of-way and schools). The local government's capital facilities plan must identify a schedule and a financing mechanism for acquiring or developing these lands and facilities.[66]

Planning counties and cities must also include in their comprehensive plans a process for identifying and siting "essential" or difficult-to-site public facilities, for example, prisons, landfills, and transportation facilities.[67] Local comprehensive plans and development regulations may not preclude the siting of essential facilities.[68]

Transmittal to State

Planning counties and cities must notify DOC of their intent to adopt plans and regulations sixty days in advance. State agencies may comment on the proposed plans and actions, but they do not have authority to approve or disapprove of them.[69] The state may appeal a comprehensive plan or implementing regulations to the Growth Planning Hearings Board.

DEVELOPMENT REGULATIONS

Local governments must adopt development regulations that are consistent with the Comprehensive Plan.[70]

PUBLIC PARTICIPATION

Local governments must establish a public participation program that identifies procedures for "early and continuous public participation" in developing comprehensive plans and development regulation.[71]

APPEALS

Administrative Appeals: Hearings Boards

The Act creates three regional Growth Planning Hearings Boards (Boards) to monitor state agency, county and city compliance with many of the Act's provisions.[72] Although separate entities, the Boards operate under a common set of procedural rules.[73]

Matters Subject to Review

The GMHB's authority to adjudicate cases is limited to (1) allegations that a state agency, county, or city is not in compliance with the GMA's requirements for comprehensive plans and development regulations,[74] not in compliance with SEPA as it relates to plans, regulations, and amendments thereto,[75] or not in compliance with the Shoreline Management Act as it relates to adoption of a shoreline master program or amendments; and (2) allegations that the twenty-year growth management planning population projections used to designate urban growth areas should be adjusted.[76] Only certain persons may file appeals.[77] Appeals regarding comprehensive plans and development regulations must be brought within sixty days of their publication by the county or city.[78] Such plans and regulations are presumed valid, and the petitioner has the burden of proving that they do not comply with the GMA.[79] Significantly, individual land use decisions, such as the granting of a building permit, may not be appealed to the GMHB.

Finding of Noncompliance or Invalidity

The GMHB, on its own motion or on motion of a petitioner, will hold hearings to determine whether the state agency, county, or city is complying with the GMA. The Boards must issue final orders within 180 days of petitions being filed.[80]

Such orders may find that the GMA action complies with the GMA, or fails to comply with the GMA.[81] A finding of non-compliance does not affect the validity of the GMA action unless the GMHB determines that the continued validity of the Plan would substantially interfere with fulfilling the goals in RCW §36.70A.020.[82] Provisions or measures found to be invalid may not be applied to project applications submitted after the GMHB's order. If the GMHB finds that the governmental entity is not complying with the GMA, the governmental entity has up to 180 days in which to comply. After 180 days, the GMHB may recommend that the Governor impose sanctions, as discussed below.[83]

Sanctions

The Governor may impose sanctions, based on a GMHB's findings, against state agencies, counties, or cities that fail to comply with the GMA. The Governor can direct the appropriate state agency to:

1. revise allotments in agency appropriation levels;
2. withhold revenues to local governments from the motor vehicle fuel tax, the transportation improvement account, the rural and urban arterial accounts, the sales and use tax, and the liquor profit and excise tax; or
3. temporarily rescind counties' or cities' authority to collect real estate excise taxes.[84]

Judicial Appeal

Parties may appeal the GMHB's decisions to superior court within thirty days of the final order from the GMHB.[85] Judicial review of GMHB decisions will be based on the administrative factual record compiled by the GMHB.

RELATIONSHIP TO OTHER LAWS

State Environmental Policy Act ("SEPA")

The requirements of SEPA must be met under the GMA.[86] SEPA review is expected for development of regional planning policies, interim regulations, comprehensive plans and final implementing regulations.[87]

Shoreline Management Act (SMA)

The goals and policies of a shoreline master program for a county or city approved under the Shoreline Management Act ("SMA") is considered to be an element of the county- or city adopted comprehensive plan.[88] All other parts of the shoreline master program, including use regulations, are considered to be part of the local government's GMA development regulations.[89]

Vesting

The GMA does not change vesting rules in existence before the GMA. The doctrine of vested rights enables a permit holder to complete a land development despite subsequent changes to the zoning code that would prohibit or otherwise affect the project. In Washington, an applicant is entitled to be governed by the zoning ordinances in effect on the date that a complete application was submitted.[90] A finding of noncompliance and an order of remand does not affect the validity of comprehensive plans and development regulations during the remand period, unless the GMHB also invalidates the provision.[91] Where the GMHB issues a determination of invalidity, the order does not extinguish rights that vested before the date of the GMHB's order.[92] Such an order subjects subsequent applications to the rules enacted in response to the remand order.

NOTES

[1] RCW §36.70A.010. Read together with the State Environmental Policy Act, the Legislature recognized that development, particularly in urban areas, affected not just the environment for the individual landowner but the environment for the community as a whole. *Erickson & Assocs., Inc. v. McLerran,* 123 Wn. 2d 864 (1994).

[2] *Kittitas County v. Kittitas County Conservation,* 176 Wn. App. 38 (2013); *Spokane County v. Eastern Washington Growth Management Hearings Board,* 173 Wn. App. 310 (2013); *Davidson Serles & Associates v. City of Kirkland,* 159 Wn. App. 616 (2011); *Futurewise v. Central Puget Sound Growth Management Hearings Bd.,* 141 Wn. App. 202 (2007); *Timberlake Christian Fellowship v. King County,* 114 Wn. App. 174 (2002), *rev. den.* 149 Wn. 2d 1013.

[3] RCW §36.70A.011.

[4] RCW §36.70A.115. *See also Gold Star Resorts, Inc. v. Futurewise,* 167 Wn. 2d 723 (2007).

[5] RCW §36.70A.020.

[6] RCW §36.70A.040; RCW §36.70A.120.

[7] RCW §43.155.070; RCW §70.146.070.

[8] RCW §36.70A.040(2).

[9] RCW §36.70A.030; RCW §36.70A.170.

[10] RCW §36.70A.060.

[11] RCW §36.70A.060.

[12] RCW §36.70A.030.

[13] *Kitsap Alliance of Property Owners v. Central Puget Sound Growth Management Hearings Bd.,* 160 Wn. App. 250, *rev. den.* 171 Wn. 2d 1030, *cert. den.* 132 S.Ct. 1792 (2011); *Honesty in Environmental Analysis and Legislation (HEAL) v. Central Puget Sound Growth Management Hearings Bd.,* 96 Wn. App. 522 (1999).

[14] RCW §36.70A.210

[15] RCW §36.70A.210(1).

[16] *King County v. Central Puget Sound Growth Management Hearings Bd.,* 138 Wn. 2d 161 (1999).

[17] RCW §36.70A.110. *See also Suquamish Tribe v. Central Puget Sound Growth Management Hearings Bd.,* 156 Wn. App. 743 (2010), *rev. den.* 170 Wn. 2d 1019.

[18] RCW §36.70A.210(3).

[19] RCW §36.70A.210(6).

[20] *Id.*

[21] RCW §36.70A.210(7).

[22] RCW §43.17.250.

[23] RCW §§47.80.010 through .050.

[24] RCW §47.80.020.

[25] RCW §§47.80.030(1)(a) and (b).

[26] RCW §47.80.030(3).

[27] RCW §36.70A.103.

[28] WAC 365-195.

[29] RCW §36.70A.190(1).

[30] RCW §36.70A.050; WAC 365-190-010 through -080.

[31] RCW §36.70A.190(5).

[32] RCW §47.80.030(3).

[33] RCW §47.80.050.

[34] RCW §36.70A.340.

[35] RCW §36.70A.100.

[36] *Miotke v. Spokane County*, 325 P. 3d 434 (2014); *Town of Woodway v. Snohomish County*, 172 Wn. App. 643 (2013); *Kittitas County v. Eastern Washington Growth Management Hearings Bd.*, 172 Wn. 2d 144 (2011); *Clark County v. Western Washington Growth Management Hearings Bd.*, 161 Wn. App. 204 (2011); *Quadrant Corp. v. State Growth Management Hearings Bd.*, 154 Wn. 2d 224 (2005).

[37] *King County v. Central Puget Sound Growth Management Hearings Bd.*, 142 Wn. App. 543 (2000).

[38] *Hapsmith v. City of Auburn*, CPSGMHB No. 95-3-0075C (1996) at 1887 (land use designation that discourages rail use discourages multimodal transportation and does not comply with transportation goal.).

[39] *Low Income Housing Institute v. City of Lakewood*, 119 Wn. App. 110 (2003).

[40] *City of Gig Harbor v. Pierce County*, CPSGMHB No. 95-3-0016 (1995) at 1325 (goal 9 met where county established minimum levels of service for parks); *Ellensburg v. Kittitas County*, EWGMHB No. 95-1-009 at 1847 (ordinance that improperly designates and conserves natural resource lands failed to maintain and enhance natural resource industries).

[41] *Brinnon Group v. Jefferson County*, 159 Wn. App. 446 (2011); *Peste v. Mason County*, 133 Wn. App. 456 (2006); *Chevron USA, Inc. v. Central Puget Sound Growth Management Hearings Bd.*, 123 Wn. App. 161 (2004), *aff'd.* 156 Wn. 2d 131.

[42] *Taxpayers for Responsible Government v. Oak Harbor*, WWGMHB No. 96-2-002 (1996)(comprehensive plan invalid where it does not analyze future capacities of public facilities auld the financial services need to ensure adequacy).

[43] RCW §36.70A.020.

[44] RCW §43.21C.

[45] RCW §90.48.

[46] *City of Arlington v. Central Puget Sound Growth Management Hearings Bd.*, 164 Wn. 2d 768 (2008); *Thurston County v. Western Washington Growth Management Hearings Bd.*, 164 Wn. 2d 329 (2007); *1000 Friends of Washington v. McFarland*, 159 Wn. 2d 165 (2006); *Clallam County v. Western Washington Growth Management Hearings Bd.*, 130 Wn. App. 127 (2005); *Whidbey Environmental Action Network v. Island County*, 122 Wn. App. 156 (2004), *rev. den.* 153 Wn. 2d 1025; *Holbrook, Inc. v. Clark County*, 112 Wn. App. 354 (2002).

[47] RCW §36.70A.070(1); *See, e.g., Swinomish Indian Tribal Community v. Western Washington Growth Management Hearings Bd.*, 161 Wn. 2d 415 (2007); *Lewis County v. Western Washington Growth Management Hearings Bd.*, 157 Wn. 2d 488 (2006).

[48] RCW §36.70A.070(2).

[49] RCW §36.70A.040(3).

[50] RCW §36.70A.070(4).

[51] RCW §36.70A.070(5); *Bremerton v. Kitsap County*, CPSGMHB No. 95-3-0039 (1995) at 1216 (plan must have variety of rural densities); *Vashon Maury v. King County*, CPSGMHB No. 95-3-0008 at 1294 (uses that otherwise meet the definition of "urban growth" are allowed in the rural area if due to their very nature they require a rural setting); Id. at 1295 (10 acre lots are clearly rural, not urban).

[52] RCW §36.70A.070(6); *City of Bellevue v. East Bellevue Community Mun. Corp.*, 119 Wn. App. 405 (2003).

53 RCW §36.70A.070; *West Seattle Defense Fund v City of Seattle*, CPSGMHB No. 95-3-0040 (1995) at 1083-84 (map and plan are inconsistent where map identifies urban village boundaries that have not yet been adopted), *Bremerton v Kitsap* at 1219 (finding lack of internal consistency between the land use element and capital facilities element).

54 RCW §36.70A.080.

55 RCW §36.70A.090; *Vashon Maury v King County* at 1273 (program allowing higher densities in exchange for open space is an innovative land use technique permitted by RCW §36.70A.090).

56 WAC 356-195-345. It would seem logical that a climate change element would be added as well.

57 RCW §36.70A.110.

58 RCW §36.70A.030(14).

59 *Bremerton v Kitsap*, CPSGMHP No. 95-3-0039 at 1216 (densities of one unit per 2.5 acres is urban in nature and may not be permitted in the rural area); *Gig Harbor v. Pierce County*, CPSGMHB No. 95-3-0016 at 1356 (provision allowing one unit per 2.5 acre shoreline development in rural areas violated RCW §36.70A.110); *Sky Valley v Snohomish County* at 1664 (densities of one unit per 2.3 acre in nature; density of one unit per 5 acre adjacent to UGA is prohibited).

60 RCW §36.70A.110; *Association of Rural Residents v Kitsap County*, CPSGMHB No. 93-3-0010 at 437 (county may not rely on outdated documents to calculate UGA).

61 RCW §36.70A.110(2).

62 RCW §36.70A 350.

63 RCW §36.70A.360.

64 RCW §36.70A.365.

65 RCW §36.70A.160.

66 RCW §36.70A.150.

67 RCW §36.70A.200(1); *Hapsmith v. City of Auburn*, CPSGMHB No. 95-3-0075c (1996) at 1884 (railroad facilities that serve the region are essential public facilities).

68 RCW §36.70A.200.

69 RCW §36.70A.106.

70 RCW §36.70A.105.

71 RCW §36.70A.140.

72 RCW §36.70A.250.

73 WAC 242-02.

74 *See, e.g., Yakima County v. Eastern Washington Growth Management Hearings Bd.*, 168 Wn. App. 680 (2012); *Olympic Stewardship Foundation v. Western Washington Growth Management Hearings Bd.*, 166 Wn. App. 172 (2012), rev. den., 174 Wn. 2d 1007; *Spokane County v. City of Spokane*, 148 Wn. App. 120 (2009); *Ferry County v. Concerned Citizens of Ferry County*, 121 Wn. App. 850 (2004); *City of Burien v. Central Puget Sound Growth Management Hearings Bd.*, 113 Wn. App. 375 (2002).

75 *City of Federal Way v. Town & Country Real Estate, LLC*, 161 Wn. App. 17 (2011).

76 RCW §36.70A.280(1).

77 RCW §§36.70A.280(2) and (4). *Stevens County v. Futurewise*, 146 Wn. App. 493 (2008)

78 RCW §36.70A.290(2).

79 RCW §36.70A.320.

80 RCW §36.70A.300(2).

81 RCW §36.70A.300(3).

[82] RCW §36.70A.300(3).

[83] RCW §36.70A.330.

[84] RCW §36.70A.340.

[85] RCW §36.70A.300(5).

[86] RCW §43.21C.

[87] RCW §36.70A.280 notes that failure to comply with SEPA is grounds for appeal to the Growth Hearings Board.

[88] RCW §90.58. *Biggers v. City of Bainbridge Island*, 162 Wn. 2d 683 (2007).

[89] RCW §36.70A.480.

[90] RCW §58.17.033. *Association of Rural Residents v. Kitsap County*, 141 Wn. 2d 185 (2000).

[91] RCW §36.70A.300(4).

[92] RCW §36.70A.302. *Weyerhauser v. Pierce County*, 95 Wn. App. 883 (1999).

CHAPTER 3

Shoreline and Coastal Zone Management

OVERVIEW

Washington established itself as a leader in managing development of its shorelines by enacting the Shoreline Management Act of 1971 ("SMA").[1] The SMA regulates "development" of "shorelines," which include all marine water areas of the state, streams with a mean annual flow of twenty cubic feet per second or more, lakes larger than twenty acres in area, and reservoirs. The SMA also applies to "shore*lands*" associated with these shorelines, including land 200 feet inland from ordinary high water mark, floodways, and all wetlands and river deltas associated with the streams, lakes, and tidal waters subject to the SMA. The SMA defines "development" broadly, applying to a host of shoreline activities, with some notable exemptions. Developments in wetlands on shorelines, defined as "critical areas" under the Growth Management Act, are regulated under the SMA within the growth Management Act permit review process.[2]

The SMA places substantive limitations on shoreline developments by prohibiting shoreline development that is inconsistent with the SMA's policies[3] or with local shoreline master programs ("SMPs")[4] using Guidelines promulgated by Ecology.[5] The SMA's policies attempt to strike a balance between development interests and the public interest by designating certain uses as "preferences" and "priorities," including single family residences, water-dependent uses, and uses that afford public access.[6] Local jurisdictions tailor the state policies to their particular circumstances through their SMPs, which enunciate their own policy goals and, like zoning codes, identify the shoreline environments to which the SMPs apply, and spell out regulations for specific uses of these environments.[7] Most disputes over SMPs' substantive and procedural compliance with the SMA and other laws are heard by the Shoreline Hearings Board (the "SHB").

Local governments ensure compliance with the SMA's policies and their local SMPs by requiring that proponents of certain "substantial" shoreline developments obtain a permit.[8] Applicants must either obtain a shoreline substantial development permit, or seek a shoreline conditional use permit or variance. Although state law establishes the framework that local permit procedures must comply with, local regulations dictate the exact shoreline permit procedure, including any available administrative appeals.[9] Any aggrieved party, including

Ecology, may appeal a permit decision to the SHB. Once final, permits are generally valid for five years.

The Act created the SHB to hear a variety of disputes related to SMPs and permit decisions, including issues related to the State Environmental Policy Act ("SEPA"). The SHB, now part of the Environmental and Land Use Hearings Office, is a quasi-judicial body with limited jurisdiction and its own rules of procedure. Appeals of SHB decisions must generally be taken to Superior Court.[10]

This chapter concludes with an overview of Washington's Coastal Zone Management Program ("CZMP"). Under the federal Coastal Zone Management Act ("CZMA"), federal activities, and private activities that require a federal license or permit within the "coastal zone" may not proceed until they are proven consistent with the CZMP. "Coastal zone" refers to water that contains a measurable quantity or percentage of sea water and the adjacent shorelands, which includes Washington's fifteen coastal counties. The heart of the CZMP's substantive requirements are the state SMA policies and local SMPs enacted under the SMA.

JURISDICTIONAL REACH OF THE SMA

"Where": Geographical Reach of the SMA

Shorelines and Shorelands

The Shoreline Management Act applies to all "shorelines of the state,"[11] which include both "shorelines"[12] and "shorelines of state-wide significance."[13] "Shorelines" include all marine water areas of the state, together with the lands underlying them, out to the western boundary of the state in the Pacific Ocean (three-mile limit), to streams with a mean annual flow of twenty cubic feet per second or more, to lakes larger than twenty acres in area, and to reservoirs. "Shorelines of state-wide significance" is a category of shorelines, and includes enumerated portions of Puget Sound and large lakes and rivers over which the state exercises greater authority. The SMA specifically requires that it be "liberally construed."[14]

The SMA also applies to the "associated shorelands" of these shorelines.[15] "Shorelands" are "those lands extending landward for 200 feet in all directions as measured on a horizontal plane from the ordinary highwater mark (the vegetation line);[16] floodways and contiguous floodplain areas landward 200 feet from such floodways; and all wetlands[17] and river deltas[18] associated with the streams, lakes, and tidal waters that are subject to the provisions of the SMA."

Lands Outside Shorelands

The SMA expressly intends that the use and development of land adjacent to the shorelines be consistent with the policy of the SMA.[19] Even when lands are inland from the boundary of "associated shorelands," the SMA may have an effect on their use. In *Merkel v. Port of Brownsville*, the court enjoined the defendant from proceeding with the development of a small boat marina complex (encompassing 12½ acres of shorelines and 10 acres of uplands) on the ground that a single, integrated project requiring development of both shoreline and upland ought not to be allowed to proceed in its upland portion prior to the granting of the SMA permit that is required for the development of the shorelines portion.[20]

"What" Actions Subject to Regulation

The SMA prohibits any "development" on shorelines not consistent with the SMA's policy and applicable SMP, even if no shoreline substantial development permit is required.[21] The SMA bans surface drilling for oil or gas outright.[22] The SMA defines "development" expansively:

> "Development" means a use consisting of the construction or exterior alteration of structures; dredging; drilling; dumping; filling; removal of any sand, gravel or minerals; bulkheading; driving of pilings; placing of obstructions; or any project of a permanent or temporary nature which interferes with the normal public use of the surface of the waters overlying lands subject to this chapter at any state of water level.[23]

Only "substantial development" requires a substantial development permit:

> "Substantial development" shall mean any development of which the total cost or fair market value exceeds five thousand dollars, or any development which materially interferes with the normal public use of the water or shorelines of the state . . . .[24]

Even though nonsubstantial developments do not require substantial development permits, local governments may regulate nonsubstantial developments through conditional use permits issued pursuant to the SMP.[25]

Certain developments are exempt from the definition of "substantial development," and therefore from the SMA's permit requirements.[26] Because the SMA is to be liberally construed to accomplish its purposes, doubts as to whether the SMA applies will probably be resolved in favor of applicability.[27] The exemptions include:

1. Normal maintenance or repair of existing structures or developments.[28]
2. Normal protective bulkheads for single family residences.
3. Emergency construction necessary to protect property from damage by the elements.
4. Ordinary construction normal or necessary to farming, irrigation and ranching . . . activities.
5. Construction or modification of navigational aids.
6. Construction on shorelands by an owner, lessee or contract purchaser of a single family residence for his or her own use or the use of his or her family, provided the residence does not exceed a height of thirty-five feet above average grade, and provided further that it meets all requirements of the state agency or local government having jurisdiction of the area.[29]
7. Construction of a pleasure craft dock for private noncommercial use by the owner, lessee or contract purchaser of a single- or multi-family residence. If the dock is located on salt water, this exception applies if fair market value of the dock does not exceed $2,500. If the dock is located on fresh water, this exception applies if the fair market value of the dock does not exceed $10,000, but if subsequent construction having a fair market value in excess of $2,500 occurs within five years of the prior construction, the subsequent construction will be considered a substantial development.[30]

8. Operation, maintenance or construction of canals, waterways, trains, reservoirs or irrigating system facilities.
9. Marking of property lines and corners on state-owned lands, when such marking does not significantly interfere with normal public use of surface water.
10. Operation and maintenance of ditches, dikes, drains and other facilities existing on September 8, 1975, which were created, developed or utilized primarily as part of an agricultural, drainage, or diking system.[31]

Holders of certifications under the Energy Facility Siting Act are also exempted from permit requirements.[32] Likewise, permit requirements do not apply to remedial action taken pursuant to a consent decree, order, or agreed order issued under the Model Toxics Control Act (MTCA),[33] or to MTCA remedial actions conducted directly by Ecology.[34]

SUBSTANTIVE REQUIREMENTS: POLICIES AND PROGRAMS

Developments subject to the SMA's jurisdiction are limited by the substantive requirements embodied in the SMA's shoreline policies and local jurisdictions' SMPs.

State Shoreline Policies

The Public Interest Test

The SHB has summarized the basic philosophy of the SMA as follows:

> Private property owners should be permitted to use their land in a manner which does not unreasonably infringe on other private rights or the public interests. Accordingly, the Shoreline Management Act was designed so that all development on the shoreline would be controlled, with priorities of use established, with natural resources preserved to the greatest extent practical and with adverse environmental impacts mitigated.[35]

The SMA must be "liberally construed."[36] The public interest is paramount to other interests,[37] but the SMA does not necessarily "mandate a calculation of equal public benefit to be offset against private benefits."[38]

Use Preferences and Priorities

The preferred and priority use policies of the SMA are particularly salient to shorelines under intense development pressure for competing industrial, commercial, recreational and residential land uses, where the shoreline resource is limited and valuable. The SMA establishes preferences for uses that protect the environment, must exist on or near a body of water, and preserve and enhance public access.[39] The SMA also creates specific, priority uses:

> Alterations of the natural condition of the shorelines of the state, in those limited instances when authorized, shall be given priority for single family residences, . . . ports, shoreline recreational uses including but not limited to . . . improvements facilitating public access to shorelines, . . . industrial and commercial developments

which are particularly dependent on their location on or use of the shorelines . . . and other development that will provide an opportunity for substantial numbers of people to enjoy the shorelines.[40]

The presence of any one of these three priority uses—single family residences, water dependent uses, and uses that afford public access—may be sufficient to establish a development as a priority use.[41] Public access is one of the highest priorities, if not the highest priority, of the SMA.[42] The SMA also favors "water dependent" uses those that cannot exist in other than a waterfront location and are dependent on the water by reason of the intrinsic nature of its operation.[43] In addition to listing single family residences as a use priority, the legislature has decided that the development of single family residences should not be subject to the same level of review as other developments.[44]

Although not an enumerated preference or priority under the SMA, aesthetics are an inherent part of both preferences and priorities.[45] Aesthetics frequently appear to be on a par with public access and water dependent concerns in SHB and court decisions.[46]

The use preferences and priorities, including the preservation of aesthetic qualities, apply to all shorelines of the state. In addition to these, the SMA establishes a set of use preferences for shorelines of state-wide significance.[47]

Local Shoreline Master Programs

Content of Shoreline Master Programs

Every local government having shorelines is required to adopt a shoreline master program (SMP). Each SMP must include:[48]

1. A statement of the jurisdiction's goals and objectives for managing its shorelines.
2. Policy statements that reflect the intent of the SMA, the goals of local citizens, and specifically relate the goals to the master program use regulations.
3. Master program elements, describing how the program will handle certain functional elements, such as public access, circulation, transportation, and minimization of flood damage.
4. Description and designation of shoreline environments, including a comprehensive use plan and map designating specific types of uses in specific shoreline environments
5. Use regulations, providing specific regulations for the types of uses allowed in each designated area.

Approval and Amendment Process

Before their SMPs or amendments to them become effective, local governments must adhere to certain procedures to develop their SMPs and amendments, to submit them for approval by Ecology,[49] and to weather any potential appeals of Ecology's decision.

The typical process for SMP adoption and revision first involves local governments formulating shoreline goals and policies in consultation with citizen advisory committees.[50] Next, government planners and citizen committees develop shoreline environment designations and use regulations.[51] Ecology Guidelines[52] and RCW §90.58.100(2) require each master program to include certain elements:

(a) An economic development element for the location and design of industries, industrial projects of statewide significance, transportation facilities, port facilities, tourist facilities, commerce and other developments that are particularly dependent on their location on or use of the shorelines of the state;
(b) A public access element making provision for public access to publicly owned areas;
(c) A recreational element for the preservation and enlargement of recreational opportunities, including but not limited to parks, tidelands, beaches, and recreational areas;
(d) A circulation element consisting of the general location and extent of existing and proposed major thoroughfares, transportation routes, terminals, and other public utilities and facilities, all correlated with the shoreline use element;
(e) A use element which considers the proposed general distribution and general location and extent of the use on shorelines and adjacent land areas for housing, business, industry, transportation, agriculture, natural resources, recreation, education, public buildings and grounds, and other categories of public and private uses of the land;
(f) A conservation element for the preservation of natural resources, including but not limited to scenic vistas, aesthetics, and vital estuarine areas for fisheries and wildlife protection;
(g) An historic, cultural, scientific, and educational element for the protection and restoration of buildings, sites, and areas having historic, cultural, scientific, or educational values;
(h) An element that gives consideration to the statewide interest in the prevention and minimization of flood damages; and
(i) Any other element deemed appropriate or necessary to effectuate the policy of this chapter.

Local planning bodies and elected officials then review and adopt the SMP and forward it on Ecology for review and approval.

Ecology must follow a specific procedure to review the SMP or amendment submitted by the local government.[53] Ecology must provide notice and a period of at least thirty days (in most cases) for written comment, during which period Ecology may conduct a public hearing on the SMP or amendment. Within fifteen days of the close of the comment period, Ecology must return the matter to the locality to review the issues raised during the comment period. The locality must provide a written response to the comments and resubmit the SMP or amendment to Ecology. Ecology then has thirty days in which to make written findings and conclusions, and to either approve the proposal as submitted, recommend specific changes, or deny approval. Ecology must approve those segments of the proposal that are consistent with the policies of the SMA and guidelines. For segments of the proposal relating to shorelines of state-wide significance, Ecology must approve them if "the program provides the optimum implementation of the policy of [the SMA] to satisfy the state-wide interest."[54] But if Ecology does not approve a proposed segment related to a shoreline of state-wide significance, Ecology may develop and, by rule, adopt an alternative. If Ecology recommends changes to any segment of any SMP or amendment, the locality has thirty days in which to assent to those changes or to submit an alternative proposal. Submitting a new proposal, however, may start the review process anew at the notice-and-comment stage.

Once Ecology approves a local shoreline master program or amendment, the program constitutes a "use" regulation that the locality may enforce through a substantial development permit.[55] In Growth Management Act jurisdictions, the goals and policies of the SMP become an element of the applicable comprehensive plan, and all other portions of the program become a part of the applicable development regulations.[56]

Appeals of SMPs or Amendments

Depending on the type of action taken by Ecology regarding a proposed SMP or amendment, different procedures dictate how aggrieved parties may appeal that action.[57] First, Ecology might "adopt" a SMP or amendment by regulation because of a locality's failure to create a SMP in a timely manner or because Ecology disapproves a proposed SMP or amendment that relates to a shoreline of state-wide significance. Appeals of these decisions must be made pursuant to the state Administrative Procedure Act, which enables appeals to be brought by any person with standing.[58]

Second, Ecology might approve, reject, or modify a proposed SMP or amendment from a jurisdiction which plans under the GMA. Appeals of that decision must be taken to the appropriate Growth Management Hearings Board (GMHB), not the Shoreline Hearings Board.[59] This provision also enables review to be sought by a range of parties, including the state, the local government whose plan is at issue, any person who appeared on the matter below, and any person who otherwise has standing under the APA.[60] The GMHB reviews the proposed SMP or amendment for compliance with the relevant portions of GMA, SEPA, and SMA. The appellant carries the burden of proof. The GMHB must uphold any Ecology decision relating to a shoreline of statewide significance, unless the GMHB determines by clear and convincing evidence that the Ecology decision is inconsistent with the policy of the SMA and its guidelines. Any aggrieved party may appeal the final decision of the GMHB to superior court.[61]

Finally, Ecology might approve, reject, or modify a proposed plan or amendment from a non-GMA jurisdiction. Appeals of that decision must be made to the SHB by filing a petition with the SHB within thirty days of Ecology's decision.[62] The SHB will review the proposal and determine its validity in light of the policy and guidelines of the SMA. The aggrieved party carries the burden of proof. The SHB must uphold any Ecology decision relating to a shoreline of statewide significance, unless the SHB determines by clear and convincing evidence that the Ecology decision is inconsistent with the policy of the SMA. Ecology or the local government may appeal an unfavorable, final Board decision to superior court under the APA.

PROCEDURAL REQUIREMENTS: SHORELINE PERMIT PROCESS

Shoreline Permits With Conditions

Shoreline substantial development permits are the primary device through which the SMA's substantive requirements are applied to a particular development or use proposal. Permit conditions are especially important. Because the SMA regulates proposals based on their consistency with shoreline policies and the relevant SMP, conditions can add the requisite measure of consistency to an otherwise inconsistent proposal. A shoreline permit may reference a SEPA document for conditions to be included in the permit.[63]

Permit conditions must be "reasonable."[64] The SHB has interpreted the requirement of "reasonable" conditions to state that the conditions must be related to the proposal's impacts and not be based on unsupportable facts or assumptions.[65]

Shoreline Conditional Use Permits

Shoreline permits with conditions are not the same as shoreline conditional use permits. The SMA authorizes local governments to include in their SMPs types of land uses and developments that may be permitted only by a conditional use permit, but are not allowed outright.[66] The purpose of a conditional use permit is to allow greater flexibility in varying the application of the use regulations of the master program. Uses that are specifically prohibited by the SMP, however, may not be authorized through a conditional use permit.

To obtain a conditional use permit, the applicant must demonstrate that the proposed use will at least:

1. be consistent with the policies of the SMA and SMP;
2. not interfere with the normal public use of public shorelines;
3. be compatible with other permitted uses within the area;
4. cause no unreasonably adverse effects to the shoreline environment designation in which it is to be located; and
5. not cause substantial detrimental effect to the public interest.[67]

Other uses that are not classified or set forth in a local SMP may be authorized as conditional uses if the applicant can demonstrate that the above criteria can be met and that "extraordinary circumstances preclude reasonable use of the property in a manner consistent with the use regulations of the master program."[68]

Shoreline Variance Permits

The SMA also authorizes shoreline variance permits for relief from specific bulk, dimensional, or performance standards of the master program. Variance permits should be granted when: (1) denial of the permit would result in thwarting the SMA's policies; (2) extraordinary circumstances exist; and (3) the public interest will suffer no substantial detrimental effect.[69]

As a practical matter, the standard has been interpreted to mean that a variance should not be granted if the owner is left with a reasonable use of the property or, conversely, that it should be granted if there is no reasonable use of the property without a variance.[70] The SHB will give deference to local interpretation in these matters.[71]

Permit Processing

State law dictates the application requirements for substantial development, conditional use, and variance permits. Local codes will still dictate the specific procedures that shoreline permit applicants, local regulators, and the public must follow, but the state requirements provide the structure around which local procedures must be built. The process generally follows a typical pattern from application to potential SHB appeal.

Application

Local planning staff usually conduct one or more pre-application conferences with the applicant, after which staff may request more information, modifications, or mitigation.[72]

Following these conferences, the applicant files a shoreline permit application. Submittal of a complete shoreline permit application "vests" the relevant use regulations.[73] SEPA compliance is required also before a locality may issue a permit.[74]

Notice

In GMA jurisdictions, public notice must be given within fourteen days of the filing of a complete shoreline application.[75] At a minimum, notice must employ at least one of the following methods:[76]

1. Mailing of the notice to the latest recorded real property owners as shown on the records of the County Assessor within at least 300 feet of the boundaries of the property on which the shoreline development is proposed.
2. Posting the notice in a conspicuous manner on the property.
3. Any other manner local officials deem appropriate to accomplish the objectives of reasonable notice to adjacent landowners and the public.

The notice requires interested persons to submit comments or requests for copies of documents within thirty days of the notice. If a hearing is to be held on the application, the notice must include a statement that any person may submit oral or written comments at the hearing. Local government is required to forward copies of the final decision to any requester in a timely manner.

Local Hearings and Decisions

Depending on the locality, the permit may be issued by an administrative official (such as a planning director), a quasi-judicial process (such as a hearing examiner), or a legislative process (such as a city council or county commission). The local jurisdiction may condition, approve, or deny an application. The local jurisdiction may also provide for an appeal to the local legislative body. After a shoreline permit decision is made, the local jurisdiction must notify the applicant, all persons requesting notification, Ecology, and the Attorney General's office.

Hearings on shoreline permits are not required under the SMA or state regulations. Where provided, the hearings may be non-adversarial (an opportunity to hear public comment) or quasi-judicial (with elements like cross-examination and rebuttal). Most local shoreline programs have a provision for hearings and typically make them optional, leaving the discretion with the local government official to decide whether a hearing is necessary.

Ecology Review

The local jurisdiction must file each permit with Ecology and the Attorney General.[77] For shoreline substantial development permits, Ecology has the opportunity to review the permits before they become effective and the appeal period runs. Ecology is not given explicit authority to reject the permits, but Ecology can use the appeal period to recommend any revisions to the local government or itself to appeal the permit to the SHB. For conditional use and variance permits, Ecology must act on the permits by approving or disapproving them.[78] Ecology may recommend that the local government modify the permit to make it consistent with the SMA.

SHB Appeal

If the local government's permit decision (or Ecology's decision to approve or disapprove a variance or conditional use decision) is not appealed, the applicant can proceed with the proposed activity.[79] Any person or entity "aggrieved" by the granting, denying, or rescinding of a shoreline permit may file an appeal with the SHB within twenty-one days from the "date of filing" of the permit decision.[80] For substantial development permits, the "date of filing" is the date that Ecology receives a copy of the decision from the locality, but for variance and conditional use permits, the "date of filing" is the date Ecology transmits its approval or disapproval of the local decision back to the local government.[81]

The SHB must render its decision within 180 days from the date that the petition for review is filed, unless the SHB extends that period by thirty days upon a showing of good cause or by stipulation of the parties.[82] Appellants carry the burden of proof in a review proceeding.[83] The SHB and its procedures are discussed in greater detail below.

Modification, Duration, and Extension of Permits

Changes are allowed within the "scope and intent" of a permit, either while the permit application is being processed or after a permit has been issued. Changes that the locality determines are within the scope and intent of the development do not require new notice or the application for a new shoreline permit.[84]

Substantial development permits, conditional use permits, and variance permits are granted for five years, unless the local government issues a shorter termination date on the permit.[85] Authorization for construction activities terminates in five years. Substantial progress toward construction of a permitted project (such as the making of contracts, completion of excavation, and the laying of major utilities), or where no construction is involved, the use activity, must begin within two years after granting the permit. Delays due to the pendency of litigation or administrative appeals will not count against either of these time limits, and the local government may authorize a single extension of no more than one year before the end of either time limit, with prior notice to parties of record and Ecology, "based on reasonable factors." Permits that have expired may nevertheless be revised, provided that applicants follow the usual revision procedures. If the revision is approved, the time limits begin running anew on the revision, but the original permit may not be extended.

APPEALS: SHORELINES HEARINGS BOARD

Jurisdiction and Authority

The SHB may hear appeals by any "aggrieved party" on the granting, denying, or rescinding of a shoreline permit, or on the adoption or approval of any shoreline rule, regulation, or guideline by Ecology.[86] The SHB may also hear appeals by a local government on Ecology's approval, rejection, or modification of a SMP for a non-GMA jurisdiction (the SMP for a GMA jurisdiction must be appealed to the GMA).[87] The SHB also has jurisdiction to hear appeals of civil penalties imposed by Ecology alone, or jointly by Ecology and a local government.[88]

Furthermore, the SHB has sole jurisdiction over both an appeal under SEPA and an appeal under the SMA, when the appeals are related to the same project or other matter. The SHB is to hear the appeals together and to issue a final order.[89] As an alternative dispute resolution process for any SEPA appeal, whether or not a shoreline issue is involved, the SHB may hear SEPA appeals upon consent of the parties to the action. If the parties invoke the process, the SEPA appeal is transferred in whole or in part to the SHB from an agency or superior court. If a party wishes to appeal the SHB's final order, the superior court is directed to certify it and the certified final order may be appealed only to an appellate court.[90]

The SHB has determined that its own jurisdiction is limited to these matters. The SHB, for example, will not review Ecology or local orders to cease and desist or to take corrective action,[91] or permit exemptions.[92] Because it reviews matters de novo, the SHB will not entertain issues of procedural errors committed by the local jurisdiction. Where it has jurisdiction, the SHB has the authority to affirm, modify, remand, or reverse a decision coming before it.[93]

Composition

The SHB has six members: the three members of the Pollution Control Hearings Board (private citizens appointed by the Governor with the advice and consent of the Senate for six-year terms) (the "PCHB"); the Commissioner of Public Lands or designee; a representative of the Association of Washington Cities; and a representative of the Association of County Commissioners. The Chair of the SHB is the Chair of the PCHB. Four members constitute a quorum for making a decision.[94] A decision of the SHB overturning the local government is not final unless four members agree.[95]

The Act provides for a smaller SHB panel to hear appeals involving a single-family residence or appurtenance to a single-family residence, such as a dock or pier.[96] For such "short-board appeals" (as opposed to "full-board appeals," which include all other types of appeals), the matter may be heard by a panel of only three SHB members, at least one and not more than two of whom must be members of the PCHB. Two members of the panel must agree to a decision.[97]

For both full- and short-board appeals, the chair of the SHB usually appoints an administrative appeals judge to serve as the presiding officer.[98]

Procedures

The SHB hears appeals *de novo*.[99] Because judicial review of SHB decisions are based on the record made before the SHB, the SHB's findings of fact and conclusions of law supersede those of local government and form the basis of future court rulings. The SMA requires that the burden of proof on appeal to the SHB rests with the party seeking review. The SHB's procedures are governed by the APA[100] and its own rules of practice and procedure.[101]

Who May Practice Before the SHB

Attorneys, legal interns admitted to practice under the applicable admission to practice rules, and officers or representatives of a firm, association, partnership, corporation, or local government may appear and practice before the SHB in a representative capacity.[102] A representative may appear either by: (1) filing a notice of appearance, a petition for review, or another pleading containing the name of the represented party and the name, address, and telephone number of the representative; or (2) entering an appearance at the time of a conference or hearing on the appeal.[103] Individuals may represent themselves before the SHB.[104] To avoid injustice, the SHB may waive any of its procedural rules, except rules relating to jurisdiction, for a party that is not represented by legal counsel.[105]

Filing a Petition For Review

A review by the SHB of a permit decision is initiated by filing an original and one copy of a petition for review with the clerk of the SHB.[106] The appellant must also serve a copy of the petition for review on Ecology, the Office of the Attorney General, and the local government concerned, unless of course the appellant is one of these parties.[107] After an aggrieved party has served a petition for review on Ecology and the attorney general, those governmental bodies have fifteen days to intervene in the proceedings.[108] If the appellant is not the permit applicant, the petition for review must also be mailed to the applicant.[109]

Even though the SHB will construe all pleadings so as to do substantial justice, the SHB requires each petition for review to contain certain specific information.[110]

Respondents' answers are due within twenty-one days of receipt of the petition for review and must generally conform to the requirements of a petition for review.[111] Any party may challenge the jurisdiction of the SHB to hear a petition for review, or the SHB may raise the question on its own.[112]

Prehearing Procedures

At his or her discretion, the presiding officer may order a prehearing conference by mailing a letter scheduling the conference at least seven days in advance.[113] The prehearing conference may be used to determine the feasibility of a settlement, or to prepare the case for hearing by scheduling prehearing deadlines and by identifying, to the extent possible, issues, witnesses, exhibits, stipulations, and admissions.[114]

The presiding officer, at the conclusion of a prehearing conference that does not result in settlement, enters a prehearing order that normally states the agreements of the parties concerning issues, admissions, witnesses, time and location of hearings, and other matters, together with any preliminary rulings of the presiding officer. The order shall control the subsequent course of the proceedings unless modified for good cause by subsequent order.[115] If the prehearing conference or a mediation results in a settlement, the parties prepare a written order of dismissal, attach a settlement agreement, and submit the order to the SHB, which must enter the order if it is in accordance with the law.[116]

Scheduling Hearings and Presenting Motions

Where the presiding officer decides not to hold a prehearing conference, he or she will mail a letter, at least seven days in advance, setting the hearing date and time. The scheduling letter will control the proceedings, unless modified for good cause, and may also set the schedule for filing motions and prehearing briefs.[117] The SHB may continue a hearing on its own motion or by the written motion of a party for an order of continuance.[118] The party moving for a continuance must seek the stipulation of all other parties to the order.[119]

All motions must be in writing and append a proposed order and any supporting affidavits, memoranda, or other documentation. Unless a party or the SHB requests a hearing, the SHB will normally decide the motion only on the parties written submissions. The party requesting a hearing must arrange and note the motion hearing with the SHB s hearing coordinator and file and serve a motion, proposed order, and note for the motion hearing. The presiding officer decides whether to hold a motion hearing and informs the parties. If a motion hearing is granted and is telephonic, the party that moved for the hearing must originate the conference call.[120]

Unless provided otherwise by a scheduling letter or order, or unless a party requests otherwise based on exigent or exceptional circumstances, all motions must adhere to the schedule outlined in WAC 46108-475(4). All dispositive motions must be filed and served at least forty-five days before the hearing on the appeal and at least twenty-eight days before the hearing on the motion itself. The response to any type of motion must be filed and served within ten days of its receipt, to which the moving party has seven days to file and serve a reply. The SHB has rules regarding filing, service and computation of time.[121]

Conduct of Hearings and Rules of Evidence

The SHB may serve a default or other dispositive order to all parties in the event a party fails to attend or participate in a hearing or other stage of the proceeding. Within seven days, the party against whom the order was entered may file a written motion to vacate the order.[122]

The order of presentation at the hearing begins with opening statements by the parties. The appealing party comes first, followed by the adverse parties with their cases in chief Rebuttal evidence is then received. Witnesses may be called out of turn only by agreement of all parties.[123] A written statement of the qualifications, experience and expertise of all expert witnesses must be submitted to the SHB and other parties at the outset of the hearing.[124]

The SHB's rules of evidence are more liberal than the rules of evidence governing superior courts.[125] The SHB may take official notice of federal law, state law, and governmental and agency organization, as well as matters involved in other SHB proceedings, and may also take official notice of business customs, notorious facts, and technical knowledge.[126] Parties may object to the introduction of evidence at the time it is offered.[127]

In addition, the SHB has a procedure for taking official notice of a material fact at the request of a party. In determining whether to take official notice of a material fact, the presiding officer is authorized to consult "any source of pertinent information," whether or not furnished by a party, and whether or not admissible under the rules of evidence. A party is entitled to challenge a request or suggestion for official notice of a material fact. The presiding officer, and SHB members, are authorized to introduce additional evidence, if they see fit, and such additional evidence may be rebutted.[128]

Disposition of Contested Cases: Reconsideration and Appeal to Superior Court

The SHB may prepare a final written decision and order containing findings and conclusions as to each contested issue of fact and law, if a majority of the SHB participated in the hearing.[129] The SHB may request counsel to prepare findings, conclusions, and orders based on the SHB's oral or memorandum opinion, or may prepare its own.[130] The parties may petition for reconsideration, but it is not a prerequisite to judicial review.[131]

The final order of the SHB is reviewable by appeal to the superior court, as provided in the APA.[132] Superior court appeals are limited to the record created in the SHB proceeding and will only be overturned upon a finding that the decision is clearly erroneous.[133] Under certain circumstances, the superior court may certify the order for direct review to the court of appeals or the court of appeals may accept a certificate of appealability issued by the

SHB.[134] The SHB may issue a certificate of appealability to the court of appeals either upon a motion of one of the parties or, if the SHB's jurisdiction is an issue on appeal, on its own motion. The SHB may issue the certificate if it finds that delay in obtaining a final and prompt determination of the issues would be detrimental to a party or the public, and if either fundamental and urgent state-wide or regional issues are raised or resolution of the issues is likely to have significant precedential value. Issues not raised before the SEIB may not be raised for the first time in during judicial review of the SHB's decision.[135]

ENFORCEMENT

Permit Rescission

If the local agency determines that a permittee has not complied with the conditions of a permit, the agency may rescind the permit, after a hearing with adequate notice to the permittee and the public. Likewise, if Ecology determines that a permittee is out of compliance, Ecology may provide written notice to the local authority and the permittee of its determination. If the local government takes no action within thirty days, Ecology has fifteen days to petition the SHB for rescission of the permit and to notify the local government and the permittee of that petition.[136]

Suits for Damages or Equitable Remedies

The state attorney general or a local government attorney may bring such injunctive, declaratory, or other actions as are necessary to ensure that no uses may be made of the shorelines that conflict with the SMA.[137] The attorney general or local government attorney may also bring suits for damages caused by violation of the SMA, to force the violator to pay the entire cost for restoring areas affected by the violation, and to recover attorneys' fees and court costs.[138]

Through a "private attorney general" provision, private persons may bring suits for damages, to force violators to restore damaged areas, and to obtain attorneys' fees and costs for such suits.[139] Yet the private attorney general action may be for damages only; only a government may seek declaratory or injunctive relief for a use that constitutes a violation of the SMA.[140]

Enforcement Orders and Penalties

Local governments and Ecology share the power to impose penalties and to take other enforcement actions. A local government or Ecology may issue orders (to cease and desist or to take corrective actions) upon those who use shorelines in violation of the SMA.[141]

Local governments and Ecology, either separately or jointly, may also impose a civil penalty of up to $1,000 per day upon anyone who uses a shoreline without a permit, violates a permit, or fails to comply with a cease and desist order, and upon those who aid or abet in such violations.[142] The civil penalty must be imposed in writing (either personally or by certified mail with return receipt requested) and must describe the violation and dates of violation. It must also contain an order to cease and desist or to take corrective action. The person incurring the violation has thirty days from receipt to apply in writing for remission or mitigation of the penalty. The local government or Ecology may remit or mitigate the penalty only upon demonstration of extraordinary circumstances. Penalties imposed by Ecology alone, or jointly by Ecology and a local government, may be appealed to the SHB. Penalties imposed by a local government alone may be appealed pursuant to that government's administrative appeals procedures.

In addition to civil penalties, the SMA provides criminal sanctions. A willful violation constitutes a gross misdemeanor, which is punishable by fine or imprisonment.[143]

COASTAL ZONE MANAGEMENT PROGRAM

Jurisdiction of the Coastal Zone Management Act

The federal Coastal Zone Management Program is a product of the Coastal Zone Management Act of 1972 ("CZMA"),[144] and is administered by the National Oceanographic and Atmospheric Administration ("NOAA") in the Department of Commerce. CZMA jurisdiction extends to federal activities and private activities that require a federal license or permit, "within or outside the coastal zone that affects any land or water use or natural resource of the coastal zone."[145] CZMA jurisdiction also covers outer continental shelf exploration, development, and production activities, and provides for federal assistance grants to state and local governments.[146] "Federal activities" means "functions performed by or on behalf of a federal agency in the exercise of its statutory responsibilities."[147] "Coastal zone" refers to water that contains a measurable quantity or percentage of sea water and the adjacent shorelands, and includes islands, transitional and intertidal areas, salt marshes, wetlands, and beaches.[148]

Activities subject to this CZMA jurisdiction must be consistent with the state coastal zone management program (CZMP). There are essentially three types of federal consistency requirements:

1. Consistency determination, which requires federal agencies to make a consistency determination for their own activities;[149]
2. Consistency certification, which requires applicants for federal licenses or permits to certify in writing, to both the federal and state agencies, that their proposed activities are consistent with the CZMP;[150] and
3. Intergovernmental consistency review, which requires a review of consistency by the state for any federal grants for activities in the coastal zone.[151]

In addition, outer continental shelf activity requires consistency certifications, but is subject to certain rules that differ in some ways from the federal consistency certification requirements for other federal permits.[152]

If a federal agency does not want to act consistently with the CZMP, the federal agency must show that its activities are mandated by federal law to be inconsistent with the state's CZMP, and that no way exists to make the activities consistent with the CZMP. The only way for an agency to proceed with a federal activity that a federal court finds to be inconsistent with the CZMP is to obtain an exemption from the President.[153] This exemption is not available, however, for federal "development projects," that are a subset of federal "activities," and that include construction, modification, or removal of public works or similar facilities.[154]

The consistency requirement maintains that the proposed activity must be consistent to the maximum extent practicable with the CZMP.[155]

The Washington Coastal Zone Management Program

Washington applies a liberal definition of coastal zone, one that embraces all relevant activities anywhere in the fifteen coastal counties of Washington. The Washington CZMP currently consists of the SMA, guidelines, and the state master program (which includes local SMMPs), as well as the state and federal Clean Water and Clean Air Acts, and the state SEPA,[156] Energy Facilities Siting Act,[157] and Transport of Petroleum Products Act.[158] Therefore, a project subject to the CZMA must demonstrate consistency with all of these state and federal authorities.

Even though the Washington CZMP embraces more than the SMA, the SMA forms the core of the Washington CZMP.[159] The Washington CZMP requires that consistency with the SMA be certified by providing Ecology with a copy of a shoreline substantial development permit, conditional use permit, variance, or a letter of exemption pursuant to the SMA. The SMA, including its permit requirements, applies independently of the CZMA[160] (1) to private activities on federal lands, so long as Congress has not preempted the SMA through some law or regulation;[161] and (2) to the activities of any federal agency that would otherwise be subject to SMA jurisdiction, whether or not those activities occur on federal lands.[162]

Consistency Determination Procedure

The consistency determination, certification, and review processes follow the same general approach in all areas:

1. *Evaluation.* The federal agency proposing an activity, or a private applicant for a federal license or permit, that is subject to CZMA jurisdiction must review the proposal and consider whether it is consistent with the CZMP.
2. *Submission to state.* The federal agency then submits a "determination" to Ecology that the federal activity will be consistent with the CZMP. Likewise, the private applicant must certify to the relevant federal agency that it is in compliance with the CZMP. In either case, the federal agency or the applicant must provide a detailed explanation of how the proposal will be consistent, and provide supporting information, including all necessary SMA permits, variances, or exemptions.
3. *State review.* Ecology reviews the proposed consistency determination or certification or funding request and informs the federal agency of its agreement or disagreement with the determination. Ecology can request the federal agency or applicant to provide more information in order to make its determination. If Ecology does not respond within a specified time period, or extend the time period, the federal agency may presume that the state has no objections.
4. *Federal-state negotiations.* In the event of disagreement, Ecology and the federal agency, along with any private applicant, attempt to develop conditions that would make the proposal consistent with the CZMP, if possible. The parties have the option of submitting a dispute between them to mediation, and may appeal their dispute if they cannot reach an agreement.
5. *Record of decision.* Certain findings or evaluations are required both by the federal agency and Ecology to issue a state concurrence with the consistency determination, certification, or review.

NOTES

[1] RCW §90.58.

[2] RCW §36.70B. *See also Futurewise w. Western Washington Growth Management Hearings Board*, 164 Wn. 2d 242 (2008); *Preserve Our Islands v. Shorelines Hearings Board*, 133 Wn. App. 503 (2006).

[3] RCW §90.58.020; *Eastlake Community Council v. City of Seattle*, 64 Wn. App. 273 (1992).

[4] RCW §90.58.140.

[5] WAC 173-26. *But see Association of Washington Business v. Ecology*, SHB No. 00-037 (2001).

[6] *Bellevue Farm Owners Assn. v. Shorelines Hearings Board*, 100 Wn. App. 341 (2000).

[7] *See, e.g., Weden v. San Juan County*, 135 Wn. 2d 678 (1998).

[8] RCW §90.58.050. *May v. Robertson*, 153 Wn. App. 57 (2009).

[9] *Citizens for Rational Shoreline Planning v. Whatcom County*, 172 Wn. 2d 384 (2011); *Samson v. City of Bainbridge Island*, 149 Wn. App. 33 (2009), *rev. den.* 166 Wn. 2d 1008; *Preserve Our Islands v. Shorelines Hearings Board*, 133 Wn. App. 503 (2006).

[10] *Herman v. State of Washington Shorelines Hearings Board*, 149 Wn. App. 444 (2009); *Kailin v. Clallam County*, 152 Wn. App. 974 (2009).

[11] RCW §90.58.030(2)(d).

[12] RCW §90.58.030(2)(d).

[13] RCW §90.58.030(2)(e). *Nisqually Delta Assn. v. City of DuPont*, 103 Wn. 2d 720 (1985).

[14] RCW §90.58.900. *Herman v. State of Washington Shorelines Hearings Bd.*, 149 Wn. App. 444 (2009); *Skokomish Indian Tribe v. Fitzsimmons*, 97 Wn. App. 84 (1999).

[15] RCW §§90.58.030(2)(d) and.030(3)(e)(vi).

[16] RCW §90.58.030(2)(b). *Thompson v. State, Dept. of Ecology*, 136 Wn. App. 580 (2007), *rev. den.* 161 Wn. 2d 1023.

[17] RCW §90.58.030(2)(h) uses the federal Clean Water Act definition of wetlands as areas that "are inundated or saturated by surface water or groundwater at a frequency and duration sufficient to support, and that under normal circumstances do support, a prevalence of vegetation typically adapted for life in saturated soil conditions."

[18] RCW §90.58.030(2)(f).

[19] RCW §90.58.340. *Preserve Our Islands v. Shorelines Hearings Board*, 133 Wn. App. 503 (2006), *as amended rev. den.* 162 Wn. 2d 1008.

[20] 8 Wn. App. 844 (1973).

[21] *Cowiche Canyon Conservancy v. Bosley*, 118 Wn. 2d 801 (1992); *Hunt v. Anderson*, 30 Wn. App. 437 (1981); *Weyerhauser Co. v. King County*, 91 Wn. 2d 721 (1979); *Putnam v. Carroll*, 13 Wn. App. 201 (1975).

[22] RCW §90.58.160.

[23] RCW §90.58.030(3)(d); *Washington Shell Fish Inc. v. Pierce County*, 132 Wn. App. 239 (2006), *rev. den.* 158 Wn. 2d 1027.

[24] RCW §90.58.030(3)(e).

[25] *Clam Shacks, Inc. v. Skagit County*, 109 Wn. 2d 91 (1987).

[26] RCW §90.58.030(3)(e).

[27] *See* RCW §90.58.900; *Ventura v. City of Seattle*, 99 F. Supp. 2d 1273 (WD WA 2000); *English Bay Enterprises, Ltd. v. Island County*, 89 Wn. 2d 16 (1977); *Mead School Dist v. Mead Education Assn.*, 85 Wn. 2d 140 (1975).

28 Yet replacement activities that go beyond normal repair and maintenance have been found not to be exempt. SHB Nos. 79-54 (1979), 80-33 (1981), 82-2 (1982), and 86-17 (1986).

29 *See Kates v. City of Seattle*, 44 Wn. App. 754 (1986) (applicability of residential exemption is a question of fact and depends on owner's intent to occupy residence for his or her own use).

30 *State, Department of Ecology v. City of Spokane Valley*, 167 Wn. App. 952 (2012).

31 RCW §90.58.030(3)(e); WAC 173-27-040(2).

32 RCW §90.58.140(9) and RCW §80.50 RCW.

33 RCW §70.105D.

34 RCW §90.58.355.

35 *Nisqually Delta Assn. v. City of DuPont*, 103 Wn. 2d 720 (1985).

36 RCW §90.58.900. *See Hayes v. Yount*, 87 Wn.2d 280, 289 (1976).

37 *Nisqually Delta Assn. v. City of DuPont*, 103 Wn. 2d 720 (1985).

38 *Jefferson County v. Seattle Yacht Club*, 73 Wn. App. 576, 589 (1994).

39 RCW §90.58.020.

40 *Id.*

41 See SHB Nos. 92-52 (1993) and 92-53 (1993).

42 SHB No. 158 (1974). *See also* SHB Nos. 114 (1974), 125 (1974), 77-30 (1978), and 82-7 (1982).

43 *See* SHB No. 88-15 (1991). Although water dependent uses are preferred, non-water dependent uses are not prohibited. *See, e.g., Eastlake Community Council v. Seattle*, 64 Wn. App. 273 1132 (1992) (office development that has no "integral relationship" to a water-dependent use may be consistent with the Act).

44 See RCW §90.58.100(6) (local SMPs must provide for use of bulkheads and similar structures to protect single family residences and appurtenant structures against damage or loss due to shoreline erosion); RCW §90.58.030(3)(e)(vi) (limited situations under which a single family residential development requires a substantial development permit); RCW §90.58.030(3)(e)(ii) (construction of normal protective bulkheads common to single family residences is exempt from the definition of "substantial development"); RCW §90.58.140(11) (more expeditious permit review and appeal process for such bulkheads).

45 *See, e.g.,* RCW §90.58.020 ("In the implementation of this policy the public's opportunity to enjoy the physical and aesthetic qualities of natural shorelines of the state shall be preserved to the greatest extent feasible consistent with the overall best interest of the state and the people generally.")

46 *See, e.g., Ecology v. Pacesetter*, 89 Wn. 2d 203 (1977); *Hunt v. Anderson*, 30 Wn. App. 437 (1981); SHB Nos. 13 (1972), 54 (1974), 120 (1974), 129 (1974), 158 (1974), 115 (1976) and 202 (1976).

47 RCW §90.58.020.

48 RCW §90.58.100. In addition to these elements, the SMPs of coastal local governments in Jefferson, Clallam, Grays Harbor, and Pacific counties must be consistent with the Ocean Resources Management Act, RCW §§43.143.005 through .030, and ocean use guidelines developed by Ecology. RCW §90.58.195.

49 RCW §90.58.090. *See also City of Bremerton v. Sesko*, 100 Wn. App. 158 (2000); *Lund. v. State Dept. of Ecology*, 93 Wn. App. 329 (1998).

50 RCW §90.58.130.

51 RCW §90.58.120.

52 WAC 173-26 and WAC 173-27.

53 RCW §90.58.090. *Buechel v. State, Dept. of Ecology*, 125 Wn. 2d 196 (1994).

54 RCW §90.58.090(4).

55 RCW §90.58.100(1). *See Clam Shacks, Inc. v. Skagit County*, 109 Wn. 2d 91 (1987); *Land Owners v. Dept. of Ecology*, 38 Wn. App. 84, 86 (1984).

56 RCW §36.70A.480.

57 RCW §90.58.190. *Batchelder v. City of Seattle*, 77 Wn. App. 154 (1995), *rev. den.* 127 Wn. 2d 1022.

58 RCW §90.58.190(1).

59 RCW §90.58.190(2).

60 See RCW §§36.70A.280(2) and 34.05.530.

61 RCW §36.70A.300.

62 RCW §§90.58.190(3) and (4).

63 *Kleinburger v. Bothell*, SHB No. 99-026 (2000).

64 SHB No. 83-17 (1983).

65 SHB Nos.155 (1975), 177 (1975) and 204 (1976).

66 *See* RCW §90.58.100(5).

67 WAC 173-27-160(1).

68 WAC 173-27-160(3).

69 WAC 173-27-170. *See also Crawford v. Mason County*, SHB No. 98-03 (1998).

70 SHB Nos. 78-7 (1978), 78-10 (1978) and 78-44 (1979).

71 SHB No. 77-18 (1977).

72 RCW §90.58.140(3).

73 *Laccinole v. City of Bellevue*, SHB No. 03-025 (2004).

74 *Sisley v. San Juan County*, 89 Wn. 2d 78 (1977) (the SMA is inextricably interrelated with and supplemented by SEPA); *Dept. of Natural Resources v. Thurston County*, 92 Wn. 2d 656 (1979) (SEPA review is generally considered broader than shoreline review). Some proposals may, however, be categorically exempt from SEPA.

75 RCW §36.70B.110(2).

76 RCW §90.58.140(4).

77 RCW §90.58.140(6).

78 RCW §90.58.140(10). Note that Ecology does not act on variance or conditional use applications that have been denied by the local government, because RCW §90.58.140(10) speaks only of a "permit."

79 *KS Tacoma Holdings, LLC v. Shorelines Hearings Board*, 166 Wn. App. 117 (2012), *rev. den.* 174 Wn. 2d. 1007.

80 RCW §90.58.180(1). *Harrington v. Spokane County*, 128 Wn. App. 202 (2005); *Samuel's Furniture, Inc. v. State, Dept. of Ecology*, 147 Wn. 2d 440 (2002); *Snohomish County v. State Shorelines Hearings Board*, 108 Wn. App. 781 (2001).

81 RCW §90.58.140(6).

82 RCW §90.58.180(3)

83 RCW §90.58.140(7)

84 See WAC 173-14-064. Under this test, "intent" refers to the type of land use, and "scope" refers to the actual structures or development activities themselves.

85 The duration of permits is guided generally by RCW §90.58.143.

86 RCW §90.58.170. *See also* RCW §43.21B.005.

87 RCW §90.58.180(3).

88 RCW §90.58.210(4).
89 RCW §43.21C.075(7).
90 *Id.*
91 SHB Nos.78-47 (1979) and 79-11 (1979).
92 See SHB No.92-49 (1992).
93 *See San Juan County v. Dept. of Natural Resources*, 28 Wn. App. 796 (1981).
94 WAC 461-08-330(2).
95 RCW §90.58.170.
96 RCW §90.58.185(1); WAC 461-08-330(1).
97 WAC 461-08-555(2).
98 WAC 461-08-330(3).
99 WAC 461-08-500.
100 RCW §34.05.
101 WAC 461-08.
102 WAC 461-08-385(2).
103 WAC 461-08-390(1).
104 WAC 461-08-385(1).
105 WAC 461-08-405.
106 WAC 461-08-340(1).
107 RCW §90.58.180(1); WAC 461-08-355 and -360(1).
108 RCW §90.58.180(1).
109 WAC 461-08-360(2).
110 WAC 461-08-350.
111 WAC 461-08-445.
112 WAC 461-08-425(2).
113 WAC 461-08-450(3).
114 WAC 461-08-455(1).
115 WAC 461-08-460.
116 WAC 461-08-465.
117 WAC 461-08-450(2).
118 WAC 461-08-480.
119 WAC 461-08-475(2).
120 WAC 461-08-475(1), (3) through (5).
121 WAC 461-08-305 and -310.
122 WAC 461-08-485.
123 WAC 461-08-495(4).
124 WAC 461-08-495(6).
125 WAC 461-08-515.
126 WAC 461-08-520 and -525(1).
127 WAC 461-08-535.

[128] WAC 461-08-525(2) through (5) and -530.

[129] WAC 461-08-555.

[130] WAC 461-08-550.

[131] WAC 461-08-565.

[132] RCW §90.58.180(3) (decisions regarding permits); RCW §90.58.180(7) (regulations, rules, and guidelines); RCW §90.58.190(3)(e) (SMMPs).

[133] *Puget Sound Water Quality Defense Fund v. Municipality of Metropolitan Seattle (Metro)*, 59 Wn. App. 613 (2000).

[134] WAC 461-08-575.

[135] *Kitsap County v. Dep't of Natural Resources*, 99 Wn. 2d 386 (1983).

[136] RCW §90.58.140(8).

[137] RCW §90.58.210(1).

[138] RCW §90.58.230. *Twin Bridge Marine Park, LLC v. State, Dept., of Ecology*, 162 Wn. 2d 825 (2008).

[139] RCW §90.58.230.

[140] *Hedlund v. White*, 67 Wn. App. 409 (1992).

[141] See RCW §90.58.210(3).

[142] See RCW §90.58.210(2) and (3). *Herman v. State of Washington Shorelines Hearings Bd.*, 149 Wn. App. 444 (2009), *rev. den.* 166 Wn. 2d 1029.

[143] RCW §90.58.220.

[144] 16 USC §§1451 *et seq.*

[145] 16 USC §1456(c).

[146] 15 CFR 930(E) and (F).

[147] 15 CFR 930.31(a).

[148] 16 USC §§1453(1) and 1453(3).

[149] 15 CFR 930(C).

[150] 15 CFR 930(D)and(E).

[151] 15 CFR 930(F).

[152] 15 CFR 930(E).

[153] 16 USC §1456(c)(1)(B).

[154] 16 USC §1456(c)(1)(A)and(c)(2); 15 CFR 930.31(b).

[155] 15 CFR 930.32(a).

[156] RCW §43.21C.

[157] RCW §80.50.

[158] RCW §88.40.

[159] *Friends of the Earth v. United States Navy*, 841 F. 2d 927 (9th Cir. 1988).

[160] The requirement to obtain a permit is driven by the SMA; the Washington CZMP merely borrows that requirement as a surrogate for demonstrating consistency with part of the CZMP. A shoreline permit, variance, or exemption is not required for all projects subject to the CZMP. Because the CZMP deals with ocean policy issues, e.g., offshore oil and gas development on the outer continental shelf, the state SMA and local SMPs do not necessarily cover all of those areas. Likewise, not all actions subject to the SMA require consistency under the CZMP. For example, the SMPs include freshwater rivers, lakes, streams, and wetlands that are beyond the scope of the CZMP, which is concerned with marine, coastal zone management.

[161] *California Coastal Comm. v. Granite Rock Co.*, 480 US 572 (1987).

[162] *Friends of the Earth v. United States Navy*, 841 F. 2d 927 (9th Cir. 1988).

CHAPTER 4

Regulation of Development in Environmentally Sensitive Areas

MANAGEMENT OF ENVIRONMENTALLY SENSITIVE AREAS IN WASHINGTON

This chapter discusses the management and regulation of development in environmentally "sensitive" areas in the State of Washington. These areas include wetlands, floodplains and other critical areas, such as sites subject to landslides and aquifer recharge zones. Federal and state law establish the framework for regulating development in these areas, while much of the responsibility for directly regulating activities in these areas has been left to local governments.

REGULATIONS TO CONTROL DEVELOPMENT IN WETLANDS AND AQUATIC ENVIRONMENTS

Wetlands provide a considerable number of environmental functions depending on their type and quality. Among other things, wetlands provide fish and wildlife habitat, enhanced water quality, flood control, and recreation opportunities. Altering wetlands can diminish their effectiveness in serving these functions.

A complex set of federal, state and local laws protect wetlands in Washington. Federal regulations define wetlands as areas that are "inundated or saturated by surface or ground water at a frequency and duration sufficient to support, and that under normal circumstances support, a prevalence of vegetation typically adapted to life in saturated soil conditions."[1] State and local laws may define wetlands differently, however, thereby creating confusion as to permissible activities.[2] State government regulates activities in wetlands or aquatic areas, although the federal 404 permit program plays the major part in wetland protection.[3]

Federal Regulations

Federal law plays a substantial role in wetlands management and regulation, primarily through the Section 404 permit program under the Federal Water Pollution Control Act (FWPCA), otherwise known as the federal Clean Water Act (CWA).[4] Section 401 of the CWA (which requires state water quality certification), the Coastal Zone Management Act (CZMA),[5] and a number of other federal regulations described below also are significant in federal wetlands management. Federal law does not regulate isolated wetlands unless there is a surface water or other actual hydrologic connection between the wetland and navigable water.[6]

CWA Section 404 (Dredge and Fill) Permits

The CWA requires a Section 404 permit for discharges of dredged or fill material into the navigable waters of the United States, which include most wetlands.[7] The courts have generally interpreted "navigable waters" broadly under the Section 404 program.[8]

The U.S. Army Corps of Engineers (the Corps) has the primary responsibility for the 404 permit program. EPA, however, may veto permits issued by the Corps.[9] Other federal, state and local agencies as well as tribes also review and comment on Corps permit applications.

The Corps is required to evaluate any project involving the discharge of dredged or fill material for compliance with guidelines developed by EPA.[10] The Corps uses a three-step approach to determine compliance with the guidelines. First, the Corps determines whether potential impacts have been avoided to the maximum extent practicable. Second, the Corps considers whether potential unavoidable impacts have been minimized to the extent appropriate and practicable. Finally, the Corps requires compensatory mitigation for unavoidable impacts that cannot be minimized.

Exemptions

There are a number of specific activities which are exempt from the 404 permit requirements: normal farming, silviculture, or ranching activities such as plowing seeding, minor drainage, and harvesting; maintenance of currently serviceable structures; construction or maintenance of irrigation ditches; maintenance of drainage ditches; construction of temporary sedimentation basins associated with construction sites; and, construction or maintenance of farm, mine, or forest roads.[11] There is a specific exemption for "prior converted croplands" but the exemption will be lost if the land is put to another use.[12]

Mitigation and Mitigation Banking

No permit will be issued that will adversely affect a wetland unless the permit applicant provides for mitigation of those impacts on a ratio of greater than 1:1 in order to maintain the requisite "no net loss" of wetland functions and values.[13] Mitigation efforts can be pooled, however, into mitigation banks. Mitigation banking has been defined as "wetland restoration, creation, enhancement, and in exceptional circumstances, preservation undertaken expressly for the purpose of compensating for unavoidable wetland losses in advance of development actions, when such compensation cannot be achieved at the development site or would not be as environmentally beneficial . . . . Units of restored, created, enhanced or preserved wetlands are expressed as 'credits' which may subsequently be withdrawn to offset 'debits' incurred at a project development site."[14]

State Water Quality Certification

Section 401 of the CWA requires state water quality certification before the Corps can issue a Section 404 permit.[15] Under the certification provision, states can veto a permit application for noncompliance with state and local water quality laws. Alternatively, states can request that the Corps place conditions on the Section 404 permit. Conditions can be imposed to ensure compliance with not only state water quality standards, but also with designated use components of water quality standards, such as a water quantity criterion.[16] A state, however, must act within a reasonable amount of time (one-year maximum) after notification of a Section 404 permit application. Otherwise, the state waives its opportunity to comment.[17]

Ecology implements the certification program for Washington and evaluates projects for consistency with the water quality standards set forth in the CWA.[18] Ecology must provide public notice for each 404 permit application to all parties having expressed an interest.[19] Persons commenting on a project must respond in writing within twenty days after the notice is published. If the public expresses sufficient interest, Ecology will hold a public hearing. An executive order issued in April 1990 by the Governor directs Ecology to condition or deny Section 404 permit applications if a proposed project adversely impacts wetlands.[20]

Nationwide Permits

The CWA authorizes the Corps to issue general permits on a nationwide, regional, or state basis for certain categories of discharges that are "similar in nature, will cause only minimal adverse environmental effects when performed separately, and will have only minimal cumulative adverse effect on the environment."[21] Currently the Corps lists forty-four nationwide permits but in Washington they are subject to regional conditions, 401 and CZMA certification, and the Puyallup Tribe's prohibition on the use of any nationwide permits on their tribal lands. A further limitation on the use of nationwide permits stems from prohibitions on activities that would affect critical habitat for endangered species or designated wild and scenic rivers.[22]

Coastal Zone Management Act (CZMA) Consistency Determination

Under the Coastal Zone Management Act (CZMA), any applicant for a federal permit for activity in a state's coastal zone must certify that the proposed activity will comply with the state's coastal zone management program.[23] Washington's program is set forth in the Shoreline Management Act (SMA).[24] The Corps ordinarily will not issue a Section 404 permit until the state has concurred with the applicant's CZMA certification.[25] The CZMA program in Washington will aplly to just about every activity in the state's 15 counties bordering salt water.

Other Federal Regulations

The federal government also regulates activities in wetlands and other aquatic environments through several other statutes. Section 10 of the Rivers and Harbors Act allows the Corps to regulate activities that will obstruct navigable waterways.[26] This includes, for example, construction of piers, bulkheads and jetties.

The "swampbuster" provision of the Food Security Act of 1985 requires federal agencies to withhold federal funds and other benefits from farmers who cultivate wetlands converted to agricultural production after December 23, 1985.[27] This measure has eliminated part of the economic incentive to drain wetlands.

State Regulations

Washington lacks a comprehensive wetlands management statute. Instead, activities occurring in wetlands and other aquatic environments are regulated through a potpourri of local ordinances, state statutes, and executive orders. The Growth Management Act serves as the integrating framework for all other land use related laws. Local governments have the lead responsibility for protecting wetlands and other aquatic environments. The state, however, has several regulatory programs relevant to wetlands and has established minimum standards for local regulation of developments in wetlands.[28] As mentioned above, the state also influences federal permitting of activities in wetlands through its CWA certifications and CZMA consistency determinations.

Wetlands Regulation Under the Growth Management Act

Wetlands are one of the defined "critical areas" under the Growth Management Act (GMA). Although Washington's GMA[29] places the duty of regulating activities in wetlands on local governments,[30] GMA requires that the Department of Commerce develop guidelines to help local governments classify wetlands and other critical areas.[31] These guidelines, which went into effect on April 15, 1991, are minimum standards that apply to all jurisdictions in Washington and are to be used by local governments to designate wetlands pursuant to GMA.[32]

The guidelines set out a process for local governments to establish a classification scheme and to determine the general distribution, location and extent of wetlands within their jurisdiction.[33] The guidelines also require local governments to involve the public and to coordinate with adjacent jurisdictions in designating wetlands.[34] CTED guidelines encourage, but do not require, local governments to use the state's wetlands rating system to classify wetlands according to specific characteristics or functional attributes.[35]

Local regulations can vary widely especially with respect to the use of the Corps 1987 Manual versus the 1989 Manual (which generally expanded the size of the regulated area), the dimension of buffer zones, and mitigation ratios, to name just a few. In addition, the GMA also covers buffer areas around wetlands, unlike federal law.

Regulation of Wetlands and other Aquatic Areas in the Shoreline Zone: Shoreline Management Act (SMA)

The Shoreline Management Act (SMA)[36] requires a permit for many of the development activities that occur within the shoreline zone.[37] Since a large proportion of the state's wetlands are located within these zones, SMA provides a key component for managing and regulating activities in Washington wetlands and other aquatic environments. Such development must be consistent with the SMA and Shoreline Management Programs established by local governments. Where there is no local program, the state retains regulatory responsibility.

Wetlands will be regulated under the SMA if they are (1) located within 200 horizontal feet from the ordinary high water mark of the shoreline they adjoin;[38] (2) located within a floodplain that is within 200 feet of a floodway;[39] or (3) associated with streams, lakes, and tidal waters subject to the SMA by a hydrologic connection via surface or groundwater.[40]

Hydraulic Project Approvals (HPA)

In order to protect populations of shellfish and food and game fish in all stages of development, as a matter of policy, a sufficient flow of water must be maintained at all times in streams.[41] The necessity of obtaining a "hydraulic project approval" or "HPA" from the Department of Fish and Wildlife is triggered whenever any construction will "use, divert, obstruct, or change the natural flow or bed of any of the salt or fresh waters of the state."[42] If the activity, however, is minor in nature, DFW has issued pamphlets authorizing the activity. Against that simple statement, there are separate regulations for some 33 different types of activities that will trigger the need for an HPA. Depending on whether the activity takes place in fresh or salt water, different regulations apply.[43] The issuance of an HPA can, under certain circumstances, be deemed complete, when another permit, such as a 404 permit, has already been approved. Failure to obtain an HPA can result in a civil penalty of up to $100 per day, which must be appealed within 30 days of receipt of notice of the penalty.

Regulation Under The Forest Practices Act RCW §76.09

The Forest Practices Act regulates activities relating to the growing, harvesting or processing timber[44] and, at the same time, achieving environmental and land use goals[45] and intergovernmental cooperation.[46] The Forest Practices Board[47] promulgates regulations which are then administered mainly by the Department of Natural Resources through a notice and permit requirement.[48] The Departments of Ecology and Fish and Wildlife have an opportunity to review forest practice notifications and permit applications.[49] The Pollution Control Hearings Board hears appeals of permits and regulatory enforcement actions.

Forest practices are divided into four classes depending on the severity of their impact on the environment,[50] with Class I being the most benign, for which notice is not required in most instances, and Class IV being the most substantial, even requiring the completion of a SEPA checklist. Activities which impact endangered species or critical areas will be deemed Class IV[51] and require special consideration.[52]

REGULATIONS TO PREVENT FLOOD DAMAGE

Most floodplain regulation occurs at the local level. These regulations often considerably restrict the allowable uses and the types of structures that property owners can construct in floodplains. The framework for these local regulations, however, comes in large part from federal and state floodplain protection programs.

Federal Programs

The National Flood Insurance Act of 1968 (the Flood Insurance Act) and the Flood Disaster Protection Act of 1973 (the Disaster Protection Act) have been the primary catalysts for development restrictions within floodplains.[53] The Flood Insurance Act established a program of federally subsidized insurance for property lying within floodplains. Under the Disaster Protection Act, the federal government conditioned the availability of the flood damage insurance on the enactment of local controls over development in floodplains.[54] These local controls must meet the minimum requirements set by the federal government. State and local governments failing to comply with the federal flood control program also risk losing other federal funding. Where state and local governments have not established flood management programs, and a risk of floods continues, private parties may find themselves unable to acquire flood insurance or even secure financing to buy property.

State Programs

State Management of Floodplains

The state participates indirectly in controlling development in floodplains.[55] Ecology facilitates local regulation of activities in floodplains by coordinating the federal requirements with efforts by local governments.[56] Ecology also must approve local floodplain ordinances and plans; ordinances failing to adequately restrict land uses in floodways, meet the requirements of the National Flood Insurance Program, or meet the state's minimum requirements will not be approved.[57]

State Regulation in Addition to Local Controls

Just as local floodplain regulations must meet state standards, state floodplain regulations must meet federal standards.[58] Federal law, however, permits states to adopt more restrictive regulations. The state also can issue regulatory orders to insure compliance with its floodplain management program.[59] In addition, Ecology reviews the design and plans of projects located on the banks of bodies of water, in or over stream channels, and in or over floodways to determine if it should prohibit such activities to prevent damage by flooding.[60]

Local Programs

Cities and counties in Washington bear the primary responsibility of regulating activities in floodplains. A local government may have a specific floodplain management program,[61] or it may include floodplain restrictions in its zoning and building codes. Zoning ordinances generally dictate the type of structures property owners can build and the activities allowed within a floodplain. Building codes typically specify the permissible characteristics of the structures allowed in the floodplain. These might include maximum allowable area of the ground floor, standards for flood proofing, and the ability to repair or alter existing structures. These zoning restrictions and building codes must meet the federal government's minimum requirements. Local restrictions, however, can exceed the federal standards. Under statutory zoning authority, local governments must integrate flood control procedures into their comprehensive land use plans.[62]

GMA identifies "frequently flooded areas" as one of the Act's critical areas. CTED guidelines define "frequently flooded areas" as "lands in the floodplain subject to a one percent or greater chance of flooding in any given year" (i.e., the 100-year floodplain).[63] As with wetlands, all cities and counties in the state must designate these areas and adopt development regulations.[64] These development regulations must conform to Ecology's standards.[65]

REGULATIONS TO PROTECT OTHER SENSITIVE AREAS

Regulation of activities in other sensitive areas is primarily a local function, although the state provides some guidance and oversight. Regulations for various sensitive areas may take the form of zoning, building and grading codes, as well as sensitive areas ordinances. Authority under SEPA to condition or deny proposals based on environmental impacts should also be considered in assessing the influence of local regulations on activities in critical areas.

GMA forced some measure of uniformity on the local regulation of sensitive areas by mandating that all cities and counties adopt regulations to protect "critical areas" and by providing common definitions.[66] "Critical areas" include wetlands, frequently flooded areas, aquifer recharge zones, fish and wildlife habitat, and geologically hazardous areas.[67]

Geologically Hazardous Areas

GMA defines geologically hazardous areas as those areas that because of their susceptibility to erosion, sliding, earthquakes, or other geological events, are not suited to the siting of commercial, residential, or industrial development consistent with public health or safety.[68] Geologically hazardous areas include steep slopes, mines, volcanic areas and seismic zones. Local restrictions for these types of areas likely include the absolute prohibition of some uses and construction standards and setbacks for allowed uses.

Aquifer Recharge Zones and Fish and Wildlife Habitat Conservation Areas

These sensitive areas are those areas for which certain land uses pose risks of environmental harm or risks to human health and safety. Local regulations for these types of areas are likely to include absolute prohibitions of some types of activities and setbacks and mitigation requirements for allowed uses.

Aquifer recharge zones are those areas where an aquifer that is a source of drinking water is vulnerable to contamination that would affect the potability of the water.[69] Factors related to vulnerability include depth to ground water, aquifer properties such as hydraulic conductivity, and gradients and soil characteristics. Local governments are likely to designate sole source aquifers designated under the Federal Safe Drinking Water Act and areas listed for special protection under ground water management programs as critical areas.[70]

"Fish and wildlife habitat conservation areas" are those areas with which endangered, threatened and sensitive species have a primary association. In addition, these areas include habitats and species of local importance, commercial and recreation shellfish areas, kelp and eelgrass beds, naturally occurring ponds of less than twenty acres and their submerged aquatic beds, waters of the state and state natural area preserves, and natural resource conservation areas.[71] Cities and counties must include all public and private tidelands or bedlands suitable for shellfish harvest, kelp and eelgrass beds, and herring and smelt spawning areas as critical areas.[72] Such areas also will include lands that are in some instances already subject to critical area regulations as wetlands, are regulated under the SMA or other statutes, or have been designated as open space corridors.[73] Local designation of, and regulations for, development in this type of critical area are likely to vary considerably among local jurisdictions.

NOTES

[1] 40 CFR 230.3(t). Under the Corps of Engineers' Wetlands Delineation Manual, Technical Report Y-87-1, three "parameters" must be present: (1) inundation or saturation in a major portion of the root zone (usually within 12 inches of the surface) during the growing seasons (when the soil temperature exceeds biologic zero); (2) hydric soils which are chemically reduced, discolored or show other evidence of anaerobic conditions; and (3) a prevalence of wetland vegetation. "Normal circumstances" excludes areas that no longer exhibit the three wetland parameters and areas that exhibit the parameters but only on a temporary basis, but includes areas that would exhibit the parameters if they had been left alone (which under the federal definition will also include man-made wetlands). *Leslie Salt Co. v. United States*, 96 F. 2d 352 (9th Cir. 1990), *cert. den.* 498 US 1126 (1991).

[2] *See e.g.*, RCW §36.70A.030 (state GMA definition of "wetlands," which is similar to the federal regulations but specifically excludes some intentionally created wetlands).

[3] Washington regulates wetlands under the Growth Management Act (including RCW §36.70A.170 which requires cities and counties to designate "critical areas" including wetlands) and RCW §36.70A.172, which requires the use of "best available science" in developing policies and development regulations), the Shoreline Management Act (RCW §90.58), and, at the federal level, the 401 certification process under 33 USC §1341 and the Coastal Zone Management Act, 16 USC §§1451 *et seq.*. The state also uses the Hydraulic Code, RCW §§75.20 *et seq.*, to regulate activities that will occur below ordinary high water mark or will divert or obstruct the natural flow or bed of state waters, the Floodplain Management Program, WAC 86.16, administered by local governments, and aquatic lands or tidelands leases under RCW §§79.90 – 79.96.

[4] 33 USC §1344. See generally Federal Water Pollution Control Act, 33 U.S.C. §§1251 *et seq.*

[5] 16 USC §1456.

[6] *Rapanos v. US*, 126 S. Ct. 2208 (2006).

[7] Some activities, including certain farming and silvicultural practices, are exempt from the Corps' Section 404 permit requirements. See 33 USC §1344(f); 33 CFR §323.4.

[8] "Navigable waters" are defined as "waters of the United States." 33 USC §1362(12). Adjacent "wetlands" are included in the definition of waters of the United States. 33 CFR 328.3(a); 40 CFR 122.3. *United States v. Riverside Bayview Homes, Inc.*, 474 US 121 (1985).

[9] 33 USC §1344(c). See *Bersani v. United States Environmental Protection Agency*, 674 F. Supp. 405 (N.D.N.Y. 1987), aff'd. 850 F. 2d 36 (2d Cir. 1988).

[10] 33 USC §1344(b); 40 CFR 230.

[11] 33 USC §1344(f)(1).

[12] 33 USC §1344(f)(2).

[13] 40 CFR 230 Subpart H.

[14] *Id. See also* RCW §90.84; 33 CFR 325 and 332; 40 CFR 230.

[15] 33 USC §1341.

[16] *PUD No. 1 of Jefferson County v. Washington Dept. of Ecology*, 511 US 700 (1994) (In PUD No. 1, the state of Washington conditioned certification upon minimum flow requirements in order to protect and enhance fish habitat. The court's upholding of such a condition suggests that CWA Section 401 may be given an extremely broad application in the future.). *But see Dolan v. City of Tigard*, 114 S.Ct. 2309 (1994) (ruling that permit conditions must be proportional to impacts, and must redress impacts actually caused by the proposed project).

[17] 33 USC §1341(a)(1).

[18] WAC 173-201A; WAC 173-225-010.

[19] WAC 173-225-030.

[20] EO 90-04 (Apr. 21, 1990).

[21] 33 USC §1344(e).

[22] 33 CFR 330.

[23] 16 USC §1456(c)(3).

[24] RCW §90.58.

[25] See 33 CFR 325.2(b)(2)(ii) (state must certify project's consistency with CZMA within six months or its concurrence with the certification statement will be conclusively presumed).

[26] 33 USC §403.

[27] 16 USC §3821.

[28] *See e.g.* RCW §90.84, Wetlands Mitigation Banking.

[29] RCW §36.70A.

[30] RCW §36.70A.060(2).

[31] RCW §36.70A.050; WAC 365-190-080(1).

[32] RCW §36.70A.050(3).

[33] WAC 365-190-040.

[34] *Id.*

[35] WAC 365-190-080(1)(a).

[36] RCW §90.58.

[37] WAC 173-16-030(3).

[38] RCW §90.58.030(2)(f).

[39] RCW §90.58.030(2)(g).

[40] RCW §90.58.030(2)(f).

[41] RCW §77.55.050.

[42] WAC 220-110-020(42).

[43] WAC 220-110-050 to 220-110-224 (fresh water projects); WAC 220-110-270 to 220-110-330 (salt water projects).

[44] RCW §76.09.020(11).

[45] RCW § 76.09.010(2). *Plum Creek Timber Co., L.P. v. Washington State Forest Practices Appeals Board*, 99 Wn. App. 579 (2000).

[46] *Ord v. Kitsap County*, 84 Wn. App. 602 (1997). *See also* WAC 222-22-010 (watershed analysis).

[47] WAC 222-08-150.

[48] WAC 222-20-010.

[49] WAC 222-50-010 and -020.

[50] WAC 222-16-050.

[51] WAC 222-16-050(1).

[52] WAC 222-16-080.

[53] 42 USC §4001 et seq. The availability of the insurance, however, may be a key catalyst in the development to begin with.

[54] 42 USC §4022.

[55] *See* RCW §86.16.

56 RCW §§86.16.010, 86.16.020 and 86.24.020. The Flood Control Assistance Account Program allows the state to help local governments financially to comply with the National Flood Insurance Program. RCW §86.16; WAC 173-145.

57 RCW §§86.16.031 and .041.

58 WAC 173-158.

59 RCW §86.16.020. Appeals and stays of regulatory orders are provided for at RCW §43.21B.310 and RCW §43.21B.320, respectively.

60 RCW §86.16.025.

61 The legislature in 1991 specifically authorized counties to adopt comprehensive flood control management plans, which must include land use regulations. RCW §86.12.200.

62 RCW §§35.63.090, 35A.63.061 and 36.70.330.

63 WAC 365-190-030(7).

64 RCW §§36.70A.060(2) and .170(1)(d).

65 RCW §86.16.041(2).

66 RCW §36.70A.060(2); WAC 365-190-080.

67 RCW 36.70A.030(5); WAC 365-190-030.

68 RCW §§36.70A.030(5) and (9).

69 WAC 365-190-030(2).

70 WAC 365-190-080(2)(d).

71 WAC 365-190-080(5).

72 WAC 365-190-080(5)(c)(iii) and (iv).

73 RCW §36.70A.160.

CHAPTER 5

Air Quality

INTRODUCTION

Air quality requirements are some of the most complex of all environmental regulations. This chapter describes key concepts that are essential to understanding how the Clean Air Act is implemented, and whether one of its programs applies to a particular business, industry or activity. It focuses on the elements of air regulation that sources in Washington are most likely to encounter: the registration and operating permit programs, new source review, air toxics requirements, emission standards, and enforcement.

SOURCES OF LAW AND REGULATION

The 1990 federal Clean Air Act and the 1991 Washington Clean Air Act are the statutory bases for air quality regulation in Washington.[1] The state Act implements the federal Clean Air Act, which establishes minimum standards for Washington's air quality programs.[2] The federal Act has spawned volumes of federal regulations, many of which apply directly to Washington facilities, and some of which have been used as models for state-level regulations. The federal air regulations are found in 40 CFR 50 through 98.

On the state level, the Washington Department of Ecology ("Ecology") and the local air pollution control authorities[3] issue regulations based on the Washington Clean Air Act.[4] In fact, Ecology has delegated most of its authority to the local authorities although it retains authority over the SIP as well as a handful of special industrial sources[5] and certain pollutants.[6] Ecology sets the minimum state-wide standards while local authorities are free to set more stringent standards.[7] The state regulations for stationary and mobile sources are found WAC 173-400 through 173-492. Local air authority regulations are available directly from each local authority.

REGULATORY FRAMEWORK

Although the scope of the Clean Air Act grew significantly when it was amended in 1990, and now includes acid rain and stratospheric ozone depletion, its basic goals are still to meet national standards for a handful of "criteria" pollutants and to limit hazardous air pollutant emissions through a federal structure. Through the Act, the federal government establishes a framework for bringing all areas in the country into compliance with national ambient air quality standards and requirements. Primary responsibility for implementing and enforcing programs designed to meet the federal standards rests with the state and local air agencies.

State Implementation Plan (SIP)

The state is required to develop a plan to implement federal air quality regulatory requirements.[8] This "State Implementation Plan," often referred to as the "SIP," is comprised of, among other things, all the state and local air quality regulations that have been approved by the EPA. The Washington SIP has developed over many years and is occasionally revised through additions or deletions. Regulations and source-specific requirements that are included in the SIP are enforceable by EPA, as well as by the state. These regulations are therefore referred to as being "federally enforceable."

National Ambient Air Quality Standards (NAAQS)

A primary goal of the Clean Air Act, and therefore of the SIP, is to establish a regulatory system designed to attain and maintain national air quality standards, known as the National Ambient Air Quality Standards, or "NAAQS." Based on health criteria, the NAAQS prescribe the permissible concentrations of particular pollutants in the ambient air.[9] Ambient air quality refers to the concentration of a pollutant in the surrounding outside air of a given area.

The NAAQS do not apply directly to individual sources. Rather emissions standards and other requirements for individual sources are the tools by which an area meets the ambient standards.

Attainment and Nonattainment Areas

Compliance with ambient air quality standards is determined by a system of monitoring stations that assess the ambient pollution concentrations in a given area. When monitoring shows that an area does not comply with an ambient standard for a particular pollutant, the area is designated as "nonattainment" for that pollutant.[10] For example, a carbon monoxide monitor in Tacoma/Pierce County indicated that the area did not meet the ambient standard for carbon monoxide, causing the area to be designated as a carbon monoxide nonattainment area. Areas that meet ambient air quality standards for particular pollutants are called "attainment" areas for that pollutant.

When an area is designated as a nonattainment area, the state must revise the SIP to implement a plan for bringing the area back into attainment.[11] This may include regulatory changes, new requirements for specific facilities in the area, or new area-wide programs. In addition, it is more difficult to obtain a permit to build new facilities and modify existing facilities in nonattainment areas. Changes that increase emissions of a nonattainment pollutant above certain amounts are subject to especially stringent requirements, as discussed in the section on major new source review below.

When ambient air monitors indicate that an area has attained a particular ambient standard, the state can petition EPA to redesignate the area to attainment.[12] To support redesignation, the state, working with the local agency with jurisdiction over the area, must prepare a plan designed to ensure that the area will continue to meet the ambient standard. This plan, known as a "maintenance plan" may impose requirements on sources, particularly new sources, that are more stringent than usually apply in attainment areas. Therefore, it is not only important to determine the attainment status of the area you are in, but also whether or not the area was recently re-designated to attainment, and thus subject to a maintenance plan. Maintenance plans cover a twenty-year time frame in two 10-year increments. The maintenance plan must demonstrate that the standards can continue to be met.

REGULATORY AGENCIES

In Washington, authority over commercial or industrial air pollution sources is divided between Ecology[13] and the local air pollution control authorities, except for permitting of larger energy facilities.[14] Although EPA has delegated authority to the state to implement most federal programs, the agency usually retains concurrent authority, and so maintains an enforcement role in the state through its Region X office in Seattle.

Ecology is primarily responsible for adopting uniform, minimum air pollution standards that form the basis for regulations issued by the local air authorities.[15] The local air authorities are the primary permitting and enforcement authorities for facilities within their jurisdictions.[16] They have the authority to set air pollution standards that are more stringent than those established by Ecology.[17] Multi-county air pollution authorities are authorized under state law.[18] In counties not covered by a local air pollution control authority, Ecology, through its Central and Eastern Regional Offices, is the primary permitting and enforcement authority. The Northwest Regional Office has authority over sources in San Juan County.

REGISTRATION AND OPERATING PERMITS

Most sources of air pollution in Washington are subject to either Registration or Operating Permit programs. In general, larger sources are required to have operating permits, while smaller sources must comply with the registration requirements.

Registration

Owners or operators of sources that emit or have the potential to emit above *de minimis* amounts one or more regulated air pollutants, must register with Ecology or with their local air authority.[19] Registration provisions of the various agencies generally fall into two groups: those that list the specific types of sources that are covered (*e.g*, Ecology,[20] ORCAA, PSCAA), and those that apply to all sources in the jurisdiction, with certain listed exemptions for insignificant sources (e.g., PSCAA, NWCAA, SWCAA). In some instances the agency may use a combination of these two approaches.

Registration generally entails providing the agency with information about the size and type of all air pollution sources at a facility, including emission control equipment. Periodic reporting regarding emissions types and amounts is usually also required. Facilities that are subject to the operating permit program are not required to comply with Registration provisions.[21]

Operating Permits

Larger sources of air pollution in the state are required to obtain operating permits.[22] An operating permit incorporates all of the local state and federal air quality requirements that apply to a facility (the "applicable requirements") into a single permit. The program is intended to facilitate compliance with and enforcement of those requirements by compiling them in one place and requiring the source itself to determine and report periodically whether or not it is maintaining compliance with each requirement. The state operating permit rule is located in WAC 173-401.

Operating permits are currently required for "major sources."[23] A major source in Washington is any source that has the potential to emit more than 100 tons per year (tpy) of any air pollutant, or twenty-five tpy of any combination of hazardous air pollutants (HAP) (established by the National Emissions Standards for Hazardous Air Pollutants or NESHAPS) or 10 tpy of any individual HAP. Facilities can avoid the operating permit program for now by accepting voluntary limits on their potential to emit to a level below the major source threshold.[24] Facilities with actual emissions that are already below the threshold are in the best position to take this approach. It is unlawful for a major source to operate without a valid operating permit, unless it has submitted a timely and complete operating permit application.

Operating permits are intended to be vehicles for implementing existing requirements. Permit writers may, however, impose new monitoring requirements through the program.[25] Operating permits must contain enforceable emission limits and requirements designed to assure that the source will remain in compliance with those limits, usually in the form of monitoring, record-keeping and reporting requirements.[26] If the monitoring that is associated with a particular limit is considered to be insufficient to assure that the source is staying in compliance with that limit, the permitting authority may impose new monitoring requirements. EPA refers to this as "gap-filling." Permits also must contain a series of standard terms and conditions.[27]

Permit holders must certify annually that their facilities are in compliance with all permit requirements.[28] A "responsible corporate official" must sign this compliance certification, attesting to its accuracy.[29] In addition, any deviations from permit requirements must be "promptly" reported to the permitting authority.[30] The reports will be available to the public. All proposed permits will be subject to public notice and comment and review by EPA.[31] Operating permits are issued for five-year terms and can carry significant fee burdens. Operating permit sources are still subject to new source permit requirements.

NEW AND MODIFIED SOURCES

An air permit is required before you can begin construction of a "new source," which includes brand new emission units, as well as modifications to existing facilities.[32] Under the Clean Air Act, the bulk of the regulatory burden falls on new rather than existing sources, based on the assumption that the most opportune time to employ technology that results in lower emissions is during initial construction or when a unit is modified. The most stringent emission limits that apply to units are usually imposed during new source permitting; usually these source-specific limits are more stringent than general limits that apply to all sources. Review and permitting of new and modifying sources is called "new source review" (NSR) or "preconstruction review."

Depending on the increase in potential emissions resulting from a change, and the location of the source different levels of review apply.[33] All changes that require review are subject to state new source permitting, known as "minor source NSR." Changes with larger emissions increases may trigger the thresholds for review under the federal new source review programs, known as "major source NSR."

Minor Source NSR

Minor source NSR applies to new sources and modifications that do not trigger a major source threshold. A "new source" is the construction or modification of a stationary source that increases the amount of any air contaminant emitted or results in the emission of any air contaminant not previously emitted.[34] The somewhat redundant definition of "modification" is any physical change in, or change in the method of, a stationary source that increases the amount of any air contaminant emitted by the source, or that results in emissions of any air contaminant not previously emitted.[35]

Before beginning construction on a new source or modification, you must apply for and obtain a Notice of Construction (NOC) Order of Approval. As with the Registration provision, the state-level NSR regulations either list the specific types of sources that must apply for an NOC, such as Ecology's NSR provision,[36] or they apply to all new or modified sources, sometimes with certain listed exemptions, such as PSCAA's NSR regulation.[37]

An NOC application typically includes general information about the anticipated emissions and any air pollution control equipment the applicant intends to use for the proposed source, including detailed engineering plans and specifications. NOC applications that would result in a significant net emissions increase, would voluntarily limit a source's potential to emit, or in which there is a substantial public interest, are subject to a thirty-day public notice and comment period.[38] Application fees apply. The terms and conditions of an NOC Order of Approval are considered "federally enforceable," meaning that EPA has authority to enforce them.[39]

To receive construction approval, a source that is not considered "major" (and thus subject to major NSR requirements) must meet three main requirements. First, the proposed new source or modification must comply with all applicable standards and requirements, including new source performance standards (NSPS), federal hazardous air pollutant standards (NESHAPS), and general state and local emission standards. These limits are usually written into the Order of Approval. Second, the proposed source must not cause any ambient air quality standard to be exceeded. Third, the source must meet the requirements of the state toxic air pollutant program if it will emit toxic air pollutants. Fourth, and most significant, the proposed new source or modification must employ "best available control technology (BACT) for all air contaminants.[40]

BACT is a technological standard, defined as an emission limit based on the "maximum degree of reduction" achievable for each regulated pollutant by using available systems and techniques to control each pollutant, taking into account energy, environmental and economic impacts.[41] BACT is usually reviewed from the "top-down," meaning that the "best" technology (i.e., the one that results in the greatest reduction in emissions of the pollutant under consideration) must be selected unless economic, environmental, and energy considerations justify the selection of the next best technology. BACT is sometimes called a "moving target," because a BACT analysis is a case-by-case review of the types of technologies and processes being used at similar facilities across the country at that given time. As technologies and processes improve, the BACT limit gets more stringent. Consequently, a BACT analysis usually results in imposing more stringent limits than those that apply through existing regulations

By requiring BACT for new non-major sources, Washington law is more stringent than federal law, which requires BACT only for "major" new sources and modifications. Under federal law, "reasonably available control technology" (RACT) is required for new sources below the major source threshold. In Washington, RACT is required for all existing sources,[42] which is also more stringent than federal law. Washington will also collect an additional fee for making RACT determinations.[43]

Major Source NSR

New sources and modifications that are considered "major" under the federal new source review regulations are subject to a more stringent review. There are two federal NSR programs: Prevention of Significant Deterioration (PSD), which applies in attainment areas; and nonattainment area new source review. These programs apply by pollutant, so it is possible that a single source would have to comply with both. For instance, a new source that will be "major" for PM-10 and carbon monoxide that is proposed to be located in an area that is nonattainment for PM-10 and attainment for carbon monoxide, would be subject to nonattainment area NSR for PM-10 and PSD review for carbon monoxide.

Key Terms

Major source NSR applicability relies on three relatively complex phrases that are unique to air quality regulation: "major stationary source;" "major modification;" and "potential to emit." NSR requirements imposed by the federal Clean Air Act apply to new "major stationary sources" and "major modifications" to existing sources.

Major Stationary Source. To make matters more complicated, the term "major" has different meanings in different contexts. For major source NSR purposes, a source is major if it on the list of twenty-eight source categories in the regulation and has the potential to emit 100 tons per year (tpy) or more of a regulated pollutant, or if it is any other type of source with the potential to emit 250 tpy or more.[44]

Potential to Emit. To determine whether a source is major, emissions are measured in terms of "potential to emit" (sometimes referred to as "PTE") rather than actual emissions. Potential to emit a particular pollutant is estimated based on a unit's maximum capacity to emit that pollutant, taking into account the unit's physical and operational design, including control equipment and enforceable limits that restrict emissions.[45] This calculation often results in potential emissions that are well above what the unit actually emits. Although facility owners are generally reluctant to limit future operations, they can avoid the additional cost of major source NSR by voluntarily limiting their potential to emit to make the source a "synthetic minor." For example, a source subject to the 100 tpy major source threshold could voluntarily assume a limit on its production rate, hours of operation, fuel input, etc. calculated to limit the unit's potential to emit to below 100 tpy. To effectively keep the source from being considered major, the limit would have to be imposed through an enforceable permit or order.[46]

Major Modification. A "major modification" is any physical change in, or change in the method of operation of, a major stationary source that would result in a significant net emissions increase of a regulated pollutant.[47] Unless one of the exceptions applies, a change at a major stationary source that causes a "net emissions increase" of a pollutant over any of the significance thresholds in the regulations will trigger major source NSR. In calculating the net increase, you take into account increases in actual emissions expected to result from the change, as well as any emission increases or decreases in actual emissions that are "contemporaneous" and "creditable."[48] Significance thresholds vary by pollutant. For the most common pollutants, a net emissions increase is "significant" if it is equal to or greater than the following amounts:[49]

Carbon monoxide	100 tons per year
Nitrogen oxides	40 tpy
Sulfur dioxide	40 tpy
Particulate matter	25 tpy
PM-10	15 tpy
VOCs	40 tpy

For a change that would otherwise be considered a "major modification," and therefore subject to major source NSR, there are two approaches to avoiding this more stringent level of review. First, you can "net out" of the review, because the definition of net emissions increase allows you offset emission increases with decreases in emissions of the same pollutant elsewhere at the facility. This would be done by making an enforceable change to decrease emissions of the pollutant that would otherwise increase by a "significant" amount, such that the facility-wide increase ends up being below the significance threshold (or relying on past decreases that qualify). Second, a facility could take the "synthetic minor" approach by voluntarily assuming enforceable limits on the modification that would ensure that the associated emissions increase would remain below the applicable significance threshold.

Prevention of Significant Deterioration ("PSD")

PSD review applies to major stationary sources and major modifications that are located within an attainment area. As the name implies, PSD review is intended to prevent the significant deterioration of air quality in regions that meet an ambient air quality standard. Preparing a PSD permit application can be significantly more costly and time consuming than preparing a notice of construction application, and the process may result in more stringent limits than the minor source NSR process. The review applies to each pollutant that is proposed to be emitted in "significant" amounts. Like a notice of construction approval, if required, a PSD permit must be obtained before beginning actual construction.[50]

EPA has delegated the authority to implement the federal PSD program to Ecology, but not to the local air authorities.[51] EPA has the authority to approve a state PSD program, but the agency has rejected Ecology's PSD regulation as insufficient. Consequently, the federal PSD regulation, not Ecology's PSD regulation, is incorporated by reference into the Washington SIP.[52] Therefore, the federal PSD provisions in 40 CFR 52.21 apply directly in Washington as of the summer of 2014. This may change in the fall of 2014.

To apply for a PSD permit one must prepare an extensive amount of information on the proposed project, including data to demonstrate that impacts from the project will be within the PSD guidelines. There are four main elements of a PSD permit application:

1. *BACT Analysis.* The applicant must show that the project will employ best available control technology ("BACT"), which is discussed in the section on minor source NSR above. Typically, the BACT review results in a set of limits that dictate or influence the type of technology and controls used in the project. The source must also comply with any applicable new source performance standards and national emission standards for hazardous air pollutants.[53]
2. *Air Quality Analysis.*[54] The applicant must be able to demonstrate that new emissions from the proposed project will not cause or contribute to a violation of any applicable NAAQS or PSD increments.[55] This evaluation of ambient air impacts generally involves an assessment of existing air quality, which may include ambient monitoring data and air quality dispersion modeling results, and predictions, using dispersion modeling, of ambient concentrations that will result from the proposed project.
3. *Additional Impacts Analysis.* For each pollutant subject to review, the applicant must prepare an analysis assessing the impacts of air, ground and water pollution on soils, vegetation and visibility caused by the increased emissions.[56]
4. *Class I Area Impact Analysis.*[57] National parks and wilderness areas are designated as Class I areas. For proposals that may affect a Class I area,[58] the applicant must analyze specific impacts that the proposal may have on the area, including impacts to "air quality related values" (AQRVs), such as soils, vegetation and visibility. PSD applicants in Washington face a higher likelihood of having to conduct this analysis due to the relatively large number of national parks and wilderness areas, especially in the western half of the state. Visibility impacts in national parks has been an especially hot issue both nationally and in Washington. Ecology is required to seek comments and input from the appropriate "federal land manager," which in Washington will be either the National Parks Service for national parks, the Forest Service for wilderness areas, or both.

Nonattainment Area NSR

For major stationary sources and major modifications proposed to be located within a nonattainment area, the most stringent level of review applies. While the PSD program allows emissions to increase as long as the impacts are not significant, a nonattainment area NSR does not allow any increases in emissions of a pollutant for which an area is designated nonattainment. Because a primary goal of the Clean Air Act is to bring such areas into attainment, the requirements are directed at reducing emissions of the problem pollutant. The nonattainment area NSR program is implemented on the state level.

There are five main requirements for obtaining nonattainment area NSR approval:

1. *LAER.* The emissions control requirement for nonattainment areas is "lowest achievable emissions rate." LAER is the most stringent emission limit available anywhere in the country, regardless of cost. The source must also comply with all applicable emissions limits.[59]
2. *Offsets.* The source must obtain actual emission reductions, known as "offsets," of the nonattainment pollutant from existing sources in the same nonattainment area, in a

number sufficient to more than offset the proposed increase. There are detailed requirements regarding the sufficiency and enforceability of the offsetting reductions relied on.[60]
3. *Alternatives Analysis.* The applicant must analyze alternative sites, sizes, production processes, and control techniques and demonstrate that the benefits of the project significantly outweigh the environmental and social costs imposed by the proposed project.[61]
4. *Compliance Demonstration.* The applicant must demonstrate that all other major stationary sources in the state owned or controlled by it are complying with all applicable emission limits and requirements.[62]
5. *Visibility Protection.* Sources impacting visibility in Class I areas must be reviewed by the appropriate federal land manager (see discussion of Class I areas above).[63]

TOXIC AND HAZARDOUS AIR POLLUTANTS

Prior to 1990, regulations implementing the Clean Air Act focused mainly on the conventional, or "criteria" pollutants. In twenty years, EPA promulgated only twelve health based standards for hazardous air pollutants (HAPs), known as National Emission Standards for Hazardous Air Pollutants (NESHAPs).[64] Congress changed all that when it completely rewrote the hazardous air pollutant section of the Clean Air Act in 1990.[65] The new federal HAP program is extensive and will be implemented on into the next century.

The slow progress of HAP regulation on the federal level before 1990 caused many states to take matters into their own hands as well. Washington implemented its own state-level regulations governing "toxic air pollutants" (TAPs). While the federal HAP program applies to new and existing HAP sources, Washington's TAP program applies only to new TAP sources.[66]

Federal HAP Program

The federal HAP program expands the list of regulated hazardous pollutants to over 180 substances. Regulations implementing the new program are being called National Emission Standards for Hazardous Air Pollutants (NESHAPs) for Source Categories.[67] Like the NSPS, the NESHAPs for Source Categories apply to specific categories of industrial sources, and contain general monitoring, recordkeeping and notification requirements applicable to all categories. The program applies to both "major" sources and "area" sources. For purposes of the HAP program, a stationary source is "major" if it emits twenty-five tons per year of any combination of HAPs, or ten tons per year of any individual HAP.[68] An "area" source is any stationary source that is not a major source.[69]

The cornerstone of the new HAPs program is the new technology-based HAP standard, called "maximum achievable control technology," or MACT.[70] The Clean Air Act defines MACT as the "maximum degree of reduction" in HAPs emissions "considering cost, non-air quality impacts and energy."[71] In establishing MACT, EPA must consider not only end-of-the-stack pollution controls, but also changes in manufacturing processes, material substitutions and design changes.[72] As they are developed by EPA, the new MACT standards will be imposed through the new operating permits program.[73]

The schedule for complying with the new MACT standards depends on whether a source is "new" or "existing." "New" sources must demonstrate immediate compliance with all final standards.[74] New sources must also demonstrate that they can comply with standards that are proposed before construction begins.[75] If the standard changes between the time it is proposed and published in final form, the source is allowed three years to comply with the final standard so long as it complies with the proposed standard during the three-year period.[76] Existing sources are allowed three years to comply with final standards.[77] An additional one-year extension is allowed if necessary to install equipment.

The new HAP section of the 1990 Clean Air Act also required EPA to develop a program to prevent accidental chemical releases.[78] The resulting Chemical Accident Prevention Provisions require sources with over threshold quantities of listed toxic substances at their sites to comply with various accident-prevention provisions, including preparing a Risk Management Plan.[79]

Washington TAP Rules

Washington's Controls for New Sources of Toxic Air Pollutants (TAPs) apply to certain listed new or modified stationary sources, including sources that emit or have the potential to emit any amount above a *de minimis* amount (with some exceptions) of any regulated pollutant, that increase the amount of any TAP emitted or results in the emission of any TAP not previously emitted.[80] TAPs are any substance listed in the regulation, which includes over 400 individual chemicals.[81] This state TAP list is significantly longer than the list of HAPs regulated under federal law.

The TAP rules are implemented through the state new source review program. There are two main requirements:

1. *T-BACT*. The applicant must show that the source will use "T-BACT," or best available control technology for toxics, to control the TAP emissions that are likely to increase.[82]
2. *ASIL analysis*. The TAP rules also require a source to control emissions such that ambient levels of TAPs meet "acceptable source impact levels" (ASILs), which are listed in tables in the rule.[83] To demonstrate compliance, the TAP emissions from the new source, after all controls are applied, must be quantified.[84] Conservative emission estimates may be used in conjunction with good engineering judgment in lieu of actual emission inventories. The quantity of each TAP emitted must be determined individually.

If a source cannot demonstrate that it will meet an applicable ASIL, it may request Ecology to conduct a "second tier" analysis, which is a site-specific risk assessment.[85] The source will be approved if it uses T-BACT and results in less than one in 100,000 increased cancer risk (10^{-5}). If it cannot meet the second tier standard, the source may petition Ecology for a "risk management decision, in which Ecology determines if the source is using "measures that would reduce community exposure, especially exposure to that portion of the community subject to the greatest additional risk, to comparable toxic air [pollutants provided that such measures are not already required.""[86] Extensive public involvement, beyond that associated with ordinary NSR, is required as part of the risk management decision-making.

EMISSION STANDARDS

Emission standards and limits are used to regulate the amount or rate at which a source releases particular air pollutants to the atmosphere. Emission limits are established by regulation or by permit. Compliance is usually measured at the point from which air emissions are released to the atmosphere, such as a stack or vent. As discussed above, emission limits for a particular source are often established in the new source review process, implementing the relevant case-by-case technology requirement, such as BACT. Other emission limits exist in state and federal regulations. This section discusses some of the most common existing state and federal emission standards, refer to the regulations for the full set of standards. Emission standards for hazardous air pollutants and air toxics are discussed separately in the previous section.

Many emission standards have associated monitoring, recordkeeping and reporting requirements, or are subject to general requirements for keeping track of a source's compliance with the standards. For example, each federal new source performance standard has very specific monitoring, recordkeeping and reporting requirements. The general monitoring, recordkeeping and reporting requirements for state emission standards are listed in WAC 173-400-105.

General Standards

The following general standards apply to all sources of air contaminants in the state.

RACT. All existing emission units are required to use "reasonably available control technology" (RACT).[87] State law requires Ecology or local authorities to determine RACT by source category for most sources.[88] This relieves most sources from having to determine on their own whether or not they comply with the RACT standard.

Opacity. All sources of visible emissions must meet the 20% general opacity standard.[89] Opacity is the degree to which an object is obscured, measured as a percentage, when viewed through an emission plume.[90] For instance, 20% opacity means that 80% an object can be seen through the plume while 20% is obscured. Opacity is considered a gross measure of particulate. Like other emission standards, there are general and source-specific opacity standards. Certain source-specific opacity standards are more or less stringent than the general standard. For instance, certain equipment at kraft pulp mills[91] is subject to a 35% opacity standard, while solid waste incinerators[92] are subject to a 5% opacity standard.

Fugitive Emissions. Operations that are sources of fugitive emissions, such as materials handling, must take reasonable precautions to prevent the release of air contaminants.[93] A similar requirement applies to sources of fugitive dust.[94] Fugitive emissions are emissions that do not, and could not reasonably, pass through a confined opening such as a stack or vent.[95]

Odors. Any source that emits an odor that unreasonably interferes with another property owner's use and enjoyment of their property must use recognized good practice and procedures to reduce those odors to a reasonable minimum.[96]

Sulfur Dioxide. All sources in the state are prohibited from emitting sulfur dioxide in excess of 1,000 parts per million in any one hour period, unless they can demonstrate there is no feasible method to achieve the reduction.[97]

Standards With Specific Applicability

Many emission standards in state and federal regulations apply to specific types of sources or activities. These source-specific standards generally take precedence over similar general standards.

New Source Performance Standards (NSPS). The NSPS are complex federal standards that establish allowable emission rates for specific pollutants from facilities in over seventy specific source categories. They are found in 40 C.F.R. §60. The standards apply to new sources built after specific dates (usually the date the standard was proposed), and to modifications that trigger applicability. EPA sets the NSPS; most NSPS have been incorporated by reference into the state regulations.[98] EPA delegated to Ecology and six of the local authorities the authority to implement and enforce the NSPS promulgated before 1993.[99]

Industry-specific State Standards. The state regulations contain several chapters devoted to specific industries, including kraft pulping mills,[100] sulfite pulping mills,[101] primary aluminum plants,[102] and solid waste incinerator facilities.[103] In addition, the state general air regulation contains emission standards for the following specific sources: combustion and incineration units;[104] general process units;[105] wigwam burners, hog fuel boilers; orchard heating; grain elevators; catalytic cracking units; other wood waste burners; and sulfuric acid plants.[106]

Outdoor Burning and Wood Stoves. New programs have sought to substantially limit outdoor burning and use of wood stoves. Outdoor burning includes residential, commercial agricultural and silviculture burning.[107] Outdoor burning is banned entirely in nonattainment areas and in any cities with populations greater than 10,000 or with an urban growth boundary. Permits with fees are required for any agricultural and silvicultural burning.[108] No permit is needed for residential burning in non-urban areas in the thirty smallest counties in the state. Permits are required in all incorporated towns and cities. Since 1995, wood stoves sold in Washington have had to meet Oregon or EPA emission standards.[109]

Asbestos. Asbestos is one of the most common hazardous air pollutants. Several of the local air pollution control authorities have their own asbestos regulations that apply generally to building construction, renovation and demolition. Asbestos is also regulated under a federal NESHAP, which generally applies to owners and operators of demolition or renovation operations.[110]

VOC Sources in Ozone Nonattainment Areas. Specifically listed sources of VOCs, such as certain types of degreasers, surface coaters, and vapor collection systems, that are located in an ozone nonattainment area are subject to specified equipment and work practice standards.[111]

Acid Rain Control. Certain electric utilities are subject to a program created by the 1990 Clean Air Act Amendments to control acid rain.[112] The program's goal is to significantly reduce national sulfur dioxide (SO_2) emissions through the issuance of a limited number of marketable allowances, each permitting one ton of SO_2 emissions. Only utility units in existence before the end of 1995 were allocated allowances. Units beginning operation after 1995, and units that want to expand, must purchase allowances to emit SO_2 in order to operate. Sources covered by the program must obtain enough emission allowances to cover their yearly SO_2 emissions, or else pay a $2,000 per ton excess emission fee.[113] The program also reduces NOx emissions through new emissions limitations for utility boilers. Permitting under the acid rain program is handled through the operating permit program.[114]

Stratospheric Ozone Protection. Requirements to protect stratospheric ozone are designed to achieve a phased reduction in the production of ozone-depleting chemicals, culminating in a complete phase-out of their use.[115] Production and consumption of fully halogenated chlorofluorocarbons (CFCs) and most other "Class I substances,"[116] that were often used in refrigeration, as solvents and as fire extinguishing chemicals, must be phased out by 2000.[117] Hydrochlorofluorocarbons (HCFCs), the "Class II substances,"[118] may serve as short term substitutes for CFCs because they are less ozone depleting, but they still harm stratospheric ozone. Restrictions on the use of HCFCs go into effect in 2015, and a full phase out of HCFC production is effective January 1, 2030.[119] Use and emission limits also affect producers of products that contain ozone-depleting substances, such as refrigerators, and those that use such substances in their production processes, such as electronics manufacturers. Since July 1992, it has been unlawful to knowingly vent or release a Class I or II substance into the environment.[120] Service providers that handle refrigerants are also subject to specific requirements.[121] State law also prohibits the sale or purchase of nonessential consumer products that contain CFCs, such as air horns, party streamers, tire inflators, noise makers and certain cleaning sprays.[122]

Motor Vehicles. Although air quality regulations focus mainly on stationary sources, in many areas, such as the Puget Sound region, motor vehicles are the single largest source of pollution, especially of VOCs, NOx and carbon monoxide. The 1990 Clean Air Act Amendments imposed numerous new requirements to address emissions of these pollutants, including tighter tailpipe emissions standards, clean fuel programs, enhanced inspection and maintenance (I/M) programs, anti-tampering measures, fuel volatility controls, controls on evaporative emissions and controls on non-road vehicles and engines.[123] Special clean fuel requirements apply in urban areas with the worst ozone nonattainment problems, and an oxygenated fuel program applies in carbon monoxide nonattainment areas.[124]

In Washington, Ecology adopted a vehicle emission inspection program to reduce emissions. In general, vehicle emission inspections are required before any vehicle garaged or operated in an emission contributing area is registered or re-registered in Washington.[125] Emission contributing areas generally include the areas in and around Tacoma, Vancouver, Spokane, Seattle and Bellevue.[126] There are several exemptions to the vehicle emission inspection requirements. Vehicles over Twenty-five years of age, farm vehicles, and motorcycles are exempt, as are diesel powered vehicles weighing less than 6001 pounds or with an engine that was certified by its manufacturer as meeting the EPA 2007 exhaust emission standards or equipped with an exhaust particle filter acceptable to Ecology (2009 and newer vehicles do not need to test), electric, propane and natural gas engines.[127]

Transportation Demand Management (TDM). TDM is an innovative approach to reducing motor vehicle emissions by reducing total vehicle miles traveled.[128] The requirements apply to certain counties and employers. Counties with over 150,000 people, or with cities with major employers,[129] are required to have county-wide TDM plans.[130] Major employers are required to have commuter trip reduction programs.[131] Private company programs may include high-occupancy vehicle parking preferences or reduced fees, higher charges for single-occupancy vehicle parking, ride matching, subsidized transit fees, van-pool or car-pool subsidies and flex-time for employees. Employers subject to the requirements must demonstrate how their programs contribute to the overall goals of the county or city TDM plan.

ENFORCEMENT AND APPEALS

State Enforcement

A local air agency may serve a Notice of Violation (NOV) on any source in its jurisdiction that it believes has violated any provision of the Washington Clean Air Act or any rule adopted by Ecology or the local agency.[132] An NOV must specify the regulatory provision allegedly violated and the facts alleged to constitute the violation, and may also include an order specifying corrective action.[133]

Any order issued by a local air authority becomes final unless appealed to the Pollution Control Hearings Board (PCHB) under RCW 43.21B.[134] The PCHB is part of the Washington Environmental Hearings Office, an independent state agency.[135] If an order is appealed, the PCHB holds a hearing under rules of practice adopted by the PCHB.[136] The PCHB issues findings of fact, conclusions of law and a decision.[137] The decision is subject to judicial review under the state Administrative Procedures Act (APA), Ch. 34.05 RCW.[138]

Local air authorities are also authorized to initiate judicial enforcement.[139] To obtain judicial relief, the local authority must first notify the alleged violator and provide an opportunity to comply.[140] If the alleged violator fails to comply, the authority may petition the superior court of the county where the violation is alleged to have occurred for a restraining order temporary injunction or a permanent injunction.[141]

Local air pollution control authorities may also seek civil penalties of $10,000 per day per violation.[142] The penalty amount may be adjusted for inflation. Upon receipt of a penalty notice, an alleged violator has fifteen days to request mitigation of the penalty.[143] An alleged violator may appeal either the penalty or a refusal to mitigate within thirty days to the PCHB.[144] The penalty becomes due if the notice of penalty or refusal to mitigate is not appealed, or when the PCHB issues a decision after an appeal.[145]

Local air agencies and Ecology may also seek criminal sanctions. Violation of any requirement enforceable by the authority is a gross misdemeanor and punishable by up to $10,000 and/or one year in jail.[146] Any person who knowingly releases a hazardous air pollutant is guilty of a Class C felony and subject to a fine of not less than $50,000 and/or by imprisonment of not more than five years.[147]

Federal Enforcement

The 1990 Clean Air Act Amendments significantly increased federal and state authority to assess penalties for violations of the Act. For instance, prior to 1990, EPA was only authorized to assess penalties for violations that "extended beyond" thirty days after a notice of violation.[148] Now EPA may issue a notice of violation with a penalty even if the violation is abated immediately.[149] Penalties up to $25,000 per day are available through an administrative process or through an action in federal court.

Substantial criminal sanctions are also available to regulators.[150] Criminal fines and imprisonment may be imposed. Jail terms are one year for knowing failure to pay a fee to EPA or negligently emitting HAPs in violation of a standard, two years for knowing submission of false information or failing to report information, five years for knowing violation of an emission standard or permit, and fifteen years and $1 million for knowing emission of HAPs that cause an imminent threat to public health. Both companies and individuals are subject to criminal sanctions. A second offense allows the court to double the maximum fines and prison terms.

EPA may assess penalties administratively if the total amount does not exceed $200,000 and the violations are not more than one year old.[151] An alleged violator has an opportunity for a contested case hearing under the federal Administrative Procedures Act (APA).[152] EPA may also issue "field citations" for "minor violations."[153] Field citations may not exceed $5,000 per day. There is no right to an APA-style hearing for such citations, only a reasonable opportunity to be heard. Judicial review "on the record" is available for both an administrative penalty and a field citation.[154]

One of the most significant changes concerns suits by third parties for violations of the Clean Air Act. Citizens may now sue under federal but not Washington state law for penalties and injunctive relief.[155] Citizen suits for violations of air quality standards are expected to increase over time as changes brought about by the 1990 Clean Air Act Amendments lead to increased monitoring and self-reporting of violations. The 1990 Amendments also authorized a new "bounty provision," which would allow EPA to award up to $10,000 to persons providing information leading to a successful criminal, civil or administrative enforcement action.[156]

NOTES

1 The federal Clean Air Act is codified at 42 USC §§7401 *et seq*. The state Act is codified in RCW §70.94.

2 *Save Our Summers v. WA State Department of Ecology*, 132 F. Supp. 2d 896 (ED WA 1999).

3 RCW §§70.94.053, 70.94.380, 70.94.331. Most of the local authorities are, in fact, formed on a regional, multi-county basis. For example, the Puget Sound Air Pollution Control Authority covers Snohomish, King, Pierce, and Kitsap counties.

4 Ecology shares regulatory authority for radioactive emissions with the Washington State Department of Health. RCW §70.98.

5 RCW §70.94.395; WAC 173-405, -410, and -415.

6 WAC 173-480 and WAC-173 481.

7 RCW §70.94.331. Certain industries, particularly energy facilities, have their own set of regulations. RCW §80.50; Residents Opposed to Kittitas Turbines v. State Energy Facility Site Evaluation Council, 165 Wn. 2d 275 (2008).

8 42 U.S.C. §7410.

9 EPA has established NAAQS for carbon monoxide, sulfur oxides, particulate matter less than 10 microns in diameter ("PM10"), ozone, nitrogen dioxide, and lead. Together, these are referred to as the "criteria" pollutants. Ecology regulations include these ambient standards, excluding lead, and add standards for fluorides and radionuclides. WAC 173-470 through -481 WAC. *See also* http://www.epa.gov/air/criteria.html.

10 WAC 173-400-030(55).

11 42 U.S.C. §7407(d).

12 *Id*.

13 *Frame Factory, Inc. v. Department of Ecology*, 21 Wn. App. 50 (1978).

14 Energy facilities with a generating capacity of 250 MW or more are permitted by the independent Energy Facility Site Evaluation Council (EFSEC). RCW §80 50.020. EFSEC's regulations are in WAC 463.

15 RCW §70.94.081; §70.94.331(2)(b). *See also* 2013 Wash. Laws Ch. 6, §§ 1 through 4 for greenhouse gas abatement; *See also* Washington Environmental Council v. Bellon, 732 F.3d 1131, *rehearing en banc den*. 741 F. 3d 1075 (9th Cir. 2013); *Utility Air Regulatory Group v. EPA*, 2014 WL 2807314 (US).

16 RCW §70. 94.141.

17 RCW §§70.94 331(2)(b) and .380(2).

18 RCW §70.94.057

19 RCW §70.94.151(2).

20 WAC 173-400-100.

21 RCW §70.94.161(17); WAC 173-400-100(4).

22 RCW §70.94.161.

23 The operating permit rule exempts non-major sources for now. Both EPA and Ecology have reserved the authority to revise the rule to apply to non-major sources. WAC 173-401-300(2).

24 WAC 173-400-091.

25 *See e.g., Bowers v. Pollution Control Hearings Board*, 103 Wn. App. 587 (2000), *rev. den*. 144 Wn.2d 1005.

26 WAC 173-401-615(1).

27 WAC 173-401-620.

28 WAC 173-401-630(5).

29 WAC 173-401-520.

30 WAC 173-401-615(3).

31 WAC 173-401-700.

32 WAC 173-400-110.

33 WAC 173-400-191, the "synthetic minor" program.

34 WAC 173-400-030(47).

35 WAC 173-400-030(43).

36 WAC 173-400-110 and -100.

37 PSCACA Regulation I, §6.03.

38 WAC 173-400-171(1).

39 The state's minor new source review process has been approved by EPA and incorporated into the SIP; the permits that result from that process are considered federally enforceable. EPA's definition of the term is at 40 CFR 52.21(b)(17).

40 *See* WAC 173-400-112 and -113.

41 WAC 173-400-030(9).

42 WAC 173-400-040. *But see also Washington Environmental Council v. Bellon*, 732 F.3d 1131 (9th Cir. 2013)

43 RCW §70.94.154(7).

44 40 CFR 52.21(b)(1); WAC 173-400-030(40).

45 40 CFR 52.21(b)(4); WAC 173-400-030(61).

46 The regulations have traditionally required such limits to be federally enforceable, but the D.C. Circuit Court of Appeals remanded this requirement in *Chemical Manufacturers Assn. v. United States Environmental Protection Agency*, 70 F. 3d 637 (DC Cir. 1995) (the court relied on its decision in *Nat'l. Mining Assn. v. United States Environmental Protection Agency*, 59 F. 3d 1351 (DC Cir. 1995), in which the court determined that EPA did not sufficiently demonstrate that federal enforceability was necessary to ensure the effectiveness of state and local controls on air emissions).

47 40 CFR 52.21(b)(2); WAC 173-400-030(39).

48 40 CFR 52.21(b)(3); WAC 173-400-030(46).

49 See 40 CFR 52.21(b)(23); WAC 173-400-030(67) for the significance thresholds of other pollutants.

50 40 CFR 52.21(i).

51 48 Fed. Reg. 48,285 (1983).

52 40 CFR 52.2479 and 52.2497.

53 40 CFR 52.21(j).

54 40 CFR 52.21(k), (l), and (m).

55 A PSD increment is a maximum allowable increase in concentration allowed to occur above a baseline concentration for a pollutant. See 40 CFR 52.21(c). As the allowable increment in an area is used, it is said to be "consumed."

56 40 CFR 52.21(o).

57 40 CFR 52.21(p).

58 This has generally been interpreted to mean that all proposed sources located within 100 km of a Class I area must conduct the analysis, although the reviewing agency can require a facility located beyond 100 km to do the analysis.

59 WAC 173-400-112(1) and (2).

60 WAC 173 400-112(5).

61 WAC 173 400-112(4).

62 WAC 173 400-112(6).

63 WAC 173-400-112(9).

64 40 CFR 61.

65 1990 CAA §112.

66 WAC 173-460-010.

67 40 CFR 63.

68 40 CFR 63.2.

69 *Id.*

70 1990 CAA §112(d)(2).

71 *Id.*

72 *Id.*

73 1990 CAA §112(i)(1).

74 1990 CAA §112(i)(1)

75 *Id.*

76 1990 CAA § 112(i)(2).

77 1990 CAA §112(i)(3).

78 1990 CAA §112(r).

79 The Provisions are in 40 CFR 68; the list of regulated substances and threshold quantities is in 40 CFR 68.130.

80 WAC 173-460-030.

81 WAC 173-460-150 and -160.

82 WAC 173-460-040(4).

83 WAC 173-460-080(2), -150 and -160.

84 WAC 173-460-050.

85 WAC 173-60-090.

86 WAC 173-460-100.

87 RCW §70.94 154(1); WAC 173-400-040.

88 RCW §70.94.154(2). *See also Longview Fibre Co. v. State, Dept. of Ecology*, 89 Wn. App. 627 (1998).

89 WAC 173- 400-040(1)(a).

90 WAC 173-400-030(5l).

91 WAC 173-405-040(6); WAC 173-410-040(3).

92 WAC 173 434-130(4)(a).

93 WAC 173-400-040(3).

94 WAC 173-400-040(8).

95 WAC 173-400-030(31).

96 WAC 173-400-040(4).

97 WAC 173-400-040(6).

98 WAC 173-400-115.

99 59 Fed Reg. 47,264 (1994).

100 WAC 173-405.

101 WAC 173-410.

102 WAC 173-415.

103 WAC 173-434.

104 WAC 173-400-050.

105 WAC 173-400-060.

106 WAC 173-400-070. As part of a new EPA regulation aimed at reducing carbon emissions from power plants nationwide, Washington will also be required to develop a plan to limit carbon dioxide production to 215 pounds per MWh (the lowest allowance in the nation). *See also United Air Regulatory Group v. EPA*, 2014 WL 2807314 (2014).

107 RCW §70.94.743; open burning regulations are in WAC 173-425, agricultural burning regulations are in WAC 173-430.

108 RCW §70.94.660.

109 RCW §70.94.457; solid fuel burning device regulations are in WAC 173-433.

110 40 CFR 61.145.

111 WAC 173-490 WAC.

112 1990 CAA §§401 through 416; 40 CFR 72 through 78; WAC 173-406.

113 1990 CAA §411.

114 1990 CAA §408.

115 1990 CAA §§601-618; 40 CFR 82.

116 1990 CAA §602(a).

117 1990 CAA §604(b).

118 1990 CAA §602(b).

119 1990 CAA §605.

120 1990 CAA §608(c).

121 1990 CAA §609(c); RCW §70.94.970(2).

122 RCW §70.94.980(2).

123 1990 CAA §§202 through 250. *See also* 42 U.S.C. §§7521 *et seq.*

124 1990 CAA §211.

125 WAC 173-422-030 and -170(10).

126 WAC 173-122-050.

127 WAC 173-422-170.

128 RCW §§70.94.521 through .551.

129 "Major employers" are those with more than 100 full-time employees at one site over a twenty-four hour period for at least six months of the year. For example, a company with three eight-hour shifts of forty full-time employees would be "major" if the facility operated for at least six months.

130 RCW §70.94.527.

131 RCW §70.94.531.

[132] RCW §70.94.211 (for local authorities); RCW §70.94.332 (for Ecology). *See also ASARCO, Inc. v. Puget Sound Air Pollution Control Agency*, 51 Wn. App. 49 (1988), *aff'd.* 112 Wn. 2d 314.

[133] *Id. See also* William Dickson Co. v. Puget Sound Air Pollution Control Agency, 81 Wn. App. 403 (1996).

[134] RCW §70.94.221.

[135] RCW §43.21B.005.

[136] RCW §43.21B.170; WAC 371-08.

[137] RCW §43.21B.100.

[138] RCW §43.21B.190.

[139] RCW §70.94.211.

[140] RCW §70.94.425.

[141] *Id.*

[142] RCW §43.21B.300; RCW §§70.94.431(1) and (3). *See also Puget Sound Air Pollution Control Agency v. Fields Products*, 68 Wn. App. 841 (1992).

[143] *Id.*

[144] RCW §43.21B.300(2).

[145] RCW §43.21B.300(3).

[146] RCW §§70.94.430(1) and .430(2).

[147] RCW §70.94.430(3).

[148] 1990 CAA, §113(a)(1); previously 42 U.S.C. §7413(a)(1).

[149] 1990 CAA §113(a)(1).

[150] 1990 CAA, §113(c).

[151] 1990 CAA, §113(d)(1) and (2).

[152] 5 USC §§501 through 554.

[153] 1990 CAA. §113(d)(3).

[154] 1990 CAA §113(d)(4).

[155] 42 USC §7604.

[156] 1990 CAA, §113(f).

CHAPTER 6

Water Quality

HISTORY OF STATE WATER POLLUTION CONTROL PROGRAMS AND RELATIONSHIP TO FEDERAL PROGRAM

Washington's water pollution control program, like many of the state's other environmental programs, is implemented and enforced partly under state law and partly under federal law. Early efforts to control water pollution by both the state and federal governments did not provide strong enforcement mechanisms. Early on, before enforcement actions could be taken, government agencies were required to demonstrate both the existence of a harmful water pollution problem and a direct link between a particular discharge and the problem.

In 1971, Washington took a new approach by enacting the Pollution Disclosure Act of 1971. This Act required pollutant dischargers to use "all known, available and reasonable methods of waste water treatment" (AKART) before discharge, regardless of the quality of the receiving water. This law was a real change in the philosophy of controlling water pollution. Instead of a remedial-approach, where regulators traced responsibility for water pollution problems to particular dischargers, the Pollution Control Disclosure Act is preventative, and requires all dischargers to implement technology-based controls, regardless of the quality of the receiving water.

This same philosophy was adopted by the federal government the following year in the Federal Water Pollution Control Act Amendments of 1972 (also known as the Clean Water Act "CWA"). The CWA stated as its ambitious goal that "the discharge of pollutants into navigable waters be eliminated by 1985."[1] To achieve this goal and the interim goal of providing "fishable, swimmable water," the CWA instituted a system of permits, called the National Pollutant Discharge Elimination System (NPDES), to limit the amount of pollutants that could be discharged into navigable waters of the United States. The CWA also provided stronger enforcement tools, including civil and criminal penalties.

The CWA shifted the focus from standards designed to protect ambient water quality to technology-based standards measured at the source of the pollution. EPA was authorized to set nationally uniform standards based on pollution control technologies, without considering the impact on receiving water quality. Based on this statutory authority, EPA has adopted technology-based effluent guidelines for major categories of industries.

In 1987, Congress substantially amended and updated the CWA. These amendments focused attention on the fact that many waterbodies were not meeting water quality standards, even after application of technology-based standards.

AGENCIES RESPONSIBLE FOR WATER POLLUTION CONTROL

The Washington Department of Ecology

Ecology has primary responsibility for controlling water pollution in Washington. It administers the NPDES and state waste discharge permit programs, and establishes effluent treatment and limitation requirements and state water quality standards in state waters.[2]

In 1973, Washington applied to EPA for authority to administer the NPDES program within the state. That same year, it became one of the first states to receive program delegation. Since then, Washington has enacted additional laws that broaden the reach of the state's permitting system and set stringent standards for water quality.

The Pollution Control Hearings Board (PCHB)

Ecology's decisions regarding water pollution control and water quality are reviewable by the Pollution Control Hearings Board (PCHB). The PCHB hears appeals of NPDES or state waste discharge permit actions (issuance, modifications, or denial), orders, rules, or regulations of Ecology.[3]

The PCHB is an independent agency of the State of Washington, composed of three members appointed by the governor for terms of six years. The members are qualified by experience or training in environmental matters. At least one member is a lawyer, and not more than two members are of the same political party.

REGULATION OF WATER POLLUTION

Discharge Permits

Under Washington's Water Pollution Control Act, the discharge of pollutants to waters of the State is unlawful. Instead, permits are required to control the discharge of pollutants into waters of the State. Any person who discharges pollutants to waters of the State without a permit, or who violates effluent or water quality standards established in a permit, is subject to civil[4] and criminal[5] penalties. In addition, there is liability to the state, counties, and cities for natural resource damages.[6]

An NPDES permit is required for discharges of pollutants from a point source into surface waters of the State.[7] The NDPES permit program was later expanded to include storm water discharges from a variety of activities.

A state waste discharge permit is required for discharges of pollutants to ground water or discharges to municipal sanitary sewer systems as part of the state-wide pretreatment program. An NPDES and a state waste discharge permit must be obtained for facilities that discharge pollutants to both surface and ground water.

NPDES Permit Program

As indicated above, an NPDES permit is required to discharge pollutants from industrial and municipal point sources into surface waters of the State.[8] NPDES permits are required under both federal and state law. Washington has been delegated full authority to issue the permit to sources within the state. Therefore, NPDES permits are federally enforceable and are governed by a combination of federal and state law. The NPDES permit sets "effluent limitations," which are limits on the amount of pollutants that can be discharged into surface waters. The discharged wastewater must be treated with the best available treatment technology that is economically achievable, regardless of the condition of the receiving water. Effluent limitations are set based on treatment technology, but more stringent limits may be imposed if the technology-based limits do not prevent violations of water quality standards.

The term "discharge of a pollutant" is defined to mean "any addition of any pollutant or combination of pollutants to surface waters of the state from any point source" or "any addition of any pollutant or combination of pollutants to the waters of the contiguous zone or the ocean from any point source, other than a vessel or other floating craft which is being used as a means of transportation."[9] Based on this language, understanding the following terms is essential to understanding whether an NPDES permit is required:

- Pollutant
- Addition
- Point source
- Waters of the state

The following sections briefly discuss each of these terms.

Pollutant

For purposes of the NPDES permit program, "pollutant" is a defined as encompassing "dredged spoil, solid waste, incinerator residue, sewage, garbage, sewage sludge, munitions, chemical wastes, biological materials, radioactive materials, heat, wrecked or discarded equipment, rock, sand, cellar dirt and industrial, municipal and agricultural waste discharged into water."[10] Case law has established that this definition is extremely broad and includes virtually every kind of waste material, regardless of whether that material had value at the time it was discharged.[11] It does not, however, include dredged or fill material which is regulated under 33 USC §1344.

Addition

The CWA requires an addition of a pollutant before an NPDES permit is required. This requirement has been successfully used in some situations to preclude the requirement of an NPDES permit when the "pollutants" in the waste stream are present only because of their presence in intake waters, if the intake waters are drawn from the same body of water into which the discharge is made and if the pollutants present in the intake water are not removed by the discharger as part of its usual operations.[12] Similarly, an "addition" does not include discharges of water from dams, even if a dam's operations adversely affect the temperature of dissolved oxygen content of the water.[13] The Ninth Circuit has held, however, that the "Act does not impose liability only where a point source discharge creates a net increase in the level of the pollution. Rather the Act categorically prohibits any discharge of a pollutant from a point source without a permit."[14]

Point Source

The term "point source" includes any discernible, confined and discrete conveyance, such as a ditch, channel, conduit, pipe, well, discrete fissure, container, rolling stock, concentrated animal feeding operation, or vessel from which pollutants may be discharged.[15] There are several exceptions to this definition, however, including irrigation return flows, the discharge of sewage from vessels regulated under Section 312 of the CWA, effluent from properly functioning marine engines, certain agricultural and silvicultural discharges, and certain discharges of dredged or fill material regulated under Section 404 of the CWA. While unconfined "sheet" runoff is theoretically not subject to the Act, in the great majority of cases, courts and agencies will find a point source under a specific exemption.

Waters of the State (or Waters of the United States)

Under the state NPDES permit program, "surface waters of the state" means "all waters defined as 'waters of the United States' in 40 CFR 122.2 that are within the boundaries of the state of Washington. This includes lakes, rivers, ponds, streams, inland waters, wetlands, ocean, bays, estuaries, sounds, and inlets."[16] The term "waters of the United States" is defined by EPA regulations to include (1) navigable waters; (2) tributaries of navigable waters; (3) interstate waters; and (4) intrastate lakes, rivers and streams (a) used by interstate travelers for recreation and other purposes, or (b) which are a source of fish or shellfish sold in interstate commerce, or (c) which are utilized for industrial purposes by industries engaged in interstate commerce."[17]

One major issue concerns whether a discharge to publicly or privately owned sewage systems constitutes a discharge to waters of the United States and thus requires an NPDES permit. A discharge to a sewage system that is not connected to an operable treatment works is a discharge subject to an NPDES permit. On the other hand, a discharge to a publicly owned treatment works (POTW) that is capable of meeting effluent limits is excluded from the NPDES permit requirement.[18] All industrial dischargers to POTWs must comply with general pretreatment standards, 40 CFR 403, and many others must also comply with industry-by-industry ("categorical") standards which have been established along with effluent limitations for each industry.

Permit Application Process

Dischargers must apply for individual NPDES permits at least 180 days before the discharge begins, or in sufficient time to ensure compliance with national and state effluent limitations and water quality standards.[19] Applications for renewal must be submitted 180 days before the expiration of an existing permit.

Under the Waste Discharge General Permit Program, Ecology may also issue general permits to cover categories of dischargers or geographic areas where there are similar operations and wastes that require the same effluent limitations, conditions, and monitoring. Dischargers who wish to be covered by a general permit must file a notification of coverage with Ecology.[20]

After receipt of an application or notification of coverage, Ecology makes a tentative determination to issue or deny the permit. If Ecology decides to issue the permit, then it issues a draft permit, and a fact sheet that contains, among other things, the legal and technical grounds for the draft permit determination.[21] Public notice of every draft permit must be given, and a public comment period follows.[22] Ecology must also notify other government agencies and provide those agencies an opportunity to submit their written views and recommendations.[23] Any interested person or entity may request a public hearing,[24] which triggers the requirement that Ecology give public notice of the hearing.[25] Permit conditions include effluent limitations, monitoring requirements, and reporting requirements (including a requirement to report any new or increased discharge of pollutants, and any conditions necessary to prevent or control pollutant discharges). Permits may also include, among other things, compliance schedules, whole effluent toxicity testing and limits, sediment monitoring, dilution analysis, and solid waste plans.

Conditions typically included in individual permits are often either negotiable or susceptible to legal attack. Because the CWA is a strict liability statute, it is crucial that permit holders either negotiate out of their permits conditions that they are unable to meet, or negotiate acceptable compliance schedules. Accepting permit conditions that a permit holder knows it cannot meet can be deadly, as case law has established that an inability to meet permit conditions is no defense to an enforcement action. Accordingly, draft permit conditions should be carefully scrutinized.[26] If proposed permits contain inappropriate or unachievable conditions, these conditions should be modified or appealed to the PCHB.

Permits are valid for a maximum of five years. Permittees must apply to renew permits at least 180 days before expiration and must demonstrate substantial compliance with all of the permits terms and conditions.[27] A timely application for renewal continues the prior permit's effectiveness until Ecology has made a final determination on the permit renewal application.

State Waste Discharge Permit Program

In general, a state waste discharge permit is required for discharges not covered by the NPDES program.[28] Specifically, state waste discharge permits are required for the following:

- Discharges of waste materials from a commercial or industrial operation to waters of the state or to a municipal sewage system.
- Any county or any municipal or public corporation operating or proposing to operate a sewage system that results in the disposal of waste material into the waters of the state.
- All lagoons containing wastewater, lined and unlined. Exceptions[29] for the requirement of a state waste discharge permit include the following:
- Discharges to municipal sewerage systems of domestic wastewater (sanitary wastewater) from residential, commercial, or industrial structures.
- Discharges to a municipal system that is already permitted by local authority.
- Discharges to a municipal system that is already permitted under a local pretreatment program.
- Discharges to municipal sewerage systems from commercial or industrial operations if the waste strength and characteristics are the same as domestic wastewater.
- Discharges that have an NPDES individual or general permit for discharges to surface water.
- Discharges from small on-site septic systems that discharge to the ground.

- Discharges from small aerobic, domestic treatment plants that discharge to the ground.

The application process for obtaining a state waste discharge permit is similar to that for obtaining an NPDES permit except that the permit application must be submitted sixty days prior to discharge.[30] Discharges to groundwater through injection wells are subject to a separate permit program.[31]

General Permits

General permits are permits that are developed for a category of discharger instead of an individual facility. Coverage under a valid Waste Discharge General Permit satisfies the requirement to obtain both an NPDES permit and a state waste discharge permit.[32] Ecology has developed general permits for the following industries: boatyards, fruit packers, dairies, sand and gravel, and fish hatcheries. Ecology has also developed a stormwater general permit for industrial and construction activities.

Applications for coverage under a general permit must be submitted no later than 90 days after the issuance of the general permit for existing operations. For new operations, applications for coverage must be submitted no later than 180 days prior to the commencement of the activity that may result in the discharge to waters of the state.[33] Unless otherwise specified in the general permit or a response by Ecology in writing, coverage of a discharger under a general permit is automatic on the later of the following:

1. The effective date of the general permit;
2. Thirty-one days following the end of any public notice and comment period on an application for coverage under the permit;
3. Thirty-one days after receipt by Ecology of a completed application for coverage; or
4. After a date specified in the general permit.[34]

Combined Permit

When a discharger requires two or more permits, the permits may be processed under WAC 173-10. Under this program, which applies to any type of permit, applicants may file a single form with Ecology to obtain all needed permits. Applicants should be aware, however, that when an NPDES permit is included among the permits applied for, the applicant must complete both a single permit application and a special NPDES permit application.

Stormwater Permits

The 1987 amendments to the CWA required EPA to develop regulations for permitting of stormwater discharges under the NPDES program.[35] EPA published final regulations regarding permitting of stormwater discharges on November 16, 1990. These regulations define stormwater as "storm water runoff, snow melt runoff, and surface runoff and drainage."[36] The new stormwater regulations require permit coverage for four types of storm water discharges to waters of the United States:

1. discharges permitted prior to February 4, 1987;
2. discharges "associated with industrial activity;"
3. large and medium municipal separate storm sewer systems; and

4. discharges determined to be causing violations of water quality standards or that significantly contribute pollutants to navigable waters.[37]

The second and third categories of discharges have been the focus of most of Ecology's efforts. These are discussed further below.

Discharges Associated With Industrial Activity

Industrial activities range from steel manufacturing to food manufacturing and include activities conducted by government entities (e.g., landfills and sewage treatment facilities) as well as private enterprises. The regulations, however, distinguish between "heavy" industries, such as the steel manufacturing and "light industries," such as food manufacturing.

Heavy Industries. "Heavy" industries such as steel manufacturing require permits whether or not the processes or materials are exposed to stormwater. Other "heavy" industries include lumber, paper, chemical, petroleum and shipbuilding and repair facilities.[38] The following activities also will require a permit whether or not the processes or materials are exposed to stormwater: hazardous waste treatment storage or disposal facilities; landfills, land application, sites and open dumps; recycling facilities; steam electric power generating facilities; and domestic sewage facilities.[39] The rules contain a special exemption for municipalities of under 100,000 people that operate heavy industrial facilities. Such facilities are generally exempt from the stormwater permit requirement. This exemption, however, does not apply to airports, power plants, or uncontrolled sanitary landfills.[40]

Light Industries. "Light" industries, such as food manufacturers, require a permit only if processes or materials are exposed to stormwater. Other "light" industries include facilities that manufacture apparel, textiles, drugs, furniture, paints, rubber and plastic products, leather products, watches, electronic equipment and transportation equipment.[41] However, the court in NRDC v. EPA held that EPA provided insufficient justification for treating "light industrial" discharges less strictly than "heavy industrial" discharges and concluded that the distinction between light and heavy industry was arbitrary and capricious.[42] EPA and Ecology are therefore not requiring permits for light industrial activities where there is no exposure to stormwater until after it completes rulemaking on these facilities.

Construction Activities. Construction activities are covered by the 1995 General Stormwater Permit for Construction Activities. Erosion control is the most prominent concern.

Permits and Notices for Industrial Discharges.

General Permit. As previously discussed, a general permit is a permit that covers a given type of activity or facility. A party conducting that activity does not need an individual permit if it complies with the general permit requirements. The Industrial and Construction Stormwater General Permit was issued by Ecology in 1995. This General Permit is intended to cover most facilities included in the stormwater program; however, it does not cover:

- stormwater discharges that are mixed with sources of non-stormwater, discharges that are subject to an existing effluent limitation guideline;
- discharges that are subject to an existing NPDES permit;
- discharges determined to be or expected to be contributing to a violation of a water quality standard;

- discharges that may adversely affect a listed or proposed to be listed endangered or threatened species or its critical habitat, and
- discharges from an inactive mining, landfill, or oil and gas operation occurring on Federal Lands.

The General Permit focuses on pollution prevention, rather than "end-of-the pipe" technology to reduce the discharge of pollutants. The General Permit, therefore, does not set effluent standards. The central requirement of the General Permit is the development and implementation of a Stormwater Pollution Prevention Plan (SWPPP) that identifies and provides a schedule for Best Management Practices (BMPs) for the facility. The SWPPPs must identify a stormwater pollution prevention team, describe potential pollutant sources, describe appropriate measures and controls to minimize stormwater contact with pollutants, and provide for compliance monitoring.

Individual Permits. Individual applicants must supply a variety of information regarding the physical layout of their facility and their industrial practices that affect the quality of storm water discharges. In addition, the applicant must furnish laboratory analyses of actual discharges from each outfall.[43] The deadline for individual applications for existing facilities was October 1, 1992.[44] Applications for new sources must be submitted 180 days before the discharge is to begin. As a result of the tiered permitting strategy, individual permits are rare in Washington.

Group Permits. A final option for stormwater permitting is to develop group permits for a number of similar facilities. Group applications were submitted, for example, for airports and log sort yards. Although group permits may be useful in limited situations, the availability of the baseline general permit for most facilities has tended to supersede the use of group permits.

Notice to Municipalities. In a major change from the rest of the NPDES permit program, industrial facilities covered by the regulations must obtain permits even if they discharge into municipal storm sewer systems, rather than directly into surface water. In addition to this permit requirement, those responsible for discharges associated with industrial activities must notify municipalities of over 100,000 if the discharge is to the municipal storm sewer system.[45] The deadline for this notice was May 15, 1991.

Discharges From Municipal Sewer Systems

Municipalities serving more than 100,000 people must have a storm water permit for the discharges from their storm sewer systems to waters of the state. Ecology is drafting three municipal storm water permits covering the Cedar-Green, South Puget Sound, and Snohomish Basin watersheds. The permits cover King, Pierce, and Snohomish Counties; Seattle and Tacoma; and the Washington Department of Transportation. To comply with these permits these municipalities may revise their current regulations regarding discharges to their storm sewer systems.

HOW PERMIT EFFLUENT LIMITATIONS ARE DERIVED

Effluent limitations restrict the amount of pollutants that may be discharged by a permittee. Effluent limitations are set by Ecology and may be based on the technology available to treat the pollutants (technology-based) or may be based on the effect of the pollutants in the receiving water (water quality-based).

Technology-Based Effluent Limitations

There are two general approaches to deriving technology-based effluent limitations. The federal effluent guidelines can be used if they are applicable and appropriate, or the effluent limitations can be set specifically for an individual discharger or pollutant. In some instances, both methods of setting effluent limitations may be employed.

Permits issued by Ecology under the NPDES and state waste discharge permit programs require the use of "all known, available and reasonable methods of treatment" (AKART) before discharge. Ecology cannot impose limitations that are weaker than federal law requires.[46] Thus, AKART generally incorporates relevant federal technology-based standards for "best conventional technology," "best available technology," and "new source performance standards." State effluent limitations, however, can be more stringent than federal regulations if necessary to meet Washington water quality standards or if Ecology determines that additional or new technology is known, available, and reasonable.[47]

AKART must be used regardless of the effect of existing discharges on water quality. Thus, water quality conditions can only require more stringent treatment than AKART, never less. Technology-based limits are intended to set a "level playing field" for sources, regardless of location.

Technology-based effluent limitations are often determined by referring to relevant federal standards. Federal technology-based effluent limitations have been promulgated for numerous categories of sources. The list of industries for which EPA has developed effluent guidelines is found in 40 CFR 122, appendix A.

As noted above, Ecology cannot select effluent limitations that are less stringent than applicable federal regulations. When federal effluent limitations are unavailable for a category of sources, or when Ecology determines that more stringent regulation is necessary, Ecology can determine AKART on a case-by-case basis. This is usually done through industry-wide surveys of what can be achieved by applying all known and available methods of treatment that improve water quality at reasonable costs.

Permit applicants should be aware, however, that "reasonable" does not mean "moderate costs" or even costs that would allow the enterprise to continue in business. Instead, the term "reasonable" reflects a determination of whether an increased expenditure is reasonable for an industry as a whole and would produce enough additional benefit to justify the cost. Arguments by the applicant that "we can't afford it" may result in a permit allowing a "phased" compliance schedule to add new facilities or equipment, but will rarely result in relaxing the ultimate effluent limitation. Facilities may have more success arguing that the marginal costs of a given level of treatment are grossly disproportional to the increased reduction over lower cost options. Although not required to, agencies are allowed to look at the "knee of the curve" in making this determination.

Water Quality-Based Effluent Limitations

In addition to technology-based effluent limitations, Ecology must consider the impact of the proposed discharge on the quality of the receiving water and how that discharge may affect the use of the receiving water. In some cases, technology-based effluent limitations are insufficient to protect water quality. In these cases, more stringent effluent limitations must be imposed or alternative disposal methods or locations must be found. To impose effluent limitations for the protection of water quality, Ecology must make a determination, by a rational and scientific process, that a discharger has a reasonable potential to violate water quality standards.

Ecology has promulgated water quality standards for ground waters[48] surface waters of the State.[49] The water quality standards allow Ecology to authorize "mixing zones" for discharges that would otherwise exceed the water quality criteria for aquatic life. Mixing zones are areas where the water quality standards may be exceeded; however, the exceedances are small enough so as not to interfere with beneficial uses. Thus, the point of compliance for water-quality-based effluent limitations is the receiving water, after allowance for a reasonable mixing zone. The mixing zone analysis is complex. Briefly summarized, however, the mixing zone is defined based on the characteristics of the outfall and the receiving water.

Total Maximum Daily Load (TMDL)

The CWA provides for TMDL restrictions as a last resort in attaining water quality standards. Initially, the CWA requires technology-based controls for point sources, which are implemented through effluent limitations in NDPES permits. If the effluent limitation approach fails to meet water quality standards, then §303(d) of the CWA requires states to identify those waters that do not meet water quality standards, after taking into account technology-based reductions of pollutant discharge.[50] The list of such water quality impaired bodies—which is known as the "303(d) list"—must include a priority ranking for each water body, taking into account the severity of the pollution and the uses to be made of such waters.

For waters identified in the 303(d) list, the CWA requires states to establish TMDLs for the pollutants causing the impairment of the water that will ensure attainment of water quality standards.[51] A TMDL defines the maximum amount of a pollutant that can be discharged (or "loaded") into a water body from all combined sources by allocating allowable pollutant loads among the point, nonpoint, and natural sources.[52] EPA has recently offered a pollutant trading rule to soften the blow of TMDLs on industrial point and agricultural nonpoint sources.

The typical TMDL methodology is as follows: First the loading capacity of the water body is determined; this is the maximum amount of a pollutant that the water body can receive without violating water quality standards. Then, the loading capacity is allocated to various pollutant sources. Load allocations (LAs) may be established for non-point sources (and also for uncertainty or a margin of safety). Waste load allocations (WLAs) are set for permitted point sources. If capacity remains, LAs and/or WLAs may be reserved for future growth. The sum of all LAs and WLAs constitutes the total maximum daily load (TMDL) for the water body.[53]

EPA must approve or disapprove a TMDL established by the state for a water body.[54] If EPA approves the TMDL, then the state incorporates the loads into its current water quality management plans.[55] If EPA disapproves the TMDL, then EPA must establish the loads necessary to implement water quality standards.[56]

When a TMDL and specific wasteload allocations for point sources have been established, any NPDES permit issued to a point source must be consistent with the terms of the TMDL and the WLA.[57]

SEDIMENT MANAGEMENT STANDARDS

Ecology's Sediment Management Standards rule, WAC 173-204, was developed by Ecology to accomplish the following:

- Establish chemical, biological, and other criteria as standards for the quality of sediments to protect beneficial uses and human health. These specific criteria values within the Sediment Management Standards are called the Sediment Quality Standards ("SQS"). The SQS are equivalent to the numerical criteria in the surface water quality standards.
- Apply the SQS as the basis for the management and reduction of pollutant discharges.
- Provide a management and decision process for the cleanup of contaminated sediments.[58]

The Sediment Management Standards address three principal issues: First, the rule establishes a narrative sediment quality goal that is defined as no acute or chronic adverse effects on biological resources and no significant health risk to humans caused by sediment contamination. The SQS establish the long-term management goal for the quality of sediments throughout the State.[59] The SQS are defined by:

- Numeric chemical concentration criteria.[60]
- Biological effects criteria.[61]
- Human health criteria[62]
- Natural source criteria.[63]

Sediments that exceed the SQS criteria are predicted to have adverse effects on biological resources or to pose significant human health risks. The SQS criteria may be revised as new data are developed regarding the toxicity of contaminants in sediments. Where sediment quality is higher, antidegradation standards apply.[64]

A significant difference between the SQS and the surface water quality standards is that the SQS can be superseded by a demonstration that no significant biological effects are occurring. A discharger who finds that the SQS are exceeded at their point of discharge may elect to let the results stand as an exceedance of the criteria or may conduct biological testing to show compliance with the standards.

GROUND WATER QUALITY STANDARDS

Ground water quality standards were adopted in December 1990.[65] These standards apply to all activities that have a potential to adversely impact ground water quality, including point and non-point sources, and regardless of whether an activity is required to have an NPDES or a state waste discharge permit. Thus, the standards could have very broad application and affect many activities, including land application facilities, landfills, mines, stormwater discharges, wastewater treatment facilities, industrial impoundments, septic systems, agricultural activities, and underground storage tanks.

Some exceptions do apply. The standards are specifically intended to protect water in the saturated zone. Additionally, Ecology wrote the regulation to protect water in the vadose, or unsaturated zone, because of the high probability that vadose zone water will migrate to the saturated zone. However, contaminants applied at rates under approved methods of land application, or applied at agronomic rates for agricultural purposes are exempt if those contaminants do not migrate below the root zone.

In April, 1996, Ecology issued a guidance document ("Implementation Guidance for the Ground Water Quality Standards"), after recognizing the need to interpret the standards and establish a standard protocol for consistent implementation. The guidance explains the intent of the ground water standards and interprets those portions of the standards that need a more precise definition for adequate implementation. The guidance details the specific requirements necessary to assure compliance with the ground water quality standards for those activities that are required to obtain a state waste discharge permit.

The guidance makes clear that the intent of the standards is not to allow degradation of ground water up to the criteria, but rather is intended to protect background water quality to the extent practical. One of the primary objectives of the guidance is to provide Ecology water quality permit managers, hydrogeologists, and engineers the necessary information to incorporate ground water quality protection provisions into water quality-based permits.

The guidance states that ground water quality standards apply to any activity that has a potential to adversely affect ground water quality. The guidance explains that the standards are to be implemented in a number of ways. First, facilities that are not covered by a general permit or regulated by an approved Ecology guideline or policy must perform a hydrogeologic study to assess the current condition of the hydrogeologic environment and characterize the facilities' activities. Second, monitoring plans will be required to define ambient conditions and to determine compliance with the standards. Compliance will be determined by demonstrating that all wastes meet AKART, and by complying with Ecology's antidegradation policy, which, while it allows an incremental increase of contaminant concentrations under specific conditions, prohibits degradation of the state's waters up to numeric and narrative criteria. Third, contingency plans will be required to describe actions necessary to remedy the impacts of a violation of the standards.

PERMIT APPEALS

The PCHB hears appeals of permits (issuance, modification, or denial), orders, rules, or regulations of Ecology. It is crucial to timely appeal any permit conditions that the permittee cannot meet.[66] Failure to challenge the conditions of a permit through the administrative appeal process causes the permit holder to forever lose the right to do so, even if an enforcement action might eventually result in the imposition of severe civil or criminal penalties.[67] Thus, if a subsequent enforcement action is brought against the permittee, there is no defense available based upon an inability to meet a permit condition.

Upon receipt of a correct appeal, the PCHB sets a hearing date.[68] Filing an appeal does not stay the requirements of the permit or order. The appealing party, however, may request a stay.[69]

The PCHB conducts a *de novo* hearing.[70] After the hearing, the PCHB issues its decision. Upon the request of the PCHB, findings, conclusions, and orders are prepared by counsel. The PCHB may then adopt the findings, conclusions, and orders, in whole or in part, or prepare their own.[71] The decision of the PCHB may be appealed within thirty days to the Superior Court,[72] and, upon certification by the PCHB, for direct review by the Court of Appeals.[73]

ENFORCEMENT

Under the CWA, it is violation of the Act to discharge a pollutant in excess of the effluent limitations in an NPDES permit or to violate other conditions in an NPDES permit. Likewise, it is a violation of the Act to discharge (add) a pollutant from a point source to waters of the United States (or waters of the State) without an NPDES permit. Similarly, it is a violation of a state waste discharge permit to violate any conditions of the permit.

When a violation occurs, an enforcement action may be brought. Under the CWA, enforcement actions may be brought by either the agency (federal or state) or a citizen group. Violations of a state waste discharge permit may only be enforced by Ecology or the Washington State Attorney General.

Agency Enforcement

With few exceptions, Ecology is responsible for establishing water quality standards and pollution control programs, monitoring compliance, and issuing orders and penalties for enforcement. The limited exceptions to Ecology's jurisdiction in this area are as follows: Permits for point source discharges by energy facilities subject to RCW §80.50 are issued and administered by the Energy Facility Site Evaluation Council, rather than Ecology.[74] Nonpoint sources of pollution that result from forest practices in compliance with RCW §§76.09.010 through 76.09.280 are not subject to permitting or enforcement by Ecology under the Water Pollution Control Act. Finally, compliance with pretreatment standards is the responsibility of a city, town, or municipality that has received authority from Ecology to issue permits to commercial and industrial entities discharging into a POTW.[75]

The Water Pollution Control Act authorizes Ecology to enter any public or private property at reasonable times to inspect or investigate conditions relating to pollution or the potential for pollution of the state's waters.[76] Ecology also has state-wide subpoena power in connection with any matter under its consideration.[77]

Ecology has broad authority, through the Attorney General, to bring actions at law or in equity to carry out the provisions of the Water Pollution Control Act.[78] The Act authorizes Ecology to levy penalties of up to $10,000 per day for each day the violator discharges without a permit, or discharges in violation of the terms of a permit, or in any other way violates the provisions of the Act.[79] In 1990 Ecology published an Enforcement Manual which classifies violations and sets minimum penalties according to the type and severity of the violation.

Notice of the penalty is given in writing by certified mail or personal service, setting out the nature of the violation. The violator may apply to Ecology within fifteen days for remission or mitigation of the penalty. Ecology may remit or mitigate the penalty only on a permittee's showing of extraordinary circumstances, such as the presence of factors not originally considered.[80] If the application for remission or mitigation is denied, or if no application is made, the violator may appeal the penalty to the PCHB within thirty days of Ecology's notice of penalty or its decision on an application for relief.[81]

The Attorney General may bring an action in Superior Court against any person who fails to comply with a final order of Ecology.[82] Under the doctrine of exhaustion of administrative remedies, the substance of the order is not reviewable in a Superior Court proceeding if the person has not timely filed an administrative challenge with the PCHB.

In addition to civil and criminal penalties and orders, the Water Pollution Control Act authorizes criminal penalties of up to $10,000 plus costs of prosecution, or imprisonment for not longer than one year, for the willful violation of any provision of the Act.[83]

The federal CWA also provides potentially severe civil and criminal penalties for violations of its provisions. Although the authority to issue and administer NPDES permits has been delegated to the state, the federal government retains its authority to take enforcement action. If the EPA decides to bring a civil enforcement action, the agency may, and often does, seek both injunctive relief and civil penalties. Concerning injunctions, the federal CWA empowers the federal district court to enter preliminary and permanent injunctions to restrain and abate violations of the statute, regulations, and permits, including state NPDES permits. If an injunction is issued and subsequently violated, not only are the criminal and civil penalty provisions of the CWA applicable, but so are the criminal and civil contempt powers of the court.

When EPA believes that a violation is serious enough for referral to the Department of Justice for civil enforcement, the agency normally seeks substantial civil penalties. The 1987 amendments increased available civil penalties from $10,000 per day for each violation, up to $25,000 per day for each violation.[84] Moreover, factors are contained in the statute for courts to weigh in assessing the appropriate amount of civil penalties to assess against a violator.[85] These factors include the following:

1. the seriousness of the violation;
2. economic benefit (if any) resulting from the violation;
3. defendant's history of violations;
4. defendant's good faith efforts to comply with the CWA;
5. the economic impact of the penalty on the violator; and
6. any other factors as justice may require.

Shortly after the 1987 amendments, the Supreme Court held that defendants in CWA civil penalty cases have a constitutional right to a jury trial on the issue of liability.[86] While the defendant is entitled to a jury trial on the issue of liability, the district judge decides the amount of penalty in the event a violation is found by a jury.[87] Felony prosecutions may be brought against any person for knowing violations of the Act or violation of any permit condition or limitation. A "person" under the CWA includes not only individuals, corporations, partnerships, states, and municipalities, but also responsible corporate officers.[88] The Ninth Circuit has recently held that to convict a person for "knowingly" violating the CWA, the government does not have to show that the person knew that the challenged conduct violated the Act. Instead, the government need only prove that the person was aware that pollutants were being discharged.[89] The U.S. Attorneys' Office for the Western District of Washington has aggressively pursued criminal prosecution of environmental violations.

Civil and criminal penalties are not deductible business expenses for federal income tax purposes, so the financial impact of these penalties on industrial dischargers can be quite severe.

Citizen Enforcement (Citizen Suit Actions)

In addition to agency enforcement, the CWA provides for "citizen enforcement," through the use of a citizen suit action.[90] The law that governs CWA citizen suits is complex, both procedurally and substantively. The material in this chapter merely provides a brief introduction to, and overview of, citizen suits.

When citizens bring an enforcement action, they effectively "stand in the shoes" of the agency and act as private attorneys general. Although they "stand in the shoes" of the agency, they must meet some additional requirements that the agency does not have to meet. For instance, citizens must give the defendant a written sixty-day notice of intent to sue before the case is filed in federal court.

Additionally, the citizen-plaintiffs must meet standing requirements. Moreover, unlike the agency, citizens may only sue to enforce "ongoing violations," which are violations that occur after the date of filing the complaint or violations that are intermittent, but reasonably likely to continue.[91] Finally, citizens may not enforce violations that have already been or that are presently being "diligently prosecuted" by an agency.[92]

Citizens may sue for violation of a permit effluent standard or limitation and may also sue to enforce violations of other permit conditions.[93] Additionally, case law has interpreted the statute to allow citizens to sue to compel a discharger to obtain an NPDES permit.[94] Finally, citizens may sue the agency for failing to enforce the CWA effectively.[95] The fact that an NDPES permit has been issued by a state agency, rather than the EPA, does not bar a citizen suit enforcement action.[96]

As with agency enforcement, citizens may seek both injunctive relief and civil penalties. However, there is no private right of action under the CWA and, therefore, the citizen-plaintiffs may not recover "damages."[97] Although "damages" are not available to the citizen-plaintiffs, the CWA does make specific provision for the payment of attorney fees.[98] Like defendants who face agency enforcement actions, defendants who are sued by a citizen group are entitled to a jury trial on the issue of liability.[99] The federal district courts have exclusive jurisdiction over citizen suit actions.

NOTES

1 33 USC §1251(a)(1).

2 RCW §90.48.260(1) describes the extent of Ecology's authority.

3 WAC 371-08-315(2) and (3) establishes the jurisdiction of the PCHB.

4 RCW §90.48.144.

5 RCW §90.48.140.

6 RCW §90.48.142.

7 *Headwaters Inc. v. Talent Irrigation Dist.*, 243 F. 3d 526 (9th Cir. 2001).

8 WAC 173-220-020.

9 WAC 173-220-030(5); see also 33 USC §1362(12).

10 Washington's definition of "pollution" is even broader. RCW §90.48.020.

11 *See Weinberger v. Romero-Barcelo*, 456 US 305 (1982) (bombs dropped on naval target range held to be pollutants); *United States v. Standard Oil Co.*, 384 US 224 (1966) (accidental discharge of gasoline held to be a pollutant under the Refuse Act).

12 40 CFR 122.45(g).

13 *National Wildlife Federation v. Consumers Power Co.*, 862 F. 2d 580, 583 (6th Cir. 1988); *National Wildlife Federation v. Gorsuch*, 693 F. 2d 156 (DC Cir. 1982).

14 *Comm. to Save Mokelumne River v. East Bay Mun. Util. Dist.*, 13 F. 3d 305 (9th Cir. 1993), *cert. den. Members of California Regional Water Quality Authority Control Bd. v. Comm. to Save Mokelumne River*, 115 S.Ct. 198 (1994).

15 WAC 173-220-030(18).

16 33 USC §1362(14); WAC 173-220-030(21).

17 40 CFR 122.2.

18 40 CFR 122.3(C)

19 WAC 173-220-040.

20 WAC 173-226-200.

21 WAC 173-220-110 and -060.

22 WAC 173-220-050.

23 WAC 173-220-070.

24 WAC 173-220-090.

25 WAC 173-220-100.

26 *Puget Soundkeeper Alliance v. State*, 102 Wn. App. 783 (2000).

27 WAC 173-220-180.

28 WAC-173-216-040.

29 WAC 173-216-050.

30 WAC 173-216-070.

31 33 USC §1342; WAC 173-218-010.

32 WAC 173-226-020.

33 WAC 173-226-200(1).

34 WAC 173-226-220(2).

[35] 33 U.S.C. §1342(p).

[36] 40 CFR 122.26(b)(13).

[37] 40 CFR 122.26(a).

[38] 40 CFR 122.26(b)(14)(i)-(ix).

[39] *Id.*

[40] 40 CFR 122.26(e)(2)(iii)(c).

[41] 40 CFR 122.26(b)(14)(xi).

[42] *National Resources Defense Council v. United States Environmental Protection Agency*, 966 F. 2d 1292 (9th Cir.1992).

[43] 40 CFR 122.26(c)(1).

[44] 40 CFR 122.26(e)(1).

[45] 40 CFR 122.26(a)(4).

[46] RCW §90.48.010; WAC 173-216-020(1), -050(3), -110(1); 173-220-130(1).

[47] WAC 173-220-130(1).

[48] WAC 173-200.

[49] WAC 173-201(A). (Water quality standards are also codified in 40 CFR 131 (the National Toxics Rule). The National Toxics Rule does not apply to those substances that are already included in the State's water quality standards.)

[50] 33 USC §1313(d); 40 CFR 130.7(b).

[51] 33 USC 1313(d)(1)(c).

[52] *See Water Quality Trading Handbook*, November 2004.

[53] See 40 CFR 130.2.

[54] 33 USC 1313(d)(2); 40 CFR 130.7(d).

[55] 40 CFR 130 7(d)(2).

[56] 33 USC §1313(d)(2).

[57] *Dioxin/Organochlorine Center v. Clarke*, 57 F. 3d 1517 (9th Cir. 1995); *see also* 40 CFR 130.2.

[58] WAC 172-204-100(2).

[59] WAC 173-204-320 through -340.

[60] WAC 173-204-320(2).

[61] WAC 173-204-320(3).

[62] WAC 173-204-320(4) and (5).

[63] WAC 173-204-320(6).

[64] WAC 173-204-120.

[65] WAC 173-200.

[66] WAC 371-08-355.

[67] *Public Interest Research v. Powell Duffryn*, 913 F. 2d 64 (3d Cir. 1990), *citing Texas Mun. Power Agency v. United States Environmental Protection Agency*, 836 F. 2d 1482 (5th Cir.1988); *Connecticut Fund for the Environment v. Job Plating Co.*, 623 F. Supp. 207 (D Conn. 1985).

[68] WAC 371-08-430 and -455.

[69] WAC 371-08-415.

[70] WAC 371-08-483(1).

71 WAC 371-08-535.

72 WAC 371-08-555.

73 WAC 371-08-560.

74 RCW §90.48.262(2).

75 RCW §90.48.165, WAC 173-216-050(1)(b) & (c); WAC 173-216-150.

76 RCW §90.48.090.

77 RCW §90.48.095.

78 RCW §90.48.037.

79 RCW §90.48.144.

80 RCW §90.48.144, RCW §43.21B.300.

81 RCW §43.21B.300.

82 RCW §43.21B.310(5)

83 RCW §90.48.140.

84 33 U.S.C. §1319.

85 33 U.S.C. §1319(d).

86 *United States v. Tull*, 481 US 412 (1987).

87 *United States v. Puerto Rico Aqueduct and Sewer Auth.*, 25 Env't. Rep. Cas. (BNA) 1921 (D PR 1987).

88 33 U.S.C §1319(d).

89 *United States v. Weitzenhoff*, 35 F.3d 1275 (1993), *cert. den.* 115 S. Ct. 939 (1995).

90 33 U.S.C. §1365.

91 *Gwaltney of Smithfield v. Chesapeake Bay Foundation*, 484 US 494 (1987); *Sierra Club v. Union Oil Co.*, 853 F. 2d 667 (9th Cir. 1988).

92 33 U S C. §§1319(g); 1365(b)(l)(B)

93 *Northwest Environmental Advocates v. Portland*, 56 F. 3d 979 (9th Cir. 1995) (citing examples of permit conditions that may be enforced).

94 *Committee to Save Mokelumne River v. East Bay Mun. Utility Dist.*, 13 F. 3d 305 (9th Cir. 1993). *cert. den. sub nom. Members of California Regional Water Quality Control Bd. v. Committee to Save Mokelumne River*, 115 S. Ct. 198 (1994); *Carr v. Alta Verde Indus., Inc.*, 931 F. 2d l055 (5th Cir. 1991); *Washington Wilderness Coalition v. Hecla Mining Co.*, 870 F. Supp. 983 (ED Wash. 1994); *Hudson River Fisherman's Assn. v. County of Westchester*, 686 F. Supp. 1044 (SDNY 1988).

95 33 U.S.C. §1365(a)(2). (Bringing a suit against the Administrator is authorized by statute when there is an alleged failure of the Administrator to perform any discretionary act or duty under the CWA. Whether an act is "discretionary" is the subject of considerable case law and is beyond the scope of this chapter.)

96 *Washington Wilderness Coalition v. Hecla Mining Co.*, 870 F. Supp. 983 (ED Wash. 1994)

97 *Walls v. Waste Resource Corp.*, 761 F. 2d 311 (6th Cir. 1985).

98 33 USC §1365(d).

99 *Tull v. United States*, 481 US 412 (1987); *Tobyhanna Conservation v. County Place Waste Fac.*, 769 F. Supp. 739 (MD Pa. 1991); *Work v. Tyson Foods, Inc.*, 720 F. Supp. 132 (WD Ark. 1989).

CHAPTER 7

Water Resources

INTRODUCTION

Historically, different legal doctrines developed for the allocation of surface water and ground water. Water from surface sources has traditionally been allocated under two doctrines—the riparian doctrine and the prior appropriation doctrine. On the other hand, appropriation of ground water has taken many forms, such as the rule of absolute ownership, the rule of reasonable use, the rule of correlative rights, and the appropriation or permit system. Many of these appropriation schemes developed out of European common law and are based on principles of property and tort law.

Surface Water Allocation: In General

The surface water allocation doctrines stem from two distinct philosophies and developed in different parts of this country. Appropriative rights developed in the arid portions of the West. This doctrine allocates the right to use relatively scarce water on a priority system: first in time, first in right. The doctrine also eliminates the absolute property right in water found under the riparian system. Instead, the concept of beneficial use developed, allowing the reallocation of water, if the water was not used by the water right holder.

In the East, where water was more plentiful, the riparian doctrine developed. The riparian doctrine allocates water rights based on land ownership. In short, all landowners bordering a common surface water source had the right to make reasonable use of the water.[1] Riparian rights ran with the land and were not subject to beneficial use requirements; however, the rights were, in some cases, limited to uses that did not adversely impact the rights of other riparian right holders.

Since the 1917 Surface Water Code, in Washington, rights to surface waters are determined by a permit system administered by Ecology. Generally, upon receipt of an application, Ecology will determine whether water is available, whether the proposed appropriation is for a beneficial use, whether the proposed appropriation will impair other existing rights, and whether the proposed appropriation will not be detrimental to the public interest or welfare.[2]

Ground Water Allocation: In General

The primary systems for allocation of ground water are appropriation-permit systems, absolute ownership, and reasonable use with correlative rights.[3] The appropriation or permit system for ground water, like the prior appropriation system for surface waters, uses priority to allocate use of water. Typically, an appropriation system will be set up by statute and require the application for a permit or other approval to appropriate water from a particular aquifer. An administrative system is required to ensure that the permitting system works efficiently to manage the ground water resources. The rule of absolute ownership derives from an old English case that held that the owner of land owns everything below that land to the center of the earth.[4] Since ground water is migratory, this rule does not work in a literal sense; instead, it is basically a rule of capture and provides that an overlying landowner may use all of the water he or she can capture on his or her land. The reasonable use doctrine, on the other hand, tempers the absolute ownership rule and provides that an overlying landowner may only take from its land the amount which he can put to reasonable use. Similarly, the correlative rights doctrine holds that an overlying user's right to take water is relative to the rights of other overlying users of the water.

ALLOCATION OF WATER: IN WASHINGTON

Washington's water allocation system developed as a dual system, combining elements of both the riparian and prior appropriation doctrines of allocating, water.[5] Under current law, the state allocates water pursuant to an administrative permit system that incorporates many principles of the prior appropriation doctrine.[6] Additionally, since large areas of the state are federal or tribal lands or are served by migration systems developed by the U.S. Bureau of Reclamation, federal and Indian water law policies have contributed to the development of the water allocation system in the state. The following sections contain an overview of the appropriation and riparian doctrines and how they fit together to form the current state of the law. Federal and Indian water law doctrines will be addressed later in this chapter.

Riparian Rights

In the early part of Washington's history, rights to use water could be obtained under the riparian system.[7] However, riparian owners were limited to reasonable use of the water and to uses that would not materially interfere with the common rights of other riparian owners and included the right to irrigate, fish, boat, and even claim title to steam beds and lakes.[8]

Riparian rights are further limited under the current law. Claims of riparian rights to appropriate water which preexisted the 1917 Water Code[9] retained validity only if they were exercised by 1932.[10] If the right was not exercised by 1932, the right was forfeited.[11] Moreover, any person claiming riparian water rights initiated before 1917 must have filed his or her claim with the Department of Ecology (Ecology) prior to 1974 or the right has been deemed waived.[12] A claim to riparian rights is subject to relinquishment if the water claimed is not put to beneficial use.[13] Now, no new riparian rights can be established. Anyone who wishes to divert surface water or withdraw ground water must comply with the statutory permitting system to obtain and perfect a water right.[14] This system is founded upon the concept that all ground and surface water belong to the public, unless and until the State appropriates water by issuing a permit for its withdrawal or diversion.[15]

Prior Appropriation Rights

The doctrine of prior appropriation was first established in Washington by the Territorial Legislature in 1873[16] and was recognized by the courts in 1879.[17] Washington's prior appropriation doctrine has been interpreted to give the water right holder a perpetual right, appurtenant to the land, which operates to the exclusion of subsequent claimants; however, the extent of the right is limited by the establishment and maintenance of a beneficial use of the water.[18] The rationale behind the beneficial use requirement "lies in the relation of available resources to the ever-increasing demands made upon them."[19]

Historically, two different methods of establishing appropriative rights to water existed in Washington. The first, the "custom" method, recognized by the state courts and local communities, provided that the customary use of water from a particular source for a particular purpose vested a right with the user against subsequent appropriators.[20] The second doctrine, the "notice" method, was statutorily based and provided that a person had to post a notice of claim to the water at the point of diversion, file a copy of the notice with the county auditor, and put the water to a beneficial use within a reasonable time in order to perfect title to the water.[21]

Statutory Laws of Water Appropriation

Water appropriation changed dramatically in 1917 with the enactment of the state's first comprehensive water code. The 1917 Water Code[22] provided a centralized program vesting the authority to allocate rights in a single state agency (currently, Ecology).[23] From this point forward, no new riparian or appropriative rights were established, and all new rights to use surface water had to be obtained through the water permitting system.[24] The Water Code, however, did retain the prior appropriation doctrine: "as between appropriators, the first in time shall be the first in right."[25] Private water right owners also have the right ot condemn rights-of-way for irrigation purposes.[26] Also, the Water Code did not "lessen, enlarge, or modify" any existing rights acquired by appropriation or as a result of riparian land ownership.

The 1917 Water Code applied to surface water, and the Legislature extended the permit system to the allocation of ground water in 1945.[27] Prior to the enactment of this law, the appropriation of ground water in Washington occurred through a prior appropriation system with a beneficial use limitation. The statute keeps the prior appropriation doctrine[28] but requires that a permit be obtained before any new ground water source is used.[29] An exemption from the permit requirement exists for certain uses of ground water not exceeding 5,000 gallons per day.[30]

Rights which were vested by prior appropriation prior to the enactment of the 1945 Water Code were not modified by the Code and could be officially documented by applying for and receiving a certificate of vested water rights from Ecology.[31] Currently, the process for appropriation and allocation of ground water and surface water is essentially the same; a permit must be obtained for new uses of water, and competing claims for the use of water may only be settled in an adjudication. Only the courts, not Ecology, have jurisdiction to resolve competing claims between holders of perfected water rights.[32]

CURRENT WATER ALLOCATION SYSTEM

Washington's Water Code is divided into several sections that address different issues of administration of Washington's water rights system. The statutes provide for a registration system that is used to record rights established prior to the current permitting system. The second part of Washington water law is a permitting system for allocating new water rights.[33] In some basins, the amount of water claimed by currently registered water users and permit holders far exceeds the water actually available, and the Water Code contains a section on adjudication. The adjudication process is the primary method of determining the proper allocation of water resources between competing claims.[34]

RCW §90.42 authorizes Ecology to institute a water banking program by which existing but unused water rights may be banked instead of forfeited, and used to offset other new water uses. The program is in its infancy but already several banks are operating in the Yakima and Columbia River basins.

WATER RIGHT APPROPRIATION PROCESS

Permitting System

A permit must be obtained from the Ecology to acquire a water right to divert surface water or withdraw ground water[35] in the state of Washington. The Water Code provides that:

> Any person, municipal corporation, firm, irrigation district, association, corporation or water users' association hereafter desiring to appropriate water for a beneficial use shall make an application to [Ecology] for a permit to make such appropriation, and shall not use or divert such waters until he has received a permit from [Ecology] as in this chapter provided. The construction of any ditch, canal or works, or performing any work in connection with said construction or appropriation, or the use of any waters, shall not be an appropriation of such water nor an act for the purpose of appropriating water unless a permit to make said appropriation has first been granted by [Ecology]: PROVIDED, That a temporary permit may be granted upon a proper showing made to [Ecology] to be valid only during the pendency of such application for a permit unless sooner revoked by [Ecology]: PROVIDED, FURTHER, That nothing in this chapter contained shall be deemed to affect RCW 90.40.010 through 90.40.080 except that the notice and certificate therein provided for in RCW 90.40.030 shall be addressed to[Ecology], and [Ecology] shall exercise the powers and perform the duties prescribed by RCW 90.40.030.[36]

Similarly, "no withdrawal of public ground waters of the state shall be begun, nor shall any well or other works for such withdrawal be constructed, unless an application to appropriate such waters has been made to [Ecology] and a permit has been granted by it as herein provided...."[37] In either case, one must generally obtain a permit and put the water to beneficial use[38] before obtaining a certificate. Only a perfected or certificated water right constitutes an interest in real property.

The application and approval process for water appropriation is set out in RCW §§90.03.250 *et seq.* and RCW §§90.44.050 *et seq.* for surface waters and ground waters, respectively. The application process is generally the same for surface and ground waters, therefore, only surface water appropriation will be described in detail here.[39]

To begin the permitting process, one must file an application with Ecology.[40] Applications to appropriate water made to Ecology must contain the following information:

- Name;
- Address;
- Source of the water supply;
- Nature and amount of the proposed use;
- Time during which the water will be required each year;
- Location and description of the proposed ditch, canal, or other work;
- Time for completion of the construction; and
- Time for complete application of the water for its proposed use.[41]

For particular types of uses, the application must include additional information. For instance, if the water is to be used for agricultural purposes, the application must contain the legal subdivision of the land, the acreage to be irrigated, and the amount of water that will be used each season.[42] Applicants may be required to provide maps, drawings or other data as well.[43] If the applicant wishes to construct and maintain a reservoir, a separate permit is required.[44]

Ecology designates the date of receipt of a complete application as the filing date to establish the claimant's priority.[45] As the next step in the permitting process, Ecology instructs the applicant to publish notice of the application in a newspaper of general circulation in the county where the water is sought to be appropriated.[46] Interested persons may file protests with Ecology.

Ecology investigates an application and determines what water, if any, is available for appropriation.[47] If the information is not available to make this determination, Ecology may issue a preliminary permit, with a term of less than three years, requiring the applicant to undertake studies, investigations, and progress reports.[48]

Ecology applies a four-part test in evaluating water right applications. The four requirements are: (1) water is available for the proposed use; (2) the proposed use constitutes a beneficial use of water; (3) the proposed use will not impair existing water rights; and (4) the proposed use will not be detrimental to the public interest.[49] This test applies to applications for both surface and ground waters.[50] More recently, the Legislature has added the requirement that the use not negatively impact instream flows necessary to maintain stocks of endangered salmon and trout.[51]

Even if Ecology determines that the application meets the four-part test, Ecology may not permit the appropriation of more water than can be put to beneficial use.[52] Ecology may issue a permit for a smaller quantity of water than that requested in the application.[53] Ecology may also place conditions on a permit.[54]

Once a permit is issued, the applicant perfects its water right by constructing the facilities needed for the diversion and applying the water to the beneficial use as provided in the permit.[55] After the applicant documents perfection of the water right, Ecology issues a water right certificate which is recorded by Ecology and the County Auditor.[56]

In the event that Ecology denies a water right application, the applicant, or any other person aggrieved by the decision, may appeal to the Pollution Control Hearings Board (PCHB).[57]

Nature of Appropriative Rights

Obtaining a permit or certificate to use water is not a guarantee that the full quantity of water allocated will be available to the user.[58] Since water is appropriated on a priority basis in a specified quantity of water,[59] new users of water from a particular source will necessarily be junior to existing users. This means that when there is insufficient water to satisfy all permitted demands, junior users may not get any water. Additionally, although Ecology is charged with determining that there is sufficient water available for the new use prior to issuing the permit, it is possible that the new use will impact the use of senior users. In such a case, an adjudication[60] may be required to determine the amount of water, if any, each claimant is authorized to appropriate.

Water Right Registration System

In order to "provide adequate records for efficient administration of the state's waters, and to cause a return to the state of any water rights which are no longer exercised,[61] a registration system was put into place. Any person making a claim of riparian rights, or other non-permitted appropriative rights, had to file a claim with Ecology no later than June 30, 1974.[62] In 1997, an additional claim window, from September 1, 1997 to June 30, 1998, was opened but the priority dates of these claims fell subordinate to prior water claims as well as to any water right embodied in a permit or certificate issued prior to the date the claim was filed.[63] If the claimant did not meet the statutory deadline, the claim is deemed to have been waived, and the claimant relinquished any rights, title or interest in the water right.[64] While the claims registered on time were presumed valid, registration is merely a recording system and is not a method of adjudicating conflicting claims.[65] A registered water right, however, can be lost due to non-use.[66]

WATER RIGHT ADJUDICATION SYSTEM

The only method to conclusively establish the water rights is to undergo an adjudication.[67] An adjudication is basically a special form of quiet title action to determine all existing rights to the use of water from a specific body of water.[68] The adjudication process is meant to determine and confirm all rights to the water whether riparian or appropriative;[69] however, the process cannot be used to lessen, enlarge or modify those rights.[70] Special adjudications are initiated by water users against other water users to determine the respective rights to water from a particular water source. General adjudications are initiated by Ecology to determine the rights of all users of a particular water source and may be used to determine the rights to water in an entire water system consisting of both ground and surface water.

To begin an adjudication process, either a person claiming the right to divert waters files a petition with Ecology, or Ecology determines that a determination of rights to certain water would serve the interests of the public.[71] In this situation, Ecology must prepare a statement of facts that includes the names of all known persons claiming the right to divert water and a statement of facts relating to the necessity of the water rights determination, together with a map or plan of the area in question and submit them to the superior court of the county in which the water rights dispute is located.[72]

The superior court causes a summons to be served on all known claimants of the water source requiring the claimants to make and file a statement of their claims to the water.[73] Because some of the water claimants may not be known, the statute also requires that the summons be published for six weeks.

After service of the summons, the superior court may refer the proceeding back to Ecology to take testimony.[74] Ecology's role is to hear testimony and advise the court as to the parties claiming a right in a body of water, as well as the priority, amount, and validity of such rights.[75] The court is charged with taking the evidence and report as filed by Ecology and entering a decree determining the water rights of the parties according to the report.[76] However, should there be exceptions to the report filed by interested parties, the court may take further evidence or remand the issue back to Ecology.[77]

Upon the conclusion of an adjudication proceeding, Ecology issues diversion certificates to the parties.[78] These certificates are evidence of the priority and purpose of a water right, the period during which the right can be used, the point of diversion of the water, the place of use, the land to which the right is appurtenant and the maximum quantity of water allowed.[79]

TRANSFER AND LOSS OF WATER RIGHTS

Water rights, even those that have been adjudicated, do not have an eternal duration and are not permanently restricted to the use, location, and quantity listed in the water right certificate. Water rights may be changed by statutory processes for the amendment of permits or transfer of rights, and water rights may be lost or reduced due to non-use, waste, or use for a non-beneficial purpose.[80]

Water Right Transfers

Once a water right has been perfected, the right to use water is appurtenant to the land or place upon which the water is used.[81] Because certificated water rights are property rights, they may be transferred and become appurtenant to other land without loss of priority of rights if the transfer does not adversely impact other existing rights.[82] Additionally, the point of diversion may be changed if the change does not impact other rights.[83] A water right holder seeking to transfer the right to use water, make changes in the point of diversion, or change the purpose of use must file an application with Ecology.[84] If Ecology determines that the change can be made without adversely impacting other water rights, the agency authorizes the change.[85] In the case of a municipal water supply, however, the water right need not be perfected prior to transfer.[86]

Loss of Water Rights

To maximize the beneficial use of waters,[87] the statutes provide several methods by which a water right holder may lose all or some of his right: non-use;[88] abandonment;[89] and failure to beneficially use.[90] Non-use, standing alone, does not necessarily prove abandonment; it is merely evidence of abandonment.[91] Non-use may also be excused for a variety of reasons.[92] The portion of the water right that is lost reverts back to the state and may become available for appropriation by other users. Ecology may issue an order to the water right holder that gives notice to the holder that the water right will revert to the state[93] unless "sufficient cause" can be shown why the right should not be relinquished.[94] The order is appealable to the PCHB.[95] The statutes provide a few exceptions to the water right relinquishment rule.

For example, if the water right is claimed for power development purposes and the annual license fees are paid, or if the water is claimed for municipal purposes, the right cannot be relinquished.[96]

Beneficial Use Requirement

Beneficial use is a term of art that encompasses two elements of a water right.[97] First, it relates to the types of activities for which the water may be used. The Washington statutes specifically define this aspect of beneficial use as including, but not limited to, the following uses: "use for domestic water, irrigation, fish, shellfish, game and other aquatic life, municipal, recreation, industrial water, generation of electric power, and navigation."[98]

The second aspect of beneficial use is the measure of the water right, i.e., the quantity of water needed to serve the purpose determined to be a beneficial use. The courts have fashioned the doctrine of "reasonable use" to determine the quantity of water necessary for a beneficial use.[99] The determination of reasonable use requires an analysis of two factors: "water duty" and "waste."[100]

Water duty is a term typically used to refer to the quantity of water needed for maximum production of crops ordinarily grown thereon, the amount of which may vary according to locality.[101] Water duty is determined by using data specific to the particular water right being investigated. Information used may include such things as the number of acres to be irrigated, the type of crops to be grown, the growing season and the type of soil. A water right which is equivalent to the water duty is considered to be a reasonable use. Water duty is a measure of the quantity of water that is needed.

Waste, on the other hand, is indicative of water that is not needed or not used. The courts have long held that the appropriation of water is not valid when the water simply goes to waste.[102] However, there is no statutory or regulatory definition of waste and there have been few cases in Washington dealing with the determination of whether or not a practice is wasteful. It is considered wasteful to divert more water than is needed for the appropriator's actual requirements.[103] Nevertheless, it is often necessary for an appropriator to divert more than his ultimate requirement due to water losses in the delivery system, particularly in irrigation systems.[104] As a result, the determination of whether a particular user is wasting water is usually made by looking at the irrigation customs in the community.[105] Thus, there is no clear uniform standard for determining when a particular use of water is wasteful.

WATER REUSE

Reuse or reclamation of water previously discharged as waste is developing as an alternative source of water supply. Such water could be beneficially used to replace potable water for many uses including: (1) direct uses such as industrial processes or irrigation; (2) ground water recharge by surface spreading or direct injection, and (3) recreational purposes such as flow augmentation in streams or wetlands and wildlife habitat.[106] Recognizing that reclaimed water could potentially be a significant resource, Washington enacted the Reclaimed Water Act in 1992 to encourage and facilitate reclaimed water uses.

The Reclaimed Water Act

The Reclaimed Water Act defines reclaimed water as "effluent derived in any part from sewage from a wastewater treatment system that has been adequately and reliably treated, so that as a result of such treatment, it is suitable for a direct beneficial use or as a controlled use that would not otherwise occur and is no longer considered wastewater."[107]

The Act requires that a permit be obtained to distribute reclaimed water and limits the availability of permits to municipal entities and wastewater discharge permit holders.[108] Unlike general water use permits issued by Ecology, Ecology and Health share jurisdiction over reclaimed water permitting. Health issues permits for commercial and industrial uses, while Ecology issues permits for land application.[109]

Water Rights in Reclaimed Water

The Reclaimed Water Act does not address issues regarding water rights in reclaimed water. Issues which are likely to arise include the determination of water rights between: (1) the water supplier and the wastewater treatment plant operator and (2) the discharger of effluent and a downstream appropriator. Ecology has issued a "Policy on Water Rights for Reclaimed Water"[110] that recognizes a water holder's right to reuse reclaimed water where the reuse is consistent with an existing water right's terms and conditions of use. Under Ecology's policy, if the place or nature of the use will change in the reuse, then an amendment to the water right must be obtained under RCW 90.03.380.

Some water reuse issues may be resolved by common law doctrines. For example, in the situation cited above of a downstream appropriator who claims water discharged upstream, the downstream user probably cannot acquire appropriative rights to discharged "foreign water" and has no right to rely on its continuation.[111] Foreign water is water which is imported into a water system and is not naturally part of the instream flow. The prior appropriation doctrine also provides for a right of recapture of water, at least in the context of irrigation, as long as the water has not escaped its place of use or been abandoned.[112]

FEDERAL AND INDIAN WATER RIGHTS

Water rights established under federal law are important because Washington state has a number of American Indian reservations, federal facilities, national parks, and national forests. Water rights on lands outside of federal lands may also be affected by federal water rights. Indian water rights emanate from treaties with the United States and the federal reserved rights doctrine. The following section briefly outlines the federal and Indian water rights doctrines and their application in Washington State.

Indian Treaty Rights

Many Indian Tribes in Washington entered into treaties with the United States government in the 19th century that reserved certain rights both on- and off-reservation.[113] Most significant for water resources, the treaties typically provided the right to fish in usual and accustomed areas. Indian treaty rights to fish have been held to include an adequate quantity of water to support the fisheries resource.[114] Thus, Indian treaty rights to fish attaches to waters located both on and off reservation lands. Indian water rights reserved in treaties predate state-issued water rights and have a priority date of "time immemorial."

Reserved Rights

The reserved rights doctrine, referred to as the *Winters* Doctrine,[115] ensures that lands set aside by the federal government have adequate water to fulfill the purpose for which they were set aside. *Winters* concerned a conflict between the Indians of the Fort Belknap Reservation in Montana and non-Indian settlers over the rights to use water from a nearby river. The court held that, although the settlers had obtained rights to the water through the state and had begun using the water prior to the Indians, the Indians had a prior right to the water. The court's rationale for this decision was stated succinctly in a later case:

> When the Federal Government withdraws its land from the public domain and reserves it for a federal purpose, the Government, by implication reserves appurtenant water then unappropriated to the extent needed to accomplish the purpose of the reservation.... [This reserved water right] vests on the date of the reservation and is superior to the rights of future appropriators.[116]

This doctrine is applicable not only to tribal lands but also to parks, wildlife refuges, national forests, military bases, or any other uses that require water for their success.[117]

Reserved water rights differ from state-approved riparian and appropriative rights in many ways; for example:

1. Federal reserved waters need not be put to use promptly or within any particular period of time.
2. Although the rights are ultimately subject to measurement by the water requirements of the purposes for which the lands were reserved, federal reserved rights need not be quantified at the time the reservation is established or within any particular period of time.
3. Federal reserved rights are not subject to loss by nonuse or abandonment.[118]

Indian Reserved Water Rights

The *Winters* doctrine determines rights to water for use on Indian reservations. The doctrine holds that reserved water rights for Indian lands vest no later than the date the reservation was created and in some cases may have an earlier priority based on historical uses of water for certain activities (aboriginal priority).[119] *Winters* rights mat attach to water sources that arise on, border, traverse, underlie, or are encompassed with Indian reservations.[120] They are not limited to waters and water sources that originate on or are physically located on the reservation.[121] Waters outside of the reservation may be reserved for reservation purposes when they are the only feasible source of supply or when the source of supply on the reservation has diminished to such an extent that a new source of water is needed.[122]

The quantity of water reserved as a federally reserved water right is based on the water needed to fulfill the "purpose of the reservation." Determining the purpose of a reservation requires studying the agreement, treaty, or executive order creating the reservation. These documents are usually interpreted broadly with any ambiguities resolved in the Indian's favor.[123] In general, Indian reservations were formed to give Indians a "homeland" with a goal of economic self-sufficiency. Thus, the "purpose of the reservation" may include a number of uses of water including water for agricultural, livestock, domestic and municipal use, wildlife, fishing, religious purposes, and aesthetic enjoyment.[124] Unless an intention to limit uses on a particular reservation is shown, a court may find rights were reserved to fulfill the broad purposes of Indian reservations, requiring development of reservation resources of every kind.

In some cases, the original agreement specified a particular purpose of the reservation. When a purpose is designated, the water right is based on the amount of water needed for that purpose. For example, in *Arizona v. California*,[125] the United States Supreme Court found that the purpose of five Indian reservations along the Colorado River was to provide agricultural land for the Tribes. The Tribes' water right quantities were then determined based on the irrigation needs of their land. However, once a federal reserved water right has been quantified, a Tribe is not limited to using the water for the particular purpose designated in the treaty.

Non-Indian Reserved Water Rights

The reserved rights doctrine is applicable not only to lands reserved by the federal government for Indian reservations, but also to any public lands set aside for a particular government purpose. The amount of water reserved by implication for public lands is limited to the reservation's specific purposes. Unlike the reservation of water for Indian lands, on non-Indian federal land, only purposes that were encompassed by the grant of congressional authority at the time of the reservation are considered in determining the quantity of water reserved.[126]

McCarran Amendment Adjudications

To resolve some of the complications that arose because of the presence of reserved water rights outside of the state appropriations systems, Congress passed the McCarran Amendment in 1952.[127] The McCarran Amendment avoids piecemeal adjudication of water rights by conferring jurisdiction on state courts for the adjudication of federal water rights, provided there are no statutory or constitutional bars to its exercise. The Amendment waives the federal government's sovereign immunity and enables joinder of the United States in suits to adjudicate all rights to use water in a basin. Thus, in a general adjudication, the federal government (including Indian Tribes) must assert its reserved right to water in the water system being adjudicated or the right may be lost in the adjudication process.[128]

NOTES

[1] Section of Natural Resources, Energy, and Environmental Law. American Bar Association, *Water Law: Trends, Policies, and Practice* xix (Kathleen M. Carr and James D. Crammond, eds. 1995).

[2] RCW §90.03.290.

[3] RCW §90.44.

[4] *Action v. Blundell*, 152 Eng. Rep. 1223 (1843). Because of its origins, this rule is sometimes called the "English Rule."

[5] *Benton v. Johncox, 17 Wn. 277 (1897)* (adopting hybrid system of appropriative and riparian water rights from *Lux v. Haggin, 69 Cal. 255 (1886)*).

[6] See RCW §§90.03 *et seq.*

[7] *Wallace v. Weitman*, 52 Wn. 2d 585 (1958); *Crook v. Hewitt*, 4 Wn. 749 (1892); *Geddis v. Parrish*, 1 Wn. 587 (1889).

[8] *De Ruwe v. Morrison*, 28 Wn. 2d 797 (1947); *Smith v. Nechanicky*, 123 Wn. 8 (1923); *Nesalhous v. Walker*, 45 Wn. 621 (1907); *Griffith v. Holman*, 23 Wn. 347 (1900). Since "pure" riparian systems do not contain a beneficial use or reasonable use limitation, the Washington system can not be considered a "pure" system.

[9] RCW §§90.03 *et seq.*

[10] *Matter of Deadman Creek Drainage Basin in Spokane County*, 103 Wn. 2d 686 (1985).

[11] *Matter of Deadman Creek Drainage Basin in Spokane County*, 103 Wn. 2d 686 (1985).

[12] RCW §90.14.041. There is no compensation for this waiver. *State Dept. of Ecology v. Adsit*, 103 Wn. 2d 698 (1985). Further, the courts are required to liberally construe §90.14 in favor of returning unused water rights to the State. *Willowbrook Farms LLP v. Dept. of Ecology*, 116 Wn. App. 392 (2003).

[13] RCW §90.14.170.

[14] *Matter of Deadman Creek Drainage Basin in Spokane County*, 103 Wn. 2d 686 (1985).

[15] RCW §90.03.010.

[16] Laws of 1873 at 520, §1.

[17] *Benton v. Johncox, 17 Wn. 277 (1897)*

[18] *Neubert v. Yakima-Tieton Irrig. Dist.*, 117 Wn. 2d 232, 237 (1991).

[19] *Dept. of Ecology v. Grimes*, 121 Wn .2d 459 (1993).

[20] *Ellis v. Pomeroy Improvement Co.*, 1 Wn. 572 (1889).

[21] Laws of 1891, ch. 142; *Grant Realty Co. v. Ham, Yearslev, and Ryrie*, 96 Wn. 616 (1917). *See also* RCW §90.14.068.

[22] Laws of 1917, ch. 117 (codified at RCW §90.03 *et seq.*).

[23] RCW §90.03.010. The power to adjudicate claims between competing water users is not within Ecology's power. *Rettkowski v. Dept. of Ecology*, 122 Wn. 2d 219 (1993).

[24] RCW §90.03.010.

[25] *Id.*

[26] *White v. Stout*, 72 Wn. 62 (1913); *State v. Superior Court of Stevens County*, 46 Wn. 500 (1907).

[27] Laws of 1945, ch. 263 (codified at RCW §90.44 *et seq.*).

[28] "Subject to existing rights, all natural ground waters of the state as defined in RCW 90.44.035, also all artificial ground waters that have been abandoned or forfeited, are hereby declared to be public ground waters and to belong to the public and to be subject to appropriation for beneficial use under the terms of this chapter and not otherwise." RCW §90.44.040. *See also Hillis v. Dept. of Ecology*, 131 Wn. 2d 373 (1997).

[29] RCW §90.44.050.

[30] *Id.*

[31] RCW §90.44.090.

[32] *Rettkowski v. Dept. of Ecology*, 122 Wn. 2d 219 (1993).

[33] This process is discussed in detail in Section 8.4.

[34] Adjudication is discussed in detail in Section 8.5.

[35] Water can also be stored and later withdrawn in underground geologic formations. RCW §90.03.370.

[36] RCW §90.03.250.

[37] RCW §90.44.050. Groundwater belongs to the public in Washington. *Pederson's Fryer Farms, Inc. v. Transamerica Insurance Company*, 83 Wn. App. 432 (1996). Small users, defined as those who withdrawn less than 5000 gallons per day, are exempt from the permit requirement, but the exemption cannot be applied to allow the collective withdrawal of more than 5000 gallons per day in a subdivision. *State v. Campbell & Gwinn, L.L.C.*, 146 Wn. 2d 1 (2002). Unperfected ground water permits may, however, be transferred. *R.D. Merrill Co. v. State*, 137 Wn. 2d 118 (1999).

[38] *See* RCW §90.13.031(2) for the definition of "beneficial use."

[39] The permit applicant may engage in cost-sharing with Ecology in which the applicant agrees to pay not only the costs of processing his or her application, but the costs of all the other applications which are prior in time. RCW §90.03.265; RCW §43.21A.690.

[40] RCW §90.03.260; WAC 508-12-100 and -110.

[41] RCW §90.03.260; *See also* WAC 508-12.

[42] RCW §90.03.260. Additional information is also required for water used for power purposes, municipal water supplies, mining purposes or construction of a reservoir.

[43] RCW §90.03.260; WAC 508-12-120.

[44] RCW §90.03.370.

[45] RCW §90.03.340; WAC 508-12-140. Priority is based on application filing date not date of permit issuance.

[46] RCW §90.03.280. An affidavit of publication of the notice must be filed with Ecology. WAC 508-12-150.

[47] RCW §90.03.290. *Swinomish Indian Tribal Community v. Washington State Dept. of Ecology*, 178 Wn. 2d 571 (2013).

[48] *Id.*

[49] RCW §90.03.290(3). *See also Hillis v. State*, 131 Wn. 2d 373 (1997).

[50] *Id.*; RCW §90.44.060; *Stempel v. Dept. of Water Resources*, 82 Wn. 2d 109 (1973).

[51] RCW §§90.22 *et seq.*; 16 U.S.C. §§1531 – 1534; 33 U.S.C. §1341.

[52] RCW §90.03.290.

[53] RCW §90.03.290. The decision of Ecology to issue a water appropriation permit is discretionary and will not be reversed absent a clear showing of abuse. *Dept. of Ecology v. United States Bureau of Reclamation*, 118 Wn. 2d 761 (1992). *See also Hillis v. State*, 131 Wn. 2d 373 (1997).

54 *Hubbard v. State*, 86 Wn. App. 119 (1997).

55 RCW §90.03.320. Ecology may also issue a construction schedule.

56 RCW §90.03.330.

57 *Postema v. Pollution Control Hearings Board*, 142 Wn. 2d 68 (2000); *Rettkowski v. Department of Ecology*, 128 Wn. 2d 508 (1996); *Schuh v. State Dept. of Ecology*, 100 Wn. 2d 180 (1983).

58 Completion of the permitting process is a "tentative determination" of water rights. To obtain a conclusive determination, a general adjudication is required. *Funk v. Bartholet*, 157 Wn. 584 (1930); *Mack v. Eldorado Water District*, 56 Wn. 2d 584 (1960); *Stempel v. Dept. of Water Resources*, 82 Wn. 2d 109 (1973).

59 Water rights must be based on actual use. Water rights based upon the capacity of a water delivery system, called the "pumps and pipes" method, are disallowed after September 9, 2003. RCW §90.03.330(3). *State Dept. of Ecology v. Theodoratus*, 135 Wn. 2d 582 (1998).

60 See Section 8.7 below.

61 RCW §90.14.010.

62 RCW §90.14.041. This provision does not apply to water rights based on the authority of a permit or certificate issued by Ecology. *Id.*

63 RCW §90.14.068.

64 RCW §90.14.071.

65 RCW §90.14.081 (A properly filed claim is prima facie evidence in an adjudication proceeding of the time of use and quantity of water used at the time of the claim's filing).

66 RCW §90.14.130; *See also Okanogan Wilderness League, Inc. v. Town of Twisp*, 133 Wn. 2d 769 (1997); *Dept. of Ecology v. Acquavella*, 131 Wn. 2d 746 (1997).

67 It should be noted that although an adjudication conclusively establishes the rights to water, the decision does not necessarily grant a permanent right to the adjudicated quantity of water. The water rights determined in an adjudication are still subject to reallocation based on beneficial use and may be subject to adjudication at some point in the future should conditions in the water supply change.

68 *McLeary v. Dept. of Game*, 91 Wn. 2d 647 (1979).

69 *Matter of Deadman Creek Drainage Basin in Spokane County*, 103 Wn. 2d 686 (1985).

70 RCW §§90.03.010 and .245.

71 RCW §90.03.110; WAC 508-12-080.

72 *Id.*

73 In an adjudication, each claimant's statement must include: (1) the name and address of the claimant; (2) the nature of the right or use on which the claim to water is based; (3) the time of the initiation of the water right and the commencement of the water use; (4) the date of the beginning and completion of any water works; (5) the dimensions and capacity of all ditches used for water diversion; and (6) the amount of land under irrigation and the maximum capacity of water used. RCW §§90.03.120, .130 and .140.

74 RCW §90.03.160.

75 RCW §90.03.170; *Rettkowski v. Department of Ecology*, 128 Wn. 2d 508 (1996).

76 RCW §90.03.200.

77 *Id.*

78 RCW §90.03.240.

79 An additional condition on a permit may be that minimum instream flows must be maintained once Ecology has established the right. *Hubbard v. State*, 86 Wn. App. 119 (1997).

80 RCW §90.03.380; RCW §90.14.130 through .180; RCW §90.44.100. *See also P.U.D. No. 1 of Pend Oreille County v. State*, 146 W.2d 778 (2002) (Ecology can impose restrictions on existing water right in order to protect instream flows for fish habitat).

81 RCW §90.03.380; *Neubert v. Yakima-Tieton Irr. Dist.*, 102 Wn. 2d 232 (1991).

82 RCW §90.03.380.

83 *Id.*

84 *Id.*; WAC 508-12-180 and -190.

85 RCW §90.03.380. In twenty counties, Water Conservancy Boards, created by RCW §§90.80 *et seq.*, expedite intra-county voluntary, uncontested transfers, changes, and amendments to water rights. *See also* WAC 173-153.

86 RCW §90.03.570.

87 RCW §90.03.005.

88 RCW §90.14.130.

89 RCW §90.14.160 (appropriative rights or rights determined by adjudication); RCW §90.14.170 (riparian rights); RCW §90.14.180 (permit or water right certificate holders).

90 *Id.*

91 RCW §90.14.160 through 90.14.180; *Okanagan Wilderness League, Inc. v. Town of Twisp*, 133 Wn. 2d 769 (1997).

92 RCW §90.14.140. *Pacific Land Partners, LLC v. State, Dept. of Ecology*, 150 Wn. App. 740 (2009), *rev. den.* 167 Wn.2d 1007.

93 RCW §90.14.130.

94 RCW §90.14.140.

95 *Id.*

96 RCW §90.14.140(2).

97 *Dept. of Ecology v. Grimes*, 121 Wn. 2d 459 (1993).

98 RCW §§90.14010 *et seq.*

99 *Dept. of Ecology v. Grimes*, 121 Wn. 2d 459 (1993).

100 *Id.*

101 *Dept. of Ecology v. Grimes*, 121 Wn. 2d 459 (1993). See also *In re Water Rights in Ahtanum Creek, Yakima County*, 139 Wn. 84 (1926).

102 *Thorp v. McBride*, 75 Wn. 466 (1913); *Dept. of Ecology v. Grimes*, 121 Wn. 2d 459 (1993).

103 *State, Dept. of Ecology v. Aquavella*, 131 Wn. 2d 746 (1997); *Dept. of Ecology v. Grimes*, 121 Wn.2d 459 (1993).

104 *Dept. of Ecology v. Grimes*, 121 Wn. 2d 459 (1993).

105 A. Dan Tarlock, *Law of Water Rights and Resources*, §5.16[3][a] (1996).

106 T.C. Richmond, *Water Reuse in Washington: Changing Our Way of Thinking on Wastewater*, Washington Water Law, Law Seminars International Proceedings (1996).

107 RCW §90.46.010(4).

108 RCW §§90.46.030 and .040.

109 *Id.*

110 Department of Ecology, *Policy on Water Rights for Reclaimed Water*, Policy 1110 (April 4, 1995).

111 *Dodge v. Ellensburg Water Co.*, 46 Wn. App 77, 80 (1986).

[112] *Dept. of Ecology v. Bureau of Reclamation*, 118 Wn. 2d 761 (1992).

[113] *Washington v. Washington State Commercial Passenger Fishing Vessel Assoc.*, 443 US 658 (1979).

[114] *United States v. Washington*, 384 F. Supp. 312 (W.D. Wash. 1975); *cert. den.* 423 US 1086 (1976).

[115] *Winters v. United States*, 207 US 564 (1908).

[116] *Cappaert V. United States*, 426 US 128 (1976).

[117] *See e.g., United States v. New Mexico*, 438 US 696 (1978) (reserved right for national forests); *Federal Power Commission v. Oregon*, 349 US 435 (1955) (reservation of land and water for power generation).

[118] American Water Works Association, *Waters Rights of the Fifty States and Territories* (Kenneth R. Wright ed. 1990), pp. 74-75.

[119] *Winters v. United States*, 207 US 564 (1908); *See also United States v. Adair*, 478 F. Supp. 336 (D Or. 1979), *aff'd.* 723 F. 2d 1394 (9th Cir. 1983); *Colville Confederated Tribes v. Walton*, 647 F. 2d 42 (9th Cir. 1981); *cert. den. sub nom. Walton v. Colville Confederated Tribes*, 475 US 1010 (1986).

[120] Sharon I. Haensly, *Overview of Tribal Concerns Regarding Use and Protection of On- and Off-Reservation Water*, Proceedings, Third Annual Sinking Creek Water Symposium (January 26, 1996).

[121] *United States v. Ahtanum Irrig. Dist.*, 236 F. 2d 321 (9th Cir. 1956), *cert. den.* 352 US 988 (1957).

[122] F. Cohen, *Handbook of Federal Indian Law* at 585, n. 51 (1982).

[123] *Id.* At 576.

[124] T. Clayton, *The Policy Choices Tribes Face When Deciding Whether to Enact a Water Code*, 17 Amer. Indian L. Rev. 523 (1994).

[125] *Arizona v. California*, 373 US 546 (1963).

[126] *See, e.g., United States v. New Mexico*, 438 US 696 (1978).

[127] 43 U.S.C. §666.

[128] *See Nevada v. United States*, 463 US 110 (1983).

CHAPTER 8

Solid Waste Management

INTRODUCTION

This chapter provides an overview of the laws affecting solid waste management in Washington. The state's principal solid waste laws are found in RCW 70.95 and 70.95A through M and their implementing regulations. RCW §§35.21 and 36.58 authorize local governments to perform various solid waste functions. Finally, RCW §81.77 and its implementing regulations govern private solid waste collection services, with oversight from the Washington Utilities and Transportation Commission ("WUTC"). At the individual compliance level, littering is prohibited and sports facilities and "official gatherings" must provide recycling programs.[1]

LOCAL GOVERNMENTS AND COMPREHENSIVE SOLID WASTE MANAGEMENT PLANNING

Local governments in Washington bear the primary responsibility for solid waste planning and management. Although the Department of Ecology ("Ecology") prepares and updates every two years a state solid waste management plan,[2] each county must prepare a comprehensive solid waste management plan (SWMP or plan), either on its own or jointly with other counties.[3] In unincorporated areas, solid waste collection is regulated by the Washington Utilities and Transportation Commission ("WUTC").[4] The WUTC also regulates the collection of solid waste from residences and businesses.

Solid Waste Management Plans (SWMPs)

The purpose of solid waste management planning is to require local governments to determine the nature and extent of the various solid waste categories in their jurisdictions and to establish local waste management concepts.[5] State law provides detailed guidance on the topics to be addressed in a local SWMP.[6] A SWMP must address:
  1. existing and long range (20 years) solid waste handling facilities and collection services;[7]

2. solid waste reduction and recycling programs;[8] and
3. the plan's effect on the costs of solid waste collection.

Local SWMPs must address Washington's statutory priorities for solid waste management, which favor waste reduction and recycling over disposal. These priorities, in descending order, are for:

1. waste reduction;
2. recycling, with source separation of recyclable materials as the preferred method;
3. energy recovery, incineration, or landfilling of separated waste; and
4. energy recovery, incineration, or landfilling of mixed wastes.[9]

Although the priorities are not mandatory duties enforceable by the courts, they may be implemented through Ecology's review and approval of SWMPs.[10]

In keeping with Washington's strong recycling emphasis, planning requirements for local recycling programs are particularly detailed. A SWMP must provide for source separation, including different source separation collection programs in "urban" and "rural" areas.[11] Collection programs for source separated material must be implemented within two years of the plan's adoption and approval.[12]

Cities, towns and counties must also prepare a plan to manage "moderate risk wastes" within their respective planning areas.[13] Moderate risk wastes are solid wastes that would otherwise be dangerous wastes under Washington's Dangerous Waste Regulations, WAC 173-303, but which are exempt from such classification because they are either generated by households or generated in amounts below regulatory thresholds.[14] Ecology has issued guidelines to assist local governments in developing and implementing moderate risk waste plans.

Planning Procedures

To obtain state financial assistance for local planning efforts, SWMPs must be developed through the active participation of properly constituted local solid waste advisory committees.[15] Final draft plans are subject to approval by Ecology. Ecology's approval or disapproval must be based on its review comments on preliminary drafts.[16] Additionally, local governments may appeal Ecology's disapproval of a SWMP under the Administrative Procedure Act, RCW 34.05.[17] The WUTC also reviews the SWMP, but for the limited purpose of advising the planning jurisdiction on the SWMP's effect on collection costs and rates.[18] SWMPs must be formally updated (with Ecology approval) at least every five years.[19]

Legal Effect of Solid Waste Management Plans

The local SWMP should guide local governments in making solid waste management decisions. In the following instances, local government decisions must specifically take the local SWMP into account:

1. as part of the permit process for siting new solid waste facilities, the local health department and Ecology must determine whether the proposed facility conforms with the approved local SWMP;[20]

2. if a city or town exercises its authority to establish a solid waste collection system under RCW 35.21.120 (contract system), the system must substantially comply with the applicable SWMP;[21]
3. if a city, town, or county contracts for use of a solid waste handling facility, the contract facility must substantially comply with the contracting jurisdiction's plan;[22]
4. if a county designates a disposal site for waste originating within its boundaries under RCW 36.58.040, the designation must be pursuant to its SWMP; and
5. if a county exercises its authority to create a solid waste collection district under RCW 36.58A, creation must follow approval of a SWMP.[23]

Implementing Local Solid Waste Management Plans

With several important exceptions, cities, towns and counties are on equal footing with respect to solid waste management authority. All are empowered to provide, by ordinance, for solid waste handling systems within their jurisdictions.[24] Only counties, however, may establish systems for unincorporated areas.

Any municipality (county, city, or town) may also own, operate or contract for the use of solid waste handling facilities or services.[25] It may select contractors for facilities and services by using either the traditional public contracting bid procedures,[26] or a more flexible negotiated contract process.[27] The latter process is intended primarily for use in negotiating contracts with private proposers.[28]

Washington authorizes its municipalities to designate a particular publicly- or privately-owned facility as the jurisdiction's exclusive disposal site.[29] Municipalities' exercise of such authority, commonly known as "flow control," must not impermissibly discriminate against interstate commerce and thereby violate the United States Constitution's dormant commerce clause.[30]

Cities and towns can provide collection themselves or by contract, and may require use of, and establish, the rates for the provided collection service.[31] Counties, on the other hand, normally may not actually operate or franchise solid waste collection services.[32] Counties are empowered to either contract for residential collection of recyclables in unincorporated areas or to notify the WUTC to carry out the county's SWMP recycling program.[33]

Waste collection services in unincorporated areas may be provided by private collectors under certification of the WUTC. Certificates are issued only if the WUTC determines that "the public convenience and necessity require such cooperation."[34] The WUTC sets service territories and rates for certified collectors.[35] Certified collectors may also serve cities and towns that elect not to require use of an established system.

If a county establishes a solid waste collection district, it may mandate use of a particular solid waste collection system within the boundaries of the district.[36] Such districts may be constituted if, after hearing, a county legislative authority determines that mandatory solid waste collection in the defined area is "in the public interest and necessary for the preservation of public health."[37] The WUTC may certify a private collector to serve the collection district, but if none are available the county may provide collection services.[38]

Financing Solid Waste Management and Disposal

Local governments have several mechanisms to fund their solid waste management and disposal activities. To fund its compliance with planning requirements, a county may impose a surcharge upon charges imposed by solid waste collection companies.[39] If a city or county owns or operates disposal facilities, it may impose tipping fees.[40] Facilities may be financed through the issuance of revenue bonds where system revenues are adequate.

Solid waste disposal and related services may also be performed and funded by a solid waste disposal district.[41] A solid waste disposal district is a quasi-municipal corporation with taxing authority under RCW 36.58. A district may engage in "providing and funding solid waste services" (except collection service), and may provide for "all aspects of disposing of solid wastes."[42] Thus, it can provide recycling and waste reduction programs, as well as disposal facilities. It is created by a county, and the county legislative body is the governing body of a disposal district. Incorporated areas may be included by agreement.

A disposal district has a number of fund-raising mechanisms available. In addition to imposing an excise tax, it may issue revenue bonds or general obligation bonds, impose tipping fees, accept funds transferred from a county, and impose a property tax.[43] With an appropriate waiver from Ecology, these funding mechanisms can also help satisfy regulatory financial assurance requirements.[44]

REGULATION OF SOLID WASTE HANDLING FACILITIES AND ACTIVITIES

Most solid waste handling facilities and activities are regulated through permit systems administered by local health districts or Ecology. More specific regulatory programs apply to particular types of wastes, like municipal solid waste, ash from waste incineration, sewage sludge and waste from cleanup actions.

General MFS Requirements

Ecology has sought, through the MFS, to require the "best available technology for siting, and all known available and reasonable methods for designing, constructing, operating and closing solid waste handling facilities."[45] The MFS are baseline regulations.[46] Local cities, counties or local health districts may adopt regulations more stringent than those in the MFS. Accordingly, one must check with the appropriate city, county and local health district to determine whether they regulate solid waste more stringently than do the MFS.

The MFS apply to facilities handling "solid waste,"[47] defined as:

> all putrescible and nonputrescible solid and semisolid wastes, including but not limited to garbage, rubbish, ashes, industrial wastes, swill, demolition and construction wastes, abandoned vehicles or parts thereof, and discarded commodities. This includes all liquid, solid and semisolid, materials which are not the primary products of public, private, industrial, commercial, mining, and agricultural operations. Solid waste includes but is not limited to sludge from wastewater treatment plants and septage, from septic tanks, woodwaste, dangerous waste and problem wastes.[48]

The MFS specifically do *not* apply to mining overburden, liquid discharge released under permits, "dangerous wastes," certain woodwaste, agricultural wastes, clean soils and clean dredge soils, septage, radioactive wastes, and timber harvesting debris.[49]

With a few exceptions, all "solid waste handling facilities"[50] are subject to the MFS's solid waste handling facility standards.[51] These standards are applied through solid waste handling facility permits issued under WAC 173-304-600.

Permits issued under WAC 173-304-600 incorporate general standards,[52] as well as standards that apply to particular types of facilities, for example, landfills;[53] energy recovery and incinerators,[54] and demolition landfills.[55] New landfills, waste piles and certain surface impoundments must be sited according to regulatory locational standards.[56] Ecology has issued guidance for moderate risk waste collection/storage facilities, a type of facility not specifically addressed by the current MFS.[57]

Municipal Solid Waste Landfill Facilities. In November 1993, Ecology issued new rules governing landfill facilities that accept municipal solid waste.[58] These rules implement EPA's RCRA Subtitle D regulation for municipal solid waste landfills.[59] Codified as WAC 173-351, Ecology's criteria for municipal solid waste landfills (MSWLF Criteria) establish standards for siting, design, operation, monitoring, corrective action, closure, post-closure and financial assurance. The MSWLF Criteria apply only to landfills that accept household waste.[60] They do not apply to waste-specific landfills (for example, woodwaste landfills) that do not accept household waste, and they do not apply to non-landfill facilities (for example, transfer stations) even if they handle household waste.

As with MFS permits, local health departments issue MSWLF permits, and Ecology has review and appeal authority.[61] Permits are also subject to appeals brought under the same procedures that govern MFS permits.[62]

Municipal Solid Waste Incinerator Ash. Ash from the incineration of municipal solid waste (MSW) receives separate regulatory treatment. Generators of such ash are responsible for determining whether their ash is a "dangerous waste" under the State Hazardous Waste Management Act.[63] If it is not a dangerous waste, MSW ash is a solid waste, and may be managed according to the MFS. If MSW ash is determined to be dangerous waste, more stringent handling and disposal requirements apply. If the ash is "state only dangerous waste,"[64] it qualifies for management as "special incinerator ash" under the Special Incinerator Ash Disposal Act (Ash Act).[65] The Ash Act and its implementing rules[66] establish a separate regulatory scheme for "special incinerator ash" which is more stringent than the MES, but less exacting than the hazardous Waste Management Act's requirements for managing dangerous wastes.

Sewage Sludge or "Biosolids." Another separately regulated solid waste is the residue from the treatment of sanitary wastewater. This material is known as "sewage sludge" or "biosolids." Biosolids that meet certain criteria are not classified as solid waste.[67] Biosolids that do not meet the criteria are considered a solid waste,[68] and their management is subject to the permit requirements and management standards of the MFS.

In addition to complying with the MFS, sewage sludge handlers in Washington must also comply with the United States EPA's *Standards for the Use or Disposal of Sewage Sludge*.[69] Often referred to as the "Part 503 Standards," EPA's sewage sludge regulations are far more complex than the MES. EPA issues any necessary permits under the Part 503 Standards, but states may take over the permitting role with EPA's approval.[70]

Cleanup and Industrial Wastes. Cleanups conducted under Washington's Model Toxics Control Act or similar authorities frequently produce solid wastes that must be managed, often by off-site treatment or disposal. A common example is contaminated soil from a cleanup site that is disposed of in a landfill. The MFS labels cleanup wastes "problem waste,"[71] but does not include specific regulations to address them.[72]

Management options for cleanup wastes therefore depend on general standards. Someone who wants to dispose of a suspected problem waste must first determine whether it is a regulated "dangerous waste" under WAC 173-303. Cleanup wastes that are "dangerous" are generally subject to the cradle-to-grave requirements of WAC 173-303,[73] although they may qualify for a conditional exemption allowing for disposal in a MSWLF.[74] If not "dangerous," cleanup wastes may be disposed of in an MSWLF or managed at an MFS facility, depending upon local ordinances or facility-specific permit limitations.

Permit Procedures

Under the MFS, permit applications are accepted and decided by the local health district, with review by Ecology.[75] Both agencies determine whether the application meets applicable laws and regulations, conforms with the approved SWMP and complies with all zoning requirements.[76] If the health department issues a permit without Ecology's approval, Ecology may appeal the issuance to the Pollution Control Hearings Board (PCHB).[77]

Solid waste permits must be renewed at least every five years.[78] The process for permit renewal is like that for initial permit approval: review and decision by the local health department, with Ecology authority to review and appeal the decision.[79]

Appeals and Enforcement

The permit applicant may request a hearing before the local health department if a solid waste handling permit is denied or suspended.[80] An appeal from such a hearing is to the PCHB and must be filed within thirty days after receipt of notice of the health officer's determination.[81] The local health department has continuing authority to suspend a permit if it determines that a facility is in violation of Ch. 70.95 RCW or applicable regulations.[82]

LAWS AFFECTING SOLID WASTE GENERATORS: HOMES, OFFICES AND BUSINESSES

Several solid waste laws and rules are directed toward the people who generate solid waste. These restrictions attempt to ensure that people use the waste disposal systems provided, and that they keep certain wastes out of the general municipal waste stream.

Solid waste generally may not be dumped or disposed of except in a permitted solid waste handling facility.[83] To assist enforcement against unlawful dumping, there is a rebuttable presumption that if a person's name appears on three items in unlawfully disposed of waste, that person committed the unlawful dumping.[84]

Each owner, operator, or occupant of a location is responsible for arranging for the proper handling of solid waste accumulated on the property.[85] Solid waste containers used on-site, such as dumpsters, must meet the standards of WAC 173-304-200.[86] Anyone transporting solid waste, including collection vehicles, must also comply with WAC 173-304-200.

Finally, special provision has been made for disposal of particularly troublesome and common consumer wastes. Waste vehicle tires may no longer be accumulated for storage or transported except by persons licensed by Ecology.[87] Waste vehicle batteries may not be disposed of except at a store selling vehicle batteries, at a secondary lead smelter, or through a person otherwise authorized by Ecology to accept them.[88] Medical wastes must be completely burned[89] and used needles must be placed in special containers.[90]

NOTES

[1] RCW §70.93.093.

[2] RCW §70.95.260, 70.95.263.

[3] RCW §70.95.080.

[4] RCW §81.77.

[5] WAC 173-304-010. *See also Klickitat County Citizens Against Imported Waste v. Klickitat County*, 122 Wn. 2d 619 (1993).

[6] RCW §70.95.090.

[7] RCW §§70.95.080, 70.95.090

[8] RCW §70.95.090.

[9] RCW §70.95.010(8). *Cf.* RCW §70.138.010(1) (priorities for solid waste management listed differently); *Citizens for Clean Air v. City of Spokane*, 114 Wn. 2d 20 (1990) (to the extent they conflict, RCW §70.95.010(8) priorities prevail over RCW §70.138.010(1) priorities because the former are the more recent and more specific enactment).

[10] *Citizens for Clean Air v. City of Spokane*, 114 Wn. 2d 20 (1990).

[11] RCW §70.95.092.

[12] RCW §70.95.110(4).

[13] RCW §70.105.220.

[14] *See* RCW §70.105.010(17).

[15] RCW §70.95.165(3) and RCW §70.95.130.

[16] RCW §70.95.094.

[17] *Id.*

[18] RCW §70.95.096.

[19] RCW §70.95.110.

[20] RCW 70.95.180(3). *Cf. Weyerhaeuser v. Pierce County*, 124 Wn. 2d 26 (1994) (zoning code required that proposed landfill conform with local SWMP). *See also Organization to Preserve Agr. Lands v. Adams County*, 128 Wn. 2d 869 (1996); *City of Everett v. Snohomish County*, 112 Wn. 2d 433 (1989).

[21] RCW §35.21.156.

[22] RCW §35.21.156 (cities and towns); RCW §36.58.040 (counties).

[23] RCW §36.58A.010.

[24] RCW §35.21.120 (cities and towns); RCW §36.58.040 (counties).

[25] RCW §35.21.152 (cities and towns); RCW §36.58.040 (counties).

[26] RCW §35.22.620, 35.23.352; 36.32.250; 39.04 and 39.30.

[27] RCW §35.21.156 (cities and towns); RCW §36.58.090 (counties). *See generally Washington Waste Systems, Inc. v. Clark County*, 115 Wn. 2d 74 (1990).

[28] RCW §35.21.156 (cities and towns); RCW §36.58.090 and RCW §36.58.040 (counties).

[29] RCW §35.21.152(3); RCW §36.58.040.

30 *C & A Carbone, Inc. v. Town of Clarkstown, N.Y.*, 511 US 383 (1994) (ordinance requiring all waste within municipality to go to transfer station unconstitutional). *Cf. USA Recycling, Inc. v. Town of Babylon*, 66 F. 3d 1272 (2d Cir. 1995) (rejecting commerce clause challenge to municipal monopoly on solid waste collection), *cert. den.* 116 S.Ct. 1419 (1996). *See also Kleenwell Biohazard Waste and General Ecology Consultants, Inc. v. Nelson*, 48 F. 3d 391 (9th Cir. 1995), *cert. den.* 515 US 1143 (1995).

31 RCW §35.21.120: RCW §35.21.130. See *City of Spokane v. Carlson*, 73 Wn. 2d 76 (1968) (upholding constitutionality of a city's police power authority to operate exclusive collection service).

32 RCW §36.58.040, RCW §70.95.160.

33 RCW §36.58.040. Counties received this authority in 1989.

34 *See* RCW §81.77.040 (factors to be considered in determining public convenience and necessity). *See also Kleenwell Biohazard Waste & General Ecology Consultants, Inc. v. Nelson*, 48 F. 3d 391 (9th Cir. 1995), *cert. den.* 115 S.Ct. 2580 (1995) (requirement of WUTC certificate of convenience and necessity to transport medical waste does not violate commerce clause); *Waste management of Seattle, Inc. v. Utilities and Transp. Comm.*, 123 Wn. 2d 621 (1994).

35 RCW §81.77.030.

36 RCW §36.58A.010.

37 RCW §36.58A.030.

38 *Id.*

39 RCW §36.58 045.

40 RCW §§35.21.130, .152; 36.58.040.

41 *See Whatcom County v Taxpayers of Whatcom County Solid Waste Disposal*, 66 Wn. App. 284 (1992) (upholding the validity of creation of a solid waste disposal district and the district's tax, in this case, a 10% excise tax on charges imposed by solid waste collection companies on their customers).

42 RCW §§36.58.100, .130.

43 RCW §§36.58.130, .150.

44 *See* WAC 173-304.

45 WAC 173-304-010(5).

46 RCW §70.95.160.

47 WAC 173-304-015.

48 WAC 173-304-100(73). The MFS definition of "solid wastes," quoted above, expands upon the statutory definition. *Cf.* RCW §70.95.030(18).

49 WAC 173-304-015.

50 While the MFS do not define the term "solid waste handling facility," the combination of two key terms provides a working definition. "Solid waste handling" means:

> the management, storage, collection, transportation, treatment, utilization, processing, and final disposal of solid wastes, including the recovery and recycling of materials from solid wastes, the recovery of energy resources from solid wastes or the conversion of the energy in solid wastes to more useful forms or combinations thereof.

RCW §70.95.030(19). A "facility" means

> all contiguous land (including buffer zones) and structures, other appurtenances, and improvements on the land used for solid waste handling.

51 WAC 173-304-400(1).

52 WAC 173-304-405 and 407.

53 WAC 173-304-460.

54 WAC 173-304-440.

55 WAC 173-304-461.

56 WAC 173-304-130.

57 *Moderate Risk Waste Fixed Facility Guidelines*, WDOE 92-13 (1992).

58 WSR 93-22-016 (Nov. 17, 1993).

59 40 CFR 257 and 258.

60 WAC 173-351-100 (definition of "municipal solid waste landfill unit"); WAC 173-351-010 (applicability of MSWLF Criteria).

61 WAC 173-351-720(1)(h).

62 WAC 173-351-760.

63 RCW §70.105. Generators should also confirm that the ash is not a "hazardous waste" under 40 CFR 261. During the 1980s, ash from municipal solid waste incinerators was widely considered to be exempt from designation as hazardous waste. In 1994, the United States Supreme Court held that it is not. *City of Chicago v. Environmental Defense Fund*, 511 US 328 (1994). If ash is designated as a "hazardous waste" in Washington, it may not be managed under the Special Incinerator Ash Disposal Act. See RCW §70.138.020(8). It would instead be subject to WAC 173-303, the dangerous waste regulations.

64 WAC 173-303-040.

65 RCW §70.138.

66 WAC 173-306.

67 WAC 173-308-060.

68 WAC 173-304-100(73).

69 40 CFR 503.

70 40 CFR 123.1 and 501.

71 WAC 173-304-100(61).

72 See WAC 173-304-463 (reserved for future problem waste landfill regulation).

73 Dangerous waste permit requirements can be relaxed for dangerous wastes that are managed at the cleanup site pursuant to consent decrees or orders. RCW §70.105D.090.

74 WAC 173-303-073

75 RCW §§70.95.180, .185.

76 *Id.*

77 RCW §70.95.185.

78 RCW §70 95.190.

79 *Id.*

80 RCW §70 95.210.

81 *Id.*

82 RCW §70.95.200.

83 RCW §70.95 240.

84 RCW §70 95.250.

85 WAC 173-304-190.

86 WAC 173-304-200.

[87] RCW §§70.95.500 through .555.
[88] RCW §§70.95.610 through .670.
[89] RCW §70.95.710.
[90] RCW §70.95.715.

CHAPTER 9

Hazardous Waste Management (RCRA)

The Resource Conservation and Recovery Act (RCRA)[1] has been called "mind-numbing."[2] Washington's Dangerous Waste Regulations are no exception.[3] This chapter aims at reducing that confusion by summarizing the key legal and scientific principles of RCRA and the Washington State regulations implementing RCRA.

INTRODUCTION

Washington's RCRA program is jointly managed by EPA and the Washington State Department of Ecology (Ecology). RCRA is a federal statute, but it allows delegation of program management and enforcement to the states, provided that the state program is consistent with the federal program and at least as stringent.[4] Any action that the state has been authorized to take has the same force and effect as if taken by EPA. Ecology has enacted certain of its own dangerous waste regulations, which, as required under RCRA, are consistent with and at least as stringent as the federal regulations. Ecology's regulations are, in part, more stringent than EPA's.

Washington has been delegated the authority to implement most of the federal RCRA program.[5] Ecology's authorization extends to issuing permits to dangerous waste treatment, storage, and disposal facilities ("TSDs") within the state, administering closures of TSDs, and regulating dangerous waste generators and transporters. EPA retains oversight authority in the event it finds that Ecology is not enforcing the law adequately.

RCRA was substantially amended by the Hazardous and Solid Waste Amendments of 1984, P.L. 98-616 ("HSWA"). The state is not authorized to enforce all regulations adopted pursuant to the HSWA,[6] however, the state has been authorized by the EPA to run the HSWA corrective action program governing the closure of RCRA facilities.[7] The HSWA program may still be enforced by EPA, including the corrective action provisions in RCRA §§3013, 3008(h), and 3004(w). Washington has not requested authorization, nor has it been given authorization, to operate the RCRA program on Indian lands; this authority remains with EPA.[8]

Because of the dual regulatory structure in Washington, regulated parties must be familiar with both federal and state requirements. The federal program is carried out pursuant to regulations that appear at 40 CFR 260-279. The state program is carried out pursuant to the federal RCRA, the state Hazardous Waste Management Act (RCW §70.105) and regulations that appear at WAC 173-303.

RCRA, and the Washington regulations implementing RCRA, set out detailed rules for managing, treating, storing, and disposing of dangerous wastes, and regulate three classes of persons:

1. dangerous waste generators;[9]
2. dangerous waste transporters;[10] and
3. owners and operators of dangerous waste TSDs.

RCRA is part of a comprehensive scheme of regulations dealing with hazardous waste issues. Two other laws are an integral part of the scheme. These are the federal Comprehensive Environmental Response Compensation and Liability Act ("CERCLA" or "Superfund")[11] and its state counterpart, the Washington Model Toxics Control Act (MTCA).[12] RCRA principally governs hazardous waste *management*, while CERCLA and MTCA govern dangerous waste *cleanup*. Over the past few years, the distinction between RCRA and CERCLA has blurred, and the two programs have, in part, begun to merge. For example, the "corrective action" provisions in Section 3008 of RCRA bear a strong resemblance to the CERCLA provisions governing hazardous waste cleanup. In fact, Ecology's clean-up regulations under MTCA are the core of its RCRA corrective action program. Likewise, treatment standards adopted under the RCRA land disposal restrictions are frequently used as cleanup standards in the state and federal Superfund programs.

DANGEROUS WASTE IDENTIFICATION

The federal RCRA statute regulates "hazardous wastes" and "acutely hazardous wastes." Ecology regulates the federal RCRA wastes, as well as additional substances that are regulated by the state alone. In Washington, the federal and state wastes together are called "dangerous wastes" and "extremely hazardous wastes."[13] Washington also conditionally regulates a category of waste called "special wastes." These are wastes that EPA does not regulate but which pose sufficient potential hazards or are sufficiently distinct to be regulated separately from dangerous or solid wastes.

The first responsibility of any person who generates, transports, or handles waste materials in Washington is to determine how those waste materials are regulated. In the federal program, this process is called "identification;" the state's equivalent term is "designation." This can be a highly technical process and requires an understanding of some key legal and scientific concepts, which are summarized below.

Definition of Solid Waste

The first step in determining how a substance will be regulated under the law is to determine if the substance is a "solid waste."[14] A "solid waste" is defined by RCRA as discarded material resulting from industrial, commercial, mining, and agricultural operations, and from community activities,[15] and in Washington as any "discarded material that is not excluded" by the regulations or by variance.[16] "Discarded" material is any material that is (1) abandoned; (2) recycled; or (3) considered "inherently waste-like."[17] These terms are further defined in the regulations.[18] Even if a waste appears to fit in one of these categories, it may be excluded from regulation as a "solid waste" if it is managed under WAC 173-303-017(2), or the waste may be excluded under a variance granted pursuant to WAC 173-303-017(5).

Definition of Dangerous Waste

If satisfied that the material in question is a "solid waste," one must next determine whether it is regulated as a "dangerous waste" or an "extremely hazardous waste."[19] Both the federal and state programs contain several methods for designating a material as a hazardous or dangerous waste. The first step in both programs is to determine if the material is a "listed waste." Under the federal RCRA program, one first looks at the federal lists contained in 40 CFR 261, subpart D. A solid waste that appears on one of these lists is "hazardous." Wastes listed with a "P" prefix are considered the most hazardous compounds on the list and are designated as "acutely hazardous wastes" with more stringent requirements for control and management.[20] Under the federal RCRA Program, if a solid waste is not on the hazardous waste lists, it may still be designated as hazardous if, using standardized procedures, it exhibits one or more "characteristics" of a hazardous waste: (1) ignitability; (2) corrosivity; (3) reactivity; or (4) toxicity. These concepts are discussed further below.

Washington uses a similar system, with listed and characteristic wastes, and adds the additional category of "criteria" wastes. Additional testing requirements are included in the regulation for determining if materials are "criteria" wastes. To determine if a waste is "dangerous" in Washington, one first looks to the dangerous waste lists contained in WAC 173-303-9903 through 9905. The lists designate materials, according to their risks to human health and the environment, as dangerous wastes (DW) or extremely hazardous wastes (EHW").[21] If the solid waste in question is not on any of the lists, it must be tested to determine if it classifies as a dangerous waste under one of the four federal characteristics (ignitability, corrosivity, reactivity, and toxicity[22]), and then under the two state criteria: (1) state toxicity; or (2) state persistence. Even if a waste passes all of the required tests without triggering designation as a dangerous waste, the waste may still be regulated in Washington as a "special waste"

Listed Wastes

A solid waste may be hazardous if it has been listed by EPA or Ecology as a dangerous waste. The dangerous waste lists appear at WAC 173-303-9903 through 9905. Certain listed wastes (those starting with the letter "F") are managed as dangerous waste regardless of how they were generated. Examples of F-wastes include common solvents, certain wastewater treatment sludges and plating baths, and other metal treatment wastes. Other waste streams (those beginning with the letter "K") are dangerous only if they come from certain industrial processes. For example, the wood preservative, pesticide, chemical, explosive, petroleum, smelting, ink, pharmaceutical, iron and steel, and manufacturing industries generally find their major waste streams listed as "K" wastes. In addition, certain discarded or off specification commercial chemical products are listed as "U" and "P" wastes under the Washington and federal regulations, if EPA determines that, because of their toxic constituents, concentrations or potential for constituents to migrate, the waste should be regulated under RCRA. Approximately 400 wastes have been listed as federal hazardous wastes, although few new wastes have been added recently. Each of these wastes is given a unique, identifying number, or "waste code."

It is possible to "delist" a listed waste, although the process is not easy.[23] EPA must go through a rulemaking procedure, which includes public notice and comment, and the process often takes years to complete. In determining whether a waste should be "delisted," EPA must determine whether the waste threatens human health or the environment if it is not properly managed. To do this, EPA uses a mathematical model that predicts the concentration of waste contaminants in groundwater, and considers their impact on a hypothetical drinking water well near a hypothetical disposal area. For purposes of the analysis, EPA takes the (usually unrealistic) worst case scenario of a well located 500 feet down gradient from an unlined municipal landfill. It then uses a model called the Vertical and Horizontal Spread ("VHS") model to predict the spread of contaminants in groundwater. If the model shows that the concentration of all contaminants of concern does not exceed a health-based threshold level at an assumed point of exposure, the waste may be delisted. EPA will typically apply a "dilution attenuation factor" ("DAF") to account for the dilution of contaminants as they migrate from their source to the point of exposure.

Ecology has a delisting process in which petitions are submitted to Ecology for approval by Ecology and EPA.

Characteristic Wastes

If a waste is not listed, it still may be "dangerous" if it exhibits any of four state dangerous waste characteristics (ignitability, corrosivity, reactivity or toxicity) or two state-only "dangerous waste" criteria (toxicity or persistence).

The ignitability test requires testing the material's "flash point."[24] If the material is a liquid, it is dangerous if it has a flash point of less than 140°F, as determined by the Pensky-Martens Closed Cup Tester, the Setaflash Closed Cup Tester, or an equivalent test approved by EPA.[25] There is an exemption for liquids containing less than 24% alcohol (e.g. wine).[26] If a material is a solid, it is ignitable if, under standard temperature and pressure, it is capable of spontaneous combustion and persistent burning.[27]

The test of corrosivity involves testing the pH of the material.[28] Corrosive wastes are those liquid or aqueous wastes with a pH of less than or equal to 2 (highly acidic) or greater than or equal to 12.5 (highly alkaline), or waste that corrodes steel faster than at a rate specified by the regulations.[29]

Wastes are considered reactive if they are unstable (i.e., could explode or release toxic gas) under normal temperature and pressure, if they react violently with water, or if they are explosives as defined in 49 CFR 173.53 or 173.88.[30]

Finally, a waste is considered toxic (i.e. having the toxicity characteristic) if under specified laboratory conditions it leaches hazardous constituents in quantities exceeding certain regulatory levels.[31] The waste may also be subjected to procedure called the Toxicity Characteristic Leaching Procedure (TCLP),[32] under which a sample of the waste is extracted under specified laboratory conditions. The leachate from the TCLP test is tested for the presence of the toxic constituents listed in the regulations.[33] The results of the leachate analysis are compared to the constituent levels specified in the regulations and, if the waste extract exceeds the regulatory levels, the waste is considered toxic. If the waste is in a liquid form, the liquid itself is analyzed for the listed constituents and the levels of the constituents found in the liquid are compared to the standard.[34]

The analysis used to set acceptable constituent levels is the same one used in the delisting process. EPA identifies health-based thresholds and establishes a Dilution Attenuation Factor (DAF) using a model. It multiplies the health-based level by the DAF to calculate allowable waste concentrations. The exposure scenario is, again, a drinking water well down-gradient from a municipal landfill site. In this case, however, EPA uses a different groundwater model (a subsurface fate and transport model called the EPACML) and some different DAF assumptions.

Mixture and Derived-From Rules

The so-called "mixture" rule provides an additional twist on waste characterization. It provides that any mixture of a listed hazardous waste and a non-hazardous waste or materials itself is a dangerous waste.[35] The mixture continues to be regulated until it is "delisted" by EPA and Ecology.[36] A mixture of a characteristic waste and a nonhazardous solid waste is also a dangerous waste but only so long as the mixture exhibits a RCRA characteristic.[37] The "derived-from" rule provides that any waste derived from the treatment, storage or disposal of a listed waste is also a listed waste.[38] A solid waste derived from a characteristic waste, however, will not be regulated as a characteristic waste if it does not itself display a characteristic.[39]

In December, 1991, the United States Court of Appeals, DC Circuit, found that the promulgation of the mixture and derived-from rules violated the notice and comment rulemaking requirements of RCRA and the federal Administrative Procedure Act.[40] The court vacated the rules and remanded them to EPA because it found that those affected by the rule had insufficient notice during the rulemaking process that EPA intended to treat mixed and derived-from wastes as hazardous.[41] As a result of this decision, EPA simultaneously removed and reinstated the rules on an interim basis pending full notice and comment.[42] A new proposal to address mixtures of hazardous and non-hazardous waste was included in the Hazardous Waste Identification Rule published in the Federal Register in 1995 and is discussed in more detail in Section 10.2.2.1 above. This proposal contains a new exemption for low risk wastes and waste mixtures.[43] The proposed rule had not been finalized at the date of this printing.

"Contained-In" Policy

The "contained-in" policy is really an interpretive rule that arises from a vague reference in EPA's original RCRA regulations.[44] EPA stated that a solid waste is no longer hazardous if it "contains a waste listed" under RCRA but is subsequently delisted.[45] According to EPA, when a "listed waste is contained in" an environmental medium such as soil or water, the contaminated medium is managed itself as the listed waste.[46] In 1989, the D.C. Circuit held that contaminated media should not be subject to the mixture rule because soil and groundwater are not a solid waste.[47] "Mixtures" currently must be delisted to avoid RCRA, whereas environmental media can be decontaminated to a site-specific, risk-based level.[48]

State-Only Dangerous Wastes

Even if a waste material passes the four federal characteristic tests just described, it may still be designated a "state-only dangerous waste" if it fails state "criteria" tests for toxicity or persistence. This is one of the areas where the state program is more stringent than federal law.

Two methods are used for determining whether a solid waste falls into the state "toxic" dangerous waste category.[49] In the first method, "book designation," data about the toxicity of various "constituents" of the waste are evaluated. To determine whether the constituents in solid wastes are "toxic," and, therefore, regulated as dangerous waste, toxicity information data on the constituents is obtained from the generator's own data or from data available from the entities listed in WAC 173-303-100(2). Based on this accumulated toxicity data, one can determine whether the waste is regulated as toxic dangerous waste. If several toxic constituents are contained in the waste, a formula can be used to calculate the overall toxicity of the waste.[50]

Alternatively, a "bioassay" procedure can be used to determine toxicity.[51] Bioassay procedures involve exposing organisms such as fish or rats to various concentrations of the waste. The toxicity of the waste is measured by counting the number of organisms which survive after exposure to the material under specified conditions.

Even if a waste is otherwise not considered dangerous, Washington requires that waste generators determine if their wastes are designated as dangerous waste under a persistence criteria. The persistence test is used for wastes containing polycyclic aromatic hydrocarbons (PAH) with two or more fused benzene rings.[52] If waste contains between 0.1 percent and 1.0 percent HOC, the waste is regulated as a DW.[53]

Exclusions

Both the federal and state hazardous waste regulations exclude from regulation certain solid wastes that might otherwise qualify as DW, AHW, or EHW. The federal statutory exclusions include, but are not limited to: (1) solid or dissolved materials in domestic sewage;[54] (2) industrial discharges that are point sources subject to permitting under Section 402 of the Clean Water Act; and (3) source, special nuclear, or by-product material as defined by the Atomic Energy Act of 1954.[55] EPA has also excluded by regulation the following materials, among others, from designation as solid wastes: (1) materials subject to in-situ mining techniques that are not removed from the ground as a part of the extraction process; (2) pulping liquors; (3) spent sulfuric acid when used to produce virgin sulfuric acid; (4) certain recycled materials; and (5) spent wood preserving solutions that have been reclaimed and are reused for their original intended purpose.[56] Many other materials, although designated by the EPA as solid wastes, have been excluded from the definition of hazardous wastes. These include, for example, household wastes, solid wastes generated in agricultural processes which are returned to the ground as fertilizers, and ash generated in the combustion of coal or fossil fuels.[57]

Washington State has established additional exclusions to the rule. Some of the state exclusions are narrower than the federal ones. For example, Ecology, but not EPA, regulates the following wastes: (1) ash, sludge, and flue gas, and emission control wastes from fossil fuel combustion; and (2) cement kiln dust waste. Other state exclusions, however, are broader than the federal exclusions, in large part to deal with state only dangerous waste. For example, asphalt would be PAH "persistent" but may be excluded from regulation,[58] as are certain PCB wastes.[59] Ecology and EPA have exempted several additional categories of waste including: arsenic treated wood that designates only for arsenic,[60] petroleum-contaminated media designating only for toxicity under certain of the TCLP tests (D018 – D043),[61] and wood ash designating only for corrosivity.[62] Ecology has exempted used oil filters.[63] A number of these materials are subject to other regulatory programs, however. For example, petroleum-contaminated media may be subject to MTCA cleanup standards. See WAC 173-340.

Special Wastes

Wastes that do not designate as DW may nevertheless be regulated in Washington as "special wastes."[64] This category has been used, albeit infrequently, to manage wastes which pose a relatively low hazard to human health and the environment.[65] Generators and transporters of special wastes, and facilities that treat, store or dispose of only special wastes, are exempted from many of the rules that apply to other waste categories.[66]

GENERATOR REQUIREMENTS

The regulation of dangerous waste generators depends on the monthly amount and type of DW generated. Predictably, there is an acronym to describe these threshold amounts, called "quantity exclusion limits" ("QELs").[67] Generally, the more DW generated, the more stringently a generator is regulated. This tracks the federal system, under which a person is regulated as a:

1. "large quantity generator" or "LQG" if he or she generates more than 1.0 kilogram (approximately 2.2 pounds) per month of acutely hazardous waste or more than 1000 kilograms (approximately 2,200 pounds) per month of hazardous wastes;
2. "small quantity generator" if he or she generates less than 1.0 kilogram (approximately 2.2 pounds) per month of acutely hazardous waste and between 100-1000 kilograms (approximately 220-2,200 pounds) per month of hazardous waste;[68] or
3. "conditionally exempt small quantity generator" if he or she generates less than 1.0 kilogram (approximately 2.2 pounds) per month of acutely hazardous waste and less than 100 kilograms (approximately 220 pounds) per month of hazardous waste.[69]

The Washington system utilizes similar concepts, but with different terms and, in some cases, lower waste quantities.

Generator Management Responsibilities

"Full regulated generators" of hazardous wastes in Washington must comply with all state requirements found at WAC 173-330-170. These require, among other things, that the generator obtain an RCRA identification number, complete a "uniform hazardous waste manifest" for each shipment of waste from the generator's site, follow certain packaging, labeling, and storage requirements for the waste, meet recordkeeping and reporting requirements, and adhere to export restrictions.

Washington's dangerous waste regulations contain several generator requirements in addition to those required under RCRA. For example, generators using containers and/or tanks to accumulate dangerous wastes must identify on the tank the major risks associated with the wastes stored inside.[70] If the waste is ignitable, that fact must be stated on the label. Shipping labels on DW or EHW are required to contain instructions to call Ecology, EPA, or local response authorities if the material is found by a third party. Also, the generator's name and address and the manifest number must appear on the shipping label.[71] In Washington, reactive and ignitable wastes must be stored in compliance with the Uniform Fire Code, as well as with DW storage requirements.[72] Also, because Washington-only "special wastes" are conditionally-regulated wastes, they have special, less stringent, requirements;[73] for example such wastes may be shipped using an alternative manifest form.[74]

Generators in Washington must file annual reports with Ecology regarding their dangerous waste activities. Under the federal program, these reports must only be submitted every other year.[75]

TRANSPORTER REQUIREMENTS

The requirements for transporters of hazardous waste in Washington are mostly identical to the federal requirements contained at 40 CFR 263.[76] Transporters are required to obtain an identification number.[77] Transporters involved in interstate commerce must use the identification number assigned to their national headquarters unless. Transporters who are only involved in intrastate transport must use the identification number assigned by the state.

Washington tracks the federal program in prohibiting transporters from accepting dangerous waste for shipment without a manifest signed by the generator.[78] Transporters of "special wastes," however, may follow the alternative manifest procedure found at WAC 173-303-073(2)(f).[79]

Transporters who spill dangerous wastes at a terminal or during transport may need to comply with the "generator" requirements described above.[80] In the event of a spill or discharge of a dangerous waste during transportation, the transporter must comply with the spill reporting requirements contained in WAC 173-303-145, in addition to providing notice to the generator of the waste, to federal authorities at the National Response Center and to the Materials Transportation Bureau of the United States Department of Transportation.[81]

REQUIREMENTS FOR OWNERS AND OPERATORS OF TREATMENT, STORAGE AND DISPOSAL FACILITIES (TSDS)

The requirements governing owners and operators of TSDs are the most detailed and complex of the Washington dangerous waste regulations.[82] The complexity of the Washington system is due to (1) the dual regulatory system, with certain RCRA provisions enforced by Ecology and others by EPA; and (2) state regulations under the Hazardous Waste Management Act that are more stringent than the RCRA requirements in several key areas. The following pages discuss the most significant areas in which the Washington system differs from the federal program.

General Performance Standards

Washington treatment, storage, and disposal regulations contain general, narrative performance standards that set the framework for the specific standards applicable to particular facilities (e.g, landfills, incinerators, waste piles, etc.). These are not found in the federal regulations. They apply to all owners and operators of TSDs.

These general standards require owners and operators of TSDs to construct, operate and maintain TSDs to prevent degradation of ground and surface water and air quality, prevent destruction of vegetation outside the active portion of the facility, and prevent excessive noise "to the maximum extent practical given the limits of technology."[83] Owners and operators of TSDs are also required to avoid "negative aesthetic impacts" and unstable hillsides or soils.[84] Operators of TSDs must also use processes that "treat, detoxify, recycle, reclaim, and recover waste material to the extent economically feasible"[85] as well as preventing endangerment of the health of employees or the public near the facility.[86]

Permit Application Process

All owners and operators of TSDs and those planning to construct new TSDs must obtain a permit.[87] RCRA permit applications contain two parts.[88] Part A of the permit is a short form containing basic information about the facility, such as the name of the owner and the operator, a description of the dangerous wastes that will be handled at the facility and a topographic map of the facility. Part B of the permit application is more extensive and must include, for example, chemical, biological and physical analyses of the dangerous waste to be handled at the facility.[89] An owner of a facility that is leased to an operator must sign the permit application and is bound by its terms and responsible for proper operation and closure along with the operator.

Existing Facilities

Owners and operators of "existing facilities"[90] must submit Part A of the permit application no later than six months after the publication of regulations that require them to comply with interim status requirements or thirty days after they first become subject to the interim status requirements.[91] An owner or operator qualifies for "interim status" if it submits Part A of the application in a timely manner and complies with certain notification requirements.[92]

Interim status allows facilities to operate pursuant to specified standards until a final permit is issued to the facility.[93] Ecology may require owners and operators of existing facilities to apply for a final facility permit at any time.[94] The owner or operator must submit Part B of the permit application within 180 days of such a demand.[95]

New Facilities

Construction of new facilities may not begin until Part A and Part B of the permit application are submitted and a final facility permit is issued.[96] In addition, construction cannot begin until at least 180 days after the submittal of the permit application.[97]

Siting Standards

Notice of Intent

The state requires that a notice of intent to site a new TSD facility or to expand an existing facility[98] be filed with Ecology at least 150 days before a TSD permit application is filed.[99] There is no similar federal requirement. The notice must include:

1. the name, address and phone number of the owner and the operator or of the planned facility or facility expansion and its corporate officers;
2. the location of the facility or a topographical map;
3. a description of the management activities and equipment proposed;

4. an "environmental checklist" prepared under the State Environmental Policy Act (SEPA);[100]
5. a demonstration that the facility will comply with Washington's siting standards (discussed below), including preliminary data characterizing groundwater;
6. a compliance history for any other TSDs operated or owned by the applicant, or by its parent or previous subsidiaries for the past ten years;
7. a statement of the need for the facility in light of state and regional TSD capacity, state dangerous waste management priorities, availability of new technologies and impacts on disposal costs; and
8. an analysis of how the planned TSD expansion will affect overall TSD capacity in the state.[101]

Ecology or the facility proponent must publish notice of the availability of this information in a local community newspaper for a minimum of fourteen consecutive days.[102] A TSD permit application may not be filed prior to 150 days following publication of the notice.[103]

Siting Restrictions

Washington's TSD facility siting standards are more comprehensive than the federal siting standards contained in 40 CFR 264 and 265. The federal standards are primarily intended to prohibit the siting of TSD facilities in floodplains, seismic areas and natural underground structures, such as caves.[104] Washington's siting standards, found at WAC 173-303-282, prohibit locating a TSD facility in wetlands and severely restrict development of TSD facilities in areas close to shorelines. For example, no new TSD facility may be located over a sole source aquifer,[105] nor in areas classified under local zoning as natural, conservancy, rural or residential.[106] Since any facility seeking a dangerous waste permit must comply with the State Environmental Policy Act (SEPA), the applicant must address potential adverse environmental impacts from the facility on (among other things) surface and groundwater, domestic water supplies, air quality, transportation, archaeological or historic sites, slope stability, endangered species habitat, and a variety of other matters. The SEPA process provides the public the opportunity to ensure that an applicant has fully addressed these matters during the permitting process.

Closure and Post-Closure

Closure is the process by which the owner or operator of a TSD facility closes out its operations. Washington dangerous waste regulations contain closure and post-closure requirements which mirror many of the federal requirements.

In Washington, TSDs must be closed in a manner that minimizes the need for further maintenance and minimizes post-closure escape of dangerous wastes.[107] A written closure plan must be submitted to Ecology as part of the TSD facility permit application,[108] and implementation of the approved closure plan is a condition of the facility's permit.[109] The closure plan must include the following:[110]

1. a description of how the facility will be closed;
2. an estimate of the maximum inventory of wastes in storage and treatment at any time over the active life of the facility;

3. a detailed description of the methods to be used during closure, including methods for removing, transporting, treating, storing or disposing of any dangerous wastes and identification of the off-site dangerous waste management units to be used;
4. a detailed description of the steps needed to remove or decontaminate dangerous waste residues and contaminated equipment, structures and soils, including procedures for cleaning equipment and removing contaminated soils, methods for sampling and testing surrounding soils, and criteria for determining the extent of decontamination required to minimize post-closure escape and protect human health and the environment; and
5. a schedule for closure.

The owner or operator must provide an estimate of the cost of closing the facility and must establish financial ability to pay for closure ("financial assurance").[111] Generally, closure must begin no later than ninety days after the facility receives its final volume of hazardous waste.[112] A certification of closure signed by the owner or operator and by an independent registered engineer must be submitted to EPA within sixty days after closure is complete.[113]

If all wastes are not removed, post-closure care must continue for thirty years after closure is complete,[114] however, a storage facility may clean-close by removing all hazardous waste and decontaminating all soil and have no post-closure care period. Ecology may shorten or extend the post-closure period, depending on site conditions. Post-closure plans must be submitted as part of the permit application and must include

1. a description of planned monitoring activities;
2. a description of planned maintenance activities to ensure the integrity of the final cap and final cover or other containment system and the integrity of the monitoring equipment; and
3. the name, address and telephone number of the person to contact about the hazardous waste disposal unit or facility during the post-closure care period. Washington also requires that the site be returned to the appearance and use of the surrounding area to the degree possible.

Corrective Action

The corrective action provisions of RCRA are set out in the statute and in 40 CFR 264.100 and 101. The Washington corrective action program utilizes the MTCA process in concert with the states dangerous waste program to fulfill the mandates of the RCRA Program.[115] The authorization for Washington's corrective action program does not extend to the entire program.[116] Instead, EPA retains authority to control several portions of the program, and where Washington's regulations exceed the federal regulations, the Washington provisions are not federally enforceable.[117] Because the Washington corrective action rules are tied to the MTCA program where they do not track the federal program, only the federal program will be addressed in this Chapter. For more information on the application of MTCA to dangerous waste corrective action please refer to WAC 173-303-645 ("Releases from regulated units") and WAC 173-303-646 ("Corrective Action").

The RCRA corrective action requirements apply at hazardous waste treatment, storage, and disposal facilities. These include facilities that have been granted or are seeking a RCRA permit,[118] facilities with a RCRA permit-by-rule,[119] facilities that are currently or previously were operated under interim status and facilities that are currently operating or have operated illegally without filing for interim status or a final RCRA permit.

Any permit issued to a treatment, storage or disposal facility after November 8, 1984, must include provisions for corrective action.[120] Permits may contain a schedule of compliance where corrective action cannot be completed before the permit is issued.[121] Facility owners or operators must demonstrate that they are financially able to complete the required corrective actions.[122] In some circumstances, EPA is authorized to require corrective action beyond facility boundaries.[123]

The provisions authorize EPA to require owners or operators of TSD facilities to clean up releases of hazardous waste or hazardous constituents from any "solid waste management unit" ("SWMU") at the facility. A "Facility" includes all contiguous property owned or controlled by the owner of the real estate on which the TSD is located.[124] For example, if a tenant applies for a permit, EPA will inspect all contiguous property of the property owner and can require corrective action on another tenant's property.[125]

ENFORCEMENT AND PENALTIES

The state and EPA exercise three types of enforcement powers:

1. to conduct inspections, issue compliance orders, and file enforcement actions;
2. to impose fines; and
3. to seek criminal penalties.

The state has the "lead" for enforcing those portions of the RCRA program that it is authorized to enforce. EPA retains oversight authority and authority for enforcing certain HSWA provisions.[126] Thus, if EPA considers Washington's enforcement posture or penalties to be insufficient, it may "over-file," even where the state has already taken an action.

In December 1994, Ecology adopted a new policy to adjust penalties for violations which are voluntarily disclosed.[127] Ecology will not, as a matter of policy, seek civil penalties for violations which are voluntarily reported to Ecology if there has been a good faith effort to comply, immediate corrective action is taken, and there is no significant threat created to the public or environment by the violation.

State administrative orders and penalties are appealable to the Washington Pollution Control Hearings Board (PCHB). Appeals from decisions of the PCHB are made to Superior Court by filing a petition to review under the state Administrative Procedure Act.[128] Appeals from PCHB decisions are "on the record," and additional evidence is not normally considered. Decisions of the PCHB will generally be overturned only where they are not supported by substantial evidence or are arbitrary or capricious.[129]

NOTES

[1] 42 USC §§6921 *et seq.*

[2] *American Mining Congress v. EPA*, 824 F.2d 1177 (DC Cir. 1987).

[3] WAC 173-303 is equally turgid.

[4] 42 USC. §6926; 40 CFR 271.

[5] 40 CFR 272, subpart WW.

[6] 51 Fed. Reg. 3782 (1986).

[7] *Washington: Final Authorization of State Hazardous Waste Management Program Revision; Final Rule*, 59 Fed. Reg. 55,322 (1994).

[8] *Id.*

[9] 40 CFR 262; WAC 173-303-170 through 173-303-230.

[10] 40 CFR 263; WAC 173-303-240 through 173-303-270.

[11] 42 USC §§9601 *et seq.*

[12] RCW §70.105D.

[13] WAC 173-303-090(8)(c).

[14] The term "solid waste" is something of a misnomer; the definition of solid waste includes wastes that are solid, liquid, semi-solid, or gaseous. *See, e.g.*, WAC 173-304-100(73).

[15] 42 USC §6903(27).

[16] WAC 173-303-016(3) through (7) gives one a taste of the complexity of this regulation.

[17] WAC 173-303-016(3)(b)(i), (ii), and (iii).

[18] *See* WAC 173-303-016(4), (5) and (6).

[19] WAC 173-303-070.

[20] 40 CFR 261.33. There are additional restrictions on storage and disposal of such wastes. *See, e.g.*, 40 CFR 268 and 262.34.

[21] Washington has also listed certain PCB wastes, which EPA regulates less stringently under the Toxic Substances and Control Act (TSCA). 15 USC §§2601, *et seq. See* WAC 173-303-9904.

[22] WAC 173-303-090.

[23] See 10 CFR 260.20, §260.22, and 261, app. IX.

[24] *See* 40 CFR 261.21; WAC 173-303-090(5).

[25] 40 CFR 261.21(a)(1).

[26] *Id.*

[27] 40 CFR 261.21(a)(2).

[28] See 40 CFR 261.22; WAC 173-303-090(6).

[29] 40 CFR 261.22(a), (b).

[30] 40 CFR 261.23; WAC 173-303-090(7).

[31] *See* 40 CFR 261.24.

[32] Method 1311 in "Test Methods for Evaluating Solid waste, Physical/Chemical Methods," EPA Publication SW-846.

[33] 40 CFR 261.24 (Table 1).

34 Note that EPA suspended some TCLP characterization and designation of certain petroleum-contaminated media (soils and water generated and re-injected in product recovery at petroleum facilities) from coverage as solid waste. 40 CFR 261.4(b)(10) and (11).

35 40 CFR 261.3(a)(2)(iv); WAC 173-303-081(3) and -082(3).

36 *Id.*

37 40 CFR 261.3(b)(3).

38 40 CFR 261.3(c)(2)(i) and (d)(2); WAC 173-303-070(2)(a).

39 40 CFR 261.3(c)(2)(ii).

40 *Shell Oil Company v. EPA*, 950 F.2d 741 (DC Cir. 1991).

41 A federal circuit court has also found that the invalidation of the mixture and derived-from rules applies retroactively, voiding the convictions of two corporate officers convicted of related violations. *United States v. Goodner Brothers Aircraft, Inc.*, 966 F.2d 380 (8th Cir. 1992), *cert. den.* 506 US 1049 (1993).

42 57 Fed. Reg. 7628 (1992).

43 60 Fed. Reg. 66344 (1995).

44 *Cf. Chemical Waste Management, Inc. v. USEPA*, 869 F.2d 1526 (DC Cir. 1989) and *Simpson Tacoma Kraft Co., v. Department of Ecology*, 119 Wn. 2d 640 (1992).

45 40 CFR 261.3(d)(2).

46 53 Fed. Reg. 31,142 (1988).

47 *Chemical Waste Management, Inc. v. EPA*, 869 F.2d 1526 (DC Cir. 1989).

48 40 CFR 261.3(i).

49 *See* WAC 173-303-100. (wastes designated as toxic under state-only dangerous waste criteria) A waste that fails the TCLP test is also considered "toxic" under both the federal and state regulations. See WAC 173-303-090(8).

50 WAC 173-303-100(5)(b)(i) - (iii).

51 WAC 173-303-110(3).

52 WAC 173-303-100(6).

53 *Id.*

54 EPA also exempts any mixture of domestic sewage and other wastes that passes through a sewer system to a publicly owned treatment works. 40 CFR 261.4(a)(1)(ii).

55 42 USC §6903(27). However, EPA and the Department of Energy have joint regulatory authority over "mixed waste," which contains exempted nuclear materials and hazardous wastes.

56 *See* 40 CFR 261.4(a).

57 See 40 CFR 261.4(b).

58 *See* WAC 173-303-071(3)(e).

59 *See* WAC 173-303-071(3)(k).

60 WAC 173 303-071(3)(i).

61 WAC 173 303-071(3)(t).

62 WAC 173-303-071(3)(v).

63 WAC 173-303-071(3)(y).

[64] "Special wastes" are defined as "any state-only dangerous waste that is solid only (nonliquid, nonaqueous, nongaseous), that is: Corrosive waste (WAC 173-303-090 (6)(b)(ii)), toxic waste that has Category D toxicity (WAC 173-303-100(5)), PCB waste (WAC 173-303-9904 under State Sources), or persistent waste that is not EHW (WAC 173-303-100(6)). Any solid waste that is regulated by the United States EPA as hazardous waste cannot be a special waste." WAC 173-303-040.

[65] WAC 173-303-073(1).

[66] WAC 173-303-073.

[67] WAC 173-303-070(7)(a).

[68] 40 CFR 262.20(e), 262.34(d), 262.44.

[69] 40 CFR 261.5(a).

[70] WAC 173-303-200(1)(d).

[71] WAC 173-303-190.

[72] WAC 173-303-200(1)(b).

[73] WAC 173-303-073(2)(f).

[74] WAC 173-303-9906.

[75] 40 CFR 262.41.

[76] WAC 173-303-240.

[77] WAC 173-303-240(1).

[78] WAC 173-303-250.

[79] WAC 173-303-240(2)

[80] WAC 173-303-240.

[81] WAC 173-303-240(1).

[82] Generators who accumulate dangerous waste on-site for more than 90 days and any transporters who store DW for more than 10 days are considered TSD "operators" and are subject to the full TSD operator regulations. See WAC 173-303-200; WAC 173-303-240(5).

[83] WAC 173-303-283.

[84] *Id.*

[85] WAC 173-303-283(3)(h).

[86] WAC 173-303-283(i).

[87] 42 USC §6925(a); WAC 173-303-800(2).

[88] 40 CFR 264, 271; WAC 173-303-806(2).

[89] WAC 173-303-806(4).

[90] An "existing facility" under the federal program is one that was in existence on November 19, 1980, or any facility in existence on the effective date of statutory or regulatory changes under RCRA which, for the first time, require the facility to have a permit. 42 USC §6925.

[91] 40 CFR 270.10(e).

[92] 42 USC §6930(a); *See also* WAC 173-303-805(5)(a).

[93] *See* WAC 173-303-805.

[94] *See* WAC 173-303-805(8).

[95] *See* WAC 173-303-805(5)(b)(i).

[96] WAC 173-303-806(5)

[97] *Id.*

98 An expansion is broadly defined as any enlargement of the surface area of an existing facility, the addition of a new process or an increase in the design capacity of existing processes at the facility. This section does not, however, apply to mobile facilities, demonstration (pilot) facilities or facilities used for CERCLA cleanups. WAC 173-303-281(2)(c).

99 WAC 173-303-281(3)(b).

100 RCW §43.21C.

101 WAC 173-303-281(3)(a).

102 WAC 173-303-281(3)(b).

103 WAC 173-303-281(3)(b).

104 40 CFR 264.18 and 265.18.

105 WAC 173-303-282(6)(c)(ii)(B).

106 WAC 173-303-280(7).

107 WAC 173-303-610(2)(a)(i) and (ii).

108 WAC 173-303-806(4)(a)(xiii).

109 WAC 173-303-610(3)(a).

110 WAC 173-303-610(3).

111 *See* WAC 173-303-620.

112 WAC 173-303-610(4)(a).

113 WAC 173-303-610(6).

114 *See* WAC 173-303-610(7)-(11).

115 59 Fed. Reg. 55,322 (1994).

116 *Id.* at 55,323.

117 *Id.*

118 40 CFR 264.101(a).

119 40 CFR 270.60(b), (c).

120 42 USC §6924(u).

121 40 CFR 264.101(b).

122 42 USC §6924(u).

123 42 USC §6924(v); 40 CFR 264.101(c).

124 40 CFR 260.10; 40 CFR 264.100; 40 CFR 264, subpart S.

125 40 CFR 260.10.

126 42 USC §6928(a)(2). Note that Ecology's HSWA type requirements were authorized to be enforced by the state by EPA in 1994. *See* WAC 173-303-050 and -960.

127 Executive Policy 1-26; "Adjusting Civil Penalties in Response to Self-Disclosure" (12/20/94).

128 RCW §34.05.

129 RCW §34.05.570(3).

CHAPTER 10

Hazardous Waste Cleanup

INTRODUCTION

Washington has adopted its own statutory "Superfund" scheme for identifying and responding to releases of hazardous substances. The Washington law, called the Model Toxics Control Act ("MTCA"),[1] supplements the federal Superfund (the Comprehensive Environmental Response Compensation and Liability Act, or "CERCLA").[2] The federal law cannot, and was not intended to, clean up all hazardous waste sites and releases, as budget limitations constrain the EPA's ability to address even some emergency situations. Therefore, many releases would go unremediated but for cleanups undertaken in conformance with state laws.

Several years of experience with the MTCA program indicates a workable system for identifying and cleaning up releases of hazardous substances, including petroleum products not covered by CERCLA. Although Ecology is experiencing resource limitations, sites continue to be cleaned up and regulatory requirements satisfied through "voluntary" actions and "independent remedial actions" undertaken by site owners, generators and transporters. The combined effect of CERCLA and MTCA has been, and will continue to be, to ensure that the vast majority of hazardous waste spills and sites at which hazardous substances have been released are cleaned up in a manner that is cost-effective and protective of the public and the environment.

HISTORY OF WASHINGTON LEGISLATION AND REGULATIONS

MTCA was the product of a voter initiative spearheaded by environmental groups dissatisfied with a site cleanup law enacted a year earlier by the Washington legislature. The voters adopted MTCA as Initiative Measure No. 97 on November 8, 1988, and it was subsequently codified at RCW §70.105D. It establishes a state cleanup program administered Ecology and is generally patterned on CERCLA.[3] The statute forcefully declares a policy, echoing RCW §43.21C.020(3) of the State Environmental Policy Act, that each person has a "fundamental and inalienable right to a healthful environment" and "a responsibility to preserve and enhance that right."[4]

Because of space limitations on the text of initiatives, MTCA's text is skeletal compared to CERCLA, and therefore depends for substance on the implementing regulations. These regulations create the basic framework for detecting, reporting, study and cleanup of releases of hazardous substances, which include (by contrast to the federal program) petroleum and petroleum products.[5] The rules also set out the "cleanup standards" that must be met at MTCA sites.[6] Experience with the regulations and with the Ecology offices that manage the program indicates that while the standards appear to set difficult targets, it is possible to develop reasonable and cost-effective cleanup plans that lead to acceptable cleanups consistent with the state standards.

OVERVIEW OF STATUTORY STRUCTURE

MTCA creates liability rules similar to those under CERCLA, imposing strict, joint and several liability on generators and transporters of hazardous substances, and on owners and operators of sites where the substances are or may be released.[7] The statute was amended in 1993 to add express provisions for contribution or cost recovery between potentially liable parties ("PLPs"), after the courts declined to imply such rights.[8] MTCA now expressly provides for recovery of attorneys' fees in contribution actions against other PLPs.[9] The amendments also grant an exemption from the procedural requirements (i.e., the permitting process) under several state environmental programs, such as the state clean water and clean air acts, although PLPs and Ecology must still comply with the processes spelled out under the State Environmental Policy Act.[10]

Ecology has drafted a number of policy and guidance documents, along with models for agreed orders, enforcement orders, and consent decrees that help explain and guide compliance with the regulations. These are available from Ecology on request, as well as from other sources.

ANALYSIS OF STATUTE

Policy Declarations

The stated purpose of MTCA is to raise funds for cleanup costs and prevent future hazards due to improper disposal of toxic wastes.[11] The actual purposes, however, reach well beyond that limited goal. MTCA encourages private party cleanups, public participation and openness in the cleanup process, information sharing by Ecology and PLPs, reasonableness in documenting and studying releases, and all deliberate speed in cleaning up releases. Recognizing that both agricultural and small business users of pesticides and other chemicals may face major liabilities for their legal use of such chemicals, MTCA establishes a policy insulating them from liability and providing potential funding to assist both pesticide users and persons harmed by such use.

Definitions

The definitions of most interest under MTCA are as follows:[12]

Potentially Liable Person ("PLP"), which includes anyone found by Ecology, on the basis of credible evidence, to be liable under RCW §70.105D.040.[13] The definition, uniquely, imposes a procedural notice requirement on Ecology to give a "PLP" notice and an opportunity to comment before the finding of potential liability is made, except in the event of an emergency.[14]

Person includes any possible legal or natural person, including federal agencies and Indian tribes.[15]

Owner or operator includes persons with ownership interests in, or control over, a facility, and all previous owners of abandoned facilities.[16] It excludes many of the same persons covered by exclusions under CERCLA, such as: (a) state agencies or units of local government that involuntarily acquire property, except where those entities caused or contributed to the release or threat of release; and (b) persons holding indicia of ownership primarily to protect a security interest.[17]

Facility covers any location, structure, or land-, air- or water-borne vehicle in the state.[18] A significant exception covers areas contaminated by consumer products in consumer use.[19]

Release is defined broadly to include "any intentional or unintentional release of any hazardous substance into the environment, including but not limited to the abandonment or disposal of containers of hazardous substances."[20]

Hazardous substance is defined to include "RCRA-type" wastes covered by the state's hazardous waste control program;[21] any hazardous substance included in CERCLA as of March 1, 1989; petroleum and petroleum products; and any "substance or category of substances, including solid waste decomposition products," that Ecology determines by rule is a threat to health and the environment if released.[22] The inclusion of petroleum and petroleum products is a major departure from CERCLA.[23]

Remedy or *remedial action* is defined both in terms of cleanup actions undertaken, and costs incurred, consistent with the statute, to identify, eliminate or minimize threats or potential threats to human health or the environment.[24]

Costs include "any investigative and monitoring activities" and "any health assessments or health effects studies" to determine risks to human health from a release.[25]

Public notice defines and requires the minimum notice to be given to persons making timely requests to Ecology, and to persons in the vicinity of a proposed action, both by mail and by publication. The definition also requires opportunity for interested persons to comment on proposed actions.[26]

Federal cleanup law references and incorporates CERCLA and its amendments.[27]

Ecology's Powers and Duties

Ecology can either investigate or require others to investigate possible releases or threats of releases of hazardous substances. If grounds exist to believe there is an actual or potential release, Ecology employees, agents or contractors can enter any property and conduct investigations, after reasonable notice, or without notice in case of emergencies. Ecology can also use subpoenas to require testimony and production of documents or other information.[28] Ecology must give notice before entering property to perform remedial work, except in emergencies, and must minimize any impact on ongoing business operations at a facility.[29] MTCA allows indemnification of Ecology contractors performing investigations or cleanups, except for their reckless or willful misconduct, and it empowers Ecology to classify hazardous substances and products for purposes of MTCA and the state's hazardous waste program.

The bulk of the MTCA program exists in regulations rather than the statute. These were adopted under the under state's Administrative Procedures Act, RCW 34.05.[30]

In addition to the "Policy" documents, Ecology has adopted a number of "guidance" documents that cover such issues as statistical and sampling methodologies to be use in site studies and remedial decisions.[31] Ecology also published a manual for ranking sites, which ranks them into five general groups by their likely threat to public health or the environment. The "Washington Ranking Method" or "WARM" forms the basis for the Washington Site Register. Sites scoring one or two (one is the highest threat, five the least) are most likely to be addressed by Ecology, due to resource limitations, but lower priority sites may be addressed sooner based on a number of factors set out in Ecology policy documents (e.g., public interest, or willingness of PLPs to pay for Ecology staff or time for review).[32] The Site Register includes the "Hazardous Sites List" and the "Confirmed and Suspected Contaminated Sites List."

To ensure that Ecology is progressing with cleanups and is adequately funded and staffed, MTCA requires regular reporting to the Legislature, with public notice and comment, on sites listed and ranked, actions planned at sites and expenditures of funds under the Act.[33]

Liability Standards

MTCA adopts CERCLA's strict, joint-and-several model of liability for releases of hazardous substances.[34] In addition, MTCA simplifies the regulatory language and broadens it to include several new categories of liable parties. Persons liable under MTCA include past and present owners of a facility, generators of hazardous substances, and persons who transported hazardous substances to a facility. MTCA's owner/operator category expressly includes not only the original site owner but any person who owned or operated the site while a release was occurring.[35] MTCA provides relatively clear protection for persons who hold security interests in property that turns out to be contaminated, and for municipalities that use condemnation authority to acquire properties for public use. Given the courts' approach to CERCLA and MTCA as "remedial" statutes, however, and the extent to which CERCLA's liability net has be stretched to fairly remote cases, there is no hard line that cuts off potential liability under either statute, whether in state enforcement actions or private party suits.[36]

Transporters are liable only if they selected the facility where the hazardous substance ended up and could not have legally accepted the material at the time of disposal or treatment (not delivery), unless they had "reasonable grounds to believe the facility is not operated in accordance with" state hazardous waste rules under Ch. 70.105 RCW.[37] To minimize or avoid liability, transporters should therefore remain current on the compliance status of TSD facilities to which they ship waste.

MTCA creates a new category of liable parties not listed in CERCLA: persons who sell and label a hazardous substance for use, if that use results in a release requiring remedial action.[38] This applies to direct sales of pesticides and specialty chemicals.

Liability under the Act extends to "all remedial costs" and "all natural resource damages" caused by a release or threat of release.[39] Defenses to liability, outside the threshold matters that the state must establish to make its prima facie case, are limited in the same way as in 42 U.S.C. §9607(b).[40] Initially, there was a question whether private parties could sue under MTCA to recover their remedial costs from other PLPs. When the Washington Supreme Court ruled they could not,[41] the Washington legislature amended MTCA to explicitly include a private right of action.[42] As a result, MTCA claims have begun to appear regularly in litigation, including contribution actions in which PLPs seek recovery of some portion of their remedial action costs from other PLPs.[43]

Many contribution or cost recovery claims may be filed under both MTCA and CERCLA. However, the party seeking recovery must show that it has complied with the federal National Contingency Plan and with MTCA in performing studies or cleanup.[44] Note that like CERCLA, MTCA preserves all other claims that might result from a hazardous substance release, whether statutory or common law. These potentially include negligence, nuisance, trespass and strict liability in tort, as well as contractual rights from indemnities or warranties.

Additional potential causes of action lie under the Washington Hazardous Waste Management Act,[45] which provides a damage remedy for persons injured by improper management of dangerous waste and also attorneys' fees, the state contribution statute,[46] and tenant waste statute, which provides treble recovery plus attorneys' fees.[47] Additionally, these environmental liabilities have given rise to actions against insurance carriers, who under Washington law have been required to defend and indemnify their insureds in a fairly broad range of circumstances.

As under CERCLA, MTCA contains an "innocent purchaser" defense, but given the exceptions and limitations to it, it will be the rare "Snow White" purchaser that will be protected by it. To take advantage of this defense, a person must have had "no knowledge or reason to know" that any hazardous substance posing a problem at a facility was "released or disposed of on, in, or at the facility" and to have made "all appropriate inquiry," taking into account the knowledge and skill of the buyer, the obviousness of contamination, the relationship between the actual purchase price and the uncontaminated value of the land and other factors.[48] The defense is not available to anyone who by any act or omission contributed to the release or who had actual knowledge of releases or threatened releases. Nor is it available to one who fails to conduct appropriate due diligence prior to acquisition of contaminated property. However, Ecology (and EPA) have instituted "brownfields" initiatives in an effort to encourage property owners and developers to place contaminated industrial lands back into productive use. Persons considering purchase of environmentally-impaired property and who are willing to undertake cleanup, can seek to insulate themselves from liability for existing contamination through "prospective purchaser" covenants not to sue and "no-further-action" letters from the agencies.

To protect home owners, farmers and others using pesticides and agricultural chemicals near their homes, MTCA provides a limited defense for any natural person who "uses a hazardous substance lawfully and without negligence for any personal or domestic purpose," but only if the person resides in the dwelling, is an unpaid assistant or a direct employee.[49] Therefore, commercial pesticide applicators, even those adhering to state and federal standards and requirements, may be incurring MTCA liability when they treat a lawn or fumigate a house.[50]

Enforcement and Settlement Provisions

MTCA departs significantly from the complicated and arguably more inflexible and arbitrary provisions governing settlements under CERCLA.[51] The range of options open to the state to resolve liability and obtain cleanup actions includes agreed orders,[52] enforcement (unilateral) administrative orders,[53] judicial actions for injunctive relief and recovery of remedial costs[54] and judicially entered consent decrees.[55] PLPs can take the initiative and control their exposure to a much greater degree than they can under CERCLA, as will be discussed below. These forms of agreement offer varying degrees of finality and protection to parties who resolve their liability to the state and other parties.

To obtain some finality and protection from claims for contribution from other parties ("contribution protection"), a PLP in MTCA's settlement process must enter into a consent decree with the state. The attorney general may agree to a settlement only if Ecology makes findings that the settlement will expedite the cleanup and will comply with cleanup standards and any existing administrative orders.[56] In a one sentence provision, MTCA also encourages *de minimis* settlements with any person "whose contribution is insignificant in amount and toxicity."[57] PLPs that qualify as *de minimis* are well advised to cash out of the cleanup process as quickly as possible and to press Ecology to follow a simplified process for persons in their position.

One of the benefits of a consent decree includes a covenant not to sue from Ecology, although this is statutorily limited to "a scope commensurate with the settlement agreement" and must contain a reopener provision requiring amendment of the decree if previously unknown factors are discovered that show a threat to human health and the environment not resolved by the decree.[58] Settlement also provides contribution protection.[59] Finally, MTCA settlement does not preempt or foreclose any person from seeking recovery for any claims or injuries compensable or remediable under other statutory or common law.[60]

The enforcement provisions of MTCA provide enforcement options similar to those of CERCLA. First, Ecology can issue orders to any PLP to compel remedial action where it is not conducting its own remedial action.[61] This authority encompasses both remedial action and immediate response orders. A PLP that refuses to comply with an order without sufficient cause may be sued by the Attorney General for a penalty of up to three times the amount of costs incurred by the state, plus an additional penalty of up to $25,000 per day for refusal to comply.[62] It is worth noting that neither MTCA nor the regulations provide an express mechanism for enforcing regulatory requirements outside the context of an order (e.g., for non-reporting).

A principal policy behind MTCA is to encourage expeditious cleanups. As is the case with CERCLA, MTCA provides a means for non-liable persons who conduct cleanups to recover remedial costs incurred and obtain reimbursement from the state cleanup fund.[63] Another purpose behind MTCA is to encourage citizen involvement in the cleanup process. The broad citizen suit provision of RCW §70.105D.050(5) encourages the most direct kind of involvement. This provision allows citizens, on thirty days' notice to Ecology, to obtain a court order requiring Ecology to perform any non-discretionary duty; it also rewards the successful citizen litigant with costs and attorneys' fees.[64]

Judicial review of Ecology's decisions on investigations, remedial actions and notification of PLPs is limited both in time and in scope. Review is possible only in three situations: (1) cost recovery or enforcement actions by Ecology; (2) actions by a PLP to recover costs incurred in responding to a release for which it was not liable from the state fund; or (3) citizen's suits.[65]

The Toxics Control Accounts

MTCA creates both state and local accounts that parallel the federal Superfund established by 26 U.S.C. §9507. The accounts are funded by various state tax levies on businesses that possess hazardous substances, including petroleum (other than crude oil); and by a hazardous waste fee chargeable to all businesses based on their gross income.[66] These accounts are used to fund a wide range of activities, including the state "RCRA" program, and the MTCA cleanup program. These accounts also provide matching funds for joint state-federal CERCLA cleanups.[67]

Ecology has developed policies for applications for "mixed funding." Mixed funding is joint funding of a cleanup by both private parties and the state, through the state account. Ecology has provided mixed or grant funding of up to 75% of response costs at several sites around the state. The mixed funding provisions are to expeditiously address any threats posed by a release. However, mixed funding is available only through a consent decree under RCW §70.105D.040(4), and only if "a substantially more expeditious and enhanced cleanup" would result and the mixed funding would prevent or mitigate unfair economic hardship.[68] While the amount of money available for mixed funding is somewhat limited, Ecology has encouraged submission of mixed funding proposals from both municipal, corporate, and individual PLPs that would qualify under this test.

OVERVIEW OF MTCA REGULATIONS

The MTCA regulations address releases or threats of releases, both retrospectively and prospectively, and establish a process for identifying, prioritizing and cleaning up such releases. The regulations are based on several underlying administrative principles.[69]

Site Reports and Cleanup Decisions

Site Discovery and Reporting

MTCA regulations require reporting of any release or threat of release of hazardous substances.[70] The initial release report must include circumstances of the release or threat, identification and location of the hazardous substances and any planned or active remedial actions.[71] Exemptions from reporting requirements include legal pesticide and fertilizer applications; lawful and non-negligent personal use of hazardous substances for personal or domestic purposes; permitted releases, (e.g., releases in compliance with air or water discharge permits); releases previously reported to Ecology or to EPA; releases in public water systems subject to the Department of Health's jurisdiction; or releases to permitted wastewater treatment facilities. Ecology states that exemption from reporting requirements does no-equate to a release from liability.[72]

PLPs have ninety days from discovery to report a release. Many PLPs have found it appropriate to undertake an independent cleanup, then report the release and the results of the cleanup to Ecology at the same time. However, CERCLA requires releases of "reportable quantities" of federally-defined hazardous substances to be reported immediately.[73] Such reports go to a variety of response agencies, including Ecology.[74] Moreover, releases from underground storage tanks, one of the largest categories of MTCA-governed releases, must be reported within twenty-four hours of discovery.[75]

A major aspect of the MTCA rules is the provision for voluntary "independent actions." Performing such an action has no absolute legal effect on liability, which can be discharged only through a cleanup performed under the oversight and control of Ecology and resolved under a consent decree.[76] However, acting quickly to mitigate the effects of a release and to contain and recover as much of the released hazardous substances as possible may make good economic, as well as environmental, sense in reducing cleanup costs. In addition, it will enhance the equitable position of the PLP with the public and Ecology.

In any event, a report of an independent action must be made to Ecology within ninety days of its completion, defined as the end of a ninety-day period of no action other than monitoring. The report must include the same basic information as the release report, and all data, cleanup actions, monitoring plans and results of the action. Ecology must respond to the report within ninety days by scheduling an initial investigation.[77]

Initial Investigation

This section of the regulations not only sets the standards and timing for an Ecology investigation of a reported release, but triggers the first official notification back to the PLP of Ecology's special interest in a site.[78] The purpose of the initial investigation is to see if a release requires further action. Ecology will conduct an investigation if it "has a reasonable basis to believe" that there is or may be a release that is a threat to human health or the environment.[79] No investigation is required of permitted releases or of releases already known to Ecology. The investigation may be nothing more than a "windshield inspection" and documentation of observations, but may also include site access and sampling.[80]

Based on the investigation, Ecology decides whether to take or require emergency action, perform a site hazard assessment, take or require interim action, or take no action at all. Ecology would take no action either because the release poses no threat to human health or the environment or because there is no release.[81] Ecology reserves the right to revisit its decision if other information surfaces.

When Ecology determines that additional action is required, it sends the first of several formal notices (the "early notice letter") to owners and operators and other PLPs known to Ecology.[82] The letter includes known information on the release and site, a description of the cleanup process under MTCA, a statement of Ecology's policy of working cooperatively with PLPs to obtain prompt and effective cleanup, contacts in Ecology and a statement that the letter is not a determination of liability and that cooperating with Ecology in planning or carrying out a cleanup is not an admission of guilt or liability. As information about the site and the connection of various parties to it develops, Ecology will at some point send "PLP status letters" to parties for which it has "credible evidence" of liability.[83] There is an opportunity to challenge Ecology's factual claims, and it has been done successfully. PLPs have also persuaded Ecology to send notices to other entities based on "credible evidence" establishing the other entities' liability under RCW 70.105D.040.[84]

Site Hazard Assessment

The site hazard assessment is intended to gather "sufficient sampling data and other information" to allow Ecology to determine whether a release has occurred; identify and quantify the hazardous substances and site characteristics that could affect migration of releases, evaluate any threats to human health or the environment, and determine the hazard ranking of the site.[85] It should be completed before any further action, other than emergency or interim action, and may be done "voluntarily" by PLPs under administrative orders or consent decrees.[86] The hazard assessment is "not intended to be a detailed site characterization."[87] It should include information on the hazardous substances present and any reaction or decomposition products, and their location on the facility; evidence of any release or threat of release; containment facilities, if any (including those installed in any independent action); any potential leaching, run-on or run-off problems; preliminary characterization of and depth to ground water that may be affected and distances to nearby water supplies; and evaluation of human or other physical factors that may affect a decision on further action.[88] Hazard assessment should be done in accordance with Ecology guidance under the Washington Ranking Method Services Manual process discussed below. If no further action is required, that determination will be incorporated in the Site Register.[89]

Hazardous Sites List[90]

If Ecology determines that additional remedial action is necessary at a site, the site will go on the list of hazardous sites.[91] Listed sites are to be collected into priority groups in accordance with Ecology guidance in the Washington Ranking Method (WARM) Scoring Manual.[92] Ranking is simply a system for prioritizing Ecology's involvement, not an actual risk or hazard assessment, which are done by the jurisdictional health department. Ecology is required to provide notification of ranking results in the Site Register.[93] Ecology may re-rank a site on receipt of new information that indicates a "significant change."

The list of hazardous sites is updated by Ecology every two weeks and contains only sites at which Ecology has determined that further remedial action, whether studies or cleanup, is warranted or under way.[94] Removing a site from the list may prove as difficult as removing one from the NPL, since "delisting" requires an Ecology finding that either all remedial actions except confirmational monitoring have been completed and cleanup standards have been met, or that the site was erroneously listed.[95] An owner or PLP may petition to have a site de-listed, but it must thoroughly document that one of the two stated conditions is satisfied, and may have to pay all costs, including an advance deposit, to cover Ecology's review of the petition.[96] Any de-listed sites will go on a separate list maintained by the department which is available to the public, and a site can go back on the site list if Ecology finds that additional remedial action is needed.

Biennial Program Report

Ecology is required to deliver to the Legislature, by November 1st of even-numbered years, its plans for conducting remedial actions during the next two years and likely expenditures from state and local toxics control funds. High-risk sites are to be addressed first, based on the hazard ranking. After public notice and comment, and legislative approval, this document becomes Ecology's program plan.[97]

State Remedial Investigation/Feasibility Study (RI/FS)

The RI/FS is the data gathering and remedial technology evaluation phase of a remedial action. It may be conducted by Ecology, by a PLP or any other person. The majority of RI/FS studies are in fact done by PLPs. The RI/FS is to be completed before selection of a remedial action, other than interim or emergency actions, and are often conducted by PLPs under an order or consent decree.[98] An RI/FS must contain the following: (1) general facility information, including location, dimensions, listing of owners and operators, history of operations and name and phone number of project coordinators; (2) a map of current site conditions, including boundaries, topography, surface and subsurface structures and utility lines and proposed "facility" boundaries; and (3) "sufficient" investigations to detail the type and extent of hazardous substances present and any threats posed to human health and the environment.[99]

The document must also address: (1) surface water and sediments, including migration routes and hydrologic features; (2) soils information, including types present and properties likely to affect migration of hazardous substances or implementability of any cleanup actions; (3) site geology and hydrogeology data adequate to characterize the extent of contamination and features affecting fate and transport; (4) air quality impacts, and local and regional climatological conditions likely to affect dispersion and migration of hazardous substances; (5) information on land use and zoning in the area; (6) information on possible impacts on natural resources and local ecology; (7) sources of hazardous substances; and (8) regulatory classifications of air, surface and ground water resources affected by the contamination.[100]

The feasibility study (FS) portion is an evaluation of the alternatives that can achieve a target protection level for human health and the environment. As with CERCLA, the criteria used to ensure protection of human health and the environment are at the heart of the evaluation and selection of an alternative.[101]
A work plan, including both a sampling and analysis plan and a safety and health plan, must also be prepared.[102]

Selection of Cleanup Actions

Before Ecology will approve the alternative selected in the FS for a site, it must be satisfied that the "preferred" alternative: (1) achieves a degree of cleanup that is protective of human health and the environment; (2) complies with applicable state, federal and local laws, (3) uses permanent cleanup strategies to the maximum extent practicable; (4) provides for adequate monitoring, (5) is appropriate to the facility; and (6) complies with cleanup standards.[103]

There is a statutory preference for on-site cleanup actions that permanently and significantly reduce volume, toxicity and mobility of the hazardous substances, and a bias against either containment as a remedy or off-site transport of untreated wastes.[104] For reasons of technical impracticability, however, Ecology has accepted many cleanups that involve on-site containment or off-site disposal.

After consideration of the alternatives presented in the FS, Ecology produces a draft cleanup action plan, similar to a CERCLA "proposed plan."[105] This document must include: (1) a description of the cleanup action and an explanation of how it meets requirements for the conduct of remedial actions and cleanup standards spelled out in the rules, (2) a brief summary of other alternatives evaluated, (3) an implementation schedule and restoration time frame; (4) identification of applicable local, state and federal requirements to be met; and (5) any institutional controls (such as deed restrictions, and justification for use of lower-preference remedial technologies. The public gets notice and an opportunity to comment on the proposed plan before it becomes final. In the case of routine actions, an order or decree can substitute for the cleanup plan. The final "cleanup action plan," like EPA's "Record of Decision," becomes the blueprint for the remedial action.

Site Cleanup and Monitoring

Cleanup Actions

Control and documentation requirements for the cleanup plan and process are spelled out in WAC 173-340-400, which is analogous to the remedial design/remedial action (RD/RA) process under CERCLA. The stated purpose of these provisions is to ensure that the cleanup action is designed, constructed and operated in a manner consistent with the cleanup action plan, accepted engineering practices and cleanup action requirements under WAC 173-340-360.[106]

Any routine or interim cleanup can be conducted by the PLP under an administrative order (unilateral or on consent) or a decree, as well as by Ecology.[107] Public participation is ensured at many stages throughout the process.[108]

In some circumstances, it may be possible to simplify or combine information and documents into a single document, but most cleanups will involve separate preparation of all required documents. For NPL sites, the full panoply of documents required by the CERCLA program will be required.[109]

These required plans include:

1. An engineering design report.[110]
2. Construction plans and specifications.[111]
3. Operation and maintenance plan to govern ongoing operation of the remedial action.[112]

Construction is required to be conducted in accordance with the above plans and specifications.[113]

Permits and approvals necessary to complete the project must also be identified.[114] In recognition of the delay caused by an earlier requirement for full permitting, the legislature amended MTCA in 1994 to eliminate the formal and procedural requirements for most permitting (e.g., air emissions and water discharges, and dangerous waste management permits) associated with site cleanups. Both MTCA and CERCLA preempt the procedural requirements (i.e., the paperwork and public participation requirements) of most laws that require a permit for any portion of the remedial work conducted completely on site.[115] However, the substantive provisions of the law—e.g., effluent guidelines or emission limitations for water or air discharges from treatment equipment installed on-site—continue to apply, as well as the full set of SEPA compliance requirements.

A Washington-registered professional engineer must supervise construction at a site. The party constructing the remedial action must keep "as-built" records, including an opinion from the engineer that the work has been performed in substantial compliance with all applicable governing documents.[116]

Changes to remedial design or construction performed under an order or decree must be approved by Ecology. If Ecology determines that there have been substantial changes, further public notice and opportunity for comment may be required.[117] Any waste generated during cleanup that requires offsite treatment, storage or disposal must be transported to an approved or permitted facility.[118]

Compliance Monitoring Requirements

MTCA regulations require monitoring to demonstrate that the remedy meets performance objectives and cleanup standards[119] and will continue to do so.[120] Monitoring must be in accordance with a plan, which must be approved by Ecology if it is part of an order or decree. This plan must include a sampling and analysis plan, a description of data analysis and evaluation procedures, a description of the statistical methodology used and, "any other information Ecology requires."[121]

Periodic Review

As under CERCLA, a periodic review to insure that human health and the environment are being protected is required at least every five years for remedial actions performed under MTCA under which hazardous substances are left on the site.[122]

Interim Actions

Ecology has recognized that cleanup activity cannot always wait until completion of all the procedural steps and planning outlined above. The rules therefore provide for interim actions.

Ecology defines an interim action as one that: (1) is technically necessary to reduce a threat to human health or the environment through the elimination of an exposure pathway; (2) corrects a problem that may become substantially worse or more costly to address if action is delayed; or (3) is needed to provide for completion of hazard assessment, RI/FS or design.[123] However, the burdens of planning, documentation and public notice spelled out in WAC 173-340-430 may prove to be a disincentive.[124]

Interim actions may do one or more of the following: (1) achieve cleanup standards for a portion of the site, (2) provide partial cleanup (e.g., source removal), but not achieve cleanup standards; or (3) provide incomplete partial cleanup but obtain information needed for final cleanup (e.g., treatability studies).[125] An interim action must be consistent with the final cleanup if the details of that cleanup are known, and if unknown, the action cannot foreclose reasonable alternatives.[126] Interim actions can occur at any time during the cleanup process, but they shall not be used to delay or supplant it. In addition, they are deemed inappropriate where insufficient technical information exists.[127] Additional remedial actions must thereafter be taken, unless the interim action has achieved cleanup standards.[128] Ecology establishes deadlines for completion, and interim actions can be taken under orders or consent decrees and are subject to public participation requirements.[129]

Although designed to be simpler than final cleanups, interim actions must still be documented via: (1) a description and justification of the action with data used in the RI/FS; (2) justification of selection of this action from among alternatives; (3) applicable information from any design and construction plans and documents; (4) a compliance monitoring plan; (5) a health and safety plan; and (6) a sampling and analysis plan.[130]

Administrative Procedures For Remedial Actions

Various administrative determinations and options are available to Ecology in connection with cleanups, including provisions for administrative and judicial settlement and orders.

Determination of PLP Status

Except in emergencies, Ecology must send an initial PLP status letter, via certified mail return receipt requested or personal service, to any person it reasonably believes, based on "credible evidence," is liable in connection with a site.[131] The letter will be sent when Ecology is ready to proceed with the remedial action (except for emergencies and initial investigations) and must include: (1) the name of the PLP, (2) information on the location of the facility; (3) the basis of Ecology's belief that the person is a PLP, (4) that a release has occurred and that human health and the environment are threatened; and (5) the names of other PLPs.[132] PLPs have an opportunity to comment within thirty days of receipt of the state's letter, and based on responses received and its own information, Ecology must then make and issue a final determination of PLP status.[133] Ecology provides an opportunity for a person to voluntarily accept PLP status through a waiver of the right to notice and comment, and there may be situations where this waiver is advisable.[134] Ecology reserves the right to notify additional PLPs, subject to its resource limitations, and obliges itself to inform existing PLPs when new PLPs are notified.[135]

Administrative Options For Remedial Actions

Ecology invites voluntary initiation of discussions and negotiations by PLPs, and in its discretion, may provide informal advice and assistance in developing proposals.[136] However, formal approval of any action can only occur through a consent order or decree.[137]

PLPs are invited to initiate remedial actions by requesting by letter that Ecology negotiate an order or consent decree.[138] Alternatively, Ecology can initiate the process by sending a letter inviting negotiations on a decree, or by issuing an administrative order.[139] Of course, Ecology reserves the right to take any appropriate action at any time, though it agrees to take reasonable steps to notify PLPs before taking its own actions.[140]

The rules also encourage independent remedial actions. However, once negotiations have begun, by issuance of an order or agreement to negotiate, PLPs are barred from independent actions unless the action (1) does not foreclose or preempt the action under discussion or foreclose selection of a cleanup action; or (2) if the PLP provides reasonable notice and Ecology does not object.[141] Of course, all such actions are purely voluntary and at the risk of the person taking the action, although in some circumstances Ecology may be willing and able to provide limited guidance to the parties conducting a remedial action.[142]

Consent Decrees

Only via a consent decree can a PLP obtain contribution protection. A PLP initiating a request for entry of a consent decree must: (1) describe the proposed action and demonstrate that settlement will lead to a more expeditious cleanup, consistent with cleanup standards and any previous orders; (2) identify the facility and describe the releases and their impacts and the particular environmental problems to be addressed, (3) summarize historical uses of and conditions at the facility; (4) provide a date for submission of a detailed proposal;[143] (5) name other PLPs not currently listed; and (6) propose a public participation plan meeting under the criteria set out in WAC 173-340-600(8).[144]

Ecology has followed EPA's lead in developing a model consent decree for MTCA cleanups. Persons proposing to resolve cleanup liability and settle cleanup requirements through a decree should obtain a copy of the model from Ecology. They should then determine what kinds of remedies have previously been accepted by Ecology for similar cleanups in previous orders and decrees, which are also available from Ecology.

The letter to Ecology may also include a waiver of procedural notice requirements, an acceptance of PLP status, and a detailed cleanup proposal per the provisions of WAC 173-340-520(1)(e).[145] The level of detail in the proposal should ideally be matched to the step in the process at which the negotiations are aimed (e.g., RI/FS or actual on-site design and action), and Ecology can waive part of the letter requirements if they have already been met by other means.[146]

Ecology must respond to the request within sixty days, unless it decides additional time is needed to determine PLP status. Ecology must make a threshold finding that entry of the decree would lead to a more expeditious cleanup.[147] Ecology's options include: (1) accepting the request and calling for a "detailed proposal;" (2) requesting additional information; or (3) denying the request and stating the reasons for the denial.[148] A "detailed proposal" must contain: (1) a technical scope of work; (2) the data and studies on which the proposal is based; (3) a recitation of the PLP's ability to conduct or fund the particular action; and (4) a schedule of proposed negotiations and time frames for implementation.[149]

The determination whether to enter into negotiations is based on the adequacy of the proposal and is made by Ecology and the Attorney General's office. The determination will be communicated in writing to the PLP within sixty days of receipt of the proposal by Ecology.[150] Negotiating time is normally 120 days, after which the "enforcement stay" lapses and Ecology can take enforcement action. Ecology may withdraw from negotiations at any time if no progress is being made or if it appears from new information that negotiations are inappropriate.[151] If Ecology believes a decree may lead to more expeditious cleanup, it may also initiate negotiations by sending a letter to the PLP, via certified mail or personal service.[152] The negotiation letter may accompany the determination of PLP status, though negotiations cannot theoretically commence until after the thirty-day PLP status comment period has elapsed. The letter must: (1) inform the PLP that Ecology and the Attorney General want to negotiate; (2) propose a draft consent decree and scope of work; (3) define the negotiation process and a schedule not to exceed ninety days; (4) mention the finding of PLP status; (5) request a written statement of the PLP's interest in and willingness to negotiate; and (6) request names of other persons the recipient believes to be a PLP. The letter may request a written response to the terms of the proposed decree and scope of work.[153] Ecology may extend the ninety-day moratorium period for an additional thirty days.[154]

If negotiations succeed and the decree survives the public comment process, Ecology will send it to the Attorney General for review and filing. If the Attorney General approves, it will be filed in the appropriate state or federal court.[155]

Agreed Orders

Either Ecology or a PLP can initiate the process leading to an agreed order covering a cleanup action. An agreed order provides no protection against contribution actions, does not allow mixed funding, and cannot include a covenant not to sue.[156] Nonetheless, agreed orders may be attractive as a means to bring PLPs to the table in the absence of a right of contribution. The request for an agreed order is much like the request for a consent decree. The PLP submits a letter containing the following: (1) description of the facility; (2) the proposed remedial action and a schedule for the work; (3) the environmental problems to be addressed, e.g, the release and its effects; (4) a summary of relevant historical use and conditions; (5) names of other PLPs; and (6) a proposed public participation plan.[157] The requesting PLP can also waive the procedural notice and comment requirements and accept, solely for purposes of the order, PLP status. The level of detail of the technical proposal that accompanies the request should be tailored to the complexity of the site, and Ecology can waive any of the requirements for the letter if they have already been met.[158]

Ecology must respond within sixty days, unless it needs additional time to determine any person's PLP status.[159] It may either grant the request, ask for additional information, or deny the request with written reasons in support of the denial. The negotiating period for the order is sixty days, unless Ecology decides a longer period is in the public interest.[160] Enforcement actions are stayed for those sixty days, unless Ecology withdraws because of lack of progress or determines that an agreed order is inappropriate.[161] Discussions on the order are essentially limited to technical issues involving the scope of and schedule for work.[162] Public notice and comment are required, and if the terms of the order change significantly, Ecology must provide another public notice and comment period.[163]

Enforcement Orders

Ecology may also issue enforcement orders to a PLP at any time after it issues a notice of potential liability under WAC 173-340-500. In deciding when or whether to issue such orders, Ecology follows its "Policy 540A." In emergencies, notice and an order can be issued concurrently. Again, except in emergencies, it appears that an order cannot be effective until after the notice and comment period on PLP status has passed and Ecology has made its final PLP determination.[164] Also, Ecology has on occasion issued enforcement orders to PLPs during negotiations over consent decrees. It appears that under WAC 173-340-520(2)(e), Ecology may not unilaterally break off negotiations with PLPs without determining that either (1) reasonable progress is not being made, or (2) that the proposal is inappropriate, and then only after providing express written notice to the PLPs of its intention to withdraw. Arguably, failure to meet these requirements would void a unilateral enforcement order in these circumstances.

Payment of Remedial Action Costs

Ecology expects to recover the costs it incurs in connection with a site essentially as they accrue. It will seek recovery not only of costs directly attributed to a site, but also "indirect costs" incurred in support of site activities and interest at a rate of 12% (per annum) on costs not paid within ninety days of submission of an itemized statement documenting its costs.[165] Ecology has adopted a policy governing the assessment and recovery of its program costs, including direct response costs and indirect program costs. See Policy 550A. The related Policy 550B governs Ecology's accounting and tracking of site costs.

Prospective Purchaser Agreements and Brownfields Redevelopment

Both nationally and locally, governments have begun to recognize that the liability structures of state and federal Superfund programs have forced large amounts of private and public land out of productive use. This was particularly true of industrial sites and waterfront property in urban commercial areas (so-called "brownfields"), leading to additional pressures to push development to "greenfields" sites in rural and suburban areas. This contributed to urban sprawl and inefficient land use patterns, and negative economic impacts on urban areas from lost jobs and tax revenues. Lenders have been unwilling to lend on contaminated property. Potential purchasers faced strict, joint and several liability for contamination placed by previous users and owners of a property. Given the large and often unknown potential liabilities associated with such properties, only the rare person with sophisticated understanding of the risks and rewards of a particular parcel was interested in undertaking redevelopment of such properties.

At the urging of a coalition of interests, the Washington Legislature modified the liability provisions of MTCA[166] to allow agreements between Ecology and prospective purchasers, under which title to contaminated sites could transfer without the new owner becoming liable for past contamination.[167] These agreements are proving to be a popular means of facilitating transactions in contaminated properties.

Public Involvement

Public Notice and Participation

In keeping with the spirit of MTCA, public involvement, input and participation provisions are central to the cleanup decision-making process. A PLP preparing a submission requiring the development of a proposed public participation plan should refer both to WAC 173-340-600 and to the section of the regulations under which the submission is being developed for specific requirements.

Ecology's goal is "to provide the public with timely information and meaningful opportunities for participation which are commensurate with each site."[168] Ecology meets this goal through early development of a participation plan, provision of public notices, public meetings and hearings, and involvement of regional citizens' advisory committees. In determining appropriate public notice opportunities, Ecology will consider: (1) health risks that could be avoided by providing the information; (2) public concerns about the facility; (3) information gathering needs that could be satisfied by the public; (4) whether future decision making will foreclose the public's opportunity to have input; (5) concerns about disclosure of confidential or sensitive information; and (6) any other factors determined by Ecology.[169]

Public notices will be given to those who make timely requests, mailed to potentially affected residents (adjacent property owners and others directly affected), published in the largest circulation newspaper in the city or county, or published through other news media. Notices must indicate the duration of the comment period, which should be at least thirty days. Where reasonable, Ecology must consolidate public notice and comment under MTCA with notice and comment under other statutes, such as SEPA, hazardous waste statutes and CERCLA.[170] Ecology must hold a public meeting if, during any comment period, ten or more persons request it.[171]

The public participation plan for each site must include: (1) a listing of applicable public notice requirements and areas and persons to be notified; (2) the location of at least one information repository, (3) means of identifying and addressing public concerns, such as interviews, questionnaires, meetings and hearings, and personal contacts; (4) provisions for coordination with other statutory public participation requirements, particularly those under CERCLA; (5) amendments as needed, and (6) other elements deemed necessary by Ecology.[172]

Implementation of the plan must be under Ecology's oversight[173] Separate provisions are set out in detail in the rules for public participation in consent decrees, agreed orders, enforcement orders, state RI/FS preparation, selection of cleanup actions, cleanup action implementation, and routine cleanup and interim actions.[174]

As noted above, Ecology must establish a Site Register for all sites in the program[175] to be published regularly and containing at least the following: (1) any no-action decision regarding a site, (2) site hazard rankings, (3) availability of annual and biennial reports, (4) notice of issuance or orders, agreed orders or proposed consent decrees; (5) notice of public meetings or hearings; (6) availability of state RI/FS scoping information and the RI/FS reports and draft and final cleanup plans; (7) notice of any changes in site listings; (8) notice of availability of engineering design reports; (10) reports of independent cleanup actions; (11) notice of commencement of negotiations for orders or consent decrees; (12) changes to deadlines for negotiations; and (13) other appropriate notices.[176]

Regional Citizens' Advisory Committees

As part of the public participation program, the rules also require Ecology to establish Regional Citizen Advisory Committees to advise Ecology about public concerns both locally and regionally, but with emphasis on regional concerns. The function of the committee is to: (1) discuss Ecology's program priorities; (2) inform regional citizens of the committee's availability as a resource; (3) timely advise Ecology of citizen concerns regarding investigative or remedial actions and suggested improvements, and (4) prepare a brief annual report to Ecology on major citizen concerns, committee proposals in response and any other information.[177]

Cleanup Standards

Overview

After considerable public discussion and debate, Ecology adopted regulations on February 28, 1991 that set cleanup standards to be achieved under MTCA—the "how clean is clean?" rules for state cleanups. These standards are subdivided according to the media affected (ground water, surface water, soil, air and sediments) and the character of the affected area (industrial versus non-industrial sites). "Cleanup standards" consist of three elements: (1) "cleanup levels," or the residual levels of contaminants that are determined to be protective of human health and the environment in a specific exposure scenario; (2) "points of compliance," or the locations at which cleanup levels must be met and maintained; and (3) "additional regulatory requirements" based on the type of cleanup and nature of the site. These are analogous to "applicable or relevant and appropriate requirements" (ARARs) under CERCLA and are determined during the remedy selection process, usually during the feasibility study.[178] The latter inquiry is intended to identify any chemical- or site-specific requirements of other laws that are more stringent than the cleanup levels specified in the MTCA rules.

Setting Cleanup Levels

Cleanup levels are generally established using standards in one of two risk-based sources. First, cleanup levels may be derived from published state and federal standards that establish legally acceptable and presumably protective concentrations of contaminants in a medium (e.g., maximum contaminant levels under the federal Safe Drinking Water Act for ground water). Second, for substances that are not on any of the existing regulatory lists, risk-based levels are set following the methodology set out in the media-specific rules. For each medium of concern (soil, surface water, ground water, air), the rules establish three methods of selecting appropriate cleanup levels: Method A, Method B and Method C. To determine cleanup levels at a given site, the PLP must:

1. identify and quantify the hazardous substances on the site;
2. identify all pathways of release and exposure; and
3. perform a risk assessment or identify published cleanup levels producing acceptable residual risk, using Method A, B, or C for substances of concern.

No single remedy is appropriate for every site. MTCA regulations provide two general ranges of cleanup options: one for "residential" property, the other for "industrial" property. The goal is to restore property to a condition that poses an acceptable risk to human health or the environment while not unduly restricting its future use. Something less than full removal of contaminants and complete restoration may be acceptable for many reasons, including past uses of the property and adjacent property, lack of effective cleanup technologies, and situations where only marginal environmental benefits would be achieved by a more stringent and costly cleanup.

After cleanup levels are established, the PLP may propose, and Ecology must determine, the point or points of compliance on the property where those cleanup levels must be met. For example, Ecology or a PLP conducting an independent cleanup must determine whether the cleanup levels identified must be met throughout the site or only at the property line; or above a containment system or at some other location based on existing contaminant plumes and technical possibilities for cleanup.[179]

State cleanup standards will, in most cases, be more stringent than the standards contained in other laws. For example, under the CERCLA program, EPA will sometimes accept a calculated carcinogenic "risk range" of up to one potential cancer case in 10,000, whereas MTCA will generally allow risks that are less than one in 100,000.[180]

Cleanup Standard Methods

Method A is based on a table of standards, derived from federal Safe Drinking Water Act standards, water quality criteria and risk assessment calculation.[181] It is to be used in situations where there are a limited number of contaminants, the site situation is relatively uncomplicated and can be addressed as a "routine" cleanup[182] and effective and well-demonstrated technologies will meet the numerical standards or cleanup levels set out in the list of chemicals for that medium.

Method B is based on a risk assessment calculation, using various numeric factors from sources outside the regulations to describe residual risk from concentrations of hazardous substances, both carcinogenic and toxic. It generally produces the most stringent cleanup standards, based on a cumulative summing of risks. Method B levels must be at least as stringent as all of the following:

1. all published and applicable state and federal standards;
2. levels that will result in "no adverse effects" on aquatic and terrestrial life; and
3. for substances without established health-based standards, "protective" levels are set based on a cumulative hazard quotient or index of less than one, a cumulative excess cancer risk of less than one in a million (10^{-6}) and concentrations that eliminate or minimize food chain contamination (bioaccumulation and bioconcentration).[183]

At a particular site, Ecology may set even more stringent levels, which must be "adjusted downward" to account for exposure via multiple pathways or exposure to multiple hazardous substances. Method B calculations may result in cleanup levels that are non-detectable by existing lab techniques. Where Ecology still deems such low levels to be "protective," it can either require that PLPs develop different sampling techniques and/or new and more sensitive analytical methods or identify surrogate measures of determining compliance and impose additional monitoring and remedial requirements.

In theory, Method C allows a PLP to develop more reasonable cleanup levels than Methods A or B.[184] It is aimed at situations where Methods A or B may be inapplicable or impossible to achieve, or where they might cause greater environmental harm if implemented. However, a PLP proposing to apply Method C must demonstrate all of the following: (1) alternate cleanup levels comply with all federal and state laws; (2) all practicable methods of treatment will be utilized; and (3) acceptable institutional controls have been implemented. Additionally, the PLP must show that at least one of the following conditions exists: (1) Method A or B levels are below area backgrounds; (2) Method C meets all applicable laws (admittedly circular); or (3) Method C produces no significant adverse effects on aquatic and terrestrial life.

Cleanup Standards For Ground Water, Surface Water, Soil, Air and Sediments

Ecology has established cleanup levels, or processes for deriving cleanup levels, for five different media: ground water, surface water, soil, air and sediments, with separate Method A, B or C processes for each. Ecology has provided slightly relaxed standards for several media for industrial properties. The description of how cleanup standards are set for the first four media is found in the MTCA regulations.[185] Cleanup standards for sediments are found in the Sediment Management Standards.[186]

MTCA ground water regulations assume that ground water should be returned to use as drinking water, its "highest beneficial use." All ground water cleanups must presumptively achieve the most restrictive risk-based standard, that is, the Method B standard. To demonstrate that a lesser standard is appropriate, Ecology must be shown that: (1) the ground water resource is not currently a drinking water resource; (2) that it is not a potential future drinking water source, e.g., due to its depth, low yield (less than 0.5 gallons per minute) or natural background contaminants that render it nonpotable; and (3) that the aquifer will not transport hazardous substances to usable ground water resources.[187]

MTCA defines the highest and best use of surface water by its current rather than potential use, a less stringent approach. Method A cleanup levels are determined by reference to water quality criteria under the state and federal Clean Water Acts rather than a table of values,[188] while Method B levels are based on a risk assessment of cumulative toxic and carcinogenic effects of all indicator substances and pathways.

Soil cleanup levels are determined based on an estimate of the "reasonable maximum exposure" of humans via ingestion, contact and inhalation and on the conservative assumption that the site will be used for residential purposes The rules allow "industrial" soil standards to be used instead of residential standards, but only in a limited number of "large industrial areas," and the PLP must overcome a significant bias in favor of residential standards.[189] To apply industrial cleanup standards for soil, a PLP must show that (1) the site is zoned or designated (e.g., by comprehensive plan) for industrial/commercial use in an area where adjacent and nearby properties are similarly used and/or designated, (2) future use of the site is expected to be commercial/ industrial based on existing uses, zoning, comprehensive plans and adjacent uses; and (3) appropriate institutional controls will be put in place, such as fencing or deed restrictions.[190] Cleanup levels for other nonresidential areas, such as recreation and agricultural areas, are to be determined on a case-by-case basis.

MTCA air quality levels assume a residential use of the property, unless it can be shown that industrial standards are appropriate using the same factors as for soil cleanups. Determinations of Method A, B or C levels follow essentially the same methodology described above for other media.[191]

Identifying "Points of Compliance"

"Points of compliance" are the geographic points at a site where cleanup levels must be met. In many instances, cleanup levels must be met throughout the site. In some cleanups, however, the point of compliance may be set at a facility boundary or other location at the site. This allows for some degree of natural attenuation. Establishment of such a "conditional point of compliance" can significantly reduce the cost of a remedy, while still providing protection of human health and the environment.[192]

The ground water point of compliance presumptively includes the entire saturated zone that is or could potentially be affected by site contamination. If Ecology allows hazardous substances to remain on-site, a conditional point of compliance may be established at the property boundary.

The surface water point of compliance is set presumptively where substances are released into the surface water. The compliance point for surface releases may in some cases be measured at the edge of an Ecology-approved mixing zone. No mixing zone is allowed in determining releases from ground water to surface water.

For soil cleanups where ingestion and contact are the pathways of concern, the point of compliance is from ground surface to a depth of fifteen feet. The point of compliance for air is presumed to be ambient air throughout the site, except for industrial sites, at which Ecology may consider a point at the site boundary.

Waiver of Cleanup Standards

There are limited circumstances under which Ecology may agree to waive strict compliance with otherwise applicable MTCA cleanup standards. The principal case is where it is not technically possible to achieve a particular numeric or health-based standard. For example, some standards for ground water cleanups may be below detection limits or may be impossible to attain due to physical and chemical characteristics of the substances, soil or ground water regime. Such "technical impossibility," however, must be based on true physical and engineering limitations, or where costs of reduction of risk by a preferred technology are "substantial and disproportionate" to the human health or environmental benefits that might be gained.

Selecting a Cleanup Remedy

The MTCA rules set out a "hierarchy" of preferred cleanup technologies, with a clear preference for technologies that minimize the amount of untreated hazardous substances remaining at the property and can be conducted on site. In descending order, the preference is for: (1) reuse or recycling; (2) destruction or detoxification (e.g., incineration); (3) separation or volume reduction, followed by reuse, recycling, destruction or detoxification of the remaining material; (4) immobilization of hazardous substances (e.g., mixing contaminated soils with concrete); (5) on-site or off-site disposal at a permitted facility (e.g., a RCRA landfill); (6) isolation or containment (e.g., capping, slurry walls); and (7) institutional controls (e.g., fencing) and monitoring.[193] Combinations of technologies may be used at a particular site for different substances and different media. The actual selection process is always site-specific.

Ecology has several "expectations" for cleanup actions recognizing that "there may be sites where these expectations are not appropriate." Ecology "expects" that: (1) treatment (as opposed to containment) will be used whenever practicable, especially with high-concentration and liquid wastes; (2) hazardous substances will be destroyed, detoxified or removed at sites containing small volumes of regulated material; (3) containment or other "engineering controls" will be used for large volumes of low-level hazardous substances where treatment is impracticable; (4) "institutional controls" (physical and legal limitations on future site use) will be used in conjunction with "engineering controls" to prevent or limit exposure and protect remedies in certain cases; (5) ground water will be returned to "beneficial uses" when practicable and within a reasonable time frame; (6) precipitation and runoff will be controlled to prevent further spread of contamination; and (7) hazardous substances left on site will be consolidated to the maximum extent practicable.

PLPs have considerable latitude to select cleanup remedies that control costs, so long as the proposed remedy meets the threshold requirement of achieving cleanup standards identified for the site.

Cleanup Cost Considerations

The MTCA rules recognize that permanent solutions will not be practicable in every case. The rules require only that permanent solutions be used "to the maximum extent practicable." Factors considered in this decision include whether a permanent remedy is technically possible and whether it can be implemented given administrative demands, scheduling, size and complexity.[194]

At least to some extent, cost of the cleanup remedy is also considered. The rules recognize that marginal gains in protectiveness may not warrant significant additional expenditures on remediation. The burden of justifying the use of a lower cost remedy that meets the protectiveness and other threshold criteria for cleanup falls on the PLPs. To ensure a lower cost remedy at a site, it must be demonstrated that the proposed remedy meets all cleanup standards and that the incremental cost of the preferred alternative is "substantial and disproportionate" to any additional environmental benefit. For example, the cost of incinerating contaminated soil may not be justified when compared to *in situ* treatment or encapsulation, and incineration may pose additional risks to human health or the environment.

Ecology disfavors lengthy remedies, especially "attenuation," dilution or natural processes. One of the "threshold" requirements is that the remedy selected provide a "reasonable" restoration time frame for both soil and ground water cleanups. A longer restoration time may be accepted, however, if a higher preference technology is used (e.g., on-site bioremediation as opposed to offsite transport to a landfill). Moreover, where off-site sources would recontaminate a site, cleanup below area background levels may be delayed until the off-site sources are controlled.

General Provisions

Property Access

MTCA provides Ecology with a right of access to any public or private real property. This right is constrained by both state and federal constitutional considerations. The MTCA rules establish reasonable procedures for written and personal notification to property owners and occupants, although in the event of an emergency, only limited notice is required.[195] Persons who enter into orders or consent decrees are required effectively to waive any objections to allowing access, but Ecology must be careful not to disrupt ongoing business or other operations at a site while exercising its right of access.[196] If access is refused, Ecology must use available state or federal authorities and if necessary, obtain a warrant.[197] Ecology agrees to make reasonable efforts to provide access to property and documents for non-owner PLPs. Ecology has also developed a policy governing its use of its authority to force access to property.[198]

As under the federal system, Ecology agrees to release to PLPs and others information it obtains. It also agrees to split any samples it takes as long as this will not interfere with the agency's activities.[199]

Worker Safety and Health

MTCA rules[200] recite state and federal worker health and safety requirements that must be complied with during remedial actions, including the Occupational Safety and Health Act[201] and the Washington Industrial Safety and Health Act.[202] This section also incorporates the requirements of Ch. 49.17 RCW as applicable to any health and safety plan submitted under this chapter.[203]

Sampling and Analysis Plans

Except for emergency actions, Ecology requires preparation of a sampling and analysis plan for all investigation and remedial activities, although it is willing to allow the detail to vary depending on the scope and purpose of the activity. Plans prepared under an order or decree must be reviewed and approved by Ecology.[204] The plan must include procedures that ensure that the quality of the data collected is sufficient to support planning, design and implementation.[205]

Laboratory Analysis Procedures

Ecology has adopted commonly used sampling and analytical guides developed by EPA and national standard-setting bodies. These cover both field and statistical techniques and laboratory methodologies.[206]

General Submittal Requirements

WAC 173-340-840 lays out general requirements for submittal of documents to Ecology. Close attention to these requirements will ensure that documents will be accepted and reviewed in the shortest possible time, an important consideration given the compressed time period in which cleanup negotiations must be concluded under the rules.

This section covers "all reports, plans, specifications, and similar information" submitted to Ecology under these rules. The submission must include: (1) a cover letter describing the submittal and identifying the desired response; (2) at least three copies, unless Ecology requires more; (3) any engineering work must be under the seal of a Washington professional engineer, and (4) compliance with specifications for visual documents such as maps and photographs, including legibility, maximum size, consistency of scale, labeling and similar clarity requirements.[207]

Recordkeeping Requirements

Ecology requires that all remedial actions, including independent actions, be carefully documented and that all records must be retained for at least ten years after completion of the action. The PLP must retain the records, unless Ecology claims them.[208]

Endangerment

Ecology retains the authority to halt any remedial action for as long as is necessary to abate any threat to human health or the environment created by that activity.[209]

NOTES

[1] RCW §70.105D.

[2] 42 USC. §§9601 et seq.; *Burlington Northern R. Co. v. Time Oil Co.*, 738 F. Supp. (WD WA 1990)(CERCLA does not preempt MTCA).

[3] *City of Seattle (Seattle City Light) v. Washington State Dept. of Transp.*, 98 Wn. App. 165 (1999).

[4] RCW §70.105D.010(1).

[5] WAC 173-340.

[6] WAC 173-340-700 to -760.

[7] See *Olds-Olympic, Inc. v. Commercial Union Ins. Co.*, 129 Wn. 2d 464 (1996); *Snokist Growers v. Washington Ins. Guar. Assn.*, 83 Wn. App. 496 (1996).

[8] RCW §70.105D.090; *Weyerhauser Co. v. Commercial Union Fire Ins. Co.*, 142 Wn. 2d 654 (2000); *Bird-Johnson v. Dana Corp.*, 119 Wn. 2d 452 (1992). Liability may also be contractually allocated. *PacifiCorp Environmental Remediation co. v. Washington State Dept. of Transp.*, 162 Wn. App. 627 (2011).

[9] RCW §70.105D.080; *William G. Hulbert, Jr. and Clare Mumford Hulbert Revocable Living Trust v. Port of Everett*, 159 Wn. App. 389 (2011) *Martin v. Johnson*, 141 Wn. App. 611 (2007).

[10] RCW §70.105D.090.

[11] RCW §70.105D.010(2); WAC 173-340-100.

[12] *See* WAC 173-340-200 for other relevant definitions.

[13] RCW §70.105D.020(16).

[14] *Cf.* CERCLA, where there is no separate definition for the equivalent "potentially responsible party" or PRP, and no notice provision or requirement for an opportunity to comment. As many PRPs and PLPs can attest, there often is simply no basis for their inclusion and little or no opportunity to escape the designation once it is attached by EPA.

[15] RCW §70.105D.020(14). Note that other portions of the statute draw clear distinctions between legal and natural persons, e.g., RCW §70.105D.040(3)(c), exempting from liability certain natural persons using hazardous substances for personal or domestic purposes around a dwelling or accessory structure. There is a question as to whether Ecology can assert its authority over Tribal lands. *See, e.g., Snohomish County v. Tulalip Tribes, et al.*, 70 Wn. 2d 668 (1967).

[16] RCW §70.195D.020(12; WAC 173-340-200. See also *City of Moses Lake v. US*, 458 F. Supp. 2d 1198 (ED WA 2006); *Taliesen Corp. v. Razore Land Co.*, 135 Wn. App. 106 (2006).

[17] RCW §70.105D.020(6). See also *Harbor Steps Ltd. Partnership v. Seattle Technical Finishing, Inc.*, 93 Wn. App. 792, *review den.*, 138 Wn. 2d 1005 (1999). The federal exemption for involuntary governmental ownership, and hence liability, is limited to situations in which the property is acquired through an exercise of the power of the sovereign. This may not protect governmental units that acquire property through gift or other noncompulsory means, although EPA's interpretations may broaden this protection.

[18] RCW §70.105D.020(4).

[19] See the related provision in the defenses to liability set forth at RCW §70.105D.040(3)(c).

[20] RCW §70.105D.020(20). Note the significant departure from the federal definition in 42 U.S.C. §9601(22), which exempts workplace exposures, engine exhaust or releases of nuclear materials. *See also Modern Sewer Corp. v. Nelson Distributing, Inc.*, 125 Wn. App. 564 (2005); *PacifiCorp Environmental Remediation Co. v. Washington State Dept. of Transportation*, 162 Wn. App. 627 (2011).

[21] RCW §70.105D.

[22] RCW §70.105D.020(7). See also *City of Seattle v. State Dept. of Transportation*, 98 Wn. App. 165 (1999).

²³ Compare 42 USC §9601(14):

> The term does not include petroleum, including crude oil or any fraction thereof which is not otherwise specifically listed or designated as a hazardous substance under [other federal statutes], and the term does not include natural gas, natural gas liquids, liquified natural gas, or synthetic gas usable for fuel (or mixtures of natural gas and such synthetic gas).

See also *Wilshire Westwood Assoc., et al. v. Atlantic Richfield Co., et al.*, 881 F. 2d 801 (9th Cir. 1989).

²⁴ RCW §70.105D.020(11). This approach differs markedly from the federal scheme, which creates many levels of cleanup activities, including statutory distinctions between "removal" and "remedial" actions, which are further subdivided in the National Contingency Plan (NCP). Removals are relatively short-term actions, limited both in time and in amount of expenditures allowed without special waivers. 42 USC §§9601(23) and 9604(c)(1). Remedial actions are only undertaken at sites that are listed on the NPL, and may include "operable units," interim remedial measures and other activities consistent with a permanent remedy. 42 USC §§9601(24) and 9604(a). Unlike CERCLA, MTCA does not impose any matching fund requirement on political subdivisions of the state. See 42 USC §9604(c)(3).

²⁵ CERCLA makes relatively clear provisions for recovery of interest on response costs, 42 USC §9607(a)(4), and attorneys' fees as governmental response costs; judicial consensus supports this conclusion. See *United States v. NEPACCO*, 579 F. Supp. 823 (WD Mo. 1984); *United States v. SCRDI*, 653 F. Supp. 984 (D SC 1984). MTCA contains an express provision for recovery of attorneys' fees in an action for contribution under RCW §70.105D.080. *Martin v. Johnson*, 141 Wn. App. 611 (2007); *Mayer v. City of Seattle*, 102 Wn. App. 66 (2000), rev. den. 142 Wn.2d 1029; *Louisiana-Pacific Corp. v. Asarco Inc.*, 131 Wn. 2d 587 (1997); *Boeing Co. v. Aetna Cas. And Sur. Co.*, 113 Wn. 2d 869 (1990).

²⁶ RCW §70.105D.020(19).

²⁷ RCW §70.105D.020(5).

²⁸ RCW §70.105D.030(l)(a).

²⁹ RCW §70.105D.030(1)(b). CERCLA's more complicated statutory structure regulates in greater detail the conduct of cleanups and use of administrative orders or judicial actions. See 42 USC §§9604, 9606 and 9607. CERCLA provides little incentive to EPA to cooperate with PRPs in the cleanup process or share information or expertise with them. To date, it appears that Ecology, perhaps as a result of significant resource limitations as well as in response to CERCLA's policies, is taking a much more cooperative tack. A considerable number of cleanups are being undertaken by PLPs as "voluntary" actions, as discussed below.

³⁰ RCW §70.105D.030(1)(j).

³¹ Available at http://www.ecy.wa.gov/programs/tcp/policies/pol_main.html.

³² Ecology's Policy 340 provides details on setting site and resource priorities.

³³ RCW §70.105D.030(3).

³⁴ RCW §70.105D.040. See also *Unigard Ins. Co. v. Leven*, 97 Wn. App. 417 (1999), rev. den. (2000); *Pedersen's Fryer Farms, Inc. v. Transamerica Ins. Co.*, 83 Wn. App. 432 (1996), rev. den., 131 Wn.2d 1010 (1997).

³⁵ RCW §70.105D.040(1)(a) and (b). Given the breadth of the "release" definition, a defense that the hazardous substance had already escaped may not stand. Compare 42 USC §9607(a)(1) and (2).

³⁶ RCW §70.105D.040(1)(c).

³⁷ RCW §70.105D.040(1)(d). The CERCLA liability formulation is stricter in the case of transporters than MTCA's, as no exceptions are provided.

³⁸ RCW §70.105D.040(1)(e).

³⁹ RCW §70.105D.040(2).

40 RCW §70.105D.040(3). MTCA takes a different approach than § 9607(b) of CERCLA, which provides:

> There shall be no liability under subsection (a) of this section for a person otherwise liable who can establish by a preponderance of the evidence that the release or threat of release of a hazardous substance and the damages resulting therefrom were caused solely by:
> (1) an act of God;
> (2) an act of war;
> (3) an act or omission of a third party other than an employee or agent of the defendant.

To escape liability under CERCLA, a PRP must establish that it acted with "due care," while the MTCA recites an "utmost care" standard. *Id.* The drafters of MTCA certainly were aware of the language of the CERCLA liability provisions, and it remains to be seen what the courts will make of the difference.

41 *Bird-Johnson v. Dana Corp.*, 119 Wn .2d 452 (1992).

42 See RCW §70.105D.080. *See also Panorama Village Condo. Owners Assn. Bd. Of Dirs. v. Allstate ins. Co.*, 144 Wn. 2d 130 (2001); *Louisiana-Pacific Corp. v. Asarco*, 131 Wn. 2d 587 (1997); *City of Seattle v. Washington State DOT*, 107 Wn. App. 236 (2001); *Mayer v. City of Seattle*, 102 Wn. App. 66 (2000); *Dash Point Village Assoc. v. Exxon Corp.*, 86 Wn. App. 596 (1997).

43 *See, e.g., Car Wash Enterprises, Inc. v. Kampanos*, 74 Wn. App. 537 (1994).

44 *See, e.g., Cadillac Fairview v. Dow Chemical Co.*, 840 F. 2d 691 (9th Cir. 1988) (party seeking recovery of response costs must prove they were necessary and incurred in a manner consistent with the National Contingency Plan). 42 USC §9607(a)(4)(B).

45 RCW §70.105D.097.

46 RCW §4.22.040.

47 RCW §64.12.020.

48 RCW §70.105D.040(3)(b)(i). The court is obliged to consider the special knowledge or experience of the purchaser, whether the price is below "clean" market value, common or readily ascertainable information about the property, whether the contamination is obvious or likely, and whether the problem could be detected by appropriate inspection.

49 RCW §§70.105D.040(3)(c) and (d).

50 MTCA's use of present tense verbs in subsections (3)(c) and (3)(d) of RCW §70.105D.040 raises the question whether courts will treat these defenses as prospective only. Many releases otherwise within the defenses have already occurred, and liability arguably would attach to users and residents in those cases regardless of the defense. The regulations contain a section on "usage," WAC 173-340-210, which covers a number of language construction points but does not address this issue.

51 RCW §70.105D.040(4)(a) through (d). *See* 42 USC §9622.

52 Regulations governing such orders are in WAC 173-340-530.

53 Regulations governing enforcement orders are in WAC 173-340-540.

54 See RCW §70.105D.040(4)(b) and RCW §§70.105D.050(1), (3) and (4).

55 RCW §70.105D.040(4).

56 RCW §70.105D.040(4)(a).

57 *Id.*

58 RCW §70.105D.040(4)(c).

59 RCW §70.105D.040(4)(d).

60 RCW §70.105D.040(6).

[61] RCW §70.105D.050(1).

[62] RCW §70.105D.050(1)(a) and (b). The parallel CERCLA section, 42 USC §9607(c)(3), allows not only recovery of treble punitive damages, but remedial costs as well. It would appear that the fundamental authority of Ecology to recover for the Toxics Control Account all of its remedial costs is also in addition to this penalty provision. See RCW §70.105D.050(3).

[63] RCW §70.105D.050(2). *See* the parallel provision contained in 42 USC §9606(b)(2), which also allows recovery of interest at the Superfund rate on such expenditures. While MTCA does not mention recovery of interest, the regulations provide for it. See WAC 173-340-550(4).

[64] The parallel CERCLA provision is 42 USC §9659, which also provides for costs and fees and which expressly permits such actions in accordance with 42 USC §9613(h) (i.e, subject to the limits on pre-enforcement review). Arguably, a citizen's suit also may be brought at any time under MTCA, assuming proper notice. Venue is proper either in Thurston County or in the county where the release or threat exists.

[65] RCW §70.105D.060. This provision tracks CERCLA's judicial review requirements, embodied in 42 USC §9613(h).

[66] RCW §70.105D.070(1) and (2).

[67] See 42 USC §9604(c)(3).

[68] RCW §70.105D.070(2)(b)(xi). *Cf.* CERCLA's mixed funding provisions at 42 USC §§9622(b)(1) through (4).

[69] WAC 173-340-130.

[70] WAC 173-340-120, 173-340-300, and 173-340-450.

[71] WAC 173-340-300(2).

[72] WAC 173-340-300(3).

[73] 42 USC §9603.

[74] WAC 173-340-300(6).

[75] WAC 173-340-300(2)(a).

[76] WAC 173-340-300(4) and (5). See also RCW §70.105D.040(4).

[77] WAC 173-340-310.

[78] Ecology's Policy 330A expands on and covers the site listing process.

[79] WAC 173-340-310(1).

[80] WAC 173 340-310(2).

[81] WAC 173-340-310(5). A proper independent action may halt the regulatory process at this point if no threat exists when the initial investigation is done.

[82] WAC 173-340-310(6).

[83] WAC 173-340-500(1).

[84] WAC 173 340-500(6).

[85] WAC 173 340-320(1).

[86] WAC 173-340-320(2) and (3). As is the case with many aspects of hazardous substances cleanups, PLPs should carefully consider performing the hazard assessment if at all possible, to control costs and have some effect on the potentially overbroad and possibly overly pessimistic scope and conclusions of an Ecology assessment. Care should be taken to obtain binding concurrence from Ecology and other agencies on the scope and coverage of the assessment.

[87] WAC 173 340-320(4).

[88] WAC 173-340-320(4)(a) through (h).

89 WAC 173-340-320(5) and (6).

90 This list is analogous to the CERCLA National Priorities List established under 42 USC §9605(a)(8) and 40 CFR 300, appendix B.

91 WAC 173-340-330(1).

92 Ecology's Policy 330A covers the listing process and prioritization of sites.

93 WAC 173-340-330(3).

94 WAC 173-340-330(4).

95 WAC 173-340-330(6). De-listing requires public notice and comment, per WAC 173-340-330(10), so satisfying Ecology will likely require proof beyond a reasonable doubt.

96 Ecology has developed an approach to the process of "de-listing" MTCA sties. *See* Policy 330B.

97 WAC 173-340-340. Ecology has indicated its ability to review and oversee cleanups of sites is limited by available resources. As a result, sites with WARM scores of 3 or more are unlikely to receive concentrated Ecology attention in the near term. These sites remain on the list, however, and may be re-ranked to higher or lower scores on receipt of more information. Completion of an effective independent cleanup may lead to a lower ranking and avoid Ecology involvement.

98 WAC 173-340-120, 173-340-350.

99 There is no guidance on how much documentation is "sufficient;" this judgment call is informed by the desire of the site manager for a comfortable level of information to support a remedial action approach, and the need to inform the public on site conditions and the possible remedies.

100 WAC 173-340-350(7)(c). The parallel federal requirements are in 40 CFR 300.430.

101 WAC 173-340-350(8).

102 WAC 173-340-355.

103 WAC 173-340-120; 173-340-360(2).

104 WAC 173-340-360. These same preferences are incorporated into CERCLA. *See* 42 USC §9621(b)(1).

105 WAC 173-340-380.

106 WAC 173-340-400(1).

107 WAC 173-340-400(2). Note that final cleanups can only be performed under a unilateral order or consent decree. See WAC 173-340-530(1).

108 WAC 173-340-400(3).

109 WAC 173-340-400(4).

110 WAC 173-340-400(4)(a).

111 WAC 173-340-400(4)(b).

112 WAC 173-340-400(4)(c).

113 WAC 173-340-400(6).

114 WAC 173-340-400(5).

115 RCW §70.105D.090; 42 USC §9621(e). An important caveat is that the state reserves the right to require full permitting where failure to do so might jeopardize its approval to administer any federal laws under delegations from EPA or other agencies.

116 WAC 173-340-400(6)(b).

117 WAC 173-340-400(7) and (8).

118 WAC 173-340-400(9).

119 WAC 173-340-700, 173-340-900.

120 WAC 173-340-410.

121 WAC 173-340-410.

122 WAC 173-340-420.

123 WAC 173-340-430(1)(a) through (c). The interim action concept under these rules appears to blend several of the immediate response, emergency and operable unit concepts provided for in the federal NCP.

124 Note that there is no separate section in the rules dealing with emergency actions, and several references within this section imply that emergency actions are a subset of interim actions. *See* WAC 173-340-430(3).

125 WAC 173-340-430(2)(a).

126 WAC 173-340-430(3).

127 WAC 173-340-430(4).

128 WAC 173-340-430(4)(b).

129 WAC 173-340-430(4)(c).

130 WAC 173-340-430(7).

131 WAC 173-340-500(1).

132 WAC 173-340-500(2).

133 WAC 173-340-500(4).

134 WAC 173-340-500(5). If a PLP wants to get on with a necessary cleanup of an acknowledged release, this waiver should be considered. Note that accepting PLP status does not entail an admission of liability for purposes of other laws or actions.

135 WAC 173-340-500(6). It is often in the best interest of a PLP, and in the interest of fairness, to ensure that all PLPs at a site are given notice and invited to participate. It is generally advisable to provide as much assistance and information as possible to Ecology when requesting that additional PLPs be notified (including liability information and a list of names and addresses in an easily usable form).

136 WAC 173-340-510(1).

137 *Id.*

138 WAC 173-340-510(2).

139 WAC 173-340-520(3). Again, sites ranking three or below on the WARM scale will probably not receive significant Ecology attention. However, Ecology has initiated a program under which a PLP or group can actually fund an Ecology staff position dedicated to that entity's sites. Companies and units of government with large and complex sites, or with several sites to address, may find it beneficial to fund a position via the required consent decree, to obtain Ecology involvement considerably earlier than would otherwise occur. The Ecology staff of course remains responsible to apply Ecology's regulations and works from the perspective of the Agency. The process is spelled out in Ecology's Policy 500C. The annual cost is about $100,000. As of this writing, there are at least five such agreements in place.

140 WAC 173-340-510(4). Note, however, that Ecology may be obliged to honor stays of enforcement where it has entered into agreed orders under WAC 173-340-520(1)(a)(i) and WAC 173-340-530(4).

141 WAC 173-340-510(5). Since this provision is directed only to PLPs, it seems to be an open question whether non-PLPs, e.g., adjacent property owners whose land is threatened by a release but not yet been directed affected, can take actions to protect their property and interests at this point in the process.

142 WAC 173-340-510(5).

¹⁴³ As should be clear from the detail demanded in this initial submission, the detailed proposal for cleanup and much of the design and study work should probably be done before the request for negotiations is sent. Given the short time period for negotiations before enforcement action may begin, with the increased transaction costs that will then ensue, the most complete submission possible should be made at the beginning. It will be a matter of judgment when sufficient information is available, and if opportunities present themselves to have informal discussions with Ecology staff to determine the adequacy of the information and the submittal, they should be taken.

¹⁴⁴ WAC 173-340-520(1)(a).

¹⁴⁵ WAC 173-340-520(l)(b).

¹⁴⁶ WAC 173-340-520(1)(e).

¹⁴⁷ WAC 173-340-520(1)(e).

¹⁴⁸ *Id.*

¹⁴⁹ WAC 173-340-520(l)(g).

¹⁵⁰ WAC 173-340-520(1)(k).

¹⁵¹ WAC 173-340-520(1)(l).

¹⁵² WAC 173-340-520(2).

¹⁵³ WAC 173-340-520(2)(c).

¹⁵⁴ WAC 173-340-520(2)(f).

¹⁵⁵ WAC 173-340-520(3).

¹⁵⁶ WAC 173-340 530(1).

¹⁵⁷ WAC 173-340-530(2)(a).

¹⁵⁸ WAC 173-340-530(2)(c) and (d). Again, to ensure acceptance of a proposal, it is probably advisable to err on the side of inclusiveness in submitting information with the request, and to discuss the request with Ecology before submitting it.

¹⁵⁹ WAC 173-340-530(3).

¹⁶⁰ WAC 173-340-530(5).

¹⁶¹ WAC 173-340-530(6).

¹⁶² WAC 173-340-530(7).

¹⁶³ WAC 173-340-530(8).

¹⁶⁴ WAC 173-340-540.

¹⁶⁵ WAC 173-340-550(1) through (4).

¹⁶⁶ RCW §70.105D.040(5); WAC 173-340-520; Department of Ecology Interim Policy 520A.

¹⁶⁷ *Id.*

¹⁶⁸ WAC 173-240-600(1).

¹⁶⁹ WAC 173 340-600(2).

¹⁷⁰ WAC 173-340-600(3). Ecology can also use other methods, including press releases, fact sheets, publications, personal contact by Ecology employees, signs at the facility and notice in the site register. WAC 173-340-600(5).

¹⁷¹ WAC 173-340-600(4)(g)(5).

¹⁷² WAC 173-340-600(9)(g).

¹⁷³ WAC 173 340-600(15).

¹⁷⁴ WAC 173-340-600(10) through (14).

[175] This register goes well beyond EPA's organized publications of site information, which are limited to the CERCLIS data base, accessible through the regional offices and the National Priorities List published in Appendix B to 40 CFR 300.

[176] WAC 173-340-600(7).

[177] WAC 173-340-610.

[178] WAC 173-340-700.

[179] *Id.*

[180] *See, e.g.,* WAC 173-340-706(2)(c)(ii).

[181] WAC 173-340-704; 173-340-720(1)(a).

[182] For example, WAC 173-340-720(2) sets out Method A cleanup levels for a limited range of contaminants in ground water. The cautions in the footnotes to this list indicate that Method A levels are appropriate only for "routine" cleanup actions. The description of such "routine" actions in WAC 173-340-130(7) seems to indicate, however, that Ecology presumes that ground water cleanups cannot be "routine."

[183] WAC 173-340-705.

[184] WAC 173-340-706.

[185] WAC 173-340-720 through 750.

[186] WAC 173-204.

[187] WAC 173-340-720.

[188] WAC 173-340-730.

[189] WAC 173-340-740. The exposure scenario is in fact based on some extremely conservative assumptions. It is worth noting that EPA, with considerably longer experience in conducting risk assessments, is now considering ways to develop more realistic assumptions. Ecology has on occasion been willing to recognize less stringent assumptions in reviewing cleanup proposals.

[190] WAC 173-340-745.

[191] WAC 173-340-750.

[192] *See, e.g.,* WAC 173-340-720(8).

[193] WAC 173-340-360(4)(a).

[194] WAC 173-340-360(4).

[195] WAC 173-340-800(1) and (6). The parallel federal authority is contained in 42 USC §9604(e).

[196] WAC 173 340-800(2) and (4).

[197] WAC 173-340-800(7). Note, however, that obstructing access is usually a futile act, since the police power of the state generally overrides private interests in property where a public danger may exist, and Ecology need only establish "administrative probable cause" under *Marshall v. Barlows*, 436 US 307 (1978), to obtain a warrant. All that refusal can accomplish, where there is a reasonable factual basis for Ecology's concern' is increased transaction costs and a short delay in obtaining access.

[198] *See* Policy 800A. The related Policy 800B spells out guidelines for Ecology when gaining access to documents and other materials on a site.

[199] WAC 173-340-800(9) and (10).

[200] WAC 173-340-810.

[201] 29 USC §§651 *et seq.*

[202] RCW §49.17.

[203] WAC 173 340-820(2).

[204] WAC 173-340-820(1).
[205] WAC 173-340-820(2).
[206] WAC 173-340-830.
[207] WAC 173-340-840.
[208] WAC 173-340-850.
[209] WAC 173-340-860.

CHAPTER 11

Oil Spill Regulation and Natural Resource Damages

INTRODUCTION

The federal government has primary responsibility for directing oil spill responses under the Federal Water Pollution Control Act (commonly known as the "Clean Water Act") and the federal Oil Pollution Act ("OPA").[1] In coastal marine areas (including Puget Sound and the Columbia River up to Pasco), the US Coast Guard directs oil spill response. EPA directs responses for all inland areas.[2] The OPA expressly allows states to impose additional and more stringent requirements although some additional requirements may still be preempted.[3] If natural resources are damaged by the spill, the federal National Oceanic & Atmospheric Administration ("NOAA") and the federal Department of Interior are charged with assessing the damage and directing restoration.

Much of Washington's regulatory scheme governing oil spills and natural resource damages was enacted contemporaneously with three separate spills. In 1985, the ARCO Anchorage ran aground in Port Angeles Harbor, Washington, spilling 239,000 gallons of oil. Just before Christmas in 1988, the barge *Nestucca* and a tug collided in heavy seas off of Grays Harbor, Washington, spilling 231,000 gallons of bunker oil. Finally, in 1989 Exxon Valdez ran aground in Prince William Sound, Alaska, spilling over ten million gallons of Prudhoe Bay crude oil along one of the most scenic sections of the Alaska coastline.

Following these spills, Washington passed the Transport of Petroleum Products—Financial Responsibility Act, which requires vessel owners to demonstrate financial responsibility covering potential liability to the state for oil spill response.[4] In 1990, the legislature passed significant amendments to the state Water Pollution Control Act,[5] imposing additional liability for oil discharges and requiring facility and vessel owners and operators to develop contingency plans for the containment and cleanup of oil spills. Some sections of the Water Pollution Control Act were recodified in 1991 into the Oil and Hazardous Substance Spill Prevention and Response Act.[6] In 1991, the legislature also enacted the Vessel Oil Spill Prevention and Response Act.[7] Together, these acts impose planning and financial responsibility requirements on many businesses not previously subject to oil spill regulation, and they establish standards for facility operation.

OIL SPILL REGULATION

Ecology is the lead state agency for oil spill responses in Washington under the direction of the US Coast Guard or EPA.[8] It does so through four different mechanisms: (1) financial responsibility requirements; (2) contingency and prevention planning requirements; (3) facility operation standards; and (4) and oil spill liability provisions.[9] Several smaller agencies also have a planning or educational role in the regulatory framework.[10]

Financial Responsibility Requirements

The state Transport of Petroleum Products—Financial Responsibility Act[11] (Oil Transport Act) establishes financial responsibility requirements for (1) barges that transport hazardous substances in bulk as cargo using any port or place in the state or the navigable waters of the state; (2) tank vessels carrying oil as cargo in bulk; (3) cargo or passenger vessels that carry oil as fuel; (4) fishing vessels;[12] and (5) onshore and offshore facilities.[13] So far Ecology has not elected to enforce its authority over facilities.

These five categories are defined as follows: (1) a "barge" is a vessel that is not self-propelled; (2) "tank vessel" is a ship that is constructed or adapted to carry, or that carries, oil in bulk as cargo or cargo residue; (3) a "cargo vessel" is "a self-propelled ship in commerce, other than a tank vessel, fishing vessel, or a passenger vessel, of three hundred or more gross tons,"[14] while a "passenger vessel" is "a ship of greater than three hundred or more gross tons with a fuel capacity of at least six thousand gallons carrying passengers for compensation;" and (4) a "fishing vessel" is a "self-propelled commercial vessel of three hundred or more gross tons that is used for catching or processing fish." An "facility" is defined as follows:

> any structure, group of structures, equipment, pipeline or device, other than a vessel, located on or near the navigable waters of the state that transfers oil in bulk to or from any vessel with an oil carrying capacity over two hundred fifty barrels or pipeline, that is used for producing, storing, handling, transferring, processing or transporting oil in bulk.[15]

An onshore facility is a facility, "any part of which is located in, on, or under any land of the state, other than submerged land, that because of its location, could reasonably be expected to cause substantial harm to the environment by discharging oil into or on the navigable waters of the state or the adjoining shorelines."[16] An offshore facility is any-facility "located in, on, or under any of the navigable waters of the state, but does not include a facility any part of which is located in, on, or under any land of the state, other than submerged land.[17]

Vessels or facilities can satisfy the financial responsibility requirements using one of four mechanisms: (1) insurance, (2) surety bonds; (3) qualification as a self-insurer; or (4) other evidence of financial responsibility.[18]

For covered vessels, the financial assurance documents must be on file twenty-four hours before the vessel enters the state's navigable waters and a copy must be kept on the vessel itself.[19]

Penalties for Failure to Meet Financial Responsibility Requirements

Several acts sanction the failure to meet financial responsibility requirements. Under the Vessel Oil Spill Prevention and Response Act (Vessel Spill Prevention Act), it is unlawful to operate a covered vessel[20] on state waters or in the state without complying with the financial responsibility requirements of the Oil Transport Act[21] and the federal OPA.[22] The first violation is a gross misdemeanor; a subsequent violation is a Class C felony.[23] Further, civil penalties of up to one hundred thousand dollars may also be assessed.[24] The Oil and Hazardous Substance Spill Prevention and Response Act provides similar penalties for facilities that fail to comply with financial responsibility requirements.[25]

Ecology must deny entry into the waters of the state to a covered vessel not in compliance.[26] Vessel owners or operators who do not meet the financial responsibility requirements are prohibited from operating the barge or vessel on state waters until such requirements are met.[27] Ecology must report violators to the U.S. Coast Guard. In addition, the Spill Prevention Act makes it unlawful for a covered vessel to transfer oil to a facility that is not in compliance with the Oil Transport Act and the OPA. A civil penalty of up to $100,000 may be assessed against the owner or operator of a vessel who violates this provision.[28] Each day is a separate violation.

Ecology can seek suspension of a facility's privilege of operating in the state if a vessel does not satisfy the financial responsibility requirements.[29] Similarly, Ecology may seek to suspend the business license and impose civil penalties of up to $100,000 upon facility owners or operators who accept cargo or passengers from a covered vessel that is not in compliance with financial responsibility requirements.[30]

Contingency Planning Requirements

The Oil and Hazardous Substance Spill Prevention and Response Act (Oil Spill Response Act) directed Ecology to prepare and annually update a Statewide Master Oil and Hazardous Substance Spill Contingency Plan.[31]

A number of other state entities are involved in spill response activities. The Washington Wildlife Rescue Coalition coordinates the rescue and rehabilitation of injured or endangered wildlife.[32] The Washington State Maritime Commission established an "oil spill first response system."[33] This system provides a mandatory emergency response network for vessels, and provides immediate response for the first twenty-four hours after an oil spill.

Another primary component of the contingency planning process is the individual facility or vessel plan. The Oil Spill Response Act and Vessel Spill Prevention Act require facilities and covered vessels, respectively, to develop contingency plans for the containment and cleanup of oil spills and for the protection of natural resources and public and private property from such spills.[34] The plans are to cover spills into "waters of the state," which are defined broadly in both Acts to include:

> lakes, rivers, ponds, streams, inland waters, underground water, salt waters, estuaries, tidal flats, beaches and lands adjoining the seacoast of the state, sewers, and all other surface waters and watercourses.[35]

Parties Subject to the Contingency Planning Requirements: Facilities and Covered Vessels

Contingency plans must be developed for all onshore and offshore facilities and covered vessels[36] and must include plans for spill notification, response organization, containment and recovery procedures, diagrams of the facility or vessel, training programs, and disposition of recovered oil.[37] The standard for reviewing the adequacy of a contingency plan is whether the vessel or facility is capable of removing the oil and minimizing environmental damage resulting from a "worst case spill," defined as "a spill of the entire cargo and fuel of the vessel complicated by adverse weather conditions."[38] Covered vessels include: (1) tank vessels that are constructed or adapted to carry oil in bulk as cargo or cargo residue and operates in waters of the state or transfers oil in a port or place subject to Washington state jurisdiction; and (2) cargo vessels and passenger vessels of 300 or more gross tons.[39]

Contingency plans for onshore and offshore facilities must be submitted to Ecology by either the owner or operator or a response contractor that meets Ecology's standards.[40] In the case of an onshore or offshore facility, the owner and operator are simply those persons owning and operating the facility. For an abandoned vessel or onshore or offshore facility, the owner is the person who owned it immediately before its abandonment.

The contingency plan for a vessel must be submitted to Ecology. The contingency plan for a tank vessel must be submitted by the owner or operator of the vessel or by the facilities at which the vessel will be unloading its cargo,[41] the resident agent for the vessel, or an approved primary response contractor.[42] An "owner or operator" is, in the case of a vessel, any person owning, operating, or chartering the vessel by demise.[43] The plan for a passenger or cargo vessel may be submitted by the owner or operator of the vessel, the agent for the vessel, or by an approved response contractor.[44] Contingency plans for onshore and offshore facilities may be submitted by the owner or operator of the facility or an approved response contractor.[45]

A copy of the plan must be kept in a conspicuous and accessible location at the facility or on the vessel, as well as at a central location accessible at any time by the Incident Commander or Spill Response Manager named in the plan.[46] Additionally, all plans must meet the statutory and regulatory requirements. A single plan may be submitted for more than one facility or more than one vessel (of the same type), provided that the plan meets the content requirements.[47]

Planning Deadlines

Covered vessels must submit a plan at least sixty-five days prior to beginning operations in waters of the state.[48] Onshore and offshore facilities shall submit a plan at least sixty-five days before the beginning of operations.[49]

Plan Requirements

The Oil Spill Response Act and the Vessel Spill Prevention Act set forth requirements for contingency plans.[50] Plans for both vessels and facilities must include: (1) a description of the methods that will be used to respond to spills of various sizes; and (2) a design that is sufficient, "to the maximum extent practicable," to remove oil and minimize environmental damage from a "worst case spill."[51] The plan must also provide for the proper disposal of recovered oil.[52] In addition, the plan must describe the amount and type of equipment available to respond to a spill, where it is located, and the extent to which other contingency plans rely on the same equipment.[53]

To the extent that Ecology regulations permit the use of dispersants, the plan must state under what circumstances and in what manner they will be applied.[54] In addition, the plan must describe how it relates to and is integrated with other contingency plans, such as those prepared by the state, regional entities, and/or the federal government.[55] The plan must also describe the features of the surrounding environment and a means of protecting it.[56]

The Ecology regulations contain specific format requirements[57] and detailed additional content requirements[58] relating to spill response planning, consistency with other plans' notification procedures, available personnel, training, use of volunteers, equipment, communication procedures, staging areas, surveillance methods and more.

Agency Review and Plan Updates

In deciding whether to approve each plan, Ecology must consider certain specific factors, including adequacy of equipment, response time, navigational hazards, vessel traffic, and the volume and type of oil transported in the area covered by the plan.[59] The agency must also consider the history of previous oil and hazardous substance spills in the plan area, the sensitivity of fisheries, wildlife, and other natural resources in the plan area,[60] and the extent to which the plan incorporates reasonable and cost effective measures to prevent spills.[61]

Ecology may execute random practice drills without prior notice in order to test the adequacy of responding entities under the plans.[62] Depending on performance, the agency can require changes in contingency plans or in their implementation.[63] Ecology "shall endeavor to review each plan in sixty-five calendar days."[64] The review period does not begin to run, however, until a complete plan is submitted. Ecology provides for public notice and comment on plans. Ecology may approve a plan conditionally, and the approved plans may be appealed within thirty days.[65] Contingency plans must be reviewed at least once every five years and updated, if necessary.[66] In addition, Ecology must be notified of any significant changes that could affect plan implementation.

Denial of approval of a vessel's contingency plan may be appealed to the Office of Marine Safety; facilities' plan denials may be appealed the Pollution Control Hearings Board.

Spill Response

In the event of a discharge of oil or a hazardous substance, the discharger is required to immediately notify the U. S. Coast Guard and Ecology's Division of Emergency Management.[67] This division maintains a twenty-four-hour statewide toll-free number for reporting such emergencies. In addition, the person owning or having control over the discharged oil is required to immediately collect and remove it.[68] If this is not feasible, such person is to take "all practicable actions" to contain, treat, and disperse the oil.[69]

One of the more sensitive environmental issues that arises immediately after an oil spill is whether to permit the use of dispersants, other chemicals or bioremediation for the containment, treatment and/or dispersal of the oil. Ecology has authority to prohibit or restrict the use of chemicals when such use would be "detrimental to the public interest."[70]

Primary Response Contractor Standards

Ecology must approve a primary response contractor[71] listed in a covered vessel contingency plan or an onshore/offshore facility plan, respectively.[72] Subcontractors to a primary response contractor do not need agency approval. The regulations listed at WAC 173-181-090 and WAC 317-10-090 list very specific requirements that a contractor must meet before he or she will be approved by Ecology. Ecology also has strict requirements it must meet when evaluating applications of primary response contractors.[73]

Spill Prevention Plans

In addition to contingency plans, owners and operators of onshore or offshore facilities and tank vessels are required to submit oil spill prevention plans.[74] Ecology is responsible for overseeing facility prevention plans under the Oil Spill Response Act. The spill prevention plan may be consolidated with a spill contingency plan.[75] Ecology and the OMS adopted rules providing prevention plan standards for facilities and tank vessels, respectively.[76]

Vessel Spill Prevention Plans

Vessel spill prevention plans must meet a list of statutory requirements. Specifically, the plan, like the facility prevention plan, must establish compliance with the OPA and applicable state and federal financial responsibility requirements.[77] Under Washington state law, the plan must also describe: (1) all discharges of oil in the prior five years of more than twenty-five barrels and measures taken to prevent a reoccurrence; (2) all accidents, collisions, groundings, and near miss incidents in which the vessel was involved in the prior five years, with an analysis of the cause and measures taken to prevent a reoccurrence; (3) vessel operations with respect to staffing standards; (4) the owner or operator's vessel inspection program; (5) the training given to vessel crews with respect to spill prevention, (6) all prevention technology that has been incorporated into the vessel; (7) the procedures used by the vessel owner or operator to ensure English language proficiency of at least one bridge officer while on duty in waters of the state; and (8) relevant prevention measures incorporated in any applicable regional marine spill safety plan that have not been adopted and the reasons for that decision.[78] In 2000, however, a number of these requirements were found to have been pre-empted by federal law. *U.S. v. Locke*, 529 U.S. 89, 120 S.Ct. 1135, 146 L.Ed.2d 69 (2000). In addition, the plan must establish compliance with federal drug and alcohol programs.[79] Ecology may require, by rule, additional information.[80]

Like the facility spill prevention plan, the vessel spill prevention plan can only be approved "if it provides the best achievable protection from damages caused by the discharge of oil into the waters of the state" and meets the requirements of the statute and any rules adopted by Ecology.[81] Ecology must review plans every five years; more frequent updates may be required where a significant change affecting the plan has occurred.[82]

Facility Spill Prevention Plans

Facility spill prevention plans are to be submitted in the time and manner as directed by Ecology.[83] The statute provides specific requirements for the plans. The plans must establish compliance with OPA and state and federal financial responsibility requirements,[84] if applicable. The plan must also certify that certain key personnel have received certification under RCW §90.56.220,[85] the facility has the required operations manual and has implemented an alcohol and drug use awareness program.[86] In addition, the plan must describe the facility's maintenance and inspection program and contain current records.[87] The plan also must describe the facility's alcohol and drug treatment program, the spill prevention technology installed, and any discharges of more than twenty-five barrels of oil to the land or water in the prior five years and measures taken to prevent a reoccurrence.[88]

Finally, the plan must describe the facility's procedures to contain and recover oil spilled during transfers to the facility and must incorporate into the facility, during the period covered by the plan, measures that will provide the best achievable protection for the public health and the environment.[89] In regulations adopted in July 1992, Ecology indicated that it will require extensive additional information, as well as a particular format. The regulations require detailed information about personnel training, planning, inspection and preventative maintenance procedures, facility technology, and facility security.[90]

Ecology can only approve a plan "if it provides the best achievable protection[91] from damages caused by the discharge of oil into the waters of the state" and meets the requirements o the statute and Ecology's rules.[92]

An approved plan must be reviewed every five years.[93] Ecology may require plan updates at any time if a "significant change" affects the plan.[94] An expedited review may be used when a plan has been approved by a federal agency or other state with equivalent criteria.[95] Ecology intends to verify compliance with its regulations through both announced and unannounced inspections under the state Water Pollution Control Act.[96]

Penalties for Violating Planning Requirements

The Spill Prevention Act and the Spill Response Act impose both criminal and civil penalties for violations of the contingency and prevention plan requirements.[97] Owners or operators who knowingly and intentionally operate an onshore or offshore facility or a covered vessel without an approved contingency or prevention plan (for facilities and tank vessels) may be found guilty of a gross misdemeanor for first convictions, and of a Class C felony for the second or subsequent convictions.[98]

In addition, if the owner or operator of an onshore or offshore facility operates without an approved contingency or prevention plan, or accepts cargo or passengers from a covered vessel that does not have the requisite approved plans, the owner or operator can be assessed a civil penalty of up to $100,000 per violation.[99] The owner or operator of a vessel in state waters is also subject to civil penalties of up to $100,000 per violation of the plan requirements.[100]

Each day that the facility or person operates without the necessary plan is considered a separate violation. Violators of the planning requirements may have their business licenses suspended by the Secretary of State,[101] and Ecology may deny entry into state waters to any covered vessel that does not have a required contingency or spill prevention plan.

The only circumstances when a facility or covered vessel is excluded from criminal and/or civil liability is where a contingency plan has been submitted to Ecology in a timely manner and is still under review or, in the case of a vessel, the vessel entered state waters after the U.S. Coast Guard determined it was in distress.[102]

Facility Operation Standards

The Oil Spill Response Act also requires onshore and offshore facilities to be operated in a manner that ensures the "best achievable protection" of public health and the environment.[103] "Best achievable protection" means "the highest level of protection that can be achieved through the use of the best achievable technology and those staffing levels, training procedures, and operational methods that provide the greatest degree of protection achievable."[104]

Ecology has adopted a facility operation standard and implemented an inspection plan to ensure compliance with the standards. In addition, Ecology has adopted rules governing the training and continuing education of facility workers and periodic certification of key personnel.[105]

Onshore and offshore facilities must also prepare an operations manual for the facility.[106] The manual must describe the equipment and procedures involving the transfer, storage and handling of oil that the operator employs or will employ for best achievable protection of the public health and the environment and to prevent oil spills in navigable waters.[107] In addition, the manual must describe equipment and procedures required for all vessels to or from which oil is transferred through use of the facility.

The manual must be approved by Ecology and is valid for five years.[108] Facility operations must comply with the manual. The owner or operator must notify Ecology of any significant change in its operations affecting the manual. Ecology may then require modification of the manual.

The Oil Spill Response Act imposes a duty on the owner or operator to "ensure that all covered vessels docked at an onshore or offshore facility comply with the terms of the operations manual for the facility."[109] However, the penalty for failure to do so is unclear.

Oil Spill Liability

Discharge of oil to state waters from a ship or any fixed or mobile facility or installation located offshore or onshore is prohibited,[110] and liability attaches regardless of fault.[111] The only exclusions are for discharges expressly authorized by Ecology and discharges authorized by operation of law where Ecology fails to act upon a waste disposal permit application within sixty days of filing.[112] Persons owning or having control over the oil have an obligation to immediately collect and remove it, or to take all practicable actions to contain, treat and disperse it.[113]

State and Private Causes of Action

Persons who unlawfully discharge oil into state waters or who pose a substantial threat of doing so are responsible to the state for all necessary expenses incurred by the state in responding to the discharge.[114] In addition, "any other person" who causes oil to enter state waters is also liable to the state for necessary expenses.[115] "Necessary expenses" include those expenses incurred by the state for the following:

1. investigating the source of a discharge;
2. investigating the extent of the environmental damage caused by the discharge;
3. conducting actions necessary to clean up the discharge;
4. conducting pre-damage and damage assessment studies; and
5. enforcing the Oil Spill Response Act and collecting for damages caused by a discharge.[116]

The state is prohibited from demanding reimbursement for any activity completed more than five years before the date of the demand.[117]

In addition to liability to the state for necessary expenses incurred in spill response, persons owning or having control over oil that unlawfully enters state waters are strictly liable for damages to persons or property, public or private, caused by such entry.[118] Responsible persons are relieved from strict liability only if they can show that the discharge was caused solely by negligence on the part of the federal or state government, an act of war or sabotage, or an act of God.[119] Persons who are liable for the costs of oil spill cleanup have a statutory cause of action to recover those cleanup costs from any other person causing the entry of oil into state waters.[120]

Notwithstanding the above, the Vessel Spill Prevention Act excludes persons from liability for removal costs or damages resulting from "actions taken or omitted to be taken in the course of rendering care, assistance, or advice consistent with the national contingency plan or as otherwise directed by the federal on-scene coordinator" or the Ecology official responsible for oil spill response.[121] This exclusion does not apply to (1) persons owning or having control over spilled oil, (2) personal injury or wrongful death claims, or (3) persons who are grossly negligent or who have engaged in willful misconduct.[122]

State Oil Spill Response Account

In 1991, the legislature created a state oil spill fund for response costs, funded by receipts from the oil spill response tax (currently set at 5 cents for every barrel brought into the state and 4 cents back for every barrel of refined product leaving the state). Response cost reimbursements are also deposited in the account.[123] The account moneys can only be used to pay for costs associated with response to spills of crude oil or petroleum products into the navigable waters of the state where the cost is likely to exceed $50,000.[124] Before expending moneys from the account, the director of Ecology must make "reasonable efforts" to obtain funding response costs from the responsible party and other sources, including the federal government. The statute defines response costs to include (1) natural resource damage assessment and related activities; (2) spill related response containment, wildlife rescue, cleanup, disposal, and associated costs; (3) interagency coordination and public information related to a response, and (4) appropriate travel, goods and services, contracts, and equipment.[125] The director of Ecology can only reimburse response costs where the funds appropriated to the agencies responsible for response activities do not cover the costs.

Civil Penalties

Persons who negligently discharge oil into or cause or permit oil to enter into state waters are subject to a penalty of up to $20,000 for each violation and for each day that the spill poses risks to the environment. If a person intentionally or recklessly discharges oil or causes or permits it to enter state waters, such person is subject to a penalty of up to $100,000 for each violation and for each day the spill poses a risk to the environment. These penalties are in addition to any other penalty provided by law. The penalty is to be determined by Ecology after considering (1) the gravity of the violation; (2) the previous record of the violator, (3)the speed and thoroughness of the collection and removal of the oil; and (4) any other considerations Ecology deems appropriate.[126]

NATURAL RESOURCE DAMAGES

In Washington, damages for injury to natural resources can be sought under either the state Water Pollution Control Act or the Model Toxics Control Act (MTCA).[127] Most of the statutory provisions discussed below were enacted in 1988, 1989 or 1991. To date, there is no case law interpreting them.

State Water Pollution Control Act

The state Water Pollution Control Act creates a cause of action on behalf of the state, counties and cities for natural resource damages. Under the Act, Ecology must follow a relatively detailed procedure for assessing damages from an oil spill.[128] First, Ecology must undertake a pre-assessment screen to determine whether damages can be quantified at a reasonable cost.[129] Depending on the results of this screen, the state can seek to recover damages either through the application of a damage compensation schedule or through a damage claim arising out of an extensive damage assessment investigation. The compensation schedule, which became effective May 24, 1992, represents one of the most comprehensive efforts in the nation to establish a simplified method for assessing oil spill damages.[130] Where damages can be quantified for a reasonable cost, a damage assessment investigation will be conducted. If, however, such an investigation is unreasonable in light of the cost and the expected damages, the compensation table will be used.

Natural Resource Damages Provision

Persons who violate the Water Pollution Control Act or the Oil Spill Response Act are liable for damages if such violation causes the death of, or injury to, fish, animals, vegetation or other resources of the state.[131] Liability for damages also flows from a failure to perform a duty under those Acts, a violation of an order or other determination by Ecology made pursuant to those Acts (including the conditions of a waste discharge permit), or an action that otherwise causes a reduction in the quality of state waters below Ecology standards or (if no standards have been set) a significant degradation of water quality, thereby damaging the same.

As originally enacted, liability under these provisions flowed solely to the state. In 1991, the Water Pollution Control Act was amended to authorize a cause of action on behalf of "affected counties and cities" as well.[132] This is significant because local governments do not have direct authority to sue for natural resource damages under comparable federal statutes.[133] Local governments are still precluded, however, from bringing a claim under the Water Pollution Control Act from an oil spill incident when the state is assessing damage for the same incident.[134]

Natural Resources Defined

The Water Pollution Control Act does not refer specifically to "natural resources." Instead, the Act addresses death or injury to "fish, animals, vegetation or other resources of the state" or a reduction in water quality. "Other resources of the state" are not defined. This is to be contrasted with the definition of "natural resources" set forth under the federal Superfund law, which covers the following:

> land, fish, wildlife, biota, air, water, ground water, drinking water supplies, and other such resources belonging to, managed by, held in trust by, appertaining to, or otherwise controlled by [the federal, state, local, or foreign governments or Indian tribes].[135]

Whether the Washington provision is as broad or broader than the federal provision is unclear. For example, it is unclear whether "other resources of the state" include only those resources "owned" by the state, or resources managed or controlled by the state as well.

Pre-assessment Screening and Damage Assessment Process

Before assessing the harm to state resources from an oil spill, Ecology is required to conduct a formal pre-assessment screening of damages.[136] A pre-assessment screening committee, known as the Resource Damage Assessment (RDA) committee,[137] decides whether the oil spill compensation schedule will be used to determine the states damages or whether, instead, a detailed damage assessment study should be conducted.[138] This committee is chaired by Ecology and includes members from the departments of Ecology, Fish and Wildlife, Natural Resources, Health, and the Parks and Recreation Commission. Ecology may also select representatives from other agencies to participate on the committee on a spill-by-spill basis.[139]

Under Ecology's regulations,[140] the screening process begins when the on-scene coordinator (OSC) makes an initial report to Ecology regarding the oil spill.[141] The committee must convene as soon as possible; no later than thirty days after Ecology is notified of the spill or the next regularly scheduled meeting following the spill.[142]

In determining whether a damage assessment investigation should be conducted, the RDA committee is to consider the following factors:

1. whether evidence from reconnaissance investigations suggests that injury has occurred or is likely to occur to publicly owned resources;
2. the potential loss in services provided by resources injured or likely to be injured and the expected value of the potential loss;
3. whether a restoration project to return lost services is technically feasible;
4. the accuracy of damage quantification methods that could be used and the anticipated cost-effectiveness of applying each method;
5. the extent to which likely injury to resources can be verified with available quantification methods; and
6. whether the injury, once quantified, can be translated into monetary values with sufficient precision or accuracy.[143]

A damage assessment investigation can be conducted only if the committee concludes after considering the factors listed above, that the damages to be investigated are quantifiable at a "reasonable" cost and that the proposed studies are clearly linked to quantifying the damages sustained.[144] The state trustee agency responsible for the potentially injured resource will conduct the studies and pursue appropriate remedies.[145] A cost is considered "reasonable" when the anticipated cost for the damage assessment is expected to be less than the anticipated damage.[146]

The compensation schedule is to be used if the committee determines that: (1) restoration is not technically feasible, (2) damages are not quantifiable at a reasonable cost,[147] and (3) the restoration and enhancement projects or studies proposed by the potentially liable parties are not adequate compensation.[148]

Under the Water Pollution Control Act, responsible parties are to be permitted ongoing involvement in the pre-assessment screening process.[149] As an alternative to selecting a damage assessment investigation or using the compensation schedule, the screening committee may accept restoration or enhancement projects or studies proposed by potentially liable parties during the pre-assessment screening period. Any proposal for such an alternative approach by a potentially liable party must, in effect, contain a "mini-assessment" with the following elements: (1) an investigation of potentially injured resources to determine exposure to oil, (2) an investigation of exposed resources to determine injury; (3) an investigation of injured resources to quantify injury; and (4) quantification of damages for injured resources.[150]

Natural Resource Damages Computation Without Compensation Schedule

If the RDA committee determines that the natural resource damages will not be calculated under the damage compensation schedule, the state can seek compensation for an amount necessary to restore any damaged resource to its condition before the injury, to the extent technically feasible, and to compensate for the lost value incurred after the injury until the time of restoration.[151] Restoration must include the cost to restock any damaged water, replenish or replace resources and to otherwise restore injured streams, lakes, or other waters of the state, including any estuary, ocean area, submerged lands, shoreline, bank or other lands adjoining such waters, to their condition before the injury, as such condition is determined by Ecology.[152]

The lost value of a damaged resource is the sum of its consumptive, non-consumptive and indirect use values, in addition to lost taxation, leasing and licensing revenues. Indirect use values may include existence, bequest, option and aesthetic values.[153] Damages are to be determined by generally accepted, cost-effective procedures.[154] The Water Pollution Control Act expressly provides that contingent valuation is a generally-accepted, cost effective valuation method. It should be noted that expenses incurred by Ecology in conducting prescreening and damage assessment studies are recoverable under the Oil Spill Response Act as "necessary expenses" of an oil spill response.[155]

Natural Resource Damages Computation Using Compensation Schedule

The state cannot both recover damages (restoration costs and lost value) and receive compensation under the compensation schedule for the same oil spill.[156] The amounts provided for in the schedule are intended to represent adequate damage compensation for adverse environmental, recreational, aesthetic or other spill effects that are otherwise unquantifiable or that cannot be quantified at reasonable cost. "Adequate compensation" is based on preexisting information regarding resource vulnerability to certain classes of oil in particular areas of the state at a particular time of year. Information collected during spill response reconnaissance is utilized as well.[157] By statute, amounts assessed under the schedule are to be no less than one dollar per gallon and no more than fifty dollars per gallon of spilled oil.[158]

The compensation schedule includes:

1. a relative ranking of six classes of oil[159] based on acute toxicity, mechanical injury and persistence in the receiving environment;
2. a series of relative vulnerability rankings for different receiving environments in the state, which takes into account spill location, habitat and resource sensitivity to oil, seasonal distribution of resources and areas of recreational, ecological or aesthetic importance;
3. a quantitative method for determining "public resource" damages resulting from an oil spill based on oil effect and vulnerability rankings;[160]

4. a method for adjusting damages calculated under the schedule based on actions taken by the potentially liable party that demonstrate acceptance of responsibility (e.g., immediate removal of the oil); or enhance or impede the detection of the spill, the extent of the spill and the damage (the amount of reduction cannot result in damages of less than one dollar per gallon).

The relative ranking scores for the oil classes range from one to five, where five represents the most harmful effect.[161] Likewise, the vulnerability scores for receiving environments in terms of the vulnerability of the habitat itself, the species present, or the ecological, recreational or aesthetic uses of habitat also range from one to five, with five representing a severe impact.

At the time of the spill, a spill vulnerability score (SVS) is calculated for the receiving environment by adding the individual scores for habitat vulnerability, vulnerability of various species present in the area (e.g., marine mammals, salmon, shellfish) during the season of the spill, and recreational vulnerability.[162] The regulations then set forth formulas that take into account the SVS; the oil scores for acute toxicity, mechanical injury and persistence; and the number of gallons spilled. Which of the formulas is to be used depends on whether the spill occurred in (1) marine and estuarine waters, excluding the Columbia River estuary; (2) the Columbia River estuary; (3) freshwater streams, rivers and lakes; (4) freshwater wetlands; or (5) more than one type of receiving environment.[163] The calculated damage amount may then be reduced in consideration of actions taken by the potentially liable party to mitigate the impact of the spill. In no event, however, can damages be reduced to less than one dollar per gallon of oil spilled.[164]

Limits on the Use of Funds Recovered

Compensation assessed under the Water Pollution Control Act must be deposited in the state Coastal Protection Fund and used for the general purposes permitted under that fund.[165] Fund moneys may be used for environmental restoration and enhancement projects, investigation of long-term oil spill effects, development and implementation of an aquatic land geographic information system, and research and development regarding oil and hazardous substance pollution. A steering committee consisting of representatives from several state agencies, including Ecology, oversees the fund. Agencies cannot be reimbursed with fund monies for the salaries and benefits of permanent employees for routine operational support. Reconnaissance and damage assessment activity may only be reimbursed from the fund if money is unavailable from other sources.[166]

Model Toxics Control Act (State Superfund)

Unlike the federal Superfund legislation, which addresses natural resource damages in a fairly comprehensive manner,[167] the state Model Toxics Control Act (MTCA) (Washington's state Superfund) only briefly mentions natural resource damages under the act's liability provision. This provision states that liable parties under MTCA are strictly, jointly, and severally liable for "all remedial action costs and for all *natural resource damages* resulting from the releases or threatened releases of hazardous substances."[168] Petroleum or petroleum products are included as "hazardous substances" under MTCA.[169] "Natural resources," however, are left undefined, as is the term "natural resource damage."

The pre-assessment screen and compensation schedule regulations discussed above apply solely to oil spills to waters of the state. MTCA does not require a compensation schedule or pre-assessment screening process to be developed for other releases of "hazardous substances." Courts applying MTCA's natural resource damages provisions to situations other than releases of oil to state waters, therefore, are likely to look to CERCLA and the federal Clean Water Act (CWA) and the federal regulations by analogy.[170] The direction the federal regulations will take has been shaped by lawsuits challenging the regulations.[171] Under the Department of the Interior's (DOI) original natural resource damage assessment regulations, trustees were requested to value the resources using the lesser of the cost of restoration or replacement, or the lost use value.[172] However, these regulations were invalidated on the basis that the statutes that authorize such damages establish a preference for using the cost of restoration as the appropriate measure.[173] DOI released revised regulations in response to the court's invalidation of the original ones in March of 1994. These too were challenged and partially invalidated in *Kennecott Utah Copper Corporation v. United States Department of the Interior*, 88 F.3d 1191 (D.C. Cir. 1996). The rules required trustees to restore both the resource as well as services lost as a result of the damage. The court thought restoration of lost services went beyond the scope of the intent of the statute, and invalidated that portion of the regulations. Additionally, the court ruled that the statute of limitations for natural resource damage claims began in 1986 when the first natural resource damage rules were promulgated, rather than 1994 when the revised rules were issued.

Therefore, the rules under CERCLA and CWA for assessing and valuing natural resource damages are still in flux. However, the National Oceanic Atmospheric and Atmospheric Administration has promulgated valuation standards pursuant to the Oil Pollution Act that trustees may be able to use to sidestep the controversial DOI rules.[174]

NOTES

[1] 33 USC §1321(c)(1)(A); 33USC §§2701 et seq.

[2] The Coast Guard and EPA are each designated as the federal On-Scene Coordinator or "FOSC". Large spills may also involve the National Response Team ("NRT") or a Regional Response Team ("RRT") to coordinate response and cleanup. Indian Tribes will be involved, too, if the spill affects their lands or resources.

[3] *US v. Locke*, 529 US 89 (2000) (invalidating certain specific WA state regulations concerning vessel operation and crew requirements).

[4] RCW §88.40.020. In 1991, these requirements were extended to onshore and offshore facilities. RCW §88.40.025.

[5] RCW §§90.48 et seq.

[6] RCW §§90.56 et seq.

[7] RCW §§88.46 et seq.

[8] The WA Department of Fish and Wildlife has also adopted procedures for rehabilitating waterfowl and wildlife affected by oil spills. RCW §§90.56.100 and 90.56.110.

[9] The state also imposes tanker escort and pilot licensing requirements (RCW §88.16 et seq.) and registration requirements (RCW §88.02 et seq.).

[10] For example, the Division of Fire Protection Services is responsible for hazardous substance incident response training and education. RCW §90.56.080. The WA Sea Grant Program also conducts oil spill prevention education. RCW §79A.60.620.

[11] RCW §§88.40 et seq.

[12] RCW §88.40.020.

[13] RCW §88.40.025.

[14] RCW §88.40.011(2).

[15] RCW §88.40.011(7)(a). Expressly excluded from the definition of a facility are railroad cars, motor vehicles or other rolling stock while transporting oil over state rail lines or highways. RCW §88.40.011(7)(b). Under the 1991 amendments, underground storage tanks regulated under RCW §§90.76 et seq. are also excluded. In addition, the amendments exclude retail motor vehicle fuel outlets, agricultural activities exempt under RCW §82.04.330, and marine fuel outlets not dispensing more than 3,000 gallons of fuel at a time to a ship that is not a covered vessel in a single transaction.

[16] RCW §88.40.011(14).

[17] RCW §88.40.011(13).

[18] RCW §88.40.030.

[19] The owner or operator of a vessel must also have certification of financial responsibility in a specified amount on the vessel under the federal OPA. 33 USC. §2716.

[20] A covered vessel is "a tank vessel, cargo vessel or passenger vessel." RCW §88.40.011(4).

[21] RCW §§88.40 et seq.

[22] RCW §88.46.080.

[23] RCW §90.56.300.

[24] RCW §88.46.090(3).

[25] RCW §§90.56.310, 90.56.330.

[26] RCW §88.44.040.

27 RCW §88.40.040.

28 RCW §88.46.090.

29 RCW §88.40.040; §90.56.310.

30 RCW §90.56.310.

31 RCW §90.56.060.

32 RCW §90.56.100.

33 In 1995 the State Legislature created a nonprofit corporation, the WA State Maritime Cooperative, to take over the State Maritime Commission's activities. RCW §§88.46.062 through .065.

34 RCW §88.46.060 (covered vessels) and RCW §90.56.210 (onshore and offshore facilities).

35 RCW §88.46.010(23); §90.56.010(27).

36 RCW §88.46.060; RCW §90.56.210. A "covered vessel" includes a tank vessel, cargo vessel, or passenger vessel. RCW §88.46.010(6) (these terms are defined above at section 12.2.1). Federal plans required under 33 CFR 154, 40 CFR 104 and 110, or the OPA may be submitted to satisfy plan requirements for both facilities and vessels if Ecology deems that such federal requirements equal or exceed those of the agency. WAC 317-10-035; WAC 173-181-035(2).

37 RCW §88.46.060; §90.56.210.

38 RCW §88.46.010; §90.56.010(29)(a). *See also* 33 USC §1321(a)(24)(B).

39 WAC 317-10-035.

40 RCW §90.56.210(3). Facilities' plans must include a "worst case spill" defined as "the largest foreseeable spill in adverse weather conditions." RCW §90.56.010(29)(b), §88.46.010(24)(b).

41 RCW §88.46.060(3).

42 WAC 173-181-035(3); WAC 317-10-035(3).

43 RCW §90.56.010(20)(a).

44 WAC 317-10-060(4).

45 WAC 173-181-060(4).

46 WAC 173-181-075; WAC 317-10-075.

47 WAC 173-181-060(5); WAC 317-10-060.

48 WAC 317-10-060(2).

49 WAC 173-181-060(2).

50 RCW §90.56.210(1); RCW §88.46.060(1). *See also* WAC 173-181-050; 317-10-050.

51 RCW §90.56.210(1); RCW §88.46.060(1).

52 RCW §90.56.210(1)(k); RCW §88.46.060(1)(l).

53 RCW §90.56.210(1)(m); RCW §88.46.060(1)(n).

54 RCW §90.56.210(1)(n); RCW §88.46.060(1)(o).

55 RCW §90.56.210(1)(c); §88.46.060(1)(c). *See e.g.,* 40 CFR 300 (National Oil and Hazardous Substance Pollution Contingency Plan).

56 RCW §90.56.210(1)(g); §88.46.060(1)(g).

57 WAC 173-181-045; WAC 317-10-045.

58 WAC 317-10-050; WAC 173-181-050.

59 RCW §90.56.210(5)(a-h); RCW §88.46.060(5)(a-h). The statute does not state what "area" the plan must cover. Presumably, this would be the area that would be affected by a worst case spill.

60 RCW §90.56.210(5)(e-f); §88.46.060(5)(e-f).

[61] RCW §90.56.210(5)(h); §88.46.060(5)(h).

[62] RCW §90.56.260; WAC 173-181-070; WAC 317-10-070.

[63] *Id.*

[64] WAC 173-181-065; WAC 317-10-065.

[65] *Id.*

[66] RCW §90.56.210(9); §88.46.060(9).

[67] RCW §90.56.280.

[68] RCW §90.56.340.

[69] *Id.*

[70] *Id*

[71] A "response contractor" is an individual, organization, association or cooperative that provides or intends to provide equipment and/or personnel for oil spill containment, cleanup and/or removal activities. A "primary response contractor" is a response contractor that is directly responsible to a contingency plan holder, either by a written contract or written agreement. WAC 173-181-030(25) and (26); WAC 317-10-030(27) and (28).

[72] WAC 173-181-090; WAC 317-10-090.

[73] WAC 173-181-096; WAC 317-10-096.

[74] RCW §88.46.040; RCW §90.56.200. Note that tank vessels, cargo vessels and passenger vessels (i.e., "covered vessels") are subject to the contingency planning requirements, while only tank vessels are subject to the prevention planning requirements.

[75] RCW §88.46.040; §90.56.200.

[76] RCW §88.46.040; §90.56.200.

[77] RCW §88.46.040(2)(a).

[78] RCW §88.46.040(2)(b)-(f), (h)-(j).

[79] RCW §88.46.040(2)(g).

[80] RCW §88.46.040(k).

[81] RCW §88.46.040(3).

[82] RCW §88.46.040(5) and (6).

[83] RCW §90.56.200. Ecology's Facility Oil Spill Prevention Plan Standards, WAC 173-180D, require that any facility that first begins operating after January 1, 1993, submit a plan at least sixty-five days prior to beginning operations. WAC 173-180D-065.

[84] RCW §90.56.200(2)(a).

[85] Operations standards are discussed below in Section 12.2.6.

[86] RCW §90.56.200(2)(b)-(d).

[87] RCW §90 56 200(2)(e).

[88] RCW §90.56.200(2)(f)-(h).

[89] RCW §90.56.200(2)(i) and (j).

[90] WAC 173-180D-060 sets forth a detailed list of what must be included in a prevention plan. WAC 173-180D-055 contains the plan format requirements.

91 "Best achievable protection" is defined as "the highest level of protection that can be achieved through the use of the best achievable technology and those staffing levels, training procedures, and operational methods that provide the greatest degree of protection achievable. The director shall consider the effectiveness, engineering feasibility, and commercial availability of the technology. RCW §90.56.010(2).

92 RCW §90.56.200(3).

93 RCW §90.56.200(5).

94 RCW §90.56.200(5). The act does not define "significant change," but Ecology has defined it in WAC 173-180D-085.

95 WAC 173-180D-070(5).

96 RCW §90.56.

97 In addition, Ecology's Facility Oil Spill Prevention Plan Standards and the contingency plan regulations impose similar penalties.

98 RCW §88.46.080; RCW §90.56.300.

99 RCW §90.56.310.

100 RCW §88.46.090.

101 *Id.*

102 RCW §88.46.090; §90.56.300.

103 RCW §90.56.220.

104 RCW §90.56.010(2).

105 WAC 173-180A (Facility Oil-Handling Operations and Design Standards); WAC 173-180B (Facility Oil Handling Operations Manual Standards); and WAC 173-180C (Facility Oil Handling Personnel Certification regulations).

106 RCW §90.56.230.

107 RCW §90.56.230(1).

108 RCW §90.56.230(4).

109 RCW §90.56.230(5).

110 RCW §90.56.320. A ship is defined as "any boat, ship, vessel, barge, or other floating craft of any kind." RCW §90.56.010(24).

111 *Id.*

112 RCW §§90.56.320 and 90.48.200.

113 RCW §90.56.340.

114 RCW §90.56.360.

115 RCW §90.56.380. While this provision is unclear, it may be addressing persons other than those owning or having control of the oil, such as owners of vessels that collide with oil-carrying vessels. The section providing exceptions to liability for some cleanup volunteers, state and local governments and others, former RCW §90.48.383, was repealed in 1991.

116 RCW §90.56.010(16).

117 RCW §90.56.400.

118 RCW §90.56.370. Liability under this provision solely applies prospectively from June 7, 1990.

119 RCW §90.56.370.

120 RCW §90.56.380.

121 RCW §90.56.390.

122 *Id.*

123 RCW §90.56.500; §82.23B.020.

124 RCW §90.56.500.

125 *Id.*

126 RCW §90.56.330.

127 Natural resource damages also can be sought under the following federal statutes: the Comprehensive Environmental Response, Compensation, and Liability Act, 42 USC. §§9601 *et seq.*; the Oil Pollution Act, 33 USC §§2701 *et seq.*; the Federal Water Pollution Control Act, 33 USC §§1251 *et seq.*; and the Marine Protection, Research, and Sanctuaries Act, 16 USC. §§1431 *et seq.*

128 Neither the Water Pollution Control Act nor MTCA directly address the assessment of natural resource damages stemming from a release of hazardous substances.

129 WAC 173-183-240.

130 WAC 173-183-320 and -330.

131 RCW §90.48.142(1).

132 *Id.*

133 See e.g., 42 USC §9607(f)(1)(a); *Town of Bedford v. Raytheon Co.*, 755 F. Supp. 469 (D. Mass. 1991); *but see City of New York v. Exxon Corp.*, 633 F. Supp. 609 (S.D.N.Y. 1986).

134 RCW §90.48.367(6).

135 42 USC §9601(16).

136 RCW §90.48.367(1).

137 WAC 173-183-100(34).

138 WAC 173-183-240.

139 WAC 173-183-230.

140 WAC 173-183.

141 The OSC or the Ecology responder must determine: (1) the quantity and type of oil spilled; (2) the extent and location of the spill; and (3) the amount of oil cleaned up on a daily basis and in total. WAC 173-183-220; WAC 173-183-810. However, the potentially liable person (PLP) may hire an independent expert to determine the volume of oil spilled. That volume may be used in calculating damages if the expert is acceptable to both Ecology and the PLP. WAC 173-183-810.

142 WAC 173-183-230.

143 RCW §§90.48.368(3)(a) through (f); WAC 173-183-240.

144 RCW §90.48.368(5).

145 RCW §90 48.368(4).

146 RCW §90.48.368(8). It may be difficult in practice to assess whether a particular assessment cost is reasonable, since the extent of any damage may not be apparent until the study is completed, or until the results of several seasons of study have been compiled.

147 "Not quantifiable at a reasonable cost" is defined in WAC 173-183-100(25) as meaning "any diminution in value of a public resource that cannot be measured with sufficient precision or accuracy by currently available and accepted procedures within a reasonable time frame."

148 RCW §90.48.367(2); WAC 173-183-240(4).

149 RCW §90.48.368(7).

150 RCW §90.48.368(1). This option is explained in greater detail in WAC 173-183-260.

[151] RCW §90.48.367(3). "Technically feasible" is defined in RCW §90.48.364 as meaning "that given available technology, a restoration or enhancement project can be successfully completed at a cost that is not disproportionate to the value of the resource before the injury." See also WAC 173-183-100(41).

[152] RCW §90.48.367(4).

[153] *Id.*

[154] *Id.*

[155] RCW §§90.56.360, .380 and .010(17).

[156] RCW §90.48.367(2).

[157] WAC 173-183-320.

[158] RCW §90.48.366.

[159] WAC 173-183-340. The six oil classes include: (1) Prudhoe Bay crude oil; (2) Bunker C; (3) No. 2 fuel oil; (4) gasoline; (5) kerosene; and (6) kerosene-type jet fuel.

[160] WAC 173-183-330.

[161] WAC 173-183-340(2).

[162] WAC 173-183-400(3).

[163] WAC 173-183-830 through -865.

[164] WAC 173-183-870.

[165] RCW §90.48.367(5); RCW §90.48.390.

[166] RCW §90.48.400.

[167] *See* 42 USC. §§9607(a)(4)(C), 9607(f)(1), 9607(f)(2)(C), and 43 CFR 11 *et seq.*

[168] RCW §70.105D.040(2) (emphasis added).

[169] RCW §70.105D.020(5)(d).

[170] *See* 42 USC §9607(a)(4)(C); 33 USC §1321(i)(4); 43 CFR 11.

[171] *See, e.g., Ohio v. United States Dept. of Interior*, 880 F. 2d 432 (DC Cir. 1989); *Colorado v. United States Dept. of Interior*, 880 F. 2d 481 (DC Cir. 1989).

[172] 43 CFR 11.35(b)(2).

[173] *See Ohio v. United States Dept. of Interior*, 880 F. 2d 432 (DC Cir. 1989).

[174] *See* 56 Fed.Reg, 19,752 (1991) (proposed rulemaking to modify the DOI's Type B damage assessment regulations pursuant to *Ohio v. Dept. of Interior*).

CHAPTER 12

Regulation of Underground Storage Tanks

INTRODUCTION

Federal UST Program

Congress enacted a federal underground storage tank ("UST") program in 1984 as part of a set of amendments to the Resource Conservation and Recovery Act (RCRA).[1] The program regulates the management and cleanup of contamination resulting from the tens of thousands of USTs that were estimated to be leaking and contaminating soil and ground water. It also contains significant measures to prevent future contamination. EPA has promulgated extensive administrative and technical regulations under the UST program.[2] Although Washington has primary regulatory and enforcement authority under its delegated UST program, EPA retains the authority to conduct inspections under 42 U.S.C. §6991d and to take enforcement actions under 42 U.S.C. §6991e.[3]

State UST Program

In 1989, the Washington legislature directed Ecology to establish a program regulating USTs.[4] Ecology promulgated UST regulations, which became effective on December 29, 1990.[5] Because Washington's UST program meets appropriate federal criteria,[6] the EPA has delegated primary regulatory and enforcement authority to the state.[7] The state program therefore operates in lieu of the federal program for all regulated UST facilities within the state, except those on Indian lands, for which the EPA retains regulatory and enforcement authority.[8] Ecology is also required to license USTs[9] and forbid the delivery of regulated substances to USTs that are unlicensed.[10]

Washington's UST program is administered by the UST section of Ecology's Toxics Cleanup Program. Information on the UST program is available from Ecology at http://www.ecy.wa.gov/programs/tcp/ust-lust/tanks. Cities and counties may also have their own regulatory programs subject to Ecology's approval.[11]

Leaking Tanks

Owners and operators of USTs should be aware that the Model Toxics Control Act (MTCA)[12] —the state Superfund program—applies to leaks and spills from all USTs, even those that are exempt from regulation under the UST program.[13] Unlike the federal Superfund program, MTCA specifically identifies petroleum and petroleum products as "hazardous substances," subject to cleanup requirements. Ecology's Toxics Cleanup Section is responsible for regulating investigations[14] and corrective actions at sites with leaking USTs.

SCOPE OF THE UST PROGRAM

What Is an Underground Storage Tank?

A UST is defined as a tank (or a combination of tanks) used for the accumulation of regulated substances with at least ten percent of the volume of the tank (including connected underground pipes) beneath the ground.[15] "Regulated substances" include liquid petroleum and petroleum-based substances (excluding propane and asphalt) and any hazardous substance as defined under the federal Superfund statute.[16] A "UST system" includes a UST, connected underground piping, underground ancillary equipment, and any containment systems.[17]

Exempt and Deferred Tanks

Several types of tanks are specifically excluded from the definition of "underground storage tank." Exemptions include UST systems that hold RCRA hazardous wastes; UST systems with a capacity of 110 gallons or less; UST systems that have never contained more than a de minimis quantity of regulated substances; certain UST systems with a capacity of 1,100 gallons or less (i.e., farm or residential USTs used for storing motor fuel for non-commercial purposes), USTs used for storing heating oil for consumptive use on the premises;[18] surface impoundments, pits, ponds or lagoons; flow-through process tanks; and tanks located in an underground area, e.g., basement, vault or tunnel).[19]

Comprehensive regulation has been deferred for several UST systems, such as for certain wastewater treatment tank systems and UST systems containing radioactive material. Deferred UST systems do not have to comply with the technical design standards and most operating requirements, but are subject to some of the basic requirements of the program discussed below, including notification and permit requirements, annual tank fees, closure requirements, release reporting requirements, and penalties.[20] In addition to these basic administrative requirements, deferred UST systems installed after December 22, 1988 must also meet specific performance standards designed to prevent leaks from the UST.[21]

To Whom Do the UST Regulations Apply?

The UST regulations apply to all owners and operators of UST systems.[22] In the case of UST systems in use on or after November 8, 1984, an "owner" is any person who owns a UST system used for the storage, use, or dispensing of regulated substances.[23] In the case of UST systems no longer in use on November 8, 1984, the person who owned the UST immediately before its use was discontinued is the "owner." If the owner of a UST system cannot be located, the owner is the person who owns the property where the UST system is located, with certain exceptions. An "operator" is any person who controls or has responsibility for the daily operation of the UST system.

PERMIT REQUIREMENTS

No UST system can be operated without a valid permit.[24] For any UST to be eligible for a permit, the owner and operator must comply with all applicable UST requirements and pay all applicable fees.[25]

Obtaining and Renewing a Permit

To obtain a permit for a new UST system (one that was installed after December 22, 1988), the owner or operator must, within thirty days of bringing the UST system into use, certify compliance with corrosion protection, financial responsibility, and release detection requirements, and must submit to Ecology a properly completed UST notification form and checklist,[26] together with the applicable annual fee at least 30 days before installation.[27]

To obtain a permit for an existing UST system (one that was installed on or before December 22, 1988) that has not been previously reported, the owner or operator must complete a UST notification form and submit it to Ecology together with the applicable fee, including any fees that should have been paid for previous years had the UST been properly registered.[28] Tanks that are temporarily out of service are not eligible for permits.[29] To obtain a new permit for a tank that previously has been temporarily out of service, the owner or operator must notify Ecology of the change in status and must comply with the temporary closure regulations.[30]

UST permits are valid for one year, provided, however, that the UST remains in compliance with regulatory requirements. In order to qualify for an annual permit renewal, the owner and operator must certify that the UST is in compliance with the applicable requirements, must provide proof of insurance, and must pay the applicable fees to the Department of Licensing.[31]

Display of Permit

Regulated substances cannot be delivered by suppliers to a UST requiring a permit unless a current and valid permit is displayed on the tank or, where appropriate, in the office or kiosk of the facility where the tank is located.[32] Suppliers are also prohibited from delivering regulated substances to a tank the supplier knows to be leaking or has leaked, regardless of whether a permit is displayed on the tank.[33] If the owner or operator knows of a confirmed release from a permitted tank, the permit must be removed from display within twenty-four hours.[34] The owner or operator may not accept regulated substances until the UST system fully complies with applicable UST regulations.

Revocation/Removal of Permit

Ecology can revoke a permit if a UST system falls out of compliance with the regulations, including the financial responsibility regulations, or if the owner or operator violates a regulation.[35] Upon revocation, the owner or operator must surrender the permit within seven days. Ecology's decision to revoke a permit may be appealed to the Pollution Control Hearings Board (PCHB).[36] When a tank is closed, any active permit must be returned to Ecology within thirty days after the closure.[37]

PROGRAM ADMINISTRATION

Investigation and Access

An "authorized representative"[38] of the state can require the owner or operator of a UST system to provide information and documents, and to monitor[39] or test a UST system in order to assess compliance with the UST regulations.[40] Ecology may also subpoena witnesses, documents and other relevant information. Upon reasonable notice (unless an emergency or other circumstances justify otherwise), an authorized representative may enter the site.[41]

Enforcement

To enforce the UST regulations, Ecology may seek injunctive or other judicial relief or issue an order to: (1) enjoin any threatened or continuing violation of the regulations; (2) restrain unauthorized activity that results in a violation and threatens public health or the environment; (3) require compliance with requests for information, access, testing or monitoring; or (4) assess civil penalties authorized under the UST statute.[42] Owners and operators are subject to civil penalties of up to $5,000 per tank for each day the UST regulations are violated.[43] Owners and operators are also subject to penalties of up to $5,000 per violation for violations of the notification requirements and for submitting false information. Penalties may be appealed to the PCHB.

NOTIFICATION, REPORTING AND RECORDKEEPING

Notification Requirements

New UST Systems

A UST owner must notify Ecology at least thirty and not more than ninety days before installing a new UST system by filing a Notice of Intent.[44] Ecology must also be notified within thirty days of startup of the new system by filing a Notification Form.[45] The owner must include a certification of compliance with the requirements for corrosion protection (if a steel tank or piping), financial responsibility and release detection.[46] The owner or operator must also certify that installation complies with new system performance standards.[47] All submittals must be on forms supplied by Ecology. One form may be used for each site.

Existing UST Systems

A UST owner must notify Ecology immediately of any existing UST systems that have not previously been reported to Ecology by filing a Notification Form.[48] If the existing UST system was installed after December 22, 1988, the Notification Form must include a certification of compliance with corrosion protection, financial responsibility and release detection requirements.

Emergency Replacement

Where a UST system is replaced in an emergency due to a release, the owner is not required to provide the thirty-day notice of intent to install a new UST system.[49] However, the owner must notify Ecology within seven days after the emergency installation.

Changes to UST System

The UST owner must submit any changes in the information initially reported to Ecology (e.g., tank closure, change in use of the UST, etc.) on a new notification form within thirty days after the change occurs.[50]

Seller Disclosure

The seller of a UST system or of property containing a UST system must inform the purchaser of the UST notification obligations.[51]

Reporting Requirements

UST owners and operators must submit the following documents to Ecology: (1) UST Notification Forms (WAC 173-360-200); (2) reports of every suspected or confirmed release (WAC 173-360-360; WAC 173-360-372), spill or overfill (WAC 173-360-375); (3) corrective action reports required under Ch. 173-340 WAC; (4) permanent closure or change in service Notification Forms (WAC 173-360-385); (5) evidence of financial responsibility (WAC 173-360-446); and (6) checklists for tank service activities, site checks, and site assessments which must be signed by certified UST supervisors and submitted to Ecology (WAC 173-360-630(2)).[52]

Recordkeeping Requirements

Owners and operators of a UST system must maintain records relating to the following topics at the UST site or a readily available alternative site: operation of corrosion protection equipment (WAC 173360-320); repairs (WAC 173-360-325(7)); release detection compliance (WAC 173-360-355); corrective actions (Ch. 173-340 WAC), financial assurance (WAC 173360-450); and permanent closure site assessments (WAC 173-360-398).[53] Permanent closure records can be mailed to Ecology if they cannot be kept at the site or an alternative site.

UST DESIGN AND PERFORMANCE STANDARDS

Ecology's regulations contain detailed technical specifications regarding UST design, operation, and testing. In particular, these standards relate to preventing corrosion of the UST, spills, and overfills. Only certified UST supervisors may provide the tank services necessary to meet these requirements, and in many cases, the supervisors must be certified in the specific task being performed.[54] UST supervisors must certify that their services comply with applicable performance standards.[55]

Design Standards

New UST Systems

The tank, piping, spill and overfill prevention equipment of a "new" UST system (any system installed after December 22, 1988) must meet specific design standards in order to prevent leaks and spills into the environment.[56] Tanks must be properly designed and constructed with material that is compatible with, and impermeable to, the stored substance.[57] In addition, any portions of the tank that are underground must be protected from corrosion so that the UST will not leak. Acceptable corrosion protection materials and methods are: fiberglass-reinforced plastic; cathodically-protected steel; a steel-fiberglass-reinforced plastic composite; or another material approved by Ecology.

Any piping that routinely contains regulated substances and is in contact with the ground must also be properly designed and constructed, and protected from corrosion.[58] Piping must be constructed of fiberglass-reinforced plastic, cathodically-protected steel, or another material approved by Ecology. Flexible metal underground hose connectors must be cathodically-protected or covered with sleeves or jackets that will ensure corrosion protection for the operating life of the system.

Spill prevention equipment, such as a spill catchment basin, is required so that the product will not reach the environment when the transfer hose is detached from the fill pipe.[59] Also required is overfill prevention equipment that either automatically shuts off flow when the UST is 95% full; restricts flow, or sounds an alarm when the UST is 90% full, or otherwise prevents overfilling.[60] Spill and overfill prevention equipment is not required if no more than twenty-five gallons is transferred into the UST at one time.[61]

Upgrading Existing UST Systems

By December 22, 1998, all "existing" UST systems (those installed on or before December 22, 1988) must either comply with the performance standards for new UST systems described above, be upgraded or be closed.[62] Steel tanks must be upgraded with internal lining, cathodic protection or both.[63] Metal piping that routinely contains regulated substances and is in contact with the ground must be cathodically protected.[64] In addition, spill and overfill equipment meeting the performance standards for new UST systems must be installed.[65]

Deferred UST Systems

A newly installed deferred UST system may not be used to store regulated substances unless the owner or operator can make the following demonstrations: (1) there will be no releases due to corrosion or structural failure for the operational life of the system; (2) the system is either cathodically protected, constructed of noncorrodible material, constructed of steel clad with a noncorrodible material, or designed to prevent releases; and (3) the system is constructed or lined with material that is compatible with the stored substance.[66]

Operating Standards for All UST Systems

Spill and Overfill Control

Before filling tanks, owners and operators must ensure that the tanks have adequate capacity.[67] Owner and operators must also constantly monitor the transfer of product into a UST to prevent overfilling and spilling and must report, investigate and clean up any spills.

Compatibility

Owners and operators must ensure that UST systems are made of, or lined with, material that is compatible with and impermeable to the substance stored in the systems.[68]

Corrosion Protection

Owners and operators of steel UST systems with corrosion protection equipment must comply with specific requirements to prevent releases due to tank corrosion.[69] These requirements include continuous operation and maintenance of corrosion protection equipment, as well as regular inspection of the equipment and retention of inspection records.

Repairs

Owners and operators of UST systems must ensure that any repairs made to the systems will prevent releases due to structural failure or corrosion for as long as the UST systems are in service.[70] If a UST system is repaired to correct a structural defect, the system must also be upgraded to meet corrosion protection and release detection requirements. Repairs must be performed by certified UST supervisors, and repair records must be retained throughout the operating life of the system.[71]

Repairs to fiberglass-reinforced plastic tanks must meet manufacturer's specifications. Corroded metal pipe sections and fittings must be replaced. Fiberglass pipes and fittings must be repaired to manufacturer's specifications. Repaired tanks and piping must be tightness tested within 30 days after the repair. Cathodically-protected UST systems must be tested within six months after the repair.

Release Detection

Owners and operators of all petroleum and other hazardous substances UST systems[72] must use an approved method to detect releases from tanks and piping that routinely contain regulated substances.[73] If release detection methods are not applied to a UST system, the system must be closed. Owners and operators of hazardous substance USTs must also install a containment system, such as secondary containment, a double-walled tank, an external liner, or another method approved by Ecology, in order to prevent releases. Release containment is mandatory for all new hazardous substance UST systems (those installed after December 22, 1988), and must be applied to all existing hazardous substance UST systems (those installed on or after December 22, 1988) by December 22, 1998.[74]

The type and frequency of release detection required depends on tank capacity and other factors relating to the particular UST system. Depending upon the UST capacity, the date of installation, and the level of compliance with upgrading requirements, a combination of the following methods may be used on existing tanks to meet leak detection requirements: (1)

daily inventory control, (2) weekly tank gauging; (3) monthly tank gauging; and (4) tank tightness testing.[75] One of the following monthly release detection methods must ultimately be used on all tanks: (1) automatic tank gauging; (2) vapor monitoring; (3) ground water monitoring; (4) interstitial monitoring; or (5) statistical inventory reconciliation.[76] Ecology may also approve other release detection methods.[77] Whatever method of release detection is selected, owners and operators must meet specific performance requirements for the particular method.[78]

For piping, the particular release detection method that must be used depends on whether the underground piping is pressurized piping or suction piping.[79] Release detection methods include automatic line leak detectors, line tightness testing and monthly monitoring. All of these methods must meet specific performance requirements.

Records of compliance with release detection requirements must be retained, typically for a period of five years or more.[80]

RELEASES AND SPILLS

What To Do If You Suspect a Release?

Report the Release

Owners and operators of UST systems must report any of the following situations to Ecology within twenty-four hours: (1) discovery of released regulated substances at the UST site or surrounding area; (2) observation of unusual operating conditions (e.g., sudden loss of product, the presence of water, or erratic operation of product dispensing equipment) unless the equipment is immediately repaired and no leak occurred; or (3) indication from monitoring results that a leak may have occurred.[81] Any confirmed release must also be reported within twenty-four hours.[82]

Investigate and Take Necessary Corrective Action

If a release is suspected, owners and operators must immediately (within seven days after discovery) investigate and confirm the suspected release.[83] Owners and operators must conduct a system test to determine whether a leak has occurred and must make any necessary repairs. Regardless of the results of the system test, if environmental contamination is the basis for suspecting the release, owners and operators must also have a certified UST supervisor take site samples and perform a site check. If at any time it is determined that a release has occurred, the UST owners and operators must report the release to Ecology and begin corrective action under the UST regulations or MTCA or both.[84] Ecology may require an investigation of off-site impacts.[85]

What Do You Do If There Is A Spill?

Contain and Cleanup

Spills must be immediately contained and cleaned up. Owners and operators of a UST must visually inspect the situation, take immediate action to prevent further release, minimize any fire hazard, absorb or otherwise contain all free product and properly dispose of the released product, soils and other materials.[86] Under MTCA's UST regulations, owners and operators must, within twenty-four hours, remove as much of the hazardous substance from the UST as is possible and necessary to prevent further release.[87]

Take Corrective Action

Additional corrective actions may be required by the MTCA regulations (Ch. 173-340 WAC) or the state Clean Water Act (Ch. 90.48 RCW) in the following cases: (1) a petroleum spill that exceeds twenty-five gallons *or* one that cannot be cleaned up within twenty-four hours; (2) a petroleum spill of any amount that causes ground water contamination or a sheen on ground water or surface water; and (3) a hazardous substance spill that exceeds the CERCLA "reportable quantity" or one that cannot be cleaned up within twenty-four hours.[88]

Report the Spill

UST system owners and operators must immediately report a petroleum spill and related cleanup efforts if the spill comes in contact with soil or water.[89] If there is no such contact but the spill is above a de minimis amount,[90] it must be reported within twenty-four hours of discovery. A hazardous substance spill and related cleanup efforts must be reported immediately if it comes in contact with soil or water or if it is above a de minimis amount.[91]

CLOSURE REQUIREMENTS

Permanent Closure

Owners and operators of USTs must notify Ecology in writing thirty days before permanently closing or changing the service of a tank or a UST system.[92] Before permanent closure or change-in-service is completed, a site assessment must be performed by a person registered with Ecology.[93] If contaminated soils, contaminated water or free product are discovered, owners and operators must ensure that appropriate corrective action is undertaken.[94] Closure must be completed by a certified UST supervisor within sixty days after expiration of the thirty-day notice period.[95] Owners and operators must return active tank permits to Ecology within thirty days after closure is completed and must submit checklists to Ecology certifying that all required tank services met the regulatory requirements.[96]

In order to elect a change-in-service or permanently close a UST system, the tank must first be emptied and cleaned of all liquids and sludges.[97] For UST systems being closed, the tank must then either be -removed from the ground or filled with inert solid material, and all piping must be either capped or removed.[98]

Temporary Closure

Temporarily closed UST systems must continue to meet certain performance standards and requirements, especially if they are to be closed for more than three months.[99] Tank owners and operators must also comply with requirements for suspected releases, spills and corrective action. Tank systems that have been temporarily closed for more than three months may not be put back into service unless they are in compliance with applicable release detection requirements or have been tightness tested. A new permit must also be obtained in order to put the system back in service.[100] After one year of temporary closure, the

UST must be permanently closed, unless it meets the performance standards for new USTs or the upgrading requirements for existing USTs.[101]

Within thirty days of temporarily closing a UST system, the owner or operator must notify Ecology and must return any active permits for the system to Ecology.[102]

Previous Closure

If Ecology believes that releases from a UST system that was closed or abandoned before December 22, 1988 pose a threat to human health and the environment, then Ecology can require the owner or operator to permanently close the UST system in accordance with the UST regulations.[103]

Closure Records

UST systems owners and operators must maintain records demonstrating compliance with the closure requirements. In addition, either the owner or operator who closed a UST or the current owner or operator of the site must maintain site assessment results for at least five years after closure or change-in-service.[104] Closure records may be mailed to Ecology if they cannot be maintained at the site.

FINANCIAL RESPONSIBILITY REQUIREMENTS FOR PETROLEUM USTS

Who Is Required to Demonstrate Financial Responsibility?

Either the owner or operator of petroleum UST systems must demonstrate financial responsibility, but both are subject to Ecology's enforcement authority for noncompliance.[105] Exempt or deferred UST systems and certain government-owned USTs are not subject to these requirements. Financial responsibility requirements must be in place until the UST system is closed, or if corrective action is required, until after corrective action has been completed and the tank has been properly closed.[106]

When?

Most petroleum UST owners and operators are currently required to have demonstrated financial responsibility.[107] The only exception is for Indian tribes that own USTs that are on Indian lands and that comply with federal technical requirements.[108] Owners and operators of these tanks must comply with federal financial responsibility requirements by December 31, 1998.

To Cover What?

Financial responsibility is required to establish financial ability to pay for corrective action and to compensate third parties for bodily injury and property damage caused by releases from petroleum UST operations.[109] Ecology can draw on the financial assurance mechanism if it suspects a release or for other specific reasons set forth in the regulations.[110]

How Much?

The owner or operator must demonstrate financial responsibility on both a per occurrence and an annual aggregate basis. These amounts do not, however, limit the liability of the owner or operator.[111]

The amount of per occurrence coverage for owners and operators of petroleum UST systems that are located at petroleum marketing facilities or that handle an average of more than 10,000 gallons per month is $1,000,000.[112] All other owners or operators of petroleum UST systems must have $500,000 of coverage per occurrence.

The annual aggregate amounts of coverage are determined by the total number of petroleum USTs[113] owned or operated by one entity. If between 1 and 100 petroleum USTs are owned or operated, the amount of aggregate coverage required is $1,000,000.[114] If an entity owns or operates 101 or more USTs, the amount of aggregate coverage required is $2,000,000. The owner or operator must review the total number of USTs owned or operated whenever an additional UST is installed to ensure that the appropriate coverage is provided.[115]

Methods of Financial Assurance

Financial responsibility requirements can be satisfied by using one or a combination of the following mechanisms (subject to some limitations): (1) financial test of self-insurance; (2) guarantee; (3) insurance and risk retention group coverage; (4) surety bond; (5) letter of credit; (6) trust fund; and (7) standby trust fund.[116] Forms for the various financial responsibility instruments are provided in appendices A-J of the regulations and must be used.[117] Under certain circumstances, the owner or operator may substitute an alternate financial assurance mechanism.[118] If the provider of financial assurance cancels or fails to renew an assurance mechanism, the owner or operator must obtain new alternate coverage, generally within sixty days.[119] If Ecology has drawn on a standby trust funded by a financial assurance mechanism and the trust falls below the full amount of required coverage, the owner or operator must either replenish the trust or obtain alternate coverage.[120]

Recordkeeping and Reporting Requirements

Specific evidence of all financial assurance mechanisms must be maintained at the UST site or the owner's or operator's place of business.[121] The owner or operator must also maintain a separate updated Certification of Financial Responsibility.[122] When installing a new UST, owners or operators must certify compliance with financial responsibility requirements. The owner or operator must submit appropriate documentation of financial responsibility to Ecology: (1) within thirty days after a reportable release; (2) within thirty days after a financial assurance provider is subject to bankruptcy proceedings or otherwise cannot provide assurance if the owner or operator cannot obtain alternate coverage; (3) in other situations where the owner or operator no longer meets the self-insurance requirement, has had coverage canceled, or cannot obtain coverage; and (4) whenever required by Ecology to do so.[123] Also, if the owner or operator is subject to bankruptcy proceedings, he or she must, within ten days, notify Ecology by certified mail and submit documentation regarding current financial responsibility.[124]

Reinsurance

The Pollution Liability Insurance Agency (PLIA) has been created to assist certain tank owners in meeting the UST financial responsibility requirements.[125] This program is intended to "reinsure" private insurance companies for losses above a stated amount specified in a contract between the insurer and the state. The PLIA also provides financial assistance to certain UST owners and operators that have limited financial resources, and to rural and remote communities.[126] Finally, the PLIA administers the newly enacted Heating Oil Pollution Liability Protection Act, which provides financial assistance to owners of active residential heating oil tanks.[127]

UST SERVICE PROVIDERS AND SUPERVISORS

UST Services Must be Performed by Certified UST Supervisors

All UST services, including installation, retrofitting, decommissioning, testing, and site checks must be performed by certified UST supervisors.[128] Site assessments may be performed by either certified UST supervisors or by Washington registered professional engineers who are otherwise competent to perform site assessments. Certified UST supervisors are persons who have been certified by the International Fire Code Institute or other nationally recognized associations identified by Ecology.[129] Ecology requires certification in five distinct areas: (1) tank installation and retrofitting; (2) tank decommissioning; (3) tightness testing; (4) cathodic protection installation and testing; and (5) site assessment.[130] UST owners and operators are responsible for ensuring that the UST supervisors they employ are properly certified.[131] Certified UST supervisors are not required for servicing tanks that are exempt from the UST rules.[132]

Responsibilities of Certified UST Supervisors

Unless otherwise determined by Ecology, a certified UST supervisor must be present on site at all times when tank service activities, including installation, retrofitting, testing, and decommissioning, are being conducted.[133] In addition, certified UST supervisors must complete checklists provided by Ecology for each regulated activity performed, and must sign the checklists within thirty days after completing the service.[134] Proof of supervisor certification must be maintained for inspection at any project site.[135] For UST system installations or retrofits, certified UST supervisors must submit to Ecology an "as-built site plan" that shows the location of the UST systems and adjacent structures.

In carrying out their obligations, certified UST supervisors must comply with all federal and state regulations when performing tank services.[136] In addition, supervisors are required to report any confirmed releases that pose a threat to human health and the environment to the UST owner or operator immediately after discovery and to Ecology within seventy-two hours after discovery.[137] If the owner or operator is not available, the supervisor should report immediately to Ecology. Finally, if a certified UST supervisor learns that a regulated UST system has not been registered with Ecology, or is otherwise out of compliance with the UST regulations' the supervisor must inform the system's owner or operator of the notification and other applicable requirements.[138]

Penalties

Any person or firm that violates these requirements is subject to civil penalties of up to $5,000 for each tank per day of violation.[139] Enforcement actions may be appealed to the Pollution Control Hearings Board.[140]

NOTES

[1] 42 USC §§6991 *et seq.*

[2] See 40 CFR 280.

[3] See Washington. Final Approval of State Underground Storage Tank Program, 58 Fed. Reg. 47,217 (1993).

[4] RCW §90.76.

[5] WAC 173-360.

[6] 42 USC §6991c; 40 CFR 281.

[7] 58 Fed. Reg. 47,217 (1993).

[8] *Id.* at 47,218.

[9] RCW §90.76.020(4). A number of categories of USTs are exempt or subject to limited regulation under WAC 173-360-110.

[10] RCW §90.76.050(2); WAC 173-360-130(4).

[11] RCW §90.76.040; WAC 173-360-500.

[12] RCW §70.105D.

[13] WAC 173-340-450(1)(a).

[14] http://www.ecy.wa.gov/pubs/04-09-088.pdf.

[15] WAC 173-360-120.

[16] *Id.*; see also 42 USC §9601(14) (Superfund definition of hazardous substances).

[17] WAC 173-360-120.

[18] Although generally exempt from regulation under the UST program, such heating oil tanks are subject to the release reporting requirements of WAC 173-360-372 if they contain more than 1,100 gallons. WAC 173-360-110(2)(h).

[19] WAC 173-360-110(2).

[20] WAC 173-360-110(3).

[21] *Id.*; WAC 173-360-300.

[22] WAC 173-360-110(1).

[23] WAC 173-360-120.

[24] WAC 173-360-130(1).

[25] WAC 173-360-130(3). Ecology has specified numerous design, construction, management, and performance standards. WAC 173-360-305 through 173-360-375.

[26] WAC 173-360-200(2).

[27] WAC 173-360-130(2)(a); WAC 173-360-400 through WAC 173-360-463.

[28] WAC 173-360-130(2)(b).

[29] WAC 173-360-130(3).

[30] WAC 173-360-130(2)(c) and -380.

[31] WAC 173-360-130(2)(d).

[32] WAC 173-360-130(4).

[33] WAC 173-360-130(6).

[34] WAC 173-360-130(7).

35 WAC 173-360-130(8).

36 WAC 173-360-130(10).

37 WAC 173-360-130(9).

38 Authorized representatives of the state include enforcement officers, employees or representatives of Ecology or of a local government with authority under RCW §90.76.030; WAC 173-360-140(4).

39 Compliance monitoring must be consistent with 40 CFR 281.40 and in accordance with WAC 173-360-150.

40 WAC 173-360-140(1)-(2).

41 WAC 173-360-140(3).

42 WAC 173-360-160. Ecology's authority to assess civil penalties is somewhat limited by the "Notice of Correction" provisions of recent technical assistance legislation. *See* RCW §90.76.080; RCW §§43.05.060 through .080; RCW §43.05.150.

43 WAC 173-360-170. Penalties for tank service providers and supervisors are contained in WAC 173-360-670.

44 WAC 173-360-200(1).

45 WAC 173-360-200(2).

46 WAC 173-360-200(2)(e).

47 WAC 173-360-200(3); WAC 173-360-305(5). The certification form must be signed by a certified UST supervisor.

48 WAC 173-360200(4).

49 WAC 173 360-200(5).

50 WAC 173-360-200(6).

51 WAC 173-360-200(7).

52 WAC 173-360-210(1).

53 WAC 173-360-210(2).

54 *See e.g.,* WAC 173 -360-305(5).

55 *See e.g,* WAC l73-360-305(5).

56 WAC 173-360-305.

57 WAC 173-360-305(1).

58 WAC 173-360-305(2).

59 WAC l73-360-305(3)(a)(i).

60 WAC l73-360-305(3)(a)(ii).

61 WAC 173-360-305(3)(b).

62 WAC 173-360-310(1).

63 WAC 173-360-310(2).

64 WAC 173-360-310(3).

65 WAC 173-360-310(4).

66 WAC 173-360-300.

67 WAC 173-360-315.

68 WAC 173-360-323.

69 WAC 173-360-320.

70 WAC 173-360-325.

71 WAC 173-325(1) and (7).

72 "Petroleum UST systems" are those that contain petroleum or a mixture of petroleum and a de minimis quantity of other regulated substances. "Hazardous substance UST systems" are all other USTs that contain regulated substances. WAC 173-360-120.

73 WAC 173-360-330 (general requirement); WAC 173-360-335 (petroleum USTs); WAC 173-360-340 (hazardous substance USTs). There is a minor exception to this requirement for emergency generator tanks installed between 1989 and 1990. However, as of December 22, 1996, even these tanks must comply with release detection requirements. WAC 173-360-330.

74 WAC 173-360-340(1).

75 WAC 173-360-345(1) through (5); (6)(a) through (6)(d).

76 WAC 173-360 345(6)(c) through (i).

77 WAC 173-360-345(6)(i).

78 WAC 173-360-345(1).

79 WAC 173-360-350.

80 WAC 173-360-355.

81 WAC 173 360-360.

82 WAC 173-360-372.

83 WAC 173-360-370.

84 WAC 173-360-370(2)(a) and (2)(b); WAC 173-360-399.

85 WAC 173-360-365.

86 WAC 173-360-375(2).

87 WAC I73-340-450(2)(b); WAC 173-360-375(3).

88 WAC 173-360-375(3).

89 WAC 173-360-375(1)(a).

90 Ecology's Guidance for Reporting Spills and Overfills of Petroleum, defines a *de minimis* amount of petroleum as "any amount of petroleum that (1) immediately evaporates or (2) is less than a gallon and has been sufficiently recovered or contained so that it will not pose a threat to human health or the environment."

91 WAC 173-360-375(1)(b). A *de minimis* amount of a hazardous substance is any amount that is below the specified reportable quantity under CERCLA. *See* 40 CFR 302.1 (reportable quantities). Note that, if the spill exceeds the reportable quantity, it also must be reported immediately to federal agencies pursuant to CERCLA reporting requirements. 42 USC §9603(a); 40 CFR 302.6.

92 WAC 173-360-385(1). "Change-in-service" is the continued use of a UST system to store a non-regulated substance. WAC 173-360-385(5).

93 WAC 173-360-390(1). In lieu of performing a site assessment, in some instances a report may be submitted to Ecology demonstrating that no leaks have been detected. WAC 173-360-390(2).

94 WAC 173-360-390(4).

95 WAC 173-360-385(2).

96 WAC 173-360-385(6).

97 WAC 173-360-385(3) and (5).

98 WAC 173-360-385(4).

99 WAC 173-360-380.

100 WAC 173-360-130(2)(c).

101 WAC 173-360-380(4).
102 WAC 173-360-200(6); WAC 173-360-380(5).
103 WAC 173-360-395.
104 WAC 173-360-398.
105 WAC-173-360-400.
106 WAC 173-360-456.
107 WAC 173-360-403.
108 40 CFR 280.91(f).
109 WAC 173-360-406.
110 WAC 173-360-453.
111 WAC 173-360-406(1), (2) and (6).
112 WAC 173-360-406(1).

113 For purposes of the financial responsibility requirements, a petroleum UST means a single containment unit, not combinations of single containment units. WAC 173-360-406(3).

114 WAC 173-360-406(2).
115 WAC 173-360-406(4).

116 WAC 173-360-410; *see* WAC 173-360-413 through -436 for the detailed requirements of various financial assurance mechanisms.

117 WAC 173-360-470 through -499.
118 WAC 173-360-440.
119 WAC 173-360-443.
120 WAC 173-360-463.
121 WAC 173-360-450.
122 WAC 173-360-450(2)(f); *see* WAC 173-360-496 for the form of the required certification.
123 WAC 173-360-446.
124 WAC 173-360-460.
125 RCW §70.148.120 through .901; WAC 374.
126 WAC 374-50; WAC 374-60.
127 RCW §70.149; WAC 374-70.
128 WAC 173-360-630 and -660.
129 WAC 173-360-120.
130 WAC 173-360-620.
131 WAC 173-360-110(1).
132 WAC 173-360-610.
133 WAC 173-360-630(4).
134 WAC 173-360-630(2).
135 WAC 173-360-630(6).
136 WAC 173-360-630(1).
137 WAC 173-360-630(3).
138 WAC 173-360-630(5).
139 WAC 173-360-670.

[140] RCW 43.21B.

CHAPTER 13

Environmental Considerations in Business Transactions

INTRODUCTION

Real estate transactions drive at least as many cleanups as do environmental agencies. A contaminated property that may not become a priority for EPA or Ecology for years, is frequently the centerpiece of negotiations between buyers and sellers, lenders and borrowers, and landlords and tenants. This chapter discusses the impact of environmental laws on real estate transactions and offers suggestions for minimizing liability in those transactions. Its focus is on "on-site" problems, as opposed to "off-site" contingent liabilities.

TYPES OF REAL PROPERTY LIKELY TO INVOLVE ENVIRONMENTAL PROBLEMS

Environmental problems are most frequently found on industrial properties, commercial and agricultural land, landfills, and environmentally sensitive areas, such as wetlands and floodplains. Determining the historical uses of the land involved in a transaction is a critical element of assessing potential environmental liabilities.

Industrial Properties

Many properties used now or in the past for manufacturing, mining, transportation, and other industrial activities have been contaminated by chemicals, petroleum and other hazardous products. In addition, many small businesses not commonly associated with hazardous waste generation have a history of waste disposal problems. For example, dry cleaners, marinas, print shops, wood refinishers and photo finishers generate hazardous wastes or byproducts. Service stations also potentially pose environmental problems, especially from leaking underground storage tanks.

Commercial Properties

Many commercial properties, including office parks, office buildings and residential apartments, contain asbestos, electrical equipment containing polychlorinated biphenyls (PCBs), leaking underground storage tanks or aboveground storage tanks.

Agricultural Land

Environmental problems occur on agricultural property because of pesticide and fertilizer use, petroleum handling, and past hazardous waste disposal.

Landfills

Many public and private landfills that were "closed" under less stringent regulatory requirements than exist today are still contaminated. In addition to licensed facilities, thousands of fills, lagoons, "bone yards," junk yards, and informal dumping grounds exist on public and private property throughout Washington.

Environmentally Sensitive Areas

Development of environmentally sensitive areas may be prohibited or restricted. Environmentally sensitive areas include shorelines, coastal areas, wetlands, floodplains, seismically active or geologically unstable areas, and historically or archaeologically significant properties.

LIABILITY CONCERNS

Concerns in the real estate community over environmental hazards stem from enactment of federal, state, and local liability laws over the past decade and the uncertainty these laws have created for lenders. The most important of these laws are the federal and state Superfund laws.

Federal and State Superfunds

Both the Comprehensive Environmental Response, Compensation and Liability Act (CERCLA), as amended by the Superfund Amendments and Reauthorization Act of 1986 (SARA) (collectively known as the federal Superfund),[1] and the Washington Model Toxics Control Act (MTCA or state Superfund)[2] were enacted to compel cleanup of contaminated property. These laws seek to impose cleanup responsibility on property owners and other presumptively liable parties.

Federal and state Superfund liability is "strict"—meaning that in order to be held legally responsible for the costs of cleaning up contaminated property, one need not have caused the contamination. Merely "owning" or "operating" the property is sufficient to establish liability.[3]

Federal and state Superfund liability is also "joint and several"—meaning that, any person legally responsible under the law can be held responsible by the government for all the cleanup costs, even if there are other persons who are equally or more responsible.[4] There is an exception from this rule under the federal Superfund if a party can show that the harm caused is "divisible" or that there is another reasonable basis for apportioning costs among liable parties.[5]

The principles of "strict" and "joint and several" liability under the federal and state Superfunds can transform real property assets into substantial liabilities.

Liabilities of Purchasers and Sellers

Purchasers and sellers of contaminated real property are potentially liable under the federal and state Superfunds. The purchaser of contaminated real property is potentially liable even if the prior owner or an adjacent property owner caused the problem.[6] A seller of contaminated real property is potentially liable for hazardous substances disposed of on the property during the seller's ownership or operation, even if the disposal was lawful at the time.[7]

Liabilities of Lenders

Lenders who are deemed to be the owner or operator of secured, contaminated property are potentially liable under the broad reach of the federal and state Superfunds. For example, lenders who come to own contaminated property through foreclosure have been held liable under the federal Superfund for cleanup costs as "owners" of that property.[8] So too, lenders who have actively managed a borrower's business or property have been held liable as "operators" (for example, by arranging for waste disposal).[9] Recently, in response to uncertainty over the liability of lenders, Congress passed legislation to clarify and limit lender liability under the federal Superfund.[10] Likewise, Washington State has also recently passed legislation to limit lender risks under MTCA.[11] Despite such legislation, however, lender liability remains a possibility under both Superfunds.[12]

Liabilities of Landlords and Tenants

Landlords are potentially liable under the federal and state Superfunds as owners of property even if the contamination was caused by tenants.[13] Landlords of contaminated property have been held liable under the federal Superfund, even if they have no knowledge that their tenants were contaminating the property.[14]

Tenants are potentially liable under the federal and state Superfunds for contamination of property occurring during their tenancy.[15] Tenants are also potentially liable as owners or operators if they maintain control over and have responsibility for, the use of the property.[16] Generally, the tenant and the landlord are held jointly and severally liable, with the allocation of cleanup costs between the two parties determined by evaluating equitable factors.[17]

Statutory Exemptions from Liability

The federal Superfund contains narrow statutory exemptions from liability, which protect the following parties:

1. interim owners—persons who owned or leased property after hazardous wastes were disposed on the property, who can demonstrate that they did not themselves contribute wastes to the site and who subsequently transferred their interest in the property before a cleanup was determined to be necessary;[18]
2. security interest holders—lenders and others who hold security instruments;[19]
3. innocent purchasers—current owners who establish by a preponderance of the evidence that (a) they did not conduct, permit, or contribute to the release of hazardous

substances on the property; (b) they acquired the property after the disposal or placement of the hazardous substances on the property; and (c) at the time they acquired contaminated property they did not know, and had no reason to know, about the disposal of hazardous substances on the property;[20]
4. government landowners who acquire property involuntarily or through eminent domain proceedings—as long as they exercise due care with respect to any hazardous substances and have not contaminated the property;[21]
5. landowners who acquire property through inheritance or bequest—as long as they did not themselves contaminate it and exercised due care to prevent contamination by third parties;[22]
6. landowners whose properly is contaminated by unrelated third parties—as long as they did not themselves contaminate it and exercised due care to prevent contamination by third parties;[23] and
7. persons whose property is contaminated solely by an act of God or an act of war.[24]

The state Superfund provides several additional exemptions from liability to those found under the federal Superfund:

1. persons who use a hazardous substance for domestic purposes, provided the hazardous substance is used in accordance with applicable laws and in a non-negligent manner;[25] and
2. persons who apply pesticides or fertilizers to food crops, provided that the pesticides or fertilizers are applied in accordance with applicable laws and in a non-negligent manner.[26]

Unlike the federal Superfund, the state Superfund applies to releases of petroleum. Because petroleum contamination is pervasive, the law has broad effects on real property transactions. Note also that the state Superfund does not exempt from liability governmental entities who acquire contaminated property through the exercise of eminent domain.

Other Environmental Laws

Environmental Management Laws

A second group of laws that create potential environmental liabilities in business transactions involving real property are environmental management laws. This group includes the Resource Conservation and Recovery Act (RCRA),[27] the Clean Air Act (CAA),[28] the Toxic Substances Control Act (TSCA),[29] the Federal Water Pollution Control Act (FWPCA),[30] the Occupational Safety and Health Act (OSHA)[31] and the various state, regional or local counterparts to these federal laws. While the federal and state Superfunds are mainly concerned with cleaning up existing disposal sites, these laws are principally concerned with managing hazardous substances and wastes so as to avoid creation of new pollution problems.

Environmental management laws are significant in real estate acquisitions because a purchaser may be liable for penalties resulting from the previous owner's regulatory violations or failure to obtain needed permits. Lenders who are deemed owners or operators may face liability under management laws as well.[32] Regulatory violations that are discovered may lead to the obligation of a new owner to report the violation, and an inability to operate a plant (due to the absence of valid permits), or to civil as well as criminal liability (operation without a valid permit). Even if the seller had the required permits, a purchaser may be liable for penalties if the seller failed to comply with the operating requirements of its permits.

Laws Governing Real Estate Development in Environmentally Sensitive Areas

A third set of environmental laws relevant to real estate transactions regulates or limits development in environmentally sensitive areas, such as shorelines, coastal areas, wetlands, floodplains, steep slopes, critical habitat, and historically or archaeologically significant properties. This group of laws includes the National Environmental Policy Act (NEPA),[33] the Coastal Zone Management Act (CZMA),[34] Section 404 of the Clean Water Act,[35] zoning ordinances and other and the various Washington State and local counterparts to these federal laws. In addition, the Growth Management Act now greatly impacts such development.

These laws can reduce the economic value of property purchased for development. When development is allowed to go forward, the owner typically must incur significant expenses to mitigate harm resulting from development.

Special State Laws Governing Real Estate Transfers

Unlike New Jersey, Massachusetts and several other states, Washington does not require purchasers to obtain the approval of environmental authorities prior to property transfer. Nor does the state Superfund law currently impose environmental disclosure requirements,[36] although common law developments have led to a conservative approach to disclosure of known environmental liabilities.

Common Law Liability

State common law could create potential environmental liability for contamination arising out of hazardous waste on an acquired property. Increased public awareness of hazardous substance management practices has given rise to a growing number of personal injury "toxic tort" cases.[37] Besides personal injury actions, property damage actions may be brought under nuisance, trespass or negligence theories. Consequently, parties to a real estate transaction must also remember to account in their negotiations for environmental disclosures and the potential for third party property damage claims, as well as cleanup actions.

STRATEGIES FOR MINIMIZING LIABILITY

As discussed above, environmental legislation, regulations, agency guidance interpreting these laws and regulations, and cases cast a broad liability net over purchasers, sellers, lenders, landlords and tenants. Given this broad liability exposure, parties to real estate transactions should investigate environmental problems and allocate the risk of environmental liability through available contractual means, including representations and warranties, indemnities and other traditional contract provisions. Although liability to governmental agencies for cleanup costs is unaffected by private agreements, CERCLA permits private parties to enter into such agreements in order to allocate liability among themselves.[38] Such agreements generally have been enforced in Superfund litigation.[39] To be enforceable, however, allocation or assumption of liability agreements should clearly make reference to the relevant environmental statutes (e.g., CERCLA).

Purchasers, sellers, lenders, landlords and tenants approach a real estate transaction with different information wants and needs regarding environmental liabilities. Purchasers must be concerned about hidden liabilities that will diminish the value of their investment and impede development. Accordingly, they will generally want to find out as much as possible about the condition of the property before purchasing and protect themselves through representations and warranties, an environmental indemnity obtained from the seller, or environmental insurance.

Conversely, sellers generally have some incentive to disclose only what they already know about property conditions. For sellers, more knowledge about environmental conditions may lead to a governmental reporting obligation, a disclosure obligation, a costly cleanup, and delay of the sale. Sellers will also want to reduce their future contingent environmental liability by limiting any representations and warranties and environmental indemnities provided to purchasers, through disclaimers and releases, and through obtaining an indemnity from purchasers for post-closing liability.

Lenders, like purchasers, generally will want to find out as much as they can before making a loan, in order to evaluate the value of the property as security. Lenders will also want to reduce their future contingent environmental liability by obtaining environmental representations and warranties and indemnities from their borrowers.

Landlords will want to find out as much as they can about the proposed activities of their tenants before entering a lease. They also will want to notice provisions regarding certain activities of their tenants to ensure that they are operating with all necessary permits, and are not employing practices that could release hazardous substances into the environment. Tenants, meanwhile, need to guard themselves against leasing commercial or industrial property that may already be contaminated by the activities of the landlord, prior tenants or tenants commonly occupying the property. Both parties will want to reduce their future contingent environmental liabilities through appropriate lease provisions. With these dynamics in mind, the following environmental information-gathering strategies and mechanisms for allocating the risk of environmental exposure should be considered.

Protecting Purchasers from Liability

Environmental Investigation

Early in the negotiation process, purchasers should do everything practical to investigate the condition of the property and necessary operating permits and licenses, even if the seller has already performed an environmental assessment. If the property is contaminated or the necessary environmental permits are not fully in place, the purchaser will then be in a position to protect itself by requiring the seller to clean up the property or secure the necessary permits as a condition of sale, by renegotiating the purchase terms, or by walking away from the sale.

Real estate purchase and sale agreements typically provide the purchaser with an opportunity to inspect the premises. From the purchaser's perspective, these provisions should be broadly written and specifically permit environmental testing including soil and groundwater sampling, and leak testing for all underground storage tanks. Closing should be made contingent upon obtaining testing results satisfactory to the purchaser. Purchasers should also obtain an explicit right to contact government agencies, environmental groups, prior owners, current and ex-employees and other third parties who may have information about operations at and environmental conditions on the property.

Environmental assessments are generally conducted in two phases: Phase I and Phase II. The purpose of the Phase I environmental assessment is to identify areas of potential contamination on the property that deserve future attention. The information needed for the Phase I assessment will vary with the transaction. Generally, the Phase I assessment will explore past ownership and uses of the property, uses of adjacent properties, and whether chemicals were used, manufactured or stored there. It will provide an explanation of all past on-site and off-site disposal practices, information about the presence and condition of asbestos, PCBs and aboveground and underground tanks, proof of the existence and status of necessary permits and government approvals, information about any pending or threatened government or third-party actions, and information about the presence of on-site environmentally sensitive areas that may limit or prevent future development or use of the property for business purposes. At a minimum, the Phase I assessment should conform to the standardized procedures of the American Society for Testing and Materials (ASTM) for environmental site assessments.

If the Phase I environmental assessment raises no warning flags, no further investigation may be warranted. If there is evidence of potential soil or groundwater contamination, or questions related to the adequacy of operating permits, a Phase II environmental assessment may be warranted.

The purpose of a Phase II environmental assessment is to confirm or deny the findings of the Phase I assessment, and to characterize the nature and extent of contamination. It generally consists of sampling of problem media, such as soils or groundwater, and laboratory analysis.

If significant environmental problems are discovered during the environmental investigation, the purchaser may still want to go ahead with the transaction.

Because the parties may be unable to predict the cost of cleaning up an environmental problem or otherwise bringing the facility into compliance, they may want to escrow funds for this purpose. A separate negotiation may be required to determine who will control disbursement of the funds in escrow. Sellers will generally want to do the cleanup as cheaply as possible, in order to recover the escrow monies. Purchasers, on the other hand, will have little incentive to keep the costs low because, in effect, they are using the seller's money. A solution might be to give the purchaser control, but to split any funds remaining after the cleanup is completed. That way, the purchaser then has an incentive to strike the best cleanup agreement with the government and the seller may move on to other projects.

In multi-site transactions, the purchaser may want to eliminate problem sites or postpone closing of the problem sites until environmental issues are resolved. Also, in a transaction involving a single parcel, it is sometimes possible to "carve out" the contaminated portion of the property. The success of pursuing this option will depend, however, on whether the environmental problem can be isolated (e.g., no adjacent groundwater contamination) and on whether the contaminated area is important to operations on the property.

Contract Mechanisms

Purchasers can also minimize their exposure by obtaining the broadest possible representations and warranties from the seller. Purchasers should ask the seller to represent and warrant that the seller is in compliance with all environmental laws and has all required permits. If misrepresentations are made, the purchaser then has the option to sue the seller for breach of these representations and warranties and recover damages. The purchase agreement should specifically state that all representations and warranties survive closing for some period of time. When possible, the purchaser should obtain representations that are absolute, i.e., not limited to the seller's knowledge. To the extent that representations are made to the best of the seller's knowledge, the purchaser should attempt to obtain language stating that the seller has made due inquiry of all persons likely to know about any environmental problems or noncompliance at the facility. The seller may attempt to resist purchaser's demands, and the price will reflect the outcome of these negotiations.

Having obtained disclosure of known liabilities in representations and warranties, the parties have a variety of mechanisms for allocating those liabilities, including a reduction in the sale price, exclusion of certain portions of the property from the transaction, placing funds in escrow, and the like. By far, the most common mechanism for allocating known liabilities is an indemnity or "hold harmless" clause.

While any party to a real estate transaction may indemnify the other, it is usually the purchaser who seeks this protection. In either case, the parties should specify that the indemnity includes liability under Superfund and related laws; however, ultimately, indemnities are interpreted using the contract law of the relevant jurisdiction.[40]

When an environmental assessment has disclosed only minor liabilities, the seller may want to offer to give the purchaser an indemnity in lieu of a reduction of the purchase price. When more substantial risks are involved, however, the indemnity alone may not be enough. If the seller does not have the resources to indemnify the purchaser, then the indemnity is of limited or no value. Therefore, where there is a potential for substantial environmental liabilities, it may be advisable to obtain the guaranty of a related, financially substantial corporation or person in the event the seller cannot pay. Another solution may be to require the seller to post a letter of credit, escrow funds, or post alternative security (other property) for a negotiated time period for the purpose of satisfying any indemnity obligation. The purchaser may also require the seller to obtain Environmental Impairment Liability (EIL) insurance and name the purchaser as an additional EIL insured, although the difficulty and expense in obtaining EIL insurance, and the ability to recover against some of the companies providing EIL, make this alternative one to undertake with care.

If the purchaser plans to continue in the seller's business, each party may want a cross-indemnity from the other. For example, if a permitted effluent discharge is known to be contributing contaminants to sediments in an urban bay, the seller and purchaser will need to negotiate a method of allocating the eventual cleanup costs Often, the parties will agree to bear a pro rata share of cleanup costs, based on their relative contribution, measured in years or volume of waste contributed. In addition, the parties may agree to share the cleanup costs associated with the contribution of prior owners, to bring a joint action against the prior owners, and to share recovery of attorneys' fees and any damages.

Prospective Purchaser Agreements

When an environmental assessment reveals that certain property is contaminated, prospective purchasers of such property face a dilemma: Superfund laws hold knowing purchasers of contaminated property strictly liable for cleanup costs.[41] In order to curb the resulting trend of abandonment and encourage redevelopment of contaminated properties (often called brownfield developments), federal and state agencies have shown increasing willingness to enter prospective purchaser agreements to limit purchasers' liability.

Prospective purchaser agreements allow prospective purchasers to determine their liability for cleanup costs prior to purchase. In this way, prospective purchasers and their successors receive assurances that they will not be liable for any further contamination they do not cause. Generally, such assurances come in the form of covenants not to sue and contribution protection within a judicially-approved consent decree. In exchange, prospective purchasers either contribute to a cleanup fund or conduct specific remedial actions. Prospective purchasers should consider the use of such agreements when appropriate. Although the application and negotiation process can be time-consuming, the trade-off may be worthwhile. In addition to benefiting themselves with a specific quantification of liability, prospective purchasers who enter these agreements can also benefit regulators (who receive necessary cleanup funds from non-responsible parties)[42] and the public (which, through the return of brownfields to beneficial use, is spared unnecessary urban sprawl and provided with local reinvestment and employment).

The Washington Legislature codified the statutory requirement for prospective purchaser agreements through a 1994 amendment of MTCA.[43] These statutory requirements include the following:

1. the settlement will provide a substantial-public benefit,
2. the settlement will yield substantial new resources to facilitate cleanup;
3. the settlement will expedite remedial action consistent with MTCA; and
4. based upon available information, Ecology determines that the redevelopment or reuse of the facility is not likely to (a) contribute to the existing release or theoretical release, (b) interfere with remedial actions that may be needed at the site, or (c) increase health risks. In addition, the purchaser cannot be currently liable for remedial action at the site.

No Further Action Letters

In many situations, prospective purchasers may be unwilling or unable to pursue prospective purchaser agreements. An alternative method exists for addressing state Superfund liability prior to purchase. Prospective purchasers can pursue a "No Further Action" letter through Washington State's voluntary cleanup program, the Independent Remedial Action Program (IRAP).[44] Through the IRAP program, prospective purchasers can have Ecology review their environmental assessments and determine the adequacy of remedial actions conducted on property that they are considering purchasing. A "No Further Action" letter may be obtained for contamination already remediated or to confirm that no contamination has occurred at a given site.

The IRAP program does not provide binding legal protection from liability under state Superfund laws. The No Further Action letter is in a sense the documentation of Ecology's current opinion, and no more. However, given that Ecology is the governing agency under state Superfund law— and that a No Further Action letter has enough weight to remove a facility from the State Hazardous Sites List—prospective purchasers may feel that such an opinion regarding liability from Ecology provides sufficient protection.

To obtain a No Further Action letter, prospective purchasers must submit a report to Ecology describing both the contamination at issue and the remedial action that has been taken. Ecology guidance must be followed in the preparation of such reports, and prospective purchasers must pay Ecology a fee for review. Upon review, Ecology will indicate whether and to what extent further remediation is necessary. If remediation is deemed inadequate by Ecology, prospective purchasers may reapply after deficiencies are addressed.

Corporate Structuring to Minimize Third-Party and Off-Site Liabilities

From an environmental standpoint, the manner of acquisition of a corporation also has an effect on the purchaser's potential liability. An asset purchase likely provides more protection for the purchaser than does a stock purchase or a merger/consolidation.

Asset Purchase. Under traditional corporate law principles, with certain exceptions, when a corporation purchases the assets of another corporation it does not assume the liabilities of the corporation purchased.[45] Those liabilities stay with the seller. For this reason, many corporate transactions are formed as purchases of corporate assets, whether to avoid successor liability or for other business reasons.[46]

The traditional exceptions to the rule protecting asset purchasers are that the seller's (predecessor's) liabilities are assumed when:[47]

1. the purchaser expressly or impliedly agrees to assume the obligation;
2. the transaction amounts to a *de facto* merger or consolidation of the seller into the purchaser;
3. the purchasing corporation is merely a continuation of the selling corporation; or
4. the transaction was entered into fraudulently to escape liability.

In light of the traditional exceptions exposing asset purchasers to their predecessor's liability, and the emerging "continuity of enterprise" and "product line" doctrines, any asset purchase from a corporation with substantial environmental liabilities should be conducted with special care. In addition, the purchaser should be sensitive to the fact that Superfund liability associated with property acquired by the purchaser ("on-site" contamination) cannot be avoided by an asset purchase, because the purchaser, as owner, is strictly liable for contamination existing on its own property.[48]

Stock Purchase and Merger/Consolidation. When a purchase is accomplished through a merger or consolidation of the purchased corporation into the acquiring corporation, liabilities ordinarily are assumed by the purchasing corporation.[49] Consequently, from an environmental perspective, this method of acquisition is less desirable to purchasers, as the purchaser avoids neither on-site nor off-site environmental liabilities.

In a straight stock purchase (without a subsequent merger), the liabilities of the purchased corporation to third parties are also retained. Any undisclosed third-party liability (e.g., for personal injury or off-site contamination) would diminish the value of the stock purchased. For this reason, from an environmental perspective, a stock purchase is also less desirable to purchasers than an asset purchase.

NOTES

1 42 USC §§9601 *et seq.*

2 RCW §70.105D.

3 42 USC §9607(a)(1)-(2); RCW §§70.105D.010(4) and .040(2).

4 *See, e.g., Reichhold Chemicals v. Textron, Inc.*, 888 F. Supp. 1116 (ND Fla. 1995); United States v. Bliss, 667 F. Supp. 1298 (ED Mo. 1987); *United States v. Chem-Dyne*, 572 F. Supp. 802 (SD Ohio 1983); RCW §§70.105D.010(4) and .040(2).

5 *See, e.g., United States v. Alcan Aluminum Corp.*, 892 F. Supp. 648 (MD Pa. 1995) (inquiries into apportionment under CERCLA are intensely factual and the defendant's burden is substantial); *O'Neil v. Picillo*, 682 F. Supp. 706, 724 (DRI 1988), *cert. den.* 493 US 1071 (1990).

6 *See, e.g., Anschutz v. Mining Corp. v. NL Indust. Inc.*, 891 F. Supp. 492 (ED Mo. 1995); *New York v. Shore Realty Corp.*, 759 F.2d 1032 (2d Cir. 1985) (prior owner); *United States v. Metate Asbestos Corp.*, 584 F. Supp. 1143 (D. Ariz. 1984) (adjacent owner).

7 *See, e.g., CP Holdings v. Goldberg-Zoino & Associates*, 769 F. Supp. 432 (D NH 1991); *Wiegmann & Rose Int'l Corp. v. NL Industries and Esselte Pendaflex Corp.*, 735 F. Supp. 957 (ND Cal. 1990); *United States v. Northeastern Pharmaceutical and Chemical Co.* (NEPACO), 579 F. Supp. 823, 840-43 (WD Mo. 1984), *aff'd in part, rev'd in part*, 810 F.2d 726 (8th Cir. 1986), *cert. den.* 484 U.S. 848 (1987).

8 *United States v. Maryland Bank & Trust Co.*, 632 F. Supp. 573 (D MD 1986) (title to property retained for four years); *Guidice v. BFG Electroplating and Mfg. Co., Inc.*, 732 F. Supp. 556 (WD PA 1989) (bank held title for less than eight months.) *But see United States v. Mirabile*, 18 Envtl. L. Rep. (BNA) 20994 (ED PA 1985) (bank within security interest exemption when it sold property four months after foreclosure). In response to this uncertainty created by case law, EPA issued an interpretive rule in 1992 to classify the type of lender ownership that will keep lenders within the security interest exemption (the "lender liability rule"). See 57 Fed. Reg. 18,344 (1992). The lender liability rule established that the "secured creditor exemption" remains available to a lender even after the lender has foreclosed upon and taken title to contaminated property, as long as the lender diligently attempts to sell, lease or otherwise dispose of the property within twelve months of foreclosure. The lender can lose the exemption if, at any time following six months after the lender acquires marketable title, the lender fails to accept a written, bona fide, firm offer of fair consideration for the property. The lender liability rule was vacated in 1994, on the ground that EPA lacked authority to issue the rule as binding authority. *Kelly v. United States Environmental Protection Agency*, 15 F. 3d 1100 (DC Cir. 1994), *cert denied, American Bankers Assn. v. Kelly*, 115 S. Ct. 900 (1995). In response, EPA announced that, despite Kelly, it intended to employ the lender liability rule as enforcement policy. 60 Fed. Reg. 63,517 (1995). Moreover, in that announcement, EPA noted that many federal courts, both before and after the *Kelly* decision, have decided cases consistent with the lender liability rule.

9 *United States v. Mirabile*, 15 Envtl. L. Rep. (BNA) 20994 (ED PA 1985). In another decision extending lender liability, one federal court decided that a bank could be held liable even without a showing that it actively participated in hazardous waste decisions, provided it participated in the financial affairs of a borrower "to a degree indicating a capacity to influence the corporation's treatment of hazardous wastes." *U.S. v. Fleet Factors Corp.*, 901 F.2d 1550 (11th Cir. 1990), *cert den.* 498 US 1046 (1991). In contrast, the Ninth Circuit stated that there is no liability absent some active participation in management. *In re Bergsoe Metal Corp.*, 910 F.2d 668 (9th Cir. 1990). EPA's lender liability rule attempted to clarify this uncertainty as well, ruling that a lender has participated in the management of a borrower, thus losing the protection of the secured creditor exemption, only if it has exercised "decision-making control" over the borrower's general operations or its program of environmental compliance. 57 Fed. Reg. 18,383 (1992).

[10] H.R. 4278, Asset Conservation, Lender Liability, and Deposit Insurance Protection (Sept. 28, 1996). The Act was passed in the wake of the D.C. Circuit vacating EPA's lender liability rule. It amends Section 101(20) of CERCLA, the "secured creditor exemption," and essentially follows EPA's lender liability rule with regard to both management participation and foreclosures. In fact, the Act deems EPA's lender liability rule to have been validly issued and to have been effective according to the terms of the final rule, despite the Kelly decision. Accordingly, the Act establishes that a lender will not be held liable under CERCLA as an "owner or operator" by merely demonstrating a "capacity" to influence company management of pollution. Rather, liability will attach only if a lender exercises actual "decision-making control over the environmental compliance" of a borrower. With respect to foreclosures, the Act establishes that a lender is not liable under CERCLA as an "owner or operator" if that person or entity sells, re-leases, liquidates, or "takes any other measure to preserve, protect, or prepare" a borrower's vessel or facility prior to sale or disposition, so long as the lender disposes of the vessel or facility at the "earliest practicable, commercially reasonable time, on commercially reasonable terms."

[11] RCW §70.105D.020(11). Under this provision of MTCA, Washington provides liability exemptions for lenders consistent with the federal amendment of CERCLA and EPA's lender liability rule. One notable difference is the time restriction imposed upon lenders in Washington: lenders must dispose of property they hold as a result of foreclosure within five years of its acquisition to remain within the MTCA security interest exemption.

[12] *See* Section 14.4.3 for a discussion of lender liability avoidance.

[13] 42 USC §9607(a)(1); RCW §§70.150D.040(1)(a) and (b).

[14] *See, e.g., South Florida Waster Management District v. Montalvo*, 26, Envtl. L. Rep. (BNA) 21,398, (SD FL 1989), *aff'd*, 84 F. 3d 402 (11th Cir. 1996); *United States v. Monsanto Co.*, 858 F. 2d 160 (4th Cir. 1988) *cert. den.*, 490 US 1106 (1989); *United States v. South Carolina Recycling and Disposal, Inc.*, 653 F. Supp. 984 (D SC 1984).

[15] 42 USC §§ 9601(20)(A) and 9607(a)(1); RCW §§70.105D.040(1)(a) and (b). *See, e.g., Weyerhaeuser Corp. v. Koppers Co.*, Inc., 771 F. Supp. 1406 (D MD 1991), *aff'd in part, rev'd in part*, 68 F. 3d 1082 (8th Cir. 1995), *cert. den.* 117 S. Ct. 50 (1996).

[16] *See, e.g., United States v. TIC Inv. Corp.*, 866 F. Supp. 1173 (ND Iowa 1994) *aff'd in part, rev'd in part*, 68 F.3d 1082 (8th Cir. 1995), *cert. den.* 117 S. Ct. 50 (1996); *United States v. Northernaire Plating Co.*, 670 F. Supp. 742 (WD Mich. 1987), *aff'd. United States v. R. W. Meyer, Inc.*, 889 F.2d 1497 (6th Cir. 1984), *cert. den. R. W Meyer, Inc. v. United States*, 494 US 1057 (1990).

[17] *See, e.g., Weyerhaeuser Corp. v. Koppers Co., Inc.*, 771 F. Supp. 1406 (D MD 1991) (present landlord responsible for 40% and former tenant liable for 60% of cleanup costs).

[18] *See, e.g., Cadillac Fairview/California, Inc. v. Dow Chemical Co.*, 21 Env't Rep. Cas. (BNA) 1108 (CD CA 1984), *aff'd in part, rev'd in part, and remanded by* 840 F. 2d 691 (9th Cir. 1988). If, however, such persons transferred their interest after learning about an environmental problem, they could be subject to suit by the government for fraudulent transfer or by the purchaser for fraud or misrepresentation. *See, e.g., United States v. Charles George Trucking Co.*, 624 F. Supp. 1185 (D MA 1985), *aff'd.* 823 F. 2d 685 (1st Cir. 1987).

[19] 42 U.S.C. §9601(20)(A). Recent legislation has strengthened this security interest exemption. H.R. 4278, Asset Conservation, Lender Liability, and Deposit Insurance Protection (Sept. 28, 1996). However, lenders will still be held liable if they participate in management to a degree that they exercise decision-making control over environmental compliance. As well, lenders will be found liable if they take possession of contaminated property through foreclosure, but then do not make efforts to dispose of the property at the earliest practicable, commercially reasonable time. *See also United States v. Wallace*, 893 F. Supp 627 (ND TX 1995); *Kemp Industries, Inc. v. Safety Light Corp.*, 857 F. Supp. 373 (D NJ 1994) (decisions issued prior to H.R. 4278, but analyzed consistent with H.R. 4278.

[20] 42 USC §9601(35)(A). To establish that they had no reason to know of the disposal of hazardous substances, lender/purchasers must show that, at the time of acquisition (i.e., foreclosure and/or purchase), they undertook "all appropriate inquiry into the previous ownership and uses of the property consistent with good commercial or customary practice." 42 USC §9601(35)(B). The appropriate level of inquiry depends on the particular circumstances, including any specialized knowledge or experience of the lender/purchaser, commonly known or reasonably ascertainable information about the property, the obviousness of the presence or likely presence of contamination at the property, and the ability to detect such contamination by inspection. *Id.* As yet, there is no regulatory standard establishing the level of "due diligence" inquiry that will qualify a landowner for the exemption; however, some courts have interpreted the standard to mean taking steps necessary to protect the public from environmental threat. *See, e.g., United States v. A & N Cleaners*, 854 F. Supp. 229 (SD NY 1994).

[21] 42 U.S.C. §9601(20)(D) and (35)(A)(ii). Although the term "governmental entity" is not defined in the statute, the exemption appears to apply broadly to any sovereign power, including the federal government, a state, any municipality, port, school district, or other governmental body. The exemption appears to be broader than for "innocent purchasers," since public owners who acquire property involuntarily or through eminent domain are not required to conduct the type of inquiry prior to taking possession that innocent purchasers must conduct in order to qualify. Compare 42 USC §9601(35)(A)(i) with 42 USC §9601(35)(A)(ii).

[22] 42 USC §9601(35)(A)(iii).

[23] 42 USC §9607(b)(3). An example of a person under this provision would be a property owner whose land was contaminated by an adjacent landowner and who exercised due care to prevent such contamination from occurring. This defense is not available to a landowner who learns of a release or threat of release after acquiring the property and then transfers the property without disclosing that information. 42 USC §9601(35)(C).

[24] 42 US. §9607(b).

[25] RCW §70.105D.040(3)(c).

[26] RCW §70.105D.040(3)(d).

[27] 42 USC §§6901 *et seq.*

[28] 42 USC §§7401 *et seq.*

[29] 15 USC §§2601 *et seq.*

[30] 33 USC §§1251 *et seq.*

[31] 29 USC §§651 *et seq.*

[32] Similar to the lender liability rule under CERCLA, an EPA rule under RCRA protects lenders who hold security interests in underground storage tanks (USTs). 40 CFR 280 and 281. Under the RCRA rule, lenders will be exempted from liability if they do not actually participate in or control the borrower's management decisions regarding the operation of the UST. Lenders who acquire USTs through foreclosure will be exempted from RCRA liability as well, so long as the acquisition at foreclosure is reasonably necessary to ensure satisfaction of the debtor's obligation and the lender actively seeks to dispose of the foreclosed-on UST.

[33] 42 USC §§4321 *et seq.*

[34] 16 USC §§1451 *et seq.*

[35] 33 USC §1344.

[36] The regulations under the Washington Model Toxics Control Act require that past releases not previously reported be covered by reports filed with Ecology by June 1, 1990, and that all future releases be reported to Ecology within ninety days of discovery. WAC 173-340-300(2).

37 See, e.g., *Ayers v. Township of Jackson*, 525 A. 2d 287 (D NJ 1987) where plaintiffs who resided near a municipal landfill that leaked toxic chemicals into a drinking water aquifer were awarded over $5 million for deterioration of their quality of life and over $8 million for future medical treatment and examinations. The jury's award of over $2 million for emotional distress was reversed on appeal only because of the municipality's statutory tort immunity.

38 Moreover, the U.S. Supreme Court has ruled that attorneys' fees are not recoverable costs under CERCLA, so contracting parties must address this provision explicitly in order to recover attorneys' fees. *Key Tronic Corp. v. United States*, 511 US 809 (1994).

39 See, e.g., *Cordova Chemical Co. v. Dept. of Natural Resources*, 536 NW 2d 860 (Mich. 1995); *Emhart Indus., Inc. v. Duracell Int'l., Inc.*, 14 Chem. Waste Lit. Rep. 817, 834 (MD Tenn. 1987) (quoting the contractual indemnification language between a seller and purchaser); *Mardan Corp. v. C.G.C. Music, Ltd.*, 804 F. 2d 1454 (9th Cir. 1986); *Caldwell v. Gurley Refining Co.*, 755 F. 2d 645 (8th Cir. 1985) (indemnification by lessee to lessor). For a contrary view, see *AM International v. International Forging Equipment*, 743 F. Supp. 525 (ND Ohio 1990), *aff'd. in part, rev'd. in part, and remanded by* 982 F. 2d 989 (6th Cir. 1993).

40 For example, failure to specify liability under CERCLA, within an indemnity, was fatal to the seller's indemnity defense in *Channel Masters Satellite Systems, Inc. v. JFD Electronics Corp.*, No. 88605-CIV-5 (ED NC 1988). In that case, the seller gave the purchaser an indemnity, which covered, among other things, violations of "state or municipal" law. The indemnity did not expressly cover violations of federal law. The purchaser allegedly incurred over $3 million to clean up the property subsequent to the purchase, and sued the seller for contribution under Section 107 of CERCLA. The seller defended on the ground that the purchaser had indemnified it at the time of sale for all damages arising from violations of state or local law. The court held, however, that since the indemnity did not specifically reference federal laws and since the purchaser's liability arose under CERCLA (a federal statute), the indemnity did not protect the seller from the purchaser's contribution action.

41 42 U.S.C. §§9607(a)(1) and (2); RCW §§70.105D.010(4) and .040(2).

42 Important to note is that prospective purchaser agreements do not in any way relieve preexisting responsible parties from liability, although presumably the potential liability for these existing PRPs is abated to the extent the condition of the site itself is improved through the prospective purchasers' efforts.

43 RCW §70.105D.040(5).

44 WAC 173-340-300 and -310.

45 15 W. Fletcher, *Cyclopedia of the Law of Private Corporations*, §§7122-23 (1983).

46 See, e.g., *Louisiana-Pacific Corp. v. ASARCO, Inc.*, 29 Envt'l. Rep. Cases (BNA) 1450 (WD Wash. 1989) (company that purchased the assets of a copper smelting, slag processing and marketing company held not liable as a successor corporation under the federal Superfund).

47 *Hall v. Armstrong Cork*, 103 Wn. 2d 258 (1984); *Martin v. Abbott Labs*, 102 Wn. 2d 581 (1984).

48 *New York v. Shore Realty Corp.*, 759 F.2d 1032 (2d Cir.1985).

49 15 W. Fletcher, *Cyclopedia of the Law of Private Corporations* §7121 (1983); see *Uni-Com N. W. v. Argus Publishing*, 47 Wn. App. 787 (1987).

CHAPTER 14

Environmental Torts: Common Law and Other Remedies

INTRODUCTION

During the 1970's and 1980's many traditional common law remedies were supplanted by federal and state statutory causes of action. Recently, however, common law theories of recovery in environmental impairment cases have made a strong comeback. This chapter describes several of the most prominent of the traditional common law theories that may be applied in actions alleging harm to persons or property due to environmental contamination. These include nuisance, trespass, negligence, strict liability and inverse condemnation.

NUISANCE

Elements of Cause of Action

Unlike most common law doctrines, nuisance claims are also addressed in statutory provisions, and this section will focus on these statutes. RCW §7.48.010 defines actionable nuisances as follows:

> The obstruction of any highway or the closing of the channel of any stream used for boating or rafting logs, lumber or timber, or whatever is injurious to health or indecent or offensive to the senses, or an obstruction to the free use of property, so as to essentially interfere with the comfortable enjoyment of the life and property, is a nuisance and the subject of an action for damages and other and further relief.

> The elements of a nuisance action are more specifically defined in RCW §7.48.120: Nuisance consists in unlawfully doing an act, or omitting to perform a duty, which act or omission either annoys, injures or endangers the comfort, repose, health or safety of others, offends decency, or unlawfully interferes with, obstructs or tends to obstruct, or render dangerous for passage, any lake or navigable river, bay, stream,

canal or basin, or any public park, square, street or highway; or in any way renders other persons insecure in life, or in the use of property.

An act or omission may be wrongful for purposes of this nuisance statute if it violates a law or permit,[1] or if it is intentional, negligent, reckless, wanton or ultra-hazardous conduct.[2] A nuisance action may be brought by "any person whose property is . . . injuriously affected or whose personal enjoyment is lessened by the nuisance."[3] However, an act that is performed under the express authority of a statute cannot be deemed a nuisance.[4] Further, the mere fact that something offends a neighbor's aesthetic sensibility or is unsightly does not qualify it as a nuisance.[5]

Most agricultural activity is protected from nuisance lawsuits by the nuisance statute.[6] If consistent with good agricultural practices and established prior to surrounding nonagricultural activities, agricultural activity conducted on farmland is presumed to be reasonable and does not constitute a nuisance unless the activity has "a substantial adverse effect on public health and safety."[7] An agricultural activity is also presumed to meet this standard if it is undertaken in conformity with federal, state and local laws and regulations.[8] The agricultural exemption has been found not to apply, however, to discharges of excess irrigation water from orchard property onto the property of others, as the court concluded that the exemption was not intended to protect agricultural activity that results in the flooding of adjoining property.[9]

Public and Private Nuisance

Nuisances are classified as public or private. "A public nuisance is one which [sic] affects equally the rights of an entire community or neighborhood, although the extent of the damage may be unequal."[10] Specific public nuisances are enumerated in the nuisance statute.[11] A private party may bring an action for a public nuisance, but only if he or she has been specifically injured.[12] Private nuisances are defined by the nuisance statute as all nuisances not included in the list of enumerated public nuisances.[13]

Recoverable Damages

In order to recover damages in a nuisance action, a plaintiff must show substantial interference with the use and enjoyment of his or her property.[14] If a plaintiff prevails in a nuisance action, he or she may recover a judgment for damages, and if the nuisance is continuing, seek an order authorizing abatement of the nuisance.[15]

The measure of recoverable damages for injury to land caused by a nuisance depends on whether the injury is temporary or permanent. Where the injury is temporary, the measure of damages is the diminished rental value if the property is to be rented, or the diminished value of its use if the property is to be used by the owner.[16] Where the injury is permanent and irreparable, the measure of damages is the difference in the market value of the property before and after creation of the nuisance.[17]

In addition to property damage, recovery may be had for sickness, suffering, mental anguish, personal discomfort, inconvenience, annoyance and bodily infirmities resulting from nuisance.[18]

Examples of Environmental Nuisance Cases

Several cases are illustrative of how environmental nuisance principles are applied in Washington. In one case, the court held that a city's discharge of raw sewage in violation of a waste disposal permit had denied the owners of lakefront properties the full use and enjoyment of their properties, and that it constituted a public nuisance for which damages were recoverable.[19] In another nuisance case, the court upheld an award of damages to owners of property near a landfill where an extremely hazardous waste had been disposed of, contaminating the property owners' drinking water.[20] Both the county operating the landfill and the manufacturer who disposed of the waste were held liable for damages involving diminished property value, annoyance and inconvenience, and mental anguish. In contrast, another case held that the lawful construction of a building or structure that merely obstructs the view from neighboring property is not an actionable nuisance.[21] A discharge of a pollutant, however, even if it is authorized by a NPDES wastewater permit, may be a nuisance if the discharge unreasonably interferes with the use and enjoyment of another's property.[22]

TRESPASS

Elements of Cause of Action

Trespass is recognized as a tort under Washington common law. Trespass consists of intentionally causing something to enter land in the possession of another.[23] Trespass is distinguished from nuisance in that trespass involves an invasion of the right of possession while nuisance involves an invasion of the right of enjoyment.

An indirect form of invasion of property, such as the presence of airborne pollutants, is recoverable in trespass if the plaintiff establishes the following elements:

1. an invasion affecting the plaintiff's interest in exclusive possession of property;
2. an intentional doing of the act resulting in the invasion;
3. reasonable foreseeability that the act could result in an invasion of the possessory interest; and
4. actual and substantial damage to the property.[24]

Unlike in nuisance actions, the reasonableness of the defendant's conduct is irrelevant.[25]

Recoverable Damages

A plaintiff must show interference with the right to exclusive possession of property to recover under a trespass claim.[26] In general, once a plaintiff has established a technical trespass, recovery of nominal damages is allowed.[27] In order to recover more than nominal damages, the plaintiff must prove the extent of such damages.[28] The measure of actual damages is the diminution in market value if the invasion was permanent, or the cost of restoring the property to its former condition, plus loss of use, if the invasion was temporary.[29]

Examples of Environmental Trespass Cases

In the most significant recent environmental trespass case, landowners sought damages in trespass for the deposit on their property of microscopic, airborne particles of heavy metals that were emitted from a copper smelter.[30] The court held that the intentional deposit of the particulates gave rise to an action for trespass if the plaintiff could prove the four elements described in Section 15.3.1 above, including actual and substantial damages.

One exception to trespass is the "common enemy rule" pursuant to which a landowner, faced with overflowing water coming onto his or her land, may erect barriers to protect his or her property but will not be held liable for an resulting damage to neighboring properties.[31]

NEGLIGENCE

Common law negligence may also be a theory that supports an action for environmental harm. The essential elements of actionable negligence are: (1) the existence of a duty owed to the complaining party; (2) a breach of that duty; (3) resulting injury; and (4) proximate cause between the claimed breach and the resulting injury.[32]

When a claimant alleges that negligent conduct resulted in a nuisance, the courts may treat the claim as an action for negligence rather than a nuisance action, and apply the rules of negligence.[33] Generally, recoverable damages are the amount necessary to adequately compensate for the loss, but where the damaged property has no market value, the measure of damages is the replacement cost.[34]

STRICT LIABILITY

Elements of Cause of Action

In Washington, strict liability is imposed for activities that are deemed to be abnormally dangerous.[35] Strict liability arises when an activity has a risk of harm of a degree that makes that activity abnormally dangerous.[36] The courts will consider the following factors when determining what is an abnormally dangerous activity:

1. existence of a high degree of risk of some harm to the person, land or chattels of others;
2. likelihood that the harm that results from it will be great;
3. inability to eliminate the risk by exercise of reasonable care;
4. extent to which the activity is not a matter of common usage;
5. inappropriateness of the activity to the place where it is carried on; and
6. extent to which its value to the community is outweighed by its dangerous attributes.[37]

Washington courts have applied the doctrine to the following activities in certain fact situations: blasting,[38] pile driving,[39] transporting gas as freight by truck,[40] aerial crop spraying,[41] and fireworks displays.[42]

Recoverable Damages

Recoverable damages for abnormally dangerous activities may involve damages for injury to property[43] or to the person,[44] depending on the nature of the loss.

INVERSE CONDEMNATION

Elements of Cause of Action

The term "inverse condemnation" applies to an action alleging a "taking" by the government, which occurs when the government interferes with the use and enjoyment of private property, with a subsequent decline in market value.[45] The basis for an inverse condemnation action is the state constitution, article 1, §16, which provides in pertinent part: "No private property shall be taken or damaged for public or private use without just compensation having first been made . . . ." In an inverse condemnation action, the claimant seeks compensation from the government for "the value of property which has been appropriated in fact, but with no formal exercise of the power."[46] There are two primary types of inverse condemnation: non-regulatory takings and regulatory takings.

Nonregulatory Takings

Nonregulatory taking claims in Washington have involved various forms of interference with private property, from intrusions upon private property by noise and vibrations due to airport operations, to a poorly designed and constructed road that resulted in chronically recurring incursions of vehicles from the road onto plaintiffs' property.[47]

In order for a plaintiff to recover, the invasion of private property must be either permanent or recurring.[48] Temporary interference with a private property right, which is not continuous or likely to be recurring, does not constitute a taking without just compensation.[49] For example, Washington courts have held that while permanent or long-term pollution of a stream resulting from sewage disposal may constitute an inverse condemnation, a single discharge of sewage into a river did not,- because it resulted in only temporary damage to property.[50] To establish a claim for inverse condemnation by physical invasion, a plaintiff must show that there has been "a chronic and unreasonable pattern of behavior by the government."[51]

Regulatory Takings

The other form of inverse condemnation are regulatory taking claims: claims of inverse condemnation by excessive regulation of property. In recent cases, the Washington Supreme Court has clarified the law of regulatory takings in this state.[52]

Exhaustion of administrative remedies is generally required before a court will resolve a regulatory taking claim.[53] The principles for analyzing regulatory taking claims under Washington law are similar to those under federal law.[54] A party challenging a land use regulation under this doctrine must overcome the strong presumption that such regulations are constitutional.[55]

The Washington courts have developed their own multi-part test for analyzing takings claims. First, the court asks whether the regulation destroys one of the fundamental attributes of ownership—the right to possess, to exclude others, to dispose of property, or to make some economically viable use of property.[56] Both "physical invasions" and "total takings" are considered in this threshold inquiry.[57] If either a "physical invasion" or a "total taking" can be established, then the owner is entitled to compensation regardless of the public purpose involved"[58] Second, the court will consider whether the regulation as applied to the challenger is part of the state's authority to protect, in a reasonable manner, the public interest in safety, morals, or health of the community, including the environment or the fiscal integrity of an area.[59] If the regulation protects the public interest and does not infringe upon a fundamental attribute of ownership, then it is insulated from a takings challenge.[60] If the regulation is not insulated from a takings claim then the court asks whether the regulation substantially advances a legitimate state interest.[61] If it does not advance a legitimate state interest, then it is a taking; if it does then the state interest in the regulation is balanced against the economic impact on the owner.[62] Finally, if any compensation was offered by the government, the challenger must establish that the compensation was not just.[63]

In *Lucas v. South Carolina Coastal Commission*, South Carolina's Beachfront Management Act was at issue.[64] The Act imposed a construction ban that prohibited the petitioner from developing previously purchased property. The petitioner claimed that application of the Act would result in an unconstitutional taking of his property under the 5th and 15th Amendments, and he sued the state for compensation. The Court affirmed the traditional takings doctrine, holding that regulations must deny the property owner all economically viable use of his or her land before compensation for a taking is required. The Court also noted the public interest exception to the compensation requirement[65] and went on to state that:

> [w]here the state seeks to sustain regulation that deprives land of all economically beneficial use, we think it may resist compensation only if the logically antecedent inquiry into the nature of the owner's estate shows that the proscribed use interests were not part of the title to begin with.[66]

Accepting the trial court's determination that the petitioner was deprived of all economically viable use of his property, the Court then remanded the case for a determination of whether any common law principles of nuisance or property law could justify South Carolina's construction ban. On remand, South Carolina found that the common law could not prohibit the owner from developing his land, and thus the owner was ordered to be compensated for a temporary taking of his property.[67]

In *Dolan v. Tigard*, the owner of a plumbing business applied to the city for a permit to expand their facility. The city approved the permit, subject to several conditions, one of which required construction of a bike path across the owner's property. The Supreme Court analyzed these conditions under a two-part test: (1) is there a reasonable relationship between the permit conditions and a legitimate public purpose (the "essential nexus" test)[68] and; (2) if there is such a nexus, are the permit requirements roughly proportional to the expected impact.[69] In applying this test, the Court held that the required bike path may be reasonably related to the mitigation of increased traffic due to the expansion of the business, however, the city would have to show on remand that this requirement was roughly proportional to the expected impact.

Recoverable Damages

The measure of recovery in nonregulatory inverse condemnation is the diminution in market value resulting from the interference. For regulatory takings, the government must pay just compensation, in the form of the leasehold value of the property for the period during which the regulation was in effect.[70] A violation of due process requires the invalidation of the regulation, but not the payment of just compensation.[71]

NOTES

[1] *Miotke v. City of Spokane*, 101 Wn. 2d 307 (1984).

[2] See *Peterson v. King County*, 45 Wn. 2d 860 (1954); *Hostetler v. Ward*, 41 Wn. App. 343 (1985), *rev. den.* 106 Wn. 2d 1004 (1986).

[3] RCW §7.48.020.

[4] RCW §7.48.160.

[5] *Mathewson v. Primeau*, 64 Wn. 2d 929 (1964).

[6] RCW §7.48.300. See, e.g., *Buchanan v. Simplot Feeders Ltd. Partnership*, 134 Wn. 2d 673 (1998).

[7] RCW §7.48.305.

[8] *Id*. Whether this presumption of reasonableness would apply to pesticide contamination is unclear.

[9] *City of Benton v. Adrian*, 50 Wn. App. 330 (1988).

[10] RCW §7.48.130.

[11] RCW §7.48.140.

[12] RCW §7.48.210; *Miotke v. City of Spokane*, 101 Wn. 2d 307 (1984)..

[13] RCW §7.48.150.

[14] *Bradley v. American Smelting & Refining Co.*, 635 F. Supp. 1154, (WD Wash. 1986) (applying Washington law) ("Bradley II"); *Highline School Dist. No. 401, King County v. Port of Seattle*, 87 Wn. 2d 6 (1976).

[15] RCW §7.48.020.

[16] *Miotke v. City of Spokane*, 101 Wn. 2d 307 (1984).

[17] *Id*.

[18] *Miotke v. City of Spokane*, 101 Wn. 2d 307 (1984); *Wilson v. Key Tronic Corp.*, 40 Wn. App. 802 (1985); *Bradley v. American Smelting & Refining Co.*, 635 F. Supp. 1154, (WD Wash. 1986); *Trail v. Civil Engineer Corps, U.S. Navy, Naval Facilities Engineering Command*, 849 F. Supp. 766 (WD Wash. 1994).

[19] *Miotke v. City of Spokane*, 101 Wn. 2d 307 (1984).

[20] *Wilson v. Key Tronic Corp.*, 40 Wn. App. 802 (1985)

[21] *Collinson v. John L. Scott, Inc.*, 55 Wn. App. 481 (1989).

[22] *Tiegs v. Watts*, 135 Wn.2d 1 (1998).

[23] Restatement (Second) of Torts §158 (1965); *Pruitt v. Douglas County*, 116 Wn. App. 547, 66 P.3d 1111 (2003); *Borden v. City of Olympia*, 113 Wn. App. 359, 53 P.3d 1020 (2002).

[24] *Bradley v. American Smelting and Refining Co.*, 104 Wn. 2d 677 (1985) (Bradley I).

[25] *Bradley v. American Smelting and Refining Co.*, 635 F. Supp. 1154 (WD WA 1986) (Bradley II).

[26] *Bradley v. American Smelting and Refining Co.*, 635 F. Supp. 1154 (WD WA 1986) (Bradley II).

[27] *Keesling v. City of Seattle*, 52 Wn. 2d 247 (1958). However, as discussed above in Section 15.3.1, indirect forms of invasion of property require actual and substantial damage to the property in order to recover in trespass.

[28] *Id*.

[29] *Id.* at 253; *Songstad v. Municipality of Metropolitan Seattle*, 2 Wn. App. 680 (1970).

[30] *Bradley v. American Smelting and Refining Co.*, 104 Wn. 2d 677 (1985) (Bradley I); *Bradley v. American Smelting and Refining Co.*, 635 F. Supp. 1154 (WD WA 1986) (Bradley II).

[31] *Lord v. Pierce County*, 166 Wn. App. 812 (2012), *rev. den.* 174 Wn.2d 1015.

32 *Hansen v. Friend*, 118 Wn. 2d 476 (1992); *Schooley v. Pinch's Deli Market, Inc.*, 80 Wn. App. 862, (1996).

33 *Kaech v. Lewis County PUD No. 1*, 106 Wn. App. 260 (2001).

34 *Puget Sound Power and Light Co. v. Strong*, 117 Wn. 2d 400 (1991).

35 *Klein v. Pyrodyne Corp.*, 117 Wn. 2d 1 (1991), *op. amended*, 817 P.2d 1359; Restatement (Second) of Torts §519.

36 Restatement (Second) of Torts §519.

37 *Kaech v. Lewis County PUD No. 1*, 106 Wn. App. 260 (2001); Restatement (Second) of Torts §520.

38 *Erickson Paving Co. v. Yardley Drilling Co.*, 7 Wn. App. 681 (1972).

39 *Vern J. Oja &Assoc. v. Washington Park Towers, Inc.*, 89 Wn. 2d 72 (1977).

40 *Siegler v. Kuhlman*, 81 Wn.2d 448 (1972), *cert. den.* 411 US 983 (1973).

41 *Langan v. Valicopters, Inc.*, 88 Wn. 2d 855 (1977).

42 *Klein v. Pyrodyne Corp.*, 117 Wn. 2d 1 (1991), *op. amended*, 817 P.2d 1359

43 See *Vern J. Oja &Assoc. v. Washington Park Towers, Inc.*, 89 Wn. 2d 72 (1977).

44 *Klein v. Pyrodyne Corp.*, 117 Wn. 2d 1 (1991), *op. amended*, 817 P.2d 1359

45 *Martin v. Port of Seattle*, 64 Wn.2d 309 (1964), *cert. den.* 379 US 989 (1965); *Lambier v. City of Kennewick*, 56 Wn. App. 275 (1989), *rev. den.*, 114 Wn. 2d 1016 (1990).

46 *Martin v. Port of Seattle*, 64 Wn.2d 309 (1964), *cert. den.* 379 US 989 (1965); *Lambier v. City of Kennewick*, 56 Wn. App. 275 (1989), *rev. den.* 114 Wn. 2d 1016, 791 P.2d 535 (1990); *Pierce v. Northeast Lake Washington Sewer & Water Dist.*, 123 Wn. 2d 550 (1994). There is no inverse condemnation cause of action against a private person. *Phillips v. King County*, 87 Wn. App. 468 (1997), *aff'd. on other grounds*, 136 Wn. 2d 946 (1998).

47 *Id.*

48 *Northern Pac. Ry. Co. v. Sunnyside Val. Irrigation Dist.*, 85 Wn. 2d 920 (1975).

49 *Miotke v. City of Spokane*, 101 Wn. 2d 307 (1984).

50 *Miotke v. City of Spokane*, 101 Wn. 2d 307 (1984).

51 *Orion Corp. v. State*, 109 Wn. 2d 621 (1987), *cert. den.*, 486 US 1022 (1988); *Lambier v. City of Kennewick*, 56 Wn. App. 275 (1989), *rev. den.*, 114 Wn. 2d 1016 (1990).

52 *Presbytery of Seattle v. King County*, 114 Wn. 2d 320, *cert. den.* 498 US 911 (1990) (owner of property containing wetland challenged county wetlands ordinance, which established buffer zones around wetland and prohibited new construction within wetland, claiming that ordinance prevented development of its property and resulted in a taking without just compensation); *Guimont v. Clarke*, 121 Wn. 2d 586 (1993), *cert den.* 114 S.Ct. 1216 (association of mobile home park owners brought suit against state claiming that statute requiring landowners to provide monetary assistance for tenant relocation costs was unconstitutional); *Margola Associates v. City of Seattle*, 121 Wn. 2d 625 (1993) (city ordinance requiring apartment house owners to pay inspection fee was found not to be a taking since it neither deprived the owners of all economic value nor amounted to a physical invasion); *Sparks v. Douglas County*, 127 Wn. 2d 901 (1995) (holding that an approval of a short plat conditioned on the widening of adjacent roads was not a takings under the *Dolan* "rough proportionality" test).

53 *Presbytery of Seattle v. King County*, 114 Wn. 2d 320, *cert. den.* 498 US 911 (1990).

54 *Orion Corp. v. State*, 109 Wn. 2d 621 (1987), *cert. den.*, 486 US 1022 (1988).

55 *Id.*

56 *Guimont v. Clarke*, 121 Wn. 2d 586 (1993) (revising *Presbytery of Seattle* analysis in light of *Lucas v. South Carolina Coastal Comm.*, 505 US 1003 (1992)).

57 *Guimont v. Clarke*, 121 Wn. 2d 586 (1993).

⁵⁸ *Guimont v. Clarke*, 121 Wn. 2d 586 (1993).

⁵⁹ *Keystone Bituminous Coal Assn. v. DeBenedictis*, 480 US 470 (1987).

⁶⁰ *Id.* Even if a regulation is insulated from a takings challenge, it must also withstand the due process test of reasonableness. Under a due process analysis, the Court considers three questions. First, is the regulation aimed at achieving a significant public purpose. Second, is the regulation reasonably necessary to achieve that public purpose. Third, is the regulation unduly oppressive on the landowner? If so, the regulation may be in violation of due process.

⁶¹ *Dolan v. City of Tigard*, 114 S. Ct. 2309 (1994); *Nollan v. California Coastal Comm.*, 483 US 825 (1987).

⁶² *Id.*

⁶³ *First English Evangelical Lutheran Church of Glendale v. Los Angeles County, Cal.*, 482 US 304 (1987).

⁶⁴ 505 U.S. 1003 (1992).

⁶⁵ *Id.* The court also affirmed the other traditional regulatory takings doctrine, which holds that where there is permanent physical occupation, compensation must be paid regardless of the weight of the public interest being asserted.

⁶⁶ *Id.*

⁶⁷ *Lucas v. South Carolina Coastal Council*, 309 S.C. 424 (1992).

⁶⁸ *See, e.g., Burton v. Clark County*, 91 Wn. App. 505 (1998).

⁶⁹ *Benchmark Land Co. v. City of Battle Ground*, 146 Wn.2d 685 (2002). *But see HEAL v. Hearings Board*, 96 Wn. App. 522 (1999; *Isla Verde Int'l. v. City of Camas*, 99 Wn. App. 127 (1999); *Largent v. Klickitat County*, 101 Wn. App. 1033 (2000).

⁷⁰ *Orion Corp. v. State*, 109 Wn. 2d 621 (1987), *cert. den.* 486 US 1022 (1988); *First English Evangelical Lutheran Church of Glendale v. Los Angeles County, Cal.*, 482 US 304 (1987).

⁷¹ *Presbytery of Seattle v. King County*, 114 Wn. 2d 320, *cert. den.* 498 US 911 (1990); *But see Sintra, Inc. v. City of Seattle*, 119 Wn. 2d 1 (1992), *cert. den.* 506 US 1028 (damages might be available under 42 USC §1983).

CHAPTER 15

Administrative Procedure and Judicial Review

INTRODUCTION

This chapter examines the scope and application of the Administrative Procedure Act and discusses procedures for rulemaking and adjudications. It also discusses judicial review of state agency action under the APA and briefly examines judicial review of other, non-APA agency actions under statutory and constitutional procedures unique to Washington.

ADMINISTRATIVE PROCEDURE IN WASHINGTON

Washington's APA: Scope and Application

Washington's Administrative Procedure Act applies to all state agencies authorized by law to make rules or adjudicate cases. Such agencies include state boards, commissions, departments and officers authorized by law to make rules or conduct adjudicative proceedings. However, they do not include those in the legislative or judicial branches, the governor or the attorney general.[1]

The Act thus applies to the principal state agencies discussed throughout this Handbook: Ecology, the Washington Department of Natural Resources and the Washington Department of Fisheries and Wildlife as well as the Pollution Control Hearings Board and the Shorelines Hearings Board.[2] The Act does not apply to local agencies making decisions of a local nature, such as cities and municipal corporations.[3] In determining whether the Act applies, Washington courts have generally looked to the function of the agency rather than its title or structure.[4] If the function performed by the agency is of statewide importance, the courts may find that the APA applies, even though the agency is not formally a creature of state statute with state employees.[5]

It is important to determine whether the APA applies, for the agency is required to follow specific procedures (i.e., for rulemaking and adjudicative proceedings) if it does. Specific procedures for obtaining judicial review must also be followed if the Act applies. The differ-

Rulemaking Proceedings

In General

The procedures for agency rulemaking are set out in considerable detail in the APA; only an overview of those procedures is provided here. Important features for parties that wish to get involved in the rulemaking process are discussed below.

Rulemaking under the APA is the process for formulating and adopting agency rules.[6] Agency rules include "any agency order,[7] directive or regulation of general applicability,"[8] (1) the violation of which subjects a person to a penalty or administrative sanction; or (2) that establishes, alters, or revokes any qualification or requirement relating to (a) agency hearings, (b) the enjoyment of benefits or privileges conferred by law, (c) the issuance, suspension or revocation of licenses to pursue any commercial activity, trade, or profession, or (d) a standard that must be met before a product or material may be distributed or sold.[9] Certain types of agency action, however, are not rules: statements relating to the agency's internal management, rulings issued under the APA, traffic restrictions, and the admission, crediting, and graduation requirements established by state institutions of higher education as well as their employment relationships and fiscal processes.[10]

Rulemaking proceedings may be initiated by agencies at any time, or they may be initiated by any person upon petition to an agency requesting the adoption, amendment, or repeal of a rule.[11] The forms and procedures for submitting such petitions are prescribed by rule.[12] Within sixty days after a petition for rulemaking is submitted, the agency must either deny the petition in writing, stating its reasons for the denial, or initiate rulemaking proceedings.[13] Where a petition is denied, the agency must specifically address the concerns raised by the petitioner and, where appropriate, the alternative means by which the agency will address those concerns.[14] Denials of petitions to repeal or amend a rule may be appealed to the governor within thirty days and, in some cases, review may be sought from the joint administrative rules review committee.[15]

Rulemaking begins with a pre-notice inquiry.[16] Pre-notice inquiry is designed to provide greater public access to administrative rulemaking and to promote consensus among interested parties. Before submitting a notice of proposed rulemaking, agencies are required to solicit comments from the public on a subject of possible rulemaking. With few exemptions,[17] the agency has to prepare an extensive statement of inquiry to be filed with the code reviser for publication in the state register at least thirty days before the date the agency files notice of proposed rulemaking.[18] Agencies are specifically encouraged to develop and use new procedures for reaching agreement among interested parties before publishing notice of proposed rulemaking. Such procedures include negotiated rulemaking and pilot rulemaking.[19]

Following pre-notice inquiry, a notice of proposed rule is filed with the code reviser for publication in the Washington State Register.[20] The notice must include a reasonably specific description of the proposed rule and its purpose and rationale, as well as a description of when, where, and how persons may comment on the proposed rule.[21] The notice must also include a statement indicating whether the rulemaking requirements for "significant legislative rules"[22] apply (or the agency elected to apply them) to the rule adoption.[23] The agency must provide a copy of the notice of the proposed rule to each person, city, and county that has made a request for a mailed copy of such notice.[24]

The scope of an agency's rulemaking authority is expressly limited for rules implementing statutes enacted after July 23, 1995. For these rules, an agency's rulemaking authority must be derived from the body of the statute. The agency may not rely solely on the section of the law stating a statute's intent or purpose, or on the enabling provisions of the statute establishing the agency, or on any combination of such provisions, for its statutory authority to adopt rules. An agency may use the statement of intent or purpose, or the agency enabling provisions, to interpret ambiguities in a statute's other provisions.[25]

To the extent practicable, any rule proposed or adopted by an agency should be "clearly and simply stated," so that it can be understood by those required to comply with it.[26]

No sooner than twenty days following the publication of the proposed rule, the agency must provide a public rulemaking hearing and an opportunity for oral comments.[27] If the agency fails to give twenty days' notice of the rulemaking, the rule will not be effective for any purpose.[28] The agency must accept written comments on the proposed rule, including supporting data, if received no later than the time and date specified in the notice.[29] Before adopting a rule, an agency must consider the written and oral submissions or any memoranda summarizing the oral submissions.[30]

A proposed rule may be revised by the agency prior to adoption. If revisions result in a rule that is "substantially different" from the rule initially proposed, however, the agency must either file a supplemental notice and reopen the comment proceedings or commence a new rulemaking proceeding.[31] If a new rulemaking proceeding is begun, relevant public comment received on the initial rule must be considered in the new proceeding.[32]

Where an agency decides to adopt a proposed rule, it must issue an order of adoption containing certain elements.[33] In addition, the agency must place in the rulemaking file[34] a concise explanatory statement, (1) identifying the agency's reasons for adopting the rule, (2) describing any differences between the text of the rule as adopted and as proposed and stating reasons for the changes, and (3) summarizing all comments received regarding the proposed rule, and responding to the comments by category or subject matter. The response to comments must indicate how the final rule reflects agency consideration of the comments, or why it fails to do so. Such a concise explanatory statement must be provided by the agency to any person upon request or from whom the agency received comment.[35]

If the agency adopts a rule that varies in content from the proposed rule, any interested person may petition the agency to amend any portion of the adopted rule that is "substantially different" from the proposed rule. Such a petition must be made within sixty days of publication of the adopted rule, must demonstrate how the adopted rule is substantially different from the proposed rule and must contain the text of a proposed amendment.[36] If a petition meets these requirements (and any general agency petition requirements), the agency must initiate rulemaking proceedings upon the proposed amendments within sixty days.

Adopted rules generally become effective thirty days after filing with the state code reviser or at a later time specified in the rule or applicable statute.[37] If it becomes apparent at any time during the course of a rulemaking proceeding that another form of proceeding would be more appropriate, the proceeding may be converted to another form pursuant to RCW §34.05.070.

Significant Legislative Rules

Special requirements apply to "significant legislative rules" adopted by certain agencies.[38] Significant legislative rules are those rules that (1) adopt substantive legal provisions the violation of which gives rise to a penalty or sanction, (2) adopt, modify or revoke qualifications or standards for licensing or permitting, or (3) adopt or significantly amend a policy or regulatory program.[39]

Before adopting a significant legislative rule, an agency must take the steps set out in RCW §34.05.328(1). In making these determinations, the agency must include in the rulemaking file sufficient documentation to persuade a reasonable person that the determinations are justified.[40] The agency must also include in the rulemaking file a rule implementation plan, which must be proposed before the rule is adopted.[41] Additional requirements apply after the agency has adopted a rule for significant agency rules regulating the same activity or subject matter as existing federal or state laws.[42]

Emergency Rules and Amendments

Agencies can adopt, amend or repeal rules on an emergency basis where the agency, for good cause, makes the findings prescribed in RCW §34.05.350. Emergency rules can be adopted without notice (including pre-notice inquiry) and opportunity for comment. They take effect immediately upon filing with the code reviser, but they may not remain in effect for longer than 120 days after filing. Within seven days after an emergency rule is adopted, any person may petition the governor requesting the immediate repeal of such rule (if adopted by an executive office agency) on the grounds that the necessary conditions (see below) were not met.[43] The governor must act on a petition within seven days.[44]

The same or substantially similar emergency rules may not be re-adopted unless conditions have changed or unless the agency is actively taking steps to adopt the emergency rule as a permanent rule. Before acting on an emergency basis, the agency must find: (1) that immediate action is "necessary for the preservation of the public health, safety, or general welfare, and that observing the time requirements of notice and opportunity to comment upon the adoption of a permanent rule would be contrary to the public interest; or (2) that state or federal law, federal rule, or a federal deadline for state receipt of federal funds requires immediate adoption of a rule.[45] The agency's findings and a concise statement of its reasons must be incorporated into the agency's order adopting the rule.[46]

Joint Administrative Rules Review Committee

Parties involved in or attempting to influence the rulemaking process should be aware of the joint administrative rules review committee.[47] This bipartisan committee consists of eight state legislators (and alternates) and functions to decide whether proposed or existing agency rules, policies or guidelines are within the intent of the legislature as expressed in the applicable enabling legislation. The committee is authorized to hire staff and establish *ad hoc* advisory boards to assist it in performing its functions.[48] The committee also possesses investigative powers, including the power to issue subpoenas.[49]

The committee may determine by a majority vote of its members that an agency's rules or other guidance materials do not meet the legislative intent of the enabling statute or were not adopted in accordance with applicable provisions of law. The committee may also determine that an agency's policies or guidelines should be in rule form.[50] If the committee raises such an objection, the affected agency must hold a hearing on the committee's objection and must fully consider all material submitted by the committee or the public.

While the committee can neither veto nor force an agency to change a rule, the committee can recommend to the governor that a rule be suspended.[51] If the suspension is approved by the governor, it is effective immediately and continues until ninety days after the expiration of the next regular legislative session.[52] In addition, if a majority of the committee finds that the agency has not modified or amended its rule to conform with legislative intent, notice of the committee's objections to the rule must be published in the state register alongside the agency's rule. The committee's objection will remain with the rule unless a subsequent adjudicatory proceeding determines that the objection is unfounded.[53]

Although the APA expressly provides that the committee's objections "in no way serve to establish a presumption as to the legality or constitutionality of a rule,"[54] the committee offers interested persons an avenue, outside of the normal agency processes discussed above, for influencing and shaping agency rulemaking. In addition, the APA provides that any person may petition the rules review committee for a review of a proposed or existing rule, or for review of a policy or interpretive statement. The committee is required to respond within thirty days and, if it rejects the petition, has to include a written statement of the reasons. A final decision on the petition must be made within ninety days.[55]

Public Access to Agency Rules, Rules Coordinator

All current, permanently effective agency rules are published in the Washington Administrative Code (WAC). The full text of proposed, emergency, and new permanently adopted rules of state agencies are published in the Washington State Register. The Register also contains a cumulative (by year) table of existing sections of the Washington Administrative Code affected by particular agency action. Public access to agency materials beyond agency rules and orders is governed generally by the Washington Public Records Act.[56]

Each agency is required to designate a rules coordinator, whose office and mailing address is to be published in the State Register. The rules coordinator must have knowledge of the subjects of rules being proposed or being prepared within the agency for proposal. The agency rules coordinator also must maintain the records of any rulemaking action and respond to public inquiries about possible or proposed rules and the identity of agency personnel working, reviewing, or commenting on them.[57]

Interpretive and Policy Statements

Where the adoption of agency rules is not feasible or practicable, agencies are encouraged by the Act to advise the public of the agency's current opinions, approaches, and likely courses of action by means of interpretive or policy statements. An "interpretive statement" is a written expression of the agency's opinion regarding the meaning of statutes, judicial decisions, agency orders or other provisions of law.[58] A "policy statement" is a written description of the agency's current approach to the implementation of statutes or other legal provisions, judicial decisions or agency orders, including (where appropriate) the agency's current practice, procedure or method of action based on that approach.[59]

The Act establishes no formal agency requirements for adopting interpretive or policy statements, except to require (1) that they be appropriately "entitled by the agency head or its designee"[60] and (2) that a statement describing the subject matter and listing an agency contact be submitted to the code reviser for publication in the state register.[61] Interpretive and policy statements are advisory only. To better inform and involve the public, the Act encourages agencies to convert long-standing interpretive and policy statements into rules.[62] The Act also provides that any person may petition an agency and request such conversion. The agency is required to notify the joint administrative rules review committee of the petition and, within sixty days after submission of a petition, either deny the petition in writing, stating its reasons for the denial, or initiate rulemaking proceedings.[63]

Agencies are required to index all interpretive and policy statements and make those materials available to the public.[64] Interested persons are entitled to receive copies of current agency materials upon written request.[65] All agency interpretive and policy statements are subject to selective review by the legislature.[66]

Challenges to Rulemaking Under the APA

Challenges to agency rulemaking are discussed in detail in the section on judicial review of agency action. However, several basic principles should be noted here. First, no state agency rule is valid unless it is adopted in substantial compliance with the provisions of the APA.[67] Procedural challenges to an agency rule must be brought within two years of the rule's effective date. Second, all state agencies must adopt rules governing their formal and informal procedures, and no person may be required to comply with any state agency procedure not adopted as a rule.[68] Third, a person whose legal rights or privileges are impaired or threatened to be impaired by an agency rule may petition the court for a declaratory ruling on the validity of a rule at any time.[69] Finally, any person may, upon making certain required showings, petition an agency for a declaratory order regarding the application of a rule to specified facts or circumstances.[70]

Adjudicative Proceedings

In General

Adjudicative proceedings under the APA encompass agency proceedings that determine the rights, duties, privileges or other legal interests of a specific person or persons. In general, adjudicative proceedings are mandated only in certain licensing proceedings or when another statute or the constitution requires a hearing. Each agency must have its own procedural rules but they must comport with the APA.[71]

Adjudicative proceedings are required for all licensing proceedings, except for uncontested license applications.[72] Agencies may not revoke, suspend, modify, annul, withdraw, or amend a license unless the agency gives notice of an opportunity for an appropriate adjudicative proceeding.[73]

When a licensee makes timely and sufficient application for the renewal of a license, an existing full, temporary or provisional license does not expire until the application has been finally determined by the agency.[74] If the application is denied or the terms of a new license limited, the existing license does not expire until the last day for seeking review of the agency order.[75]

Licenses may be summarily suspended if an agency finds (and incorporates a finding in its order) that public health, safety or welfare "imperatively requires emergency action."[76] Summary suspension of a license may be ordered pending proceedings for revocation or other action.

Outside of licensing proceedings, the Act does not itself require adjudicative proceedings. Instead, whether a hearing is required is determined by authority outside the APA.[77] The Act provides that an agency (acting within its authority and on matters within its jurisdiction) may commence an adjudicative proceeding at any time but is required to do so only when a hearing is required by "law or constitutional right."[78] While there is ambiguity in the Act regarding the scope of adjudicative proceedings "required by law,"[79] it is fair to assume that adjudicative proceedings are required when mandated by an agency's enabling legislation or by its own regulations. Adjudicative proceedings are also mandated when required by constitutional due process concerns.

When adjudicative proceedings are required, an agency must commence a hearing upon timely application (consistent with agency procedures) by the person seeking the hearing.[80] Within thirty days of receipt of an application for adjudication, the agency must notify the applicant of any obvious errors or omissions in the application and must request any additional information that the agency wishes to obtain.[81] Within ninety days of the receipt of the application for adjudication, the agency must either commence an adjudicative proceeding or furnish notice to the applicant in writing denying the application.[82]

Adjudicative proceedings commence with specific written notice to all parties (and to all persons who have petitioned to intervene) not less than seven days before a hearing.[83] A party cannot be said to have waived its right to a hearing unless it fails to request a hearing within the time limits established by agency rule. The Act requires that agencies give parties a minimum of twenty days' notice of an opportunity to request a hearing.[84]

If it becomes apparent at any time during the course of an adjudicative proceeding that another form of proceeding would be more appropriate, the proceeding may be converted to another form.[85]

Procedures for Adjudicative Proceedings

The APA establishes only minimum procedural standards applicable to agency hearings. Detailed procedural regulations are left to agency rule. To encourage consistency between agency procedures, the Act directs the state's chief administrative law judge to adopt model rules of procedure and requires each agency to adopt as much of the model rules "as is reasonable.[86] Any agency adopting procedural rules different from the model rules is required to explain the reasons for the difference in its order adopting the rule. The Model Rules of Procedure are published in the Washington Administrative Code and should be read in conjunction with the APA.[87]

Pre-Hearing Proceedings. Adjudicative proceedings commence with written notice to all parties not less than seven days before the hearing.[88] Pre-hearing pleadings and discovery are guided by the presiding officer. The agency head, or his or her designee, serves as the presiding officer unless disqualified.[89] Except where agency rules provide otherwise, the presiding officer is authorized to allow discovery consistent with the procedures found in Washington Superior Court Civil Rules 26 to 36. The presiding officer has authority to issue subpoenas and discovery orders and to grant petitions to intervene.[90] Agency subpoenas can be enforced by petition to superior court.[91] Pre-hearing or other conferences for settlement or simplification of the issues are authorized; such conferences may be conducted by telephone or other electronic means.[92]

At appropriate stages of the proceeding, all parties must be given full opportunity to submit and respond to pleadings, motions, objections, and offers of settlement.[93] The presiding officer may give all parties an opportunity to file briefs, proposed findings of fact and conclusions of law, and proposed initial and final orders, but is not required to do so.[94]

Hearings. The presiding officer regulates the course of the hearing, which is open to the public. At the hearing, all parties must be afforded the opportunity ("to the extent necessary for full disclosure of all relevant facts and issues") to present evidence and argument, respond, conduct cross-examination and submit rebuttal evidence.[95] Parties may participate at the hearing personally, through an authorized representative, or through counsel. Where not prejudicial to the parties, electronic communications may be used to conduct the hearing. A record of the hearing must be kept by the agency, although transcription is not required.[96]

At the hearing, the parties are not bound by the strict judicial rules of evidence, but the presiding officer is directed to use the rules as "guidelines" for evidentiary rulings. Evidence, including hearsay evidence, is admissible if the presiding officer concludes it is the kind of evidence "on which reasonably prudent persons are accustomed to rely in the conduct of their affairs."[97] The agency may take official notice of judicially cognizable facts, technical or scientific facts within the agency's specialized knowledge, and codes or standards of other state and federal agencies.[98] Parties must be notified that official notice is being taken and must be given an opportunity to respond.

Decisions. Following the hearing, the agency must provide the parties with a reasoned decision based on the record. When the hearing is conducted by the agency head or by a presiding officer authorized by the agency to make a final decision, an initial or a final order may be entered. In all other cases (such as those presided over by an administrative law judge), an initial order must be entered.[99] Parties are entitled to file exceptions to the initial order.[100]

Initial and final orders must include a statement of reasoned findings and conclusions on all material issues of fact, law or discretion presented on the record.[101] Initial or final orders must be served in writing within ninety days after conclusion of the hearing or after submission of memos, briefs, or proposed findings.[102] Findings relating to credibility of witnesses must be expressly identified. Findings of fact must be based exclusively on the evidence of record or on matters officially noticed, but the agency may use its experience, technical competence and specialized knowledge to evaluate the evidence.[103]

Initial orders are reviewed internally by the agency, unless the agency provides by rule that internal orders become final without further agency action.[104] If the agency so provides, the agency may review the initial order upon its own motion and must review the order if a party files exceptions to the initial order. The agency head may appoint a person to review initial orders and to prepare and enter final orders.[105]

The reviewing officer is given relatively broad powers on review. He or she must "personally consider the whole record" (or such portions cited by the parties), and can "exercise all the decision-making power that the reviewing officer would have had to decide and enter the final order had the reviewing officer presided over the hearing."[106] In reviewing factual matters, the reviewing officer must give "due regard to the presiding officer's opportunity to observe the witnesses."[107] Parties are afforded an opportunity to present written argument and may be given an opportunity for oral argument by the agency.

The reviewing officer must either enter a final order disposing of the proceeding or remand the matter with instructions for further proceedings. Upon remand, the reviewing officer is empowered to order temporary relief, as authorized and appropriate.[108] Final orders are effective when signed, although compliance is not required until a party is served with or has actual notice of the order.[109]

Within ten days of the issuance of a final order, a party may petition the agency for reconsideration or a stay of effectiveness of the order.[110] Petitions for reconsideration are generally decided by the same person entering the final order. The petition is deemed denied if not disposed of within twenty days, unless the time limit is extended by the agency for "good cause."[111] Petitions for reconsideration are not required prior to seeking judicial review of a final order. Petitions for reconsideration do not stay the effectiveness of an order.[112] Petitions for a stay of effectiveness may be heard by the reviewing officer, presiding officer or agency head, as provided in agency rule. A decision on the petition may be made before or after the effective date of the order. A decision denying a stay is not subject to judicial review.[113]

Brief and Emergency Adjudicative Proceedings

Under certain circumstances, the Act authorizes agencies to use "brief" adjudicative proceedings rather than the more formal procedures described above. Brief adjudicative proceedings are generally authorized where the interests involved do not warrant a formal adjudicative proceeding, where the agency has provided by rule for such proceedings and where the public interest does not require that the agency give public notice and an opportunity to participate to persons other than the parties involved.[114] The procedures for brief adjudicative proceedings are set out at RCW §§34.05.482 through .494.

Emergency adjudicative proceedings are authorized in situations involving an immediate danger to the public health, safety or welfare and requiring immediate agency action. The agency may only take such action as is necessary to prevent or avoid the immediate danger. Following issuance of an emergency order, the agency is required to proceed "as quickly as feasible" to complete any proceedings that would be required if the matter did not involve an immediate danger.[115]

Administrative Safeguards

The Act contains a number of administrative safeguards designed to ensure the fairness and integrity of the administrative process. These safeguards relate principally to the presiding officer, *ex parte* communications, and separation of functions.[116]

The Act requires that the presiding officer be either an accountable official from the agency or an independent administrative law judge from the Office of Administrative Hearings. Presiding officers are subject to disqualification, upon petition, for bias, prejudice, interest or any other cause for which a judge can be disqualified.[117]

Ex parte communications on non-procedural matters are expressly prohibited under the APA. A presiding officer may not communicate directly or indirectly, with very limited exceptions, with certain types of persons within the agency or with persons outside the agency who have an interest in the outcome of the proceeding.[118] Similarly, certain identified persons may not communicate with the presiding officer. *Ex parte* communications received by a presiding officer in violation of the Act must be disclosed and placed on the record of the pending proceeding and are subject to written rebuttal.[119] If necessary to eliminate the effect of a prohibited communication, a presiding officer can be disqualified.

The Act also attempts to ensure impartial decision-making by requiring the separation of agency functions. The Act prohibits any person who has served as (or who is subject to the authority, direction or discretion of) an investigator, prosecutor or advocate in an adjudicative proceeding from later presiding over that adjudication. Persons, including agency heads, who have participated in certain preliminary agency determinations may later serve as a presiding officer unless a party demonstrates grounds for disqualification, such as bias, prejudice or other cause.[120]

JUDICIAL REVIEW OF AGENCY ACTION

Judicial Review Under the APA

In General

The APA establishes the exclusive means for judicial review of agency action, except in cases relating solely to money damages, ancillary procedural matters, or to the extent that *de novo* review or jury trial is expressly authorized by other provisions of law.[121]

"Agency action" reviewable under the Act includes the implementation or enforcement of a statute; the adoption or application of an agency rule or order; the issuance, denial or suspension of a license; the imposition of sanctions; or the granting or withholding of benefits.[122] Among the matters expressly excluded from agency action are "any sale, lease, contract, or other proprietary decision of the Department of Natural Resources in the management of public lands."[123] Judicial review of certain agency inaction is also available under RCW §34.05.570(4).

Review Procedures. Review of agency action is obtained by filing a petition for review in superior court along with a filing fee. The petitioner selects from among three statutory options.[124] The contents required of the petition for review are set out in detail in the statute,[125] and the timing of the petition is governed by the type of agency action sought to be reviewed.[126]

Direct review of agency action by the Court of Appeals may be obtained in two general cases: First, it is available upon certification by the superior court that review of the agency action is limited to the record and that the four criteria set out in RCW §34.05.518(2) are met. Second, in the case of appeals from a final decision of an environmental board,[127] direct review is available if certain regulations are met, including the issuance of a certificate of appealability by the environmental board that rendered the final decision.[128] An agency may grant a stay or other temporary remedy during the pendency of judicial review, and a party may move the court for such relief after filing a petition for review. If judicial relief is sought from agency action based on public health, safety or welfare grounds, the court may not grant relief without finding that the applicant is likely to succeed, that the applicant will suffer irreparable injury absent the relief that other parties to the proceedings will not be substantially harmed and that the threat to public health and safety is sufficiently serious to merit relief.[129]

Standing & Exhaustion of Remedies. Standing to petition for review is granted to all persons "aggrieved or adversely affected" by the agency action.[130] The Act sets forth three criteria for establishing standing, all of which must be met in order to obtain review.[131] The Act also requires, with three exceptions, that petitioners exhaust their administrative remedies prior to seeking judicial review.[132] Petitioners seeking judicial review of a rule need not have participated in the rulemaking process, petitioned for the rule's amendment or repeal, or have appealed to the Governor a petition for amendment or repeal. Additionally, petitioners need not exhaust administrative remedies where the Act or another statute does not require exhaustion. The court may also waive the exhaustion requirement upon certain showings by petitioner.[133]

Issues on Appeal. Issues not raised before the agency may not be raised on appeal, with certain exceptions set out in the rule.[134] When new issues are properly raised, the court must remand the matter to the agency for the agency's determination. Similarly, judicial review of facts is generally confined to the agency record.[135] The court may take new evidence only with respect to various procedural matters and must remand the matter to the agency if other supplemental fact-finding is required.[136]

Scope of Judicial Review. The scope of judicial review varies with the nature of the agency action being reviewed. In all actions for judicial review, the burden of proof lies with the party trying to establish the invalidity of an agency action. The validity of the agency's action is to be determined at the time the agency action was taken. The court must make separate and distinct rulings on every material issue, and it may grant relief only where the complainant demonstrates substantial prejudice resulting from the agency action.[137]

The validity of any agency rule may be determined upon petition for declaratory judgment or upon review of agency orders or other agency action.[138] Procedural challenges to a rule are barred two years after the rule becomes effective.[139] Agency rules may be declared invalid only if a court finds that the rule violates constitutional provisions, exceeds the agency's statutory authority,[140] was adopted without compliance with statutory rulemaking procedures, or is arbitrary and capricious.[141] Standards for reviewing a challenge to the application of a rule are governed by the paragraphs that follow regarding agency orders and other agency actions.

A court may grant relief from an agency order only if it determines that the order violates constitutional provisions, or is (1) outside the agency's authority, (2) the product of unlawful procedure,[142] (3) the result of an erroneous interpretation of the law, (4) not supported by substantial evidence, (5) arbitrary and capricious, (6) the product of incomplete decision-making, (7) inconsistent with agency rules (unless the agency explains the inconsistency) or (8) the product of persons who were properly subject to disqualification.[143]

Finally, a court may grant relief from all other agency action where the action is unconstitutional, outside the agency's statutory authority, arbitrary and capricious or taken by persons not lawfully entitled to take such action.[144] Agency action reviewable under this section can also include agency inaction where a person's rights are violated by an agency's failure to perform a duty required by law to be performed.[145] A court is specifically empowered to order the agency to "take action required by law."[146]

Following review of agency action, a court may grant a variety of relief. The court may order the agency to take action required by law, order an agency to exercise discretion required by law, affirm or set aside agency action, remand the matter for further proceedings or enter a declaratory judgment order.[147] Where a court reviews matters within an agency's discretion, the court must limit its review to assuring that the agency exercised its discretion in accordance with law. The court may not itself undertake to exercise that discretion but must instead remand the matter to the agency.[148] A court may award damages, compensation or other ancillary relief only to the extent expressly authorized by other provisions of law.[149] Frivolous petitions for judicial review are to be treated like frivolous civil actions under RCW §4.84.185, which allows a court to award reasonable expenses, including attorneys' fees, incurred in opposing a frivolous action or defense.[150]

Civil Enforcement of Agency Rules and Orders

The Act provides that both agencies and private parties may seek civil enforcement of agency rules and orders in superior court.[151] An agency can seek civil enforcement by petitioning the court and may request declaratory relief, temporary or permanent injunctive relief, any other civil remedy provided by law or a combination of these remedies.[152] Private parties with standing may file a petition for civil enforcement, but they must first give the agency sixty days' notice of the alleged violation.[153] If the agency cures the violation, the petition is mooted. An agency whose order is sought to be enforced may move to dismiss the petition on grounds that enforcement would be contrary to the policy of the agency. Dismissal must be granted unless the petitioner can demonstrate that the agency's failure to enforce its order is based on an exercise of discretion that is arbitrary or capricious.[154]

Defenses to civil enforcement proceedings are stated in RCW §34.05.586 which also allows the court to consider new issues or take new evidence (to the extent necessary for the determination of the matter). Proceedings for civil enforcement are governed by RCW §34.05.590, and they are subject to review by a higher court as in other civil cases.[155]

Judicial Review of Actions by Local Agencies

Judicial review of agency action not covered by the APA (such as review of action by local agencies) is beyond the scope of this chapter. However, a brief outline is appropriate here. Judicial review of local agency action is usually initiated by the filing of an extraordinary writ, either under Washington's writ statute (RCW §7.16) or under the court's inherent constitutional power of review. Such review is discretionary and is generally available only when an agency acts in a "judicial" capacity. Judicial review of local agency action may also be available by declaratory judgment or through injunctive relief.

Three statutory writs are available for review of local agency action: certiorari, mandamus and prohibition. A writ of certiorari (also called a "writ of review") may be granted by any court when an inferior tribunal, board or officer, exercising judicial functions, has exceeded its jurisdiction or acted illegally, and when there is no appeal or any plain, speedy and adequate remedy at law.[156] If the writ is granted and the record of the agency's proceedings is certified to the court, the issues that the court may resolve upon hearing are limited by statute.[157]

A writ of mandamus may be issued by a court to any inferior tribunal, corporation, board or person to compel the agency to perform an act required by law.[158] Generally, a writ of mandamus will issue only where the act to be performed is ministerial as opposed to discretionary. Courts can nonetheless order the agency to at least make a decision, even though they cannot dictate how the agency will exercise its discretion.[159]

Finally, the writ of prohibition is the counterpart of the writ of mandamus. It arrests the proceeding of any tribunal, corporation, board or person when such proceedings are outside, or in excess of, that agency's jurisdiction.[160]

Courts may also review the actions of local agencies under their "inherent power of review." That power is based on a right of review derived from the Washington Constitution.[161] A constitutional writ of review is available only where the agency action is not otherwise reviewable. Accordingly, constitutional writs are used principally to review legislative or administrative agency action. The scope of review by constitutional writ is quite narrow. Courts will only review the agency's action to determine if it was arbitrary and capricious or otherwise contrary to law.[162]

Review of local agency action may also be obtained through actions for declaratory relief (RCW §7.24 and Superior Court Civil Rule 57), or actions for injunctive relief (RCW §7.40 and Superior Court Civil Rule 65).

NOTES

¹ RCW §34.05.010(2) defines an "agency" as "any state board, commission, department, institution of higher education, or officer, authorized by law to make rules or to conduct adjudicative proceedings, except those in the legislative or judicial branches, the governor, or the attorney general except to the extent otherwise required by law and any local governmental entity that may request the appointment of an administrative law judge under chapter 42.41 RCW." While a number of state agencies are expressly excluded from all or parts of the Act's coverage, none of these exclusions are relevant to the environmental practitioner. See RCW §34.05.030.

² *See, e.g., Snohomish County v. State Shorelines Hearings Bd.*, 108 Wn. App. 781 (2001); *DOT v. Inlandboatmen's Union of Pac.*, 103 Wn. App. 573 (2000).

³ *See, e.g. Kitsap County Fire Protection Dist. No. 7 v. Kitsap County Boundary Review Bd.*, 87 Wn. App. 753 (1997), *rev. den.* 134 Wn. 2d 1027 (1998). A local governmental agency may be treated as a state agency when it requests the appointment of an administrative law judge under RCW §42.41 (local government whistleblower protection).

⁴ For example, a County Board of Valuation was found to be subject to the APA because it functioned to review property values for the purpose of levying a state tax. Because the agency acted in furtherance of the state's taxing power, the court held that the APA applied. *State v. Board of Valuation, King County*, 72 Wn. 2d 66 (1967). In contrast, even though established by a state statute, the Seattle Housing Authority was not found to be a state agency administering a statewide program. *Riggins v. Housing Authority of Seattle*, 87 Wn. 2d 97 (1976).

⁵ But see *Plumbers and Steamfitters Union Local 598 v. WPPSS*, 44 Wn. App. 906 (1986), *cert. den.* 432 US 905 (1987) (finding that the Washington Public Power Supply System was a "local agency" and hence not subject to the APA, even though the agency engaged in functions of statewide importance).

⁶ RCW §34.05.010(17). Unlike the federal APA, which establishes procedures for "formal" and "informal" rulemaking, there is only one kind of rulemaking under Washington's APA. It is akin to "informal" rulemaking under the federal APA, and it covers all rulemaking by state agencies. *See also Budget Rent A Car Corp. v. State*, 144 Wn. 2d 889 (2001); *Hunter v. University of Wash.*, 101 Wn. App. 283 (2000); *McGee Guest Home, Inc. v. Department of Soc. & Health Servs.*, 142 Wn. 2d 316 (2000).

⁷ "Order" means a written statement of particular applicability that finally determines the legal rights, duties, privileges, immunities or other legal interests of a specific person or persons. RCW §34.05.010(10)(a).

⁸ Action is of "general applicability" if it is applied uniformly to all members of a class. See *Failor's Pharmacy v. Dept. of Social and Health Services*, 125 Wn. 2d 488 (1994).

⁹ RCW §34.05.010(15).

¹⁰ *Id.*

¹¹ RCW §34.05.330.

¹² See §§RCW 34.05.330(1) and (4).

¹³ RCW §34.05.330(1).

¹⁴ RCW §34.05.330(1).

¹⁵ RCW §§34.05.330(2) and (3).

¹⁶ See §RCW 34.05.310.

¹⁷ See §RCW 34.05.310(4).

¹⁸ RCW §34.05.310(1).

¹⁹ RCW §34.05.330(2) & (3). *See also* RCW §34.05.313 (pilot project feasibility studies).

[20] RCW §34.05.315; RCW §34.05.320(1); RCW §34.08.020(1). Advance notice of agency rulemaking may be obtained by reviewing each agency's rulemaking docket. The docket contains a listing of the subject of each rule currently being prepared by the agency for proposal, the name and address of agency personnel responsible for the proposal, and an indication of the proposal's present status. The docket also contains a listing of each pending rulemaking proceeding and its status. RCW §34.05.315.

[21] *In re McCrea*, 28 Wn. App. 777 (1981).

[22] *See* RCW §34.05.328.

[23] RCW §34.05.320(1); RCW §34.05.325 (5)(d). *See State v. Squally*, 78 Wn. 2d 475 (1970) (finding notice of a proposed rule deficient); *Pan Pacific Trading Corp. v. Dept. of Labor and* Industries, 88 Wn. 2d 347 (1977); *Clark v. Horse Racing Comm.*, 106 Wn. 2d 84 (1986) (same).

[24] RCW §34.05.320(3).

[25] RCW §34.05.322.

[26] RCW §34.05.220(5).

[27] RCW §34 05.325.

[28] RCW §34.05.345.

[29] RCW §34.05.325. Comments may be submitted by facsimile if permitted by the agency. *See* RCW §34.05.325(3).

[30] RCW §34.05.335(2).

[31] RCW §34.05.340.

[32] RCW §34.05.340(1). The factors to be considered in determining whether a rule is "substantially different" from a proposed rule are set out in RCW §34.05.340(2).

[33] *See* RCW §34.05.360.

[34] Each agency is required to maintain an official rulemaking file. *See* RCW §34.05.370 (prescribing file contents). Upon judicial review, the official file is considered by the court. The Act, however, makes clear that the rulemaking file need not be the exclusive basis for agency action on a rule.

[35] RCW §34.05.325(6).

[36] RCW §34.05.340(3).

[37] RCW §34.05.380(2).

[38] The agencies relevant to environmental practitioners include Ecology, DNR, the Environmental Hearings Office, and the Department of Fish & Wildlife, when implementing RCW §75.20 (construction projects in state waters). Any agency can voluntarily apply these requirements to its rulemaking. RCW §34.05.328(5)(a).

[39] RCW §34.05.328(5)(c)(iii).

[40] RCW §34.05.328(2).

[41] RCW §34.05.328(3).

[42] *See* RCW §34.05.328(4).

[43] The executive office agencies are listed in RCW §42.17.010 and include all the key environmental agencies.

[44] RCW §34.05.350(3).

[45] RCW §34.05.350(1).

[46] RCW §34.05.350(1)(b). *See Mauzy v. Gibbs*, 44 Wn. App. 625 (1986) (striking down an emergency rule where the agency failed to set forth sufficient specific reasons for an emergency; also noting that considerations of administrative and fiscal convenience alone are generally not sufficient to satisfy standards for emergency rules).

47 *See* RCW §§34.05.610 through .681.

48 RCW §34.05.671.

49 *See* RCW §§34.05.675 and .681.

50 RCW §34.05.630.

51 RCW §34.05.640(3).

52 RCW §34.05.640(3).

53 RCW §34.05.640(4) and (5).

54 RCW §34.05.660.

55 RCW §34.05.655.

56 RCW §§42.17.250 through .340.

57 RCW §34.05.312.

58 RCW §34.05.010(8).

59 RCW §34.05.010(14).

60 RCW §34.05.010(8) and (14).

61 RCW §34.05.230(4).

62 RCW §34.05.230(1).

63 RCW §34.05.230(2).

64 *See* RCW §42.17.460.

65 RCW §34.05.230(3).

66 RCW §34.05.630(2).

67 RCW §34.05 375.

68 RCW §34.05.220(1)(b).

69 RCW §34.05.542(1); RCW §§34.05.570(2)(a) and (b).

70 RCW §34.05.240.

71 RCW §34.05.250 and WAC 10-08.

72 "Licenses" include franchises, permits, certificates, approvals, registrations, charters or similar forms of authorization required by law. RCW §34.05.010(9). *See also Wash. Indep. Tel. Ass'n v. Wash. Utils. & Transp. Comm.*, 110 Wn. App. 498 (2002), *aff'd*, 149 Wn. 2d 17 (2003); *Watershed Defense Fund v. Riveland*, 91 Wn. App. 454 (1998).

73 RCW§§34.05.01, 34.05.422.

74 RCW §34.05.422(3).

75 *Id.*

76 RCW §34.05.422(4).

77 In this respect, the Washington Act follows the federal APA. *See* 5 USC §554(a) (establishing procedures for adjudications "required by statute to be determined on the record after opportunity-for an agency hearing").

78 RCW §34.05.413.

79 The ambiguity arises from the differences in language used in RCW §34.05.010(1) (mandating hearings when "required by statute") and RCW §34.05.413 (mandating hearings when "required by law").

80 RCW §34.05.413.

81 RCW §34 05.419.

82 RCW §34.05.416.

83 RCW §34.05.434.

84 RCW §34.05 440.

85 RCW §34.05.070.

86 RCW §34.05.250.

87 WAC 10-08.

88 RCW §34.05.434.

89 RCW §34.05.425. The Pollution Control Hearings Board, Shorelines Hearings Board, Forest Practices Appeal Board and the Environmental Hearings Office are among the agencies exempted from this requirement and are permitted to select organizational inferiors to serve as presiding officers. RCW §34.05.425(2). *See also Ritter v. Board of Comm'rs. Of Adams County Public Hospital Dist. No. 1*, 96 Wn. 2d 503 (1981).

90 RCW §§34.05.443; 34.05.446.

91 RCW §§34.05.446; 34.05.588.

92 RCW §34.05.431.

93 RCW §34.05 437.

94 RCW §34.05.437.

95 RCW §34.05.449. *See also Chmela v. State Dept. of Motor Vehicles*, 88 Wn. 2d 385 (1977).

96 RCW §34.05.449.

97 RCW §34.05.452. *See also Weyerhauser v. Pierce County*, 124 Wn. 2d 26 (1994); *Nisqually Delta Assn. v. City of DuPont*, 103 Wn. 2d 720 (1985).

98 RCW §34.05.452.

99 RCW §34.05.461.

100 RCW §34.05.464.

101 RCW §34.05.461.

102 RCW §34.05.461(8). The ninety day period may be waived or extended for good cause shown.

103 RCW §34.05.461(4) and (5).

104 RCW §34.05.464(1).

105 RCW §34.05.464(2).

106 RCW §34.05.464(4). *See Northwest Steelhead and Salmon Council of Trout Unlimited v. Washington State Dep't of Fisheries*, 78 Wn. App. 778 (1995) (agency head may substitute his or her own findings of fact and conclusions of law for those made by hearing officer).

107 RCW §34.05.464(4).

108 RCW §34.05.464.

109 RCW §34.05.473.

110 RCW §34.05.470(1).

111 RCW §34.05.470(3).

112 RCW §34.05.470.

113 RCW §34.05.467.

114 RCW §34.05.482.

115 RCW §34.05.479.

116 RCW §34.05.455.

117 RCW §34.05.425(3).

[118] RCW §34.05.455.

[119] RCW §34.05.455. Quasi-judicial local land use decisions made by boards, commissioners, or examiners are also subject to the state appearance of fairness statute. See RCW §42.36.

[120] RCW §34.05.458. See *Matter of Johnston*, 99 Wn. 2d 466 (1983).

[121] RCW §34.05.510. In the environmental area, *de novo* review is provided for appeals from all decisions and orders of Ecology. See WAC 173-04-010. Such appeals are under the jurisdiction of the Pollution Control Hearings Board, the practice and procedure of which is governed by WAC 371-08. Declaratory proceedings under the Shoreline Management Act of 1971 are under the jurisdiction of the Shoreline Hearings Board and are governed by WAC 461-08.

[122] RCW §34.05.010.

[123] RCW §34.05.010(3).

[124] See RCW §34.05.514. The petition may be filed in Thurston County Superior Court, the petitioner's county of residence or principal place of business, or the county where the affectred property is located.

[125] See RCW §34.05.546. Strict compliance with these procedural requirements is necessary. See *City of Seattle v. Public Employment Relations Comm.*, 116 Wn. 2d 923 (1991).

[126] RCW §34.05.542. Generally, petitions for judicial review of agency orders and other agency action must be filed with the court within thirty days of the action from which review is sought. The time period for petitioning for review of other agency action is extended during any period that a petitioner does not know of (and should not have reasonably discovered) the agency's action or its effect on petitioner. Petitions for judicial review of an agency rule can be brought at any time, RCW §34.05.542, although procedural challenges to a rule must be brought within two years of the rule's effective date. RCW §34.05.375. Petitions for judicial review must be served on the agency in question, the Office of the Attorney General, and all parties of record. RCW §34.05.542. See also *Suquamish Indian Tribe v. Kitsap County*, 92 Wn. App. 816 (1998).

[127] Environmental boards are defined to include the Pollution Control Hearings Board, the Shorelines Hearings Board, other boards in the Environmental Hearings Office (*see* RCW §43.21B.005), as well as the growth planning hearings boards (*see* RCW §36.70A.250). RCW §34.05.518(3).

[128] See RCW §34.05.518(3) (setting out the standards and process for obtaining such review). The Court of Appeals may refuse to accept direct review of a case if it finds that the case does not meet the applicable standards. Review is then by superior court. RCW §34.05.522.

[129] RCW §34.05 550.

[130] RCW 34.05.530; See also *Wash. Indep. Tel. Assn. v. Wash. Utils. & Transp. Comm'n.*, 110 Wn. App. 498 (2002), *aff'd.* 149 Wn. 2d 17 (2003); *Allan v. University of Wash.*, 140 Wn. 2d 323 (2000).

[131] RCW §34.05.530. See also *KS Tacoma Holdings, LLC v. Shorelines Hearings Board*, 166 Wn. App. 117 (2012); *Biggers v. City of Bainbridge* Island, 124 Wn. App. 858 (2004); *Project for Informed* Citizens, 92 Wn. App. 290 (1998).

[132] *See, e.g., Beard v. King County*, 76 Wn. App. 863 (1995); *Citizens for Clean Air v. Spokane*, 114 Wn. 2d 20 (1990); *Estate of Friedman v. Pierce County*, 112 Wn. 2d 68 (1989).

[133] RCW §34.05.534. *Dioxin/Organochlorine Center v. Dept. of Ecology*, 119 Wn. 2d 837 (1992).

[134] RCW §§34.05.554; 34.05.558; 34.05.562; 34.05.570. See also *King County v. Washington State Boundary Review Bd. for King County*, 122 Wn. 2d 648 (1993).

[135] RCW §34.05:558. See, e.g., *Batchelder v. City of Seattle*, 77 Wn. App. 154 (1995), *rev. den.* 127 Wn. 2d 1022.

[136] RCW §34.05.562.

[137] RCW §34.05 570.

[138] RCW §34.05.570(2).

[139] RCW 34.05.375.

[140] See *Washington Indep. Tel. Assn. v. Telecommunications Ratepayers Assn. for Cost-Based and Equitable Rates (TRACER)*, 75 Wn. App. 356 (1994) (invalidating agency rule in excess of statutory authority).

[141] RCW 34.05.570(2)(c).

[142] See *Failor's Pharmacy v. Dep't of Social and Health Serv.*, 125 Wn. 2d 488 (1994) (invalidating agency action for failure to comply with APA rulemaking procedures).

[143] RCW §34.05.570.

[144] *Id. See also Neah Bay Chamber of Commerce v. Dept., of Fisheries*, 119 Wn. 2d 464 (1992)

[145] *Id.*

[146] RCW §34.05.570.

[147] RCW §34.05.574.

[148] *Manke Lumber Co., Inc. v. Diehl*, 91 Wn. App. 793 (1998).

[149] RCW §34.05.574(3).

[150] RCW §34.05.598.

[151] RCW §§34.05.578; 34.05.582.

[152] RCW §34.05.578.

[153] RCW §34.05.582.

[154] RCW §34.05.582(3).

[155] RCW §34.05.594.

[156] RCW §7.16.040.

[157] RCW §7.16.120.

[158] RCW §7.16.150 through .280.

[159] *See, e.g., Norco Constr. v. King County*, 97 Wn. 2d 680 (1982).

[160] RCW §7.16.290 through .320.

[161] *Pierce County Sheriff v. Civil Service Comm.*, 98 Wn. 2d 690 (1983).

[162] See *Williams v. Seattle School District*, 97 Wn. 2d 215 (1982).

About the Author

Theda Braddock has been an environmental and securities attorney for over 20 years. She is the author of the *Washington Environmental Law Handbook* (Government Institutes, 2005), *Wetlands Regulation: Case Law, Interpretation & Commentary* (Government Institutes, 2003), and *Wetlands: An Introduction to Ecology, the Law, and Permitting* (Government Institutes, 2007 [1995]). She is also a FINRA arbitrator.

Ms. Braddock is admitted to practice before the state and federal courts in California, Maryland, Massachusetts, and Washington. She is also admitted to practice before the United States Court of Federal Claims and the United States Supreme Court.

Ms. Braddock attended the Great Books Program at St. John's College in Annapolis, Maryland, and received her B.A. from Mills College in Oakland, California. She received her Juris Doctor from Golden Gate University in San Francisco, California.

Ms. Braddock is also a sailor and has served as a racing skipper and tactician on the Chesapeake Bay and Puget Sound. She taught sailing for the Command, Seamanship, and Navigation Training Squadron at the U.S. Naval Academy and is qualified as an Offshore Skipper by the U.S. Naval Sailing Squadron.

Praise for *A Voice in the Wilderness*

"Archbishop Viganò is that rarest of mortal men: one who speaks the truth whatever the cost to his career or his standing with his fellow bishops. To be sure, his writings cast light on some of the darker corners of the institutional Church and on the abuses of some of its officials, but they are also suffused with hope by a prelate whose vibrant Christian faith shines through on every page."—STEVEN W. MOSHER, president of the Population Research Institute

"Angelico Press has done an important service in gathering together in one volume Archbishop Carlo Maria Viganò's stunning August 2018 Memorandum and his subsequent writings, in which he details his personal knowledge of how the Holy See has failed to deal effectively with grave immorality in the Church's hierarchy, particularly in the case of ex-cardinal Theodore McCarrick. Viganò decided in conscience to expose the ways in which clerical expediency, self-interest, and a misplaced desire to avoid public scandal have in fact done grave harm to the Church and her mission. These collected interventions give a clear insight into Viganò's thinking and allow readers to judge for themselves the cogency of his analysis of the causes, and the remedies, of the present crisis in the Church."—FR. GERALD E. MURRAY, pastor of Church of the Holy Family

"In an era of increasing moral darkness, Archbishop Viganò soars as a meteoric light for the Children of Light. Within these pages lies the call to action by the Oracle of Christian Truth. God has not abandoned his flock. Archbishop Viganò leads them out of the desolate desert into the sustaining waters of faith, truth, and hope with the courage and clarity of a modern-day prophet. His bold and steadfast witness elevates the weary, rescues the lost, and leads the disheartened to Christ. This paragon of moral clarity and courage belongs among the pantheon of great Catholic thinkers and saints."—LIZ YORE, founder of Yore Children

"What would we do without Angelico Press! Once again, it presents us with a collection of documents that speak most closely to the needs of the Catholic Church at this exact moment. As we face the imminent prospect of a Conclave, the voice of His Grace Archbishop Viganò makes a decisively synthetic contribution to understanding where we are now, and offers an analytic exploration of the possibilities that lie before God's Church Militant. In these documents, usefully supported by explanatory notes, we behold an Archbishop, a man of the Holy Spirit, gradually discerning from contemporary events what must be offered to thoughtful Catholics. Papa Bergoglio has spoken about the 'God of surprises.' One of the biggest surprises, however, must surely be that a highly intelligent member of the Vatican's diplomatic service should emerge to offer, on the basis of his own careful observations, a critical judgement of the Church's problems and needs as she awaits her next supreme Pastor. Timely and most welcome!"—FR. JOHN HUNWICKE, moderator of "Fr Hunwicke's Mutual Enrichment" blog

"St. Matthew tells us that the crowds were astonished by Christ's words because He taught them 'as one having authority and not as the scribes did.' Tragically, we believing Catholics have come to expect our leaders, from the top on down, to offer us the 'mess of pottage' provided by our pathetic contemporary media scribes, handing us over in the process to be devoured by their wolf-like political, economic, technocratic, and medical allies. I felt the crowd's astonishment anew when reading the words of Archbishop Viganò in this book. For he shows us that there are still true shepherds of the flock who know that their task is that of repeating the Master's unchangeable authoritative teaching in all its fullness, and of driving those who do not do so from the temple precincts. Viva Viganò!"—JOHN RAO, director of the Roman Forum

"I first met Archbishop Viganò in 2013 to present him with a request to the Holy Father to declare Planned Parenthood an enemy of the Catholic Church. Even in that first meeting, though he never said it, he seemed aware that something was amiss and that the pope would not be amenable to such a request. When I saw him again in Rome, just before he published his first testimony regarding Theodore McCarrick, I could tell something weighed heavily on his heart. Since that time, his missives have been a beacon of light and a freshening spring to souls thirsting for the light-infused waters of Truth."—MICHAEL HICHBORN, president of the Lepanto Institute

"Archbishop Viganò's willingness while he was U.S. nuncio to relay messages from us at the Covenants Initiative (a Muslim peace movement) to Pope Francis about the newly-rediscovered Prophetic Covenants was very helpful to our efforts. These Covenants, authored by Muhammad himself, place groups like ISIS under the curse of God and command all Muslims not to attack or rob or damage the buildings of Christians living in peace with Islam, or even to prevent their Christian wives from going to church, but rather to defend the Christians until the end of time. Seeing that ISIS has massacred more Muslims than Christians, this is a sterling example of the 'united front ecumenism' against the common enemies of religion so necessary in our times."—CHARLES UPTON, co-founder of the Covenants Initiative

A Voice in the Wilderness

*Archbishop Carlo Maria Viganò
on the Church, America, and the World*